Mehrdad Amanat is an independent scholar with a PhD in History from UCLA. He is a regular contributor to the *Encyclopaedia Iranica*.

JEWISH IDENTITIES IN IRAN

Resistance and Conversion to Islam and the Baha'i Faith

MEHRDAD AMANAT

I.B. TAURIS

LONDON · NEW YORK

New paperback edition published in 2013 by I.B.Tauris & Co. Ltd
6 Salem Road, London W2 4BU
175 Fifth Avenue,
New York NY 10010
www.ibtauris.com

Distributed in the United States and Canada
Exclusively by Palgrave Macmillan
175 Fifth Avenue, New York NY 10010

First published in hardback in 2011 by I.B.Tauris & Co. Ltd
Copyright © Mehrdad Amanat, 2011, 2013

ISBN: 978 1 78076 777 2

A full CIP record for this book is available from the British Library
A full CIP record is available from the Library of Congress

Library of Congress catalog card: available
Printed and bound by Page Bros Ltd, UK
from camera-ready copy edited and supplied by the author

To the Memory of Mousa Amanat

CONTENTS

Map of Iran in the Nineteenth Century

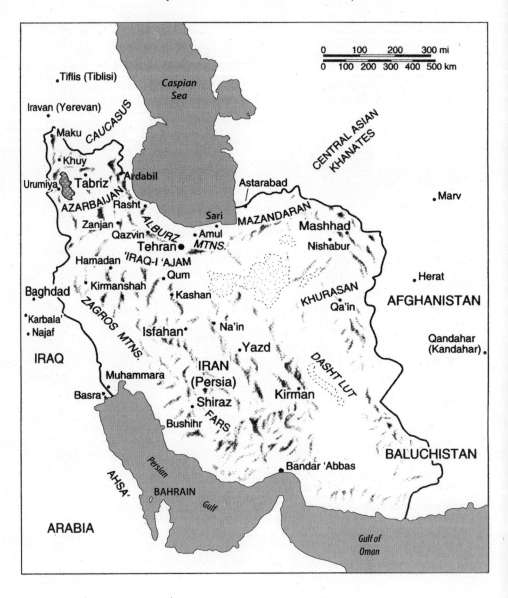

FOREWORD

This book is an attempt to examine the roots of conversion to Islam and the Baha'i faith among Iran's Jews during the past two centuries, and the related question of the changing nature of religious identity during this period. Despite its continuing relevance, conversion is marked with shame and its mention is even considered "impolite" among both converts and the loyal faithful. Converts generally wish to present a homogeneous community free of past differences, while defenders of tradition see conversion as apostasy and a betrayal of age-old traditions which causes harm to their ancestral faith. Losing members to a new religion carries a negative weight and shaming nonconformists is a potent means of protecting conventions. This may explain why Baha'is are at times accused of providing financial incentives to converts. Obviously, such a reductive theory does not do justice to the complex process of conversion and cannot be supported by the accounts of a number of converts discussed in this book who faced the risk of persecution and financial devastation and struggled with finances almost their entire lives (see Chapters 6 and 7).

Like many other societies with a history of anti-Jewish sentiments, Iran's mistreatment of Jews has added an additional layer of stigma to Jewish converts as many try to hide their Jewish past. The conformist reading of Shi'ism has ironically prevented the full acceptance of genuine converts to Islam by labeling them as "new converts" (jadid ul-Islam), clinging to an unrelenting memory of conversion, sometimes for centuries. A need for acceptance may thus explain why some converts have become hostile critics of their ancestral religion.

To a history of religious conformity one might add the dominance of class-conscious and Tehran-centered modern sensibilities. An obsession with national unity—itself a byproduct of the Pahlavi nation-building project—dismisses and ridicules longstanding ethnic and religious diversity. The fixation on a bourgeois image suppresses any memory of the widespread poverty and illiteracy in Iran's past. Some of these same concerns may be clues to the attention paid to forced (as opposed to voluntary) conversion in the field of Iranian Jewish studies. Conventional narratives, including some Baha'i sources, generally emphasize coincidental events, dreams, and sudden spiritual transformations. They underplay the role of long-term developments and historical forces which contributed to such personal spiritual milestones.

This study is a product of years of reflection on these questions and may be at variance with conventional approaches to the subject. Aside from an interest in my own family history, I was initially inspired by the memoirs of a number of early Jewish Baha'i converts. Their ease in discussing their modest past and the rawness of their accounts were particularly refreshing. Even more striking was the confidence with which converts defined their new selves in defiance of conventions and clerical authority. Through the unusual experience of writing their memoirs, they asserted their individuality and constructed a modern self. It is these creative moments of self-definition that I have tried to capture.

In writing this book, I am greatly indebted to my late father Mousa Amanat for his tireless efforts in building a rich archival collection of biographies, family histories, images, memoirs and correspondence, as well as his own historical contributions. Unless otherwise noted, all images in this book are from this collection. I am also indebted to the numerous contributors to this collection whose detailed accounts I have benefited from. In particular, I am thankful to the Rayhani, Hafezi and Abizadeh families for contributing copies of family memoirs to this collection.

Professor Nikki Keddie's support of what started out as a translation project was vital in developing it into a dissertation and later into this book. I am grateful to her for teaching me a historical perspective and for her careful readings of the original dissertation. I am also thankful to Professors Michael Morony and Yona Sabar for their supervision over the course of my studies. The support and encouragement of my brother Professor Abbas Amanat, including his numerous suggestions, observations and source materials and his detailed attention to my drafts, have been crucial to the quality of this work. I have also benefited from the assistance of a number of friends. Dr. Anthony Lee carefully read and edited the manuscript. His thoughtful comments and dialogue over the years have inspired a number of the ideas in this book. I have also benefited from the exchange of ideas with Professor Afshin Matin-Asgari. Professor Daniel Tsadik's generous assistance in reading and commenting on parts of the manuscript, providing me with archival material, and translating passages from Hebrew has been greatly beneficial. Professor Touraj Daryaee's kind assistance was particularly important for the pre-Islamic period. Professor Mehdi Bozorgmehr provided me with valuable references in sociological theory. Ms. Diane James' editorial work greatly improved the dissertation manuscript. Mr. Steve Scholl's help was vital in the book's design. Dr. Jalal Jalali, Mr. Ranin Kazemi, Professor Feraydoun Vahman, Professor Farzin Vejdani, Mr. Erfan Sabeti, Dr. Manouchehr Sadeghi, Ms. Haleh Emrani and Mr. Ala Qods have kindly provided me with references and source material for which I am most thankful. Dr. Olga Vasilyeva and Mr. Asef Ashraf assisted me with access to archival material, for which I am grateful. Needless to say, all errors and omissions are mine. Finally, to my dear wife Sholeh, I owe my earnest gratitude for her enduring patience, unremitting encouragement and thoughtful dialogue over the course of this project.

Mehrdad Amanat
Los Angeles, California

INTRODUCTION

During the late nineteenth and early twentieth centuries, a substantial number of Iranian Jews converted to the new Baha'i religion. As the noted Orientalist and scholar Walter J. Fischel observes, these conversions amounted to a revolution in Iranian Jewry:

> Small wonder, therefore, that Jewish adherents flocked to the Bahai movement. It was a revolution in the true sense of the word. The new ideas had the same effect on Persian Jewry that the French revolution had on western Jewry and, as in the case of the French revolution, Persian Jews were seized by a profound enthusiasm and admiration for their new faith.[1]

A sizable percentage of the Jews of Iran, and especially large numbers of young Jewish men, became Baha'is and enthusiastically promoted their new faith. This mass conversion was all the more remarkable since the Jewish converts were motivated primarily by ideas and a commitment to modernity.

Founded by Mirza Hosein 'Ali Nuri (1817–92), commonly known as Baha'u'llah (Arabic, glory of God), the Baha'i faith emerged in the 1860s from the messianic Babi movement which was started in 1844 by Mirza 'Ali Mohammad Shirazi (1819–50), known as the Bab (Arabic, the gate). The Bab attracted large numbers of Shi'i Muslim followers before he was executed as a heretic and his movement suppressed. The great majority of his followers eventually became Baha'is.

This book seeks to explore the causes and examine the circumstances of Jewish conversions within the broad context of the social and religious history of the late Qajar period. Chapter One attempts to trace the enduring dialogue and exchange of ideas between Jews and other

Persians that has played a role in Iranian history since ancient times. The mutual influences between Judaism and mainstream Zoroastrianism are one longstanding result. Sectarian movements of the early Islamic period also shared common themes with their Jewish counterparts—most notably in the area of messianic expectation.[2] These cultural and religious interactions intensified during a period of what has been called "religious ambiguity" under Ilkhanid rule (1256–1335), when a number of Jewish administrators became prominent statesmen under the Mongol khans. Later, during the Safavid and Qajar periods, as discussed in Chapter Two, this process of interfaith exchange and dialogue was disrupted as an exclusivist and politicized version of Shi'i Islam came to serve as the main source of legitimacy for the state. Especially during the Qajar period, Jews gradually lost much of their social status and economic influence, and trends towards integration became more restrained. Jewish participation in Iran's cultural discourse in this period was limited to scant liteary expressions and some involvement in Sufi orders.[3]

Attraction to a minority religion was a novel phenomenon among Iranian Jewry. While the Jewish presence in Iran's religious discourse is deep-rooted and its interaction with other sectarian and heterodox faiths particularly extensive, conversion to religions and sects outside of mainstream Islam has never been widespread among Jews. As discussed in Chapter Two, the forced conversion of large Jewish communities did take place during both the Safavid and Qajar periods, but these were usually only nominal conversions, subject to reversal once coercive pressures were lifted. The conversion of Jews to Christianity in the late nineteenth century was scant and restricted to a few communities. Although it was common for religious minorities in Iran to adopt the religion of the dominant culture or the ruling establishment, the story of the disadvantaged Iranian Jews who converted to the even more persecuted Baha'i faith presents an important, and perhaps unique, exception to earlier trends.

Voluntary conversions to Islam were not unusual in this period. Aside from genuine conviction, these conversions are often attributed to social and economic pressures, reinforced by a resurgence of messianic yearnings. Another type of conversion among a small group of aspiring and mostly privileged Jews also took place; and for these converts, joining mainstream Shi'ism was a means of immediate access to political, social, and economic advancement. However, for ordinary Jews who converted to Islam, out of force or necessity, or even out of personal conviction, the stigma and shame associated with being a new-convert (*jadid al-Islam*) could not be easily erased, even after generations.

It can therefore be argued that conversions to the Baha'i faith in the nineteenth and twentieth centuries were an extension of a somewhat forgotten cultural discourse among Jews within the Iranian environment. Messianic expectations were a primordial common theme of this discourse, with influences that are obvious in Jewish-Baha'i conversions. For many converts, the coming of a Savior instilled a new sense of optimism and hope for an end to age-old miseries. As discussed in Chapter Three, the all-embracing Baha'i message of "progressive revelation" inspired a sense of religious egalitarianism, regarding all past religions as equals, and created new possibilities for the meaning and boundaries of Jewish identity.

Jews in mid-nineteenth-century Iran faced severe discrimination and segregation based on the Shi'i doctrine of "impurity" (*nejasat*).[4] Most significantly, they were not allowed to engage in certain economic activities. By the turn of the twentieth century, conversion was facilitated by an increasing sense of optimism that Jews would be able to overcome old restrictions. Baha'i tolerance of fluid religious identities meant that converts could maintain their past communal and family ties, and even observe their previous ritual practices, after conversion to the new faith.

Unlike instances of forced conversions of Iranian Jews to Islam, Baha'i conversions were the result of conscious and voluntary individual choices, with characteristic personal and spiritual dimensions. As discussed in Chapter Four, conversion was also a complex process closely tied to the larger social and intellectual trends in Iran during this period. It came at a time of significant historical transformation, with the advent of modernity, foreign encroachment, political awakening, and national integration.[5] During this time of emerging "national" identity, many Jews migrated from ancient ghettos to newer or larger cities and became the beneficiaries of economic and social mobility within the emerging modern sector of society.

The voluntary nature of Baha'i conversions becomes even more significant in light of the long history of Baha'i persecutions. Beginning in the 1860s, at the urging of influential British Jews, Iranian Jews, like their Christian counterparts, sought a level of legal protection guaranteed by European powers. Even Zoroastrians found support among their coreligionists in India. Yet despite widespread conspiratorial beliefs that Babis and Baha'is were supported by various foreign nations, they lacked any such external allies and were almost entirely vulnerable to mob attacks and staged riots aimed at murder, looting, confiscation of property, and rape or the forced marriage of surviving women.

It is in this context of persecution that Jewish conversion to a socially deprived community appears remarkable. This book attempts to answer the vital question of why a sizable group of Persian Jews, who had a long history of mistreatment themselves, instead of seeking the relative security of conversion to Islam, would choose to join a new religion that was subject to even harsher persecution. This is a seemingly paradoxical development for which very few historical parallels may be found. It also defies any theories that explain conversion as an easy means of obtaining direct social and economic benefit.

Jewish-Baha'i conversions were mostly concentrated in certain communities with cultural and socio-economic characteristics that influenced conversion patterns. Although reliable statistics are hard to find, foreign observers have made estimates about the number of Jewish Baha'i converts in Iran. Ephraim Neumark (1860), a Jewish traveler and a native of Poland who visited Iran in 1884, gives the unlikely estimate of two million followers of the new religion, including "many Jews." Some fifty years later, the Jewish Ukrainian geographer Dr. Abraham J. Brower estimated the number of followers in the mid-1930s to be "thousands and perhaps ten thousand of Jews." He reports the converts to be "around a quarter of the Jews of Hamadan," while he estimates the Jewish population of Hamadan at the time to be 8,000. He also reports that as many as 700 Jews in Tehran converted to the Baha'i faith. Even these figures at first may seem inflated. Yet given the fluidity and range of Jewish-Baha'i identity in this period, ranging from sympathizers to community leaders, these estimates may not be entirely unreasonable.

The British diplomat Lord Curzon's estimates in the 1880s, prior to the early-twentieth-century wave of conversions, are perhaps representative of those converts who publicly confessed their Baha'i convictions. His figures for Kashan, Hamadan, and Tehran range from 50 to 100 to 150 Jewish families respectively. His estimate of as many as 75 per cent of the Golpayegan Jewish population having "formally joined the Bahai movement and their numbers have since increased considerably," indicates mass conversions among certain Jews.[6]

Any assessment of the number of converts is complicated by the fact that many converted as migrants while away from their hometowns. A recent study extending to the 1950s contains an expanded list of converts numbering some 150 families and individuals originally from Kashan, most of whom converted outside their city of origin. The study finds over 600 families and individual converts from Hamadan, including members of extended families. These figures compare to a Jewish community estimated in Hamadan at about 5,000 around the turn of the century, and 8,000 by the mid-1930s; and in Kashan some 400 Jewish households and individuals (including converts) prior to the mid-twentieth century wave of migration to Tehran.[7]

This book provides a survey of patterns of conversion among Jews based on the experiences of particular converts and their encounters with other Jews, Christians, Muslims, and Baha'is. As discussed in Chapter Five, many Jews underwent multiple conversion experiences. Some of those who were initially attracted to the message of the American Presbyterian missionaries in Hamadan, for example, overcame an important identity barrier and became Baha'is shortly thereafter. A sizable number of Jews also converted to Islam, either nominally or through genuine conviction, but later became Baha'is.

Such multiple conversions may provide clues to the question of why many Jewish converts to Islam would become committed members of the new and persecuted Baha'i faith. The anticipated advantages of being part of the majority Muslim community were often overshadowed by a deep sense of distrust and shame that attached to Jewish converts to Islam. Jewish identity was not so easily escaped. Converts who were labeled as "new-Muslims" could face serious disabilities, even after generations. This obsession with conversion history persists up to this day, as public figures are stigmatized in the Islamic Republic for their real or assumed Jewish ancestry.[8]

Beyond this, for those Jewish converts to Islam who sought freedom from what they saw as archaic fixations and oppressive clerical authority and who had paid the heavy price of abandoning family and community ties, becoming Muslims may have come to seem like exchanging one system of oppression for another. Many felt a pressing need to connect with a universal idea free from legalistic restraints, clerical restraints, and (what they saw as) archaic practices. In a social environment where self-definition was inconceivable outside of a religious community, conversion became a vital link to the emerging modern, secular mindset. There was also an important generational element, as younger, more mobile Jews tended to be attracted to a Baha'i community that represented modern ways and challenged traditional views of religion.

In fact a layered and multifaceted religious identity was not unusual among a number of Jewish converts. To some, Christianity initially offered a right of entry to western education and culture through missionary schools. Becoming a Muslim provided the legal protections necessary to an emerging propertied class. The Baha'i community, on the other hand, was the key to a faith-based belief in a modern mindset, which might allow the convert to escape at least the psychological control of all clerical authority and construct an autonomous self.

Like Baha'is, the Jews mostly tolerated fluid identities. However, when it came to public expressions of faith and open challenges to conventions, tension and confrontation intensified, especially with the rabbis. The Baha'i conversion experience, as a means of dealing with modernity and restoring ancient Iranian connections, was thus a more complex process than it is assumed to be in the works of earlier commentators.

Sources and Studies

This book is inspired by a number of autobiographical accounts written by Jewish Baha'i converts with a range of social backgrounds and geographic origins. Rayhan Rayhani (1859–1943) was an orphan from Kashan, an ancient town on the outskirts of Iran's central desert, who became a Jewish peddler with keen historical insight and later underwent a religious transformation.[9] As discussed in Chapter Six, his memoir gives voice to the experience of a disadvantaged, marginalized, and evolving Jewish community. The self-educated Rayhani may at times seem obscure, lacking the style and sophistication of his more literate contemporaries. Yet his rawness also makes him more transparent.

Chapter Seven is an overview of the life of Aqajan Shakeri (1884–1964) based on his autobiography (completed in 1961). He was also a self-educated convert from Iran's northwest region of Hamadan. He came from a modest background and earned a living as a textile merchant with modest and ephemeral success. His father was a bank-rupt merchant turned day laborer and his mother worked three jobs to barely make ends meet. Shakeri's account of Jewish family life captures the harsh reality of their miseries and includes invaluable information on a convert's struggle for faith and economic survival.[10]

In contrast to Shakeri, Yuhanna Khan Hafezi (1870–1951) who is the subject of Chapter Eight was a well-educated physician and entre-preneur from a privileged family of Hamadan Jewish physicians with close ties to the local ulama and nobility. His multi-volume memoir (written between 1925 and 1950) provides a view of a privileged and successful Jewish convert in Iran. It is a meticulously detailed account of the Baha'i community of Hamadan and the family lives of Hama-dani Jews, Muslims, and Baha'is of various social backgrounds.[11]

These unconventional accounts fill an important gap in the existing historical sources for this period of Iranian history, which are otherwise mostly concerned with the lives of the elite. Standard Qajar chronicles such as the *Rowdat al-safa* and *Nasekh al-tawarikh* contain little infor-mation about the experiences and persecution of the Iranian Jews. Their silence may speak to a lack of concern on the part of the official chroniclers to include non-Muslims in the official narrative. Important information relating to the forced conversions in Mashhad is found in E'temad al-Saltaneh's *Matla' al-shams*.[12] Works by Hasan Naraqi, a member of a prominent Kashan family of ulama and merchants, are scholarly contributions with valuable personal insight on social history and the history of the Constitutional Revolution in Kashan.[13]

Most notable among the general primary sources dealing with Kashan during the Qajar period is *Mer'at ul-Qasan* (Mirror of Kashan), written in 1871 by 'Abd al-Rahim Kalantar Zarrabi who, as indicated by his name (*kalantar*, mayor), was a member of a Kashan ruling family. The book was composed in response to a questionnaire sent around to urban officials and notables throughout Iran in the Naseri period to collect national data. It contains valuable information on geography, industries, agriculture and ethnography, as well as a history of the elite ulama, merchant, bureaucrat, and landowning families.[14] Muhammad 'Ali Ghaffari's *Khaterat va asnad* contains important information about the state of the economy and society and agricultural development in mid-nineteenth century Kashan.[15] However, the above primary sources say little about Kashan's Jewish community.

There have been few efforts to examine the lives, and especially the religious experiences, of ordinary Iranians. Nor has the critical voice of the converts looking from the outside of the Jewish community received the attention it deserves. At the turn of the century, when most commoners were illiterate, members of the Iranian elite produced the vast majority of autobiographies, journals, and other personal narratives. Starting in the 1940s an increasing number of autobiographies of mostly elite figures were published. This trend accelerated during the 1980s, when a great number of memoirs, including that of many clerics were published. Also, more common folk such as Aqa Najafi Quchani and 'Abdu l-Hosein Owrang (Shaykh al-Mulk), as well as Ahmad Kasravi, all of whom were poor *tullab* (religious students) trying to cope with a changing environment, produced fascinating accounts of the obstacles they faced trying to achieve social mobility through education. 'Abd ul-Hosein San'atizadeh-Kermani's narrative is, among other things, the story of the challenges in the life of an orphan.[16] Sheikh Ebrahim Zanjani's autobiography, written at the onset of Reza Shah's rule (mid-1920s) and published in 2000, is remarkable for its blatant anti-clerical views by a reform-minded thinker and constitutional advocate with a clerical facade.[17] Memoirs of Mo'ez al-Din Mahdavi (b. 1910?) reflects the viewpoint of a Pahlavi period mainstream religious family in Isfahan with modern education, but in touch with a traditional past.[18]

Like Mahdavi, his contemporary Mash'allah Farivar, the son of a Jewish rabbi, is also a product of a traditional religious family and a modern education. His extensive memoir provides valuable details about the life of Jews in Shiraz, a major center of Jewish population. His account contains valuable details on the impoverished, uneducated, and stratified nature of the Shiraz Jewish community and its efforts to build schools and provide itself with basic services. His description of the Jewish ghetto, its internal divisions and poor state of public health, are described with remarkable sophistication and with a personal touch relatively free from usual efforts to hide unpleasant realities.[19]

Among unpublished accounts by other Baha'is, Muzaffar Berjis's narrative, written in the 1970s, contains information about Kashan's Baha'i history.[20] *Tarikh-e amri-ye Kashan* was written in in 1930 by Mohammad

Nateq-e Isfahani, the principal of Vahdat-e Bashar, the Baha'i boy's school in Kashan. This work was part of a larger project initiated in the 1920s by the Baha'i world leader Bahiyyeh Khanom (1846–1932), the sister of 'Abdu'l-Baha, and continued by Shoghi Effendi Rabbani— known as the "Guardian" of the Baha'i faith (ministry 1921–57)—to collect local histories of Baha'i communities throughout Iran.[21] It is an important account of the development of the Kashan Baha'i commu- nity, its institutional history, and the persecutions it endured. Despite its usefulness, Nateq's history lacks the personal dimension and level of detail of the accounts by Rayhani, Shakeri, and Hafezi.[22]

The prominent Baha'i historian Fazel Mazandarani (1880–1957) produced a monumental nine-volume study of Babi-Baha'i history that contains valuable information on Kashan and Hamadan, based on interviews and accounts by Baha'i participants and eyewitnesses such as Rayhani and Hafezi. Remarkable for its thoroughness, this work provides evidence of the Baha'i movement's rapid growth in Iran and elsewhere through the 1940s. Yet to date, unfortunately, it remains mostly unpublished.[23]

In addition to the accounts of Baha'i authors, Yazghel Yerusha- laymi's history of Kashan and Arak, written in the 1980s, presents a Jewish perspective and contains important details about the lives of the Jews of Kashan, their motives for migrating to other cities, the lives of their young Jewish migrants, and internal communal tensions.[24] Yedidia Shofet's account contains the valuable firsthand experiences of a leading rabbi in Kashan and Tehran (and later Los Angeles). It focuses on the lives of the community elite, often at the expense of ordinary people who are largely absent from his narrative.[25]

In contrast to the frank accounts of Jewish miseries in pre-Pahlavi Iran penned by Baha'i converts, the published autobiographies by con- temporary Jewish authors tend to emphasize the social and economic advances of Iran's Jews under the Pahlavis and present sanitized accounts picturing a mostly successful past, free of misery and discrimination. This characteristic is even more pronounced in post-revolutionary writing from exile. For example, Heshmatullah Kermanshahchi's book focuses on the history of various Jewish organizations, but contains relatively little on the author's personal experiences in his hometown of Kermanshah. He makes virtually no mention of the family's origins prior to its arrival in Kermanshah. Instead, the volume's editor reports that the author's "ancestors came from one of Iran's central cities." This is presumably a euphemistic reference to a less glamorous Jewish center, such as Isfahan or Kashan.[26]

Yousef Cohen's short autobiography, though void of personal or family details, offers important information relating to the institutional formation and the changing legal position of the Jewish community since the 1950s. A newcomer to politics, Cohen was one of the Iran's first Jewish graduates of law. In 1975, at age 48, he won the seat reserved for the Jewish representative in Iran's parliament, previously held only by prominent Jewish families. His description of his close association with prominent political figures of the late-Pahlavi era, especially during the years leading to the 1979 Revolution, demonstrates the Pahlavi officials' sensitivity towards protection of the Jewish community against real and even imaginary threats. Nevertheless, his account is typical in its elite orientation to community history.[27]

A number of Persian sources that have dealt with Baha'i conversions have been written either by excommunicated Baha'is or by highly biased authors who revel in bizarre conspiracy theories. Some of these accounts are reflective of deep-rooted anti-Baha'i and anti-Jewish sentiments that persist through modernist narratives, be they nationalist, Marxist, or Islamic. One shared theme is their tendency to discount Baha'i success in attracting converts by pointing to the "Jewish element" (onsor-e jahud) as a corrupting force. For example, they blame the rise in the price of land and property in Tehran during the post-World War II boom on speculation by Jewish Baha'i converts, a stereotype that conveniently serves their double bias against Jews and Baha'is.[28] Such raw prejudices, tracing historical developments to Jewish-Baha'i conspiracies, persist not only in the works of influential popular historians such as Esma'il Ra'in, whose writing can hardly be called objective, but also in the works of contemporary historians familiar with Western-style scholarship, such as Fereydun Adamiyat who writes:

> The Baha'i factor, like the Jewish factor, became an instrument for the advancement of British policy in Iran. What is new is that some Jews (jahudan) also joined this sect and the same heritage of the British policy has now been handed over to America.[29]

More recently, the work of the prolific internet blogger 'Abdullah Shahbazi is noteworthy for its wide use of Baha'i secondary sources.

He deconstructs and dismisses the standard Marxist interpretations of the early Babi movement as a popular revolutionary uprising, only to replace them with yet another conspiracy theory that is indiscriminately hostile to Jews and Baha'is—yet more in line with established currents in the Islamic Republic.[30]

One common criticism raised in the above category of sources is that Baha'is have created division within the Iranian nation and have somehow been disloyal to the Iranian sense of patriotism. Ironically, both secularists and their traditionalist enemies have promoted these charges. This convergence suggests the usefulness of fringe groups in providing an element of "Otherness" which can be used as a point of contrast to the imagined unity of the national self. Baha'is reject these charges and in response tend to see such accusations as a misrepresentation of the Baha'i principle of universal peace and of Baha'u'llah's critique of extreme nationalism.

A related accusation has to do with Baha'is having somehow hindered the cause of liberal democracy in Iran by identifying it with religious heresy, thereby causing a reaction against reform among the ranks of Iran's traditionalists. The idea faults the Baha'is for presenting progressive ideas in a religious, rather than in a secular, framework. This argument fails to recognize the preeminence of religion in Iranian society and the indispensable historical role it continues to play. In the context of nineteenth-century Iran—and arguably up to this day—no meaningful voice of change could avoid addressing religion as a fundamental aspect of Iran's social and psychological structure.[31]

A somewhat different critique is presented by the reformist Islamic thinker 'Abd ul-Karim Sorush, who in a recent passing reference assessed Baha'i thought as "anachronistic." This evaluation is based on references to Baha'i religious obligations and rituals (takalif) as being out of place in a contemporary age of reason and rights (hoquq) and implies that Baha'is maintain a Shari'ah-style orientation toward religion.[32] However, one may question whether there was ever such a clear-cut division between religion and reason in mid-nineteenth-century Iran, or for that matter even in European thought. It can be argued that the Baha'i scriptures offer ample room for rational thinking and usually minimize ritual obligations when compared to other organized religions. In historical context, this may be seen as a radical departure from the Shi'i legalistic mindset of the nineteenth century, preoccupied as it was with matters such as "ritual impurity." In several instances, the relatively few ritual obligations ordained in Baha'i scriptures were reversed, abrogated, or simplified, while much room is left for reinterpretation of such laws in the future.[33]

Jewish Baha'i converts have also received some attention in Western scholarship.[34] Walter Fischel attributes the appeal of the Baha'i faith for Persian Jews to its "cosmopolitan outlook on life," its belief in "peaceful relations between the different faiths," and its rejection of the Shi'i principle of the uncleanness of non-Muslims. As proponents of religious tolerance and equality, Baha'is were seen as natural allies with Jews in their struggle against "the Shi'i clergy for freedom and tolerance."[35]

Hayyim J. Cohen attributes the general trend of Jewish conversions to Islam and the Baha'i faith to the "humiliation and persecution, suffering and torture" the Jews endured as a result of the Shi'i doctrine of ritual impurity.[36] He also cites a number of other factors including Baha'i acceptance of "Moses and his Torah," the absence of "a formal act of conversion," the fact that the Jews saw the new religion as one that spread a message of hope and promise for the improvement of their situation, and the "hope that Muslim Baha'is would furnish protection against persecution by the Muslims, at a time when authorities' protection was not sufficient, particularly outside of Tehran."[37] In Cohen's view, however, "ignorance in matters of religion" among Jews was a more significant factor in their attraction to the new religion.[38]

The charges of "ignorance" and "simplemindedness" leveled against Iranian Jews, originating with European observers, are also exressed in the works of scholars such as Fischel and Cohen. According to Fischel, for example:

> Had Persian Jews had spiritual leaders of high cultural standing in the last centuries, had the rabbis and schools taught and asserted a Judaism free from superstitious notions, empty formalism and medieval prejudices, had they shown a true sense for Judaism and its ethics, its national aspirations, its contribution to world culture, Bahaism would hardly have won so many Jewish hearts.[39]

Even Iranian scholars such as Habib Levy seem to be influenced by such views. His three-volume work was among the first to document the history of the Jewish presence in Iran.[40] In his autobiography, he

deplores the sad state of affairs among Iranian Jews around the turn of
the twentieth century. As an example, he cites an incident in which some
Jews sacrificed a sheep as a vow to the eighth Shi'i Imam Reza, portray-
ing this incident not as a case of religious and cultural give-and-take
with Islamic popular practice, but as a sign of decaying Jewish traditions.[41] In fact, such religious and cultural exchanges were common in
Iran. Many Jews in the community of Siahkal in Gilan province, for
example, fasted during Ramadan.[42] The Jews of Kurdistan celebrated
the Jewish festival of Simha-tura with familiar Sufi dances in order to
reach a state of *sama'* (trance).[43]

Such essentialist notions that present an idealized "true sense of Judaism" being weakened by the "ignorance" of Iranian Jews who needed
protection from various "threats" may be regarded as a Eurocentric
legacy that assumes an ahistorical, static, and monolithic Jewish identity which must be immune to the forces of change. Such views allow
little room for diversity within the Jewish community, discount cultural
borrowings from Iran's greater Perso-Islamic heritage, and leave little
room for interaction or for fluid identities.

A more complex alternative to this paradigm has been developed by
scholars, such as Mercedes Garcia-Arenal, who view religious identity
as a dynamic phenomenon in constant interplay with various cultural
forces, social interactions, and economic and political necessities. Her
brilliant work follows the sixteenth- and seventeenth-century history
of Spanish Jews who were forced to move from their homeland to
Morocco and then back to Spain.[44] The story of their forced conversions to Christianity, and later their return to Judaism and conversion
to Islam, is a fascinating and paradoxical example of how religious
identities can be negotiable and yet remain resilient.

An alternate view is possible to that of Cohen, who sees Iranian
"ignorance" as a function of "the absence of higher Torah institutions" and of isolation from other Middle Eastern Jews due to language
barriers. That is to acknowledge the Iranian Jewish community pos-
sesses a unique history and religious tradition. Its isolation from
rabbinic Judaism, one can argue, has deep historical roots that reach
back over centuries. Iranian Jews, especially in certain communities
such as Kashan, were influenced by alternative traditions such as the
Karaite movement, a medieval anti-rabbinic reading of Judaism with
Shi'i and pre-Islamic Iranian influences.[45] Iranian Jews had long held

a tangible sense of Iranian identity and had been active participants in the cultural life of their society.

In Fischel's view, Christian missionary activities and Baha'i conversions among Jews constituted "the two main dangers threatening Jewish survival" in Iran.[46] Conversions in this period were in fact part of a reach toward modernity and a response to changes in nineteenth-century Iran which became more pronounced after the 1906 Constitutional Revolution. The opening of modern schools meant better Persian language skills for Jews, and mastery of foreign languages—advantages that were not otherwise available to them. New economic opportunities required a physical and mental departure from the ghetto to exploit a new work environment that was opening up, especially after the gradual lifting of legal restrictions around the turn of the century. These factors increased the Jewish tendency to assimilate and gave some Jews a greater desire to rid themselves of the stigma of the "uncleanliness" and a willingness to re-evaluate their traditional belief systems.

The late Amnon Netzer's thoughtful essay stands in contrast to the usual treatment of the subject by observers unkind to Persian Jews and unsympathetic to converts.[47] He provides an extensive and useful summary of the arguments presented in the Jewish sources in various languages and finds them inadequate in answering many fundamental questions. However, his treatment of the Baha'i sources is limited to a couple of secondary books, including an apologetic work by Mirza Mehdi Arjomand.[48] He therefore leaves out the firsthand accounts and the viewpoints of the converts. Yet Netzer's religious and cultural approach leads him to a reformulation of Fischel's thesis that attraction to the Baha'i movement in Iran was analogous to the impact of the French Revolution on European Jews. Lacking the intellectual tradition of the European Jews to reform itself, Netzer argues, Persian Jewry had to search beyond its antiquated boundaries for a "Reform Judaism." The antiquated, "almost empty, broken vessel" of nineteenth-century Persian Judaism had little to offer to "the youth searching for intellectual meanings."

To the vital question of why Persian Jews would embrace a persecuted faith, Netzer admits having no definitive answers. He suggests, however, that conversion to the Baha'i religion among Jews (presumably, instead of to Islam) is part of a deep-rooted desire to subvert the dominance of Shi'ism, which Persian Jews saw as the source of their oppression. Netzer goes on to argue that the deep "Iranian" aspiration for "replacing Islam in Iran with a reformed, or perhaps eclectic, 'Iranian religion'" has long been an aspect of the history of the nation. However, this book argues that one main source of tension in Iran's religious history, extending back to the pre-Islamic era, has always been the conflict between a conformist, legalistic form of religion and an eclectic approach favoring tolerance, diversity, and dialogue. This interpretation rejects an unchanging Iranian struggle to oppose an essentialized notion of Islam.

As Netzer admits, the rise of a centralized and secular state under Pahlavi rule brought political protection and economic improvement for Jews. It also brought new "threats" to the Jewish community in the form of intellectual challenges, mainly from state-sponsored secularism and leftist intellectuals. For many Jewish leaders, such as Habib Levy, the only proper response to these challenges to tradition from secularism (*bi-dini*) was to adopt a new, Western Jewish identity heavily influenced by the ideology of Zionism. By the 1940s, the traditional Iranian Jewish practice was increasingly giving way to a new, modern Jewish identity with Zionism as a significant component. As Fischel foresaw, the establishment of the state of Israel as the fulfillment of Jewish "national aspirations" (perhaps in combination with the Jews' economic transformation under the Pahlavis) drastically reduced Baha'i conversions, instilled a new sense of self-confidence among Jews, and served to counter forces of secularism and modernity.

This book is an attempt to explore how Iranian Jews tried alternative ways of coming to terms with modernity. While some converted to Islam, many others adopted the dominant Western or secular model of assimilation, and others took the path of an indigenous form of modernity rooted in the Iranian cultural tradition and consistent with an ancient yet somewhat forgotten tradition of inclusiveness and tolerance.

1

THE JEWISH PRESENCE IN
PRE-ISLAMIC AND MEDIEVAL IRAN

The Jews of Iran have been an integral part of the Iranian milieu since its very inception and have always had a presence in various spheres of Iranian life. Western observers, influenced by their own nineteenth-century experience of Jewish life, drew a picture of isolated and often persecuted Jewish communities in Iran with little interaction with the larger society. A deeper perspective on the Jewish experience, however, reveals a very different, though somewhat forgotten, pre-modern past when long coexistence with other Iranians involved a good deal of engagement, interaction, and borrowing of ideas and practices, that resulted in profound mutual influences. [1] A brief overview of the long history of the Jewish community in Iran will provide an historical context that is necessary to better understand some of the social transformations that took place during the modern period.

As a marginalized "religious minority" (as they are often referred to in the literature), the rich history of the Jews of Iran has not always been fully acknowledged and their role and accomplishments have gone largely unrecognized. Yet their wide-ranging contributions have indeed been crucial to what can be called Iran's socio-cultural "eco-system," an environment often endangered by the threat of cultural and religious conformity. In a society that exhorted considerable pressure to conform to a single dominant religion, communities with a different religious identity provided much-needed diversity that served a variety of economic and cultural functions. Such functions varied from preservation of aspects of the culture forbidden by dominant norms to reaffirmation of the dominant identity, whether Zoroastrian or Islamic, by providing an example of "Otherness."

Jews in the Pre-Islamic Period

As one of Iran's oldest ethnic groups, Jews are reported to have lived within Iran's historical boundaries some two hundred years prior to the establishment of the Persian Empire. By the time of Achaemenid rule in the sixth century BCE, Jewish colonies were reportedly "scattered over all provinces and among all peoples of the Persian Empire."[2] For over a millennium, from the Achaemenid to the late Sassanid era, and with few exceptions, the Jews enjoyed relative freedom and religious toleration. They were an active part of Iran's diverse religious scene and became a component in the ecumenical equilibrium that preserved the Sassanid social fabric.[3] This equilibrium began to change after the Arab invasion as a whole new set of rules were applied to non-Muslims.

The Assyrian invasion of the Northern Kingdom of Israel in 722 BCE is believed to have started the first wave of Jewish migration to Iran. The invasion of the Southern Kingdom of Judea and the destruction of the first Temple in Jerusalem by Babylonians in 586 BCE were accompanied by forced exile and captivity (*galut*) in Babylonia that lasted a half-century. This was the beginning of what came to be known as the Jewish Diaspora. The Jews interpreted this course of events as God's punishment for their failure to keep their covenant with Moses. The destruction of the Temple was a major blow to Jewish identity, as the required sacrifices that were crucial to Jewish religious life could only be performed there.

A major turning point, one with profound consequences to the history of Judaism, came with the conquest of Babylon by Cyrus in 539 BCE. Founder of the Achaemenid Empire, Cyrus (d. 529 BCE) was noted for allowing Jews and other religious communities to practice their religions more freely. He ended the exile of Babylonian Jewry and allowed many of them to return to Jerusalem and rebuild their Temple. The reconstruction of the Temple, which actually took place under Darius the Great (520–516 BCE), became a symbol of the freedom of the Jews and their acceptance as subjects of the empire on an equal footing with other nationalities. Some observers have even compared the role of Cyrus as a liberator of the Jews to that of Moses. In fact, Cyrus is the only foreign ruler with a positive image in the Bible, where he is referred to as "God's anointed." Based on this, the Jews regarded him as a messiah (*masih*).[4]

Under Artaxerxes II, a second wave of Jewish settlements led by

Ezra returned to ancient Palestine in 398 BCE.[5] However, many Jews remained in today's western Iran and Mesopotamia-Babylonia, and were influential in the formation of Talmudic law.[6] On many occasions, the Jews of Palestine and Babylonia saw Persians as their allies and even their liberators vis-à-vis the often-intolerant Greeks and Romans who ruled Palestine from 330 BCE and 63 BCE respectively. While there is plenty of propaganda in Jewish texts against Babylonian, Roman, and Greek rule, there are no such derogatory references to the Persians. The natural alliance between Jewish elites and Achaemenid Persians against common enemies is an underlying current throughout the period. The cultural interaction of Jews and Iranians is evident from the early stages of their contact and influenced several central eschatological beliefs found in Judaism.

This pattern of interaction and tolerance became more evident during the Parthian era, which coincided with severe persecutions of Jews in the neighboring Roman Empire. The tolerant policies of the Parthians are believed to have convinced a large number of Jews to migrate to Iran. The position of exilarch (*rash galuta*; lit., head of the exiles) was established in 70 CE under King Vologeses I (Valaxsh, 51–77 CE), whereby the Jews of Parthian Iran enjoyed a form of self-governing authority with independent political, administrative, and juridical powers. There were Jews with Persian names among the Parthian cavalry officers and administrators. Indeed, the earliest extant record of today's city of Isfahan is a tablet inscription in Hebrew, dated 130 CE, commemorating Jewish atonement.[7]

As promoters and protectors of the Zoroastrian religion, the early Sassanid rulers (224–651 CE) reduced the autonomy that Jews and other non-Zoroastrians had previously enjoyed, and as a result the exilarch exercised less power. An example of this change of status can be observed in the reign of Shapur I (240–70 CE), when the Jewish community under the leadership of Samuel was forced to accept Sassanid laws and the imposition of new taxes.[8] However, as their Parthian predecessors had learned, the Sassanids found that it was impossible to control their vast empire without allowing considerable autonomy to diverse religious and ethnic groups. By the beginning of the fifth century, the Jews had regained much of their independence and their position had improved. This is evident in the marriage of Yazdgird I (399–420 CE) to Shoshan-dokht, daughter of the Jewish exilarch.[9]

Yet by the mid-fifth century, the conditions of the Jews changed again. Under Yazdgird's successors, observance of the Sabbath was banned and Hebrew schools were closed. The rise of a number of Jewish messianic movements, with their call to rebuild the Temple in Jerusalem, had political implications. Such movements symbolized the evolving messianic trend and its alarming consequences even for the Jewish rabbis. The enthusiasm of the Jews for the advent of the Messiah may have been an expression of their aspirations for improved conditions. In 364 CE, for instance, Jews who had been deported from Armenia to Gay (or Jay: Isfahan) attacked and killed two Zoroastrian priests, which led to the massacre of a community of Armenian Jews on the orders of Shapur II (309–79 CE).[10] This brutal suppression may have been in part a response to the actions taken by some Iranian Christians who had vandalized Zoroastrian fire temples and defied Sassanid legitimacy by refusing to pay taxes. Yet at the same time there was a level of political alliance and political collaboration. As conditions changed for the better yet again in the mid-sixth century under Khusrow I (531–70 CE), Yemeni Jews collaborated with the Persians against the Byzantines' Ethiopian vassalage.

By the seventh century, there was much discontent with the archaic and extremely restrictive Sassanid social structure, which was dominated by a clerical elite with ties to an exclusionist and corrupt ruling class. Just as many Iranians in the early Islamic period saw hope in the arrival of conquering Arab armies and their promises of social equality, the Jews also responded positively to the advance of the Arabs.[11]

Economic and Cultural Spheres

The symbiotic relationship between Jews and non-Jews was able to fill gaps in vital areas of the economy. This is particularly evident where Islamic law discouraged or prohibited such activities as money-lending, dealing in gold and silver, and even the production of wine, an indispensable element in Persian social life as reflected in Persian poetry. Jewish financiers, goldsmiths and silversmiths, and traders with long-distance connections who served as retailers and distributors of merchandise, made up a significant part of Iran's economy.

Examples of long-distance traders among Jews are found throughout Iranian history. As early as the Parthian period, Jews played a vital role in Babylonia and Palestine, particularly in the silk trade from China to the Roman Empire. One major advantage of the Jews in Islamic times was their crucial economic function as interregional commercial agents. Their right to travel and their freedom of economic enterprise were guaranteed by their *dhimma* status. In contrast to the majority Muslims whose travel to non-Muslim lands was restricted, the Jews of the Islamic world utilized their network of coreligionists to establish trade links and facilitate financial transactions within and beyond Islamic boundaries.

Through most of the Islamic period, cross-regional trade connections remained a marker of the Jewish economy and commercial character. Jewish traders played a crucial role in the Khorasan and Central Asian trade even as late as the eighteenth and early nineteenth centuries. As long as the Iran-Basra trade was in existence (as late as the 1930s), it was largely dependent on connections between the large and affluent Iraqi Jewish community and their coreligionists all over the region, including western and central Iran.

Even in later Islamic times, when the social status of Jews declined in Iranian society, small merchants and peddlers (such as Rayhan Rayhani, who provides a case study for this book) maintained their integral function. Jewish artisans ranging from goldsmiths, silversmiths, and silk weavers to those with more menial skills such as women who sorted silk threads, possessed specialized skills that were crucial to such major industries as the manufacture of carpets and textiles.[12]

The Jewish contribution to Iran's performing arts is especially noteworthy. The role of Jewish musicians, entertainers, comedians, and dancers—as well as composers and instructors of music—in preserving and promoting the Persian musical tradition is particularly visible. Their role became significant during periods of increased social pressure from conservative elements within the Shi'i ulama, who in such times launched broad attacks on musical entertainment as a whole and tried to prevent the Muslim majority from taking part in performing or even learning music.[13]

In the area of science and scholarship during the Islamic period, knowledge of Hebrew placed many literate Jews in the privileged position of being the custodians of what was considered to be esoteric knowledge, ranging from holy scriptures to medicine, astrology, and white magic. This in part explains the image of the Jewish physician and the substantial contribution of Persian Jews to the preservation of Galenic and Indo-Persian traditions of medicine. As part of a movement that was crucial to the development of Western science and philosophy in later centuries, Jewish translators in twelfth- and thirteenth-century Spain helped to expand as well as preserve many Perso-Islamic texts by translating them from Arabic and Persian into Hebrew and Latin.[14]

Knowledge of Hebrew and the biblical tradition also accounts for many contributions of prominent Jewish converts to the development of what are often defined as "Islamic" sciences. Chief among them is Rashid al-Din Fazlullah, the great minister and historian of the Ilkhanid period who is well known for his monumental contributions in the fields of historiography, scientific research, and urban development. His work as a scholar and thinker was built on a Jewish tradition of scholarship going back several generations. Rashid al-Din's grandfathers collaborated with the "Sevener" or Shi'i Isma'ili scholars assembled in the fortress of Alamut in northern Iran.[15]

Iranian Jews were also important in the fields of Persian language and literature. One early contribution is the introduction of terms from Aramaic, the language of the Jews, into Persian, especially in the fourth century BCE when the Jews were increasingly adopting Persian vernacular.[16] As poets, mystics and literary figures who reflected on their individual and community experiences, they wrote mostly in Judeo-Persian (Persian written in Hebrew characters).[17] Their literary work represents one important aspect of diversity within Iran's cultural landscape. This is evident in the way Judeo-Persian aided in the preservation and development of the middle-Persian vernacular during the two "silent" centuries following the Islamic conquest. This was a critical time for the evolution of Middle Persian into the modern Persian language. The archaic Pahlavi script, which had been intentionally complicated for the exclusive use of the Zoroastrian priesthood, was abandoned almost of necessity. The Judeo-Persian script, in which the oldest known example of modern Persian was written, played a vital conservational role during this transitional period prior to the emergence of the modern Persian script which consists mostly of a modified Arabic alphabet. The first known examples of the modern Persian language, dating back to the eighth and ninth centuries and discovered in northwestern China (Khutan), are written in Hebrew script.[18] Moreover, the first known example of a printed Persian text, being a translation of the Pentateuch, was published in Hebrew characters in Constantinople in 1456.[19]

A remarkable literary contribution during the first half of the nineteenth century was accomplished through interfaith cooperation in Hamadan, later a center of Jewish conversion to the Baha'i faith. The first known joint publication of the Old and the New Testaments in Persian translation was commissioned by the British and Foreign Bible Society and completed through collaboration of Christian missionaries, Jewish rabbis, and the renown Qajar literary figure Fazel Khan Garrusi (1784–1843), with whom the term *fazelkhani* is associated. Published in 1856, this text had important religious significance for the Persian Jews, who for the first time had access to the scripture in their spoken language. This access to Torah texts may have reduced the authority of the rabbis as the sole source of scriptural knowledge. The book is also notable for its literary significance as part of Iran's mid-nineteenth century literary revival. Its lasting influence can be traced in mid-twentieth century Persian poetry.[20]

Encounters with Other Religions

Another area of interaction with immense historical significance is that of the mutual influences between Zoroastrian and Jewish cosmology and eschatology, which are believed to have begun early, in the sixth century BCE, when Jews and Persians first came into contact. A number of fundamental aspects of what later came to be the mainstream beliefs and doctrines were absent in pre-Babylonian Judaism. Such basic principles as a clear definition of life after death, angels, demons (and "the devil," including the figure of Satan, who later became a central part of Christian and Muslim demonology), a personal sense of responsibility and ethics as distinct from the responsibility of the community, a "linear" notion of time with an apocalyptic end, even the notion of a messiah as savior—all of these concepts were introduced into Judaism during this period and are believed to be the product of interaction and borrowing between the two religious traditions.[21]

Among many similarities between the two traditions, the idea of the first man committing sin in the story of Adam and Eve corresponds to that of Yima and Yami, the brother and sister who sinned together in the Avestic tradition. Other parallels with Iranian myths can be observed in the story of Noah and the flood and the biblical theme of expectation of the ultimate savior, which was profoundly influenced by the idea of Saoshyant and the notion of the renewal of the world (*farashkart*) in the Zoroastrian tradition. In the Islamic era too, one area of interreligious exchange with somber consequences for Persian Jews was the Zoroastrian influence on the development of the laws of purity and pollution, particularly after the ascendancy of legalistic Shi'ism in the Safavid period.[22]

The engagement between the two religious traditions on apocalyptic themes is also evident in the Book of Daniel and other writings contemporary with it, such as the Book of the Secrets of Enoch (which was discarded in the first century CE by rabbis responsible for the establishment of Jewish orthodoxy). Written in Aramaic, then the official language of the Parthian Empire, the Book of Daniel contains a number of Persian loanwords, including key words such as *raz*, a familiar term in Zoroastrianism and early Christianity that refers to "knowledge of God's plan for the world and especially for the end of time."[23] Despite the pretense of these texts to an earlier origin, they are believed to be products of the second century BCE, when in 167 Judaism was banned in Palestine under Greek rule and Jewish persecutions continued under their Roman successors.[24]

There are striking parallels in these Jewish scriptures with Zurvanism, a monistic form of Zoroastrianism. Itself in part influenced by Judaism, Zurvanism modified the Zoroastrian view of the course of history as a struggle between the powers of good and evil culminating in the destruction of all forces of evil, to a predetermined course dictated by a single determined primordial power of Time. It has been argued that the Zurvanic influence on Judaism is evident in ideas such as the resurrection of the dead on the Day of Judgment (which is to come within "limited time"), when individuals are punished for their sins or rewarded for good deeds with eternal life, which many saw as physical life on earth. The idea of the imminent coming of the Day of Judgment that would put an end to the rule of oppressors against whom the Jews had no recourse was appealing to the persecuted Jews of the time. This differs sharply from the "Day of Yahweh" foretold in the Old Testament, when Israel and its enemies would both be the recipients of God's wrath. Enoch presents an image that is radically different from the wrathful and often merciless God of the Old Testament, in the form of a teacher with secret knowledge to pass on to others, a familiar presentation of the "Lord of Wisdom," Ahura Mazda.[25] With the ascendancy of rabbinic orthodoxy, however, the active presence of the human agent in the realm of the sacred, itself a prominent feature of the Zoroastrian religion, was largely forgotten.[26]

In a fascinating case of Jewish influence on the Iranian religious environment, the Zoroastrian rulers of the Parthian vassal state of Adiabene in Mesopotamia were converted to Judaism by Jewish missionaries during the lifetime of Jesus. They went on pilgrimage to Palestine, built mausoleums there and later sent troops to reinforce the defense of Jerusalem against Roman attack.[27] This is one of many examples of state-subject relations between the Jewish clients and Persian overlords.

The Early Islamic Period

Though Jews initially welcomed the Arab invasion of Iran in the seventh century, some Jewish communities soon joined forces with other resistance movements—many with common messianic tendencies—to oppose foreign rule and seek political and religious independence. The establishment of Islamic rule required more conformity and placed serious restrictions on Jews, inhibiting their social and cultural participation in public life. Yet Islamic law provided Jews, as "People of the Book" (*ahl al-kitab*), a measure of protection that, while at times overlooked or violated, nevertheless resulted in overall conditions for Persian Jews that were far superior to those of Jews in pre-modern Europe.

The Arab invasion, at least initially, led to more religious diversity, as Iran experienced a variety of messianic revivalist movements. The collapse of Sassanid rule and the disintegration of the authority of the Zoroastrian priestly establishment provided the necessary space for otherwise suppressed sectarian tendencies to emerge. Aside from heterodox Zoroastrian movements, a whole range of Jewish sects (supposedly as many as seventy-one) evolved during this period—from messianic rebellions to anti-rabbinic movements and even radical atheism. They shared some common characteristics with other crypto-Zoroastrian and Manichean movements of the time, such as a strong expectation of the advent of a savior and the call for regional independence. A natural reaction to the Arab occupation, such aspirations for political independence characterized Persia's great social transformation in the two centuries following the Arab conquest. The widespread appeal of these movements within the Islamic context eventually culminated in the Abbasid Revolution of 750.

Yet the significance of these movements went beyond their political role of resisting foreign rule. Perhaps more importantly, they resisted the threat of religious and cultural conformity. As alternatives to a dominant religious identity, they helped develop a distinct "Perso-Islamic" religious culture which, contrary to the established religion, was non-dogmatic, intellectually dynamic, and "negotiable" at individual and communal levels. Chief among the non-Islamic movements was the crypto-Mazdakite Khurramiya movement (816–36) led by the charismatic Babak Khorramdin in Azerbaijan.[28]

The flexibility embedded in these movements allowed them to act simultaneously as agents of change and instruments of continuity. While at times they facilitated the process of conversion to Islam by acting as "stepping stones," they did so by infusing a substantial Iranian element into the Islamic message. Iran's early religious mosaic produced a vibrant interfaith discourse with considerable exchange among diverse Jewish, Christian, Zoroastrian, Manichean, and Muslim groups, as well as a range of heterodoxies within which the lines of religious identity were more freely drawn. Although many surviving sources have dismissed the role of sectarian movements and concealed or distorted information about them in an attempt to present an historical narrative free of "heresies" and nonconformities, these movements and the participation of the Jews in Iranian religious life remain an important influence in the Islamic discourse. The heresiographical genre (*al-milal wa al-nihal*) that emerged in the early Islamic centuries demonstrates the preoccupation of the writers of the time with the richness of the religious environment and often with the dangers of heretical diversity.[29]

The Militant Jews of Isfahan

The Jewish community of Isfahan presents a valuable example of messianic aspirations and sectarian participation in the early Islamic period. The very founding of Isfahan was closely associated with the Jewish settlement in the area, giving rise to one of the city's appellations as *Yahud-bareh* (Jewish Borough, known today as Jubareh). At the time of the arrival of the Arab armies around 642, which they presumably saw as the prelude to the coming of the "Jewish King," the Jews (who formed a sizable sector of the city's population) reportedly celebrated the event with music and dancing. Such accounts of rising expectations point to continuity in messianic aspirations among Jews of the Sassanid period before the Arab invasion.[30]

Decades later, probably toward the end of the seventh century, Jewish messianic hopes in Isfahan resurfaced in the form of an armed rebellion against Arab rule. The movement was led by Abu 'Isa, a tailor with apparently no formal education, but presumably possessing esoteric knowledge. He proclaimed himself the Messiah and revealed books of his own, giving birth to a movement that came to be known as 'Isawiyya. Abu 'Isa defended the station of Jesus and of Mohammad as true divine prophets, while he advocated innovations in Jewish law, thereby challenging rabbinic authority. His proposed reforms included a prohibition against the consumption of meat and wine (indicating a possible Manichean influence) and a call for the recitation of prayers seven to ten times daily. The movement attracted a large number of adherents who engaged in armed conflict against the Arab forces stationed in the city. Abu 'Isa was reportedly killed in a battle with the caliph's troops in Ray, some 200 miles north of Isfahan—itself evidence of the spread of the conflict beyond the area of the city. For many years after the death of Abu 'Isa, his followers continued to await his "return." His movement spread beyond Iran to Syria where a community of his followers is reported to have survived as late as the eleventh century. Like many other movements for communal autonomy in the early Islamic period, Abu 'Isa sought to come to terms with the new religious realities of an increasingly Islamicized Iran.[31]

An even more radical form of Jewish heterodoxy of this period found expression in one of Abu 'Isa's followers, the Yudghan of Hamadan, and in Hiwi al-Balkhi who went much further in breaking with convention. Their skepticism went beyond questioning rabbinic authority and extended to doubting the validity of the Torah and even to denying the existence of God. These radical Jews fought for their new creeds and questioned the conventional approach to their religion.

But other more conservative Persian Jews also resisted the ascendancy of rabbinic orthodoxy. One important product of dialogue between "reformist" Jews and the early Islamic sectarian movements was the rise of the Karaite movement. Originating in Iraq of the eighth century, a hotbed of sectarian debate, the Karaites showed clear Shi'i and Iranian influences. They were intensely messianic and preoccupied with the mourning of saints; they rejected the authority of the Talmud as an unchanging body of law and relied on *ijtihad*, interpretation of the Torah by living experts. Iran became an important center of the Karaite movement and was home to a number of its leaders. Despite continuous opposition from the Talmudic/rabbinic orthodoxy, Karaite communities continued to survive throughout Iran into the sixteenth century, and their influence is discernible as late as the nineteenth century. Karaite debates were known to congregants in Kashan synagogues as late as the 1920s and influenced Baha'i conversions there. Karaite communities survive to this day in Israel.[32]

After the establishment of the Pax Islamica, improved means of communication facilitated contacts with Baghdad's Jewish rabbinic authority and in turn gave Iran's rabbis greater authority over eastern communities through the appointment of judges, the establishment of religious schools (*yeshivas*), and the collection of religious taxes. This led to protests from the already overtaxed Iranian Jews, such that the Babylonian Jewish rabbis even engaged the assistance of Muslim government officials to collect delinquent taxes. This may shed light on anti-rabbinic tendencies within the Jewish sectarian movements of the early Islamic period.

Early Conversions to Islam

Messianic non-conformism aside, from the early days of the Islamic era, conversion to Islam in the Iranian world has been a multifaceted process whose diversity and complexity remain largely unexplored. Apart from the widespread ambivalence in the Islamic sources about the entire subject of conversion, the early Islamic chronicles and biographical dictionaries were mostly written, as suggested by Richard Bulliet, during the tenth century, after most mass conversions had already taken place.

Conversion was for the most part a social phenomenon. Aside from the recitation of a creed in a liturgical language that most Iranians did not understand, the main expressions of adherence to Islam were made through social symbols, such as public prayer, changing one's name, and adopting Arab-style clothing. Such public expressions were not easy things to accomplish in the presence of friends and relatives, many of whom had not converted. The need for Muslim converts to start a new life with a new identity in a new setting under Islamic rule may well explain the increased rate of urbanization during the early Islamic centuries, which was in the main due to the growth of immigration from the countryside. The emerging Islamic world gave rise to a rapid rate of economic expansion, eliminated rigid class distinctions, broadened social mobility, and enhanced migration trends.[33]

At least during the early decades of the Islamic conquest, the Zoroastrian community was under more pressure to convert than were other religious groups, such as the Jews. The Zoroastrian elites, concerned with maintaining their position of privilege and leadership, were more inclined to convert to Islam and attach themselves to the new Muslim aristocracy as their *mawali* (clients). On the other hand, Jewish and Christian leaders had less to lose and did not have to become Muslims in order to maintain their social standing. Moreover, as Claude Cahen has pointed out, unlike the Sassanid Zoroastrian elite, whose community ties were weakened because of schisms within the Zoroastrian establishment, Jewish and Christian elites were "more successful in restraining their adherents from yielding to the temptations of Islam."[34]

With respect to the timing of mass conversions, and contrary to the conventional view, the course of the Arab conquest was not swift and without resistance, nor did it lead to instantaneous mass conversions. In fact, according to recent scholarship, few Persians converted to Islam before the mid-eighth century. Mass conversions only reached their zenith in the early part of the tenth century and were "completed" by the early eleventh century. Even then, Zoroastrians, Christians, and Jews continued to form a substantial part of Iran's population.[35] This was a time when Islamic society had become much more homogenized and for the most part dress codes had lost their religious significance. The reappearance of Persian names during this period indicates a decline in religious naming, while the emergence of the written modern Persian language meant that Arabic was no longer the only written language of Muslims. These developments led to a shift in the meaning of conversion from social and political assimilation to an expression of one's religious belief. Believers were now expected to have a deeper knowledge of Islam. This trend indicates more resistance to conversion and resulted in fewer mass conversions in general. However, as indicated below, this did not mean that conversions came to a halt. We can assume that, although throughout the early Islamic centuries there were some conversions to Islam among the Jews along with the majority of the Iranian population, the communal identity of a sizable sector of the Jews of Iran was further solidified by their assigned status as People of the Book.

Much has been made of the inferior status of the Jews under early Islamic rule. Their non-Muslim status (*dhimmi*) has often been considered a form of second-class citizenship. Yet it is important to note that, at least in some ways, the conditions of Persian Jews improved after the Muslim conquest. Unlike their situation in the Sassanian period, the Jews were no longer required to perform forced labor and military service, while the non-Muslim tax (*jizya*) was not much more than the mostly voluntary *zakat* expected of Muslim believers. On the other hand, a long list of discriminatory restrictions were placed upon the Jews in some periods under Islam—although their level of enforcement varied—including a dress code, limitations on the size of Jewish houses, and prohibitions on the propagation of their faith and marriage to Muslim women. Jews were prohibited from allowing the sound of their prayers to reach the ears of Muslims and were forced to perform their burial rituals in secret. Nevertheless, as *dhimmi*s, they were a recognized minority protected under Islamic law, as people whose protection was the responsibility of the Muslim community, a position the Zoroastrians did not enjoy until decades after the Arab conquest. As a result, Jews and Christians received more lenient treatment from the Muslim conquerors than did their Zoroastrian counterparts.[36]

Religious Diversity under Mongol Rule

The real change in Jewish social status came about in the late Middle Ages. After the Mongol invasion in the thirteenth century, Iran was ruled for the first time since the Arab conquest by non-Muslims, often with shamanistic and Buddhist persuasions. For decades after the initial invasion, the Mongol Ilkhans, as they were known, remained indifferent and at times even hostile to Islam. With the weakening of the dominant Islamic establishment and the Shari'a legal order it represented, the Jews opted for greater socio-cultural assimilation and even political participation. The Mongol rulers, as a minority community with limited political or agrarian bases coming to dominate a largely alien territory, more easily trusted the Jews than the majority Muslims who had stronger political roots. A number of Jewish physicians and administrators rose to positions of administrative prominence and played leading roles in the political life of Ilkhanid

Iran. This prepared the ground for a period of greater openness and religious dialogue among Jewish and Muslim scholars. We can also observe a number of voluntary conversions to Islam among Jewish scholars and statesmen in this era.[37]

The fall of the Abbasid Caliphate in 1258, and the further consolidation of non-Muslim rule, lasting some seventy years, gave rise to fundamental changes in the religious and political life of the eastern Muslim world. The new ruling elite with its shamanistic beliefs was initially uninterested in monotheistic religions, and least of all in Islam as a viable social force. Gradually, however, the Ilkhanids became attracted to other religions, and at various periods many eventually converted to Buddhism, Christianity, and Islam along with their Mongol tribal leadership. Muslim rule was re-established in earnest in Iran after the conversion of Ghazan Khan in 1295.

The fall of the caliphate also strengthened sectarian groups such as the Shi'is and the Sufi orders. They entertained a wide range of belief systems alternative to Sunni Islam, and fresh intellectual tendencies gained currency among the Muslim populace and the Ilkhanid elite in the later Middle Ages. These groups included moderate Shi'is who tried to win over the Ilkhanid rulers and their administration, at times even seeking reconciliation with Sunni Islam. On the other end of the spectrum stood various forms of "extremist" Shi'i-Sufi orders with ambitions to power. It was this latter tendency that eventually contributed to the ascendancy of the Safavid dynasty in the beginning of the sixteenth century.

During the Mongol period then, Iran became a land of religious diversity, home to many Nestorian churches (especially popular among elite Mongol women) and Buddhist temples led by priests invited from India. Adding to this fascinating picture was the rise of a wide variety of popular religious figures, ranging from those with claims to magical powers and sorcery (an accepted practice among the Mongols) to mystics with ancient Iranian tendencies such as Mazdakism about which very little is known.

Part of this environment of religious experimentation may be attributed to the reigning pagan culture of the period and its tolerant approach to various monotheistic traditions. Examples of religious fluidity and curiosity include rulers like Tagdur (also known by his Muslim name, Ahmad; r. 1282–84), who converted to Islam but reverted back to Buddhism toward the end of his life, and Baydu (r. 1295), a Buddhist who was baptized and later confessed his belief in Islam. This fluidity may be attributed to a natural attempt by Mongol rulers to find meaning in a much more complex monotheistic culture that was drastically different from their own and to try to connect to it. Politically, experimentation with various religious traditions was an attempt to find legitimacy in alternative models. In the end, none of these experiments in religious innovation could compete with what had become by then the deep-rooted belief in Islam held by most Iranians, which dominated many spheres of life including law and education.

A turning point in the era of religious tolerance and innovation came with Ghazan (r. 1295–1304), when at the outset of his reign his entire army converted to Islam in the midst of intense dynastic conflicts. This event virtually put an end to seventy years of ecumenical rule and established the state's recognition of Islam as Iran's dominant religion. Ghazan's conversion, which was initially followed by the destruction of churches and Buddhist temples (including one built for his own father), at least superficially ended religious fluidity and multiple identities among the Mongol rulers. However, others within the governing class maintained their diverse identities or, as Rashid al-Din put it, "persevered in their hypocrisy."[38] Ghazan's dramatic public utterance of the Islamic confessional creed (*shahada*) represented a definitive step toward Mongol assimilation into Perso-Islamic culture. It also signaled a reversal of previous Mongol anti-Islamic policies toward Muslim notables whose support Ghazan needed to consolidate his rule during the dynastic conflicts.[39]

Emergence of Jewish Notables

One of the issues that contributed to the prominence of Islam in this period was the controversy that developed over the rise of Jewish statesmen to the highest political offices in the Ilkhanid administration, one of the most remarkable developments in the history of Iranian Jewry. The most notable example is the rise to power of Sa'd al-Dowleh (d. 1291), a minister under Arghun (r. 1284–91) and the most influential Jewish political figure in Islamic Iran. Arghun himself was a convert to Buddhism and favored Jewish administrators at the expense of Muslims. Sa'd al-Dowleh, a native of Abhar nobility and a physician about whose background little is known, is often accused of discriminating against Muslim notables and even murdering them.[40] He is also portrayed as the architect of Arghun's religious innovations, notably the establishment of shamanist temples (bot-khaneh) with Genghis Khan as the primary deity, a belief based on Genghis Khan's presumed claim to a divine mission. However, Sa'd al-Dowleh's main contribution was his vision as a statesman defending the sedentarization of Ilkhanid Iran, a policy in which he was supported by the landowning faction within the Mongol ruling elite.

Reading against the dominant narrative of Muslim historians, Sa'd al-Dowleh should be seen as a champion of cultural diversity (including paganism) and of resistance to the hegemony of the religious majority. His support of a sedentarized economy favored development and benefited workers on the land. He should also be credited for his financial integrity, his administrative skills, and his campaign against destructive Mongol taxation and other oppressive practices—and above all, for his desire to infuse a new spirit of cohesion into the empire. His downfall and execution immediately after the death of Arghun was largely due to factional rivalries within the administration (divan) and had dire consequences for Jews of high administrative rank within the Ilkhanid administration.[41]

The fall of Sa'd al-Dowleh and the persecution of his Jewish clique was not without its after-effects on the Jewish presence in public life and perhaps on the course of conversion of high officials to Islam. According to a majority of sources, this period coincides with the conversion to Islam of one of the most celebrated figures in the Mongol period. Rashid al-Din Fazlullah of Hamadan (1247–1318). This great historian, physician, ethicist, and accomplished statesman is also credited for his vital contribution in the extensive reconstruction scheme after the Mongol invasion. As a member of the Jewish educated elite, his acceptance of Islam along with a number of his relatives and other high-ranking Jewish officials at this time (c. 1291, after the execution of Sa'd al-Dowleh) would be consistent with the dominant narrative of elite Jewish administrators converting to Islam out of force or political necessity.[42]

However, if we were to assign an earlier date to Rashid al-Din's conversion as supported by other sources, we would then be faced with the question of why, in the midst of unprecedented political power of Jewish administrators, a promising member of the Jewish elite would choose to convert to Islam.[43] Such a seemingly puzzling conversion must be explained by factors other than sheer political expediency. The complex dynamics of intellectual and social mobility and a desire to participate in the dominant discourse within the Islamic world may have played a role.

It is important to note that unlike many elite conversions to the dominant religious system, which are often tied to expediency, neither contemporary sources nor modern observers have considered Rashid al-Din's conversion to be anything but wholehearted. A case in point is his unwavering loyalty to the Shafi'i school: This during a period of volatile political change coinciding with the rise of Shi'ism under the Mongol Ilkhan Uljaito, which contributed to Rashid al-Din's downfall and eventual execution. His highly praised scholarship in Islamic history and ethics and his authentic expressions of his faith also speak to his genuine devotion.

His conversion and that of his elite relatives can thus be assumed to have been a natural culmination of a long process of contact and dialogue with an accomplished Muslim elite over the course of generations, a discourse deeply engaged with the sources of power both temporal and intellectual. In a world where Islamic civilization at its zenith dominated global intellectual and scientific discourse, conversion may have seemed a natural choice for those who sought to participate in and contribute to this discourse of power.

Fazlullah Ibn Abu'l-Khayr, known as Rashid al-Dowleh and later (after his conversion) as Rashid al-Din, was born into a learned and prominent Jewish family of Hamadan, an ancient Iranian city and home to a large Jewish population with an ancient cultural heritage, centered in the city's Yeshiva. His family had been known for producing physicians and philosophers for at least three generations. Around the time of the Mongol invasion, Fazlullah's grandfather, Mowaffaq al-Dowleh, along with his brother Ra'is al-Dowleh, were prominent physicians and close associates of the celebrated Shi'i minister and leading philosopher and scientist of his time, Khawjeh Nasir al-Din Tusi (1201–74), to whom the revival of many Islamic sciences is attributed.[44] Although they specialized primarily in medicine and pharmacology, they were well versed in literature (Rashid al-Din's father 'Emad al-Dowleh was an accomplished poet) and presumably in other fields of knowledge as well. During the terror years of the first Mongol invasion, the three associates found refuge in the Isma'ili castle of Alamut in northern Iran, where Tusi was given the post of minister. During the second Mongol invasion starting in the 1250s, the besieged Isma'ili governor Khur Shah, encouraged by Tusi, decided not to resist the vastly superior Mongol army and sent a delegation including members of his own family with Tusi and Rashid al-Din's father and uncle to surrender to Hulegu in 1256. Soon after, Tusi and his associates were serving as physicians and administrators in the Mongol court.[45] Similar to Sa'd al-Dowleh, Rashid al-Din was part of the pro-settlement indigenous Iranian faction within the Ilkhanid ruling establishment and was opposed to the faction that favored nomadic tribalization of the countryside. As with notables of landowning background such as the celebrated Jowayni family, Rashid al-Din's vision was a natural outcome of an urban order in which non-Muslim communities found greater security and means of preserving generational wealth. This was where Jewish urban notables found common ground with their Muslim counterparts. These alliances could and did cross confessional lines to the extent of facilitating conversions from the Jewish to the majority Muslim confession. If the tide of Ilkhanid conversions was toward adopting Islam, and with it the values of an urban culture, it was understandable that the supporting Jewish enclave of administrating notables would fully embrace the Muslim cultural universe.

As one of Iran's leading historians, it is ironic that not a great deal is known about Rashid al-Din's early years or the circumstances of his conversion. His path was typical of high-profile converts who tried to efface the stigma of conversion by stressing their Islamic identity and projecting it into their past. We know for a fact that following his family tradition, Rashid al-Din received his education in medicine, an area dominated by Jews. He also studied literature, philosophy, and science, fields traditionally related to medicine. Judging from his extended treatment of Jewish history in his masterful collaborative work, the universal history *Jame' al-tawarikh*, he seems to have been well versed in Hebrew and biblical studies. He also mastered Arabic and Turkish, wrote poetry in Mongolian, was familiar with Chinese, and even used European (*farang*) sources, perhaps with the help of associates.

Rashid al-Din's belief in Islam did not stop his enemies from trying to stigmatize him by bringing up his Jewish past, even several decades after his death. After his execution in 1318, at the age of 70, his head was displayed by his enemies who said "this is the head of the Jew who abused us in the name of God; may God's curse be upon him."[46] Some one hundred years after his burial, his remains were exhumed from the Muslim cemetery on the order of Miran Shah, the mad son of Timur, and reburied in the Jewish cemetery.[47] By doing so his enemies tried to deny him his belief in Islam and re-assign him a Jewish identity, possibly a strategy to invalidate his endowment and confiscate its vast assets.

As contemporaries, Rashid al-Din and Sa'd al-Dowleh represent the kinds of options that became available to the Jewish elite. The life stories of the two ministers are full of ambiguities, and they are divergent in their religious identities—one was accused of being an enemy of Islam and one was recognized as a devout Muslim convert—yet they also have many commonalities. They were both literate and capable Jewish court physicians who rose to the highest levels of state administration, demonstrated superior managerial skills, fought the excesses of the nomadic Mongol elite, strove for financial stability, reformed the treasury and fiscal system, and helped Iran reconstruct itself physically and culturally. As statesmen, their involvement in the perilous political game of court intrigue was inevitable, and they eventually paid with their lives. They seem to have been equally victimized by the common practice of executing powerful ministers. They both were also targets of rampant anti-Jewish sentiments, even long after their deaths.

2

JEWISH CONVERSIONS
IN THE SAFAVID AND
EARLY QAJAR PERIODS

The Safavid period (1509–1722) is seen as a threshold in Iran's modern history in a variety of ways: in the realms of economy, society, and religion. It was during this period that the notions of an Iranian identity and of Iran as a political entity began to take shape. Safavid society preserved most of the cultural, ethnic, and religious characteristics of the previous centuries, especially the Ilkhanid and Timurid eras, and added new dimensions to the culture's confessional and ethnic complexities of which the establishment of the Twelver (*ithna 'ashari*) Shi'i creed is the most enduring.

During this era, Iran experienced some periods of tolerance, economic prosperity, and even an influx of non-Muslims—as well as Shi'i indoctrination of the Sunni population—sporadic persecutions, and attempts to forcefully convert Jews and Christians to Shi'ism. The "religious ambiguity" of the Mongol period gave way to pervasive pressures toward conformity as a means of solidifying a form of "imperial identity."[1] Nonetheless, the more oppressive the state administrators became in forcing religious conformity upon non-Muslims, the more entrenched their original identities became.

Religion and Politics under the Safavids

The Safavid state established its political authority with an exclusivist approach to religious identity that strove to define the state and the society. Shi'ism became a cornerstone of Safavid legitimacy. The creation of a state religion in turn put an end to the religious fluidity and confessional ambiguity that had prevailed for more than two centuries.[2] Even before the rise of the Safavids, it can be argued, Shi'ism was long present and deeply rooted in Iran, and beginning with the Mongol period there was increasing interchange among Iranians of Shi'i and Sunni persuasions. Yet the new Safavid ruling elite had a distinct agenda in provoking the extreme polarization of the two sects for the political purpose of constituting a predominantly Shi'i base of support for its own survival. It has been has argued that Safavid public cursing of the Sunni caliphs "was an effective tool in setting sharper boundaries between Sunnism and Shi'ism. It made allegiance to the latter almost inconceivable without a rejection of the former."[3]

It has also been argued that after much of Iran's Sunni population had converted to Shi'ism, the proponents of conversion then turned their attention to other minorities "in an effort to further the 'Shi'itization' of the Safavid kingdom."[4] Conversions of non-Muslim communities thus seem to have been a by-product of "a more pronounced atmosphere of intolerance." No doubt deep changes did affect Iran's social fabric under Safavid rule. One primary change relevant to the condition of the Jews was that the prevalence of the doctrine of ritual "impurity" (*nejasat*)—present in Sunni Islam but more emphatically emphasized in Shi'ism—served as a cornerstone of relations between Muslims and non-Muslims. The expansion of clerical power under the *mojtahed*s (legal scholars) as the embodiment of Shi'i legal authority further defined the boundaries of a segregated society. These circumstances coincided with a number of instances of forced conversion directed in particular toward indigenous Jews and to a lesser extent toward indigenous Christian communities. Immigrant Christians and Jews were generally less exposed to such intolerant practices. In some instances, forced conversions were conducted openly and in direct violation of Shari'a law mandating the protection of the *dhimmi*s. At other times they were done indirectly and by means of intimidation and harassment.

Yet religious motivation cannot by itself explain the often complicated processes leading to these incidents of forced conversion. Zoroastrians, who unlike some Jews and Christians did not have a high profile in Iran's commercial economy or its international trade, were more immune to such practices. This may point to the possibility of economic and political components working in combination with religious motives to give rise to an environment of intolerance toward non-Muslim communities.

The conditions of Jews under Safavid rule were dependent on the attitude of the ruling shah, attitudes that became generally more orthodox toward the latter part of the Safavid era. At least as far as Shah 'Abbas I (1571–1629) was concerned, the laws of non-Muslim ritual "impurity" were conveniently overlooked when economic and political considerations were at stake. He encouraged Georgian and Armenian Christians, as well as Jewish silk producers and merchants with connections in Europe, to live and work in Iran under royal aegis. He is reported to have freely associated with them, including sharing meals (a clear breach of the doctrine of ritual "impurity"), and to have visited their churches and taken part in their religious festivals. Contrary to the apparent injunction of the Shari'a, he also patronized the construction of an Armenian cathedral in Julfa. In a gesture of friendship consistent with his ecumenical approach to religion, Shah 'Abbas I is reported to have engaged in inter-confessional religious debates and even to have made a pilgrimage on foot to a Jewish shrine, accompanied by a great number of Jews. This seems to have been consistent with his fondness for performing pilgrimage on foot to Muslim shrines. Nevertheless, there were also instances of persecution and the forced conversion of Jews throughout his reign.[5]

Some cases of mass conversion in the Safavid period are easier to explain than others. One such case of the mass conversion of Jews occurred in Farahabad in Mazandaran province sometime around 1620. Beginning in 1615, some 8,000 Jews who were "accustomed to tend the laborers of [silk] worms"[6] and whose leaders suffered under Christian rule, collaborated with Iranian troops during the shah's campaigns in the Caucasus.[7] Consequently, they were transplanted to the newly established town of Farahabad. The new settlement was adjacent to the province of Gilan recently annexed by the entrepreneurial shah. The relocation of Jews was accompanied by massive investments in silk production in the region, where forests were cut down to house the new population, to make way for the planting of a great number of mulberry trees, and to build the shah's favorite Caspian resort. The Jews soon became the beneficiaries of the region's lucrative silk production and trade.[8] The Jews of Farahabad are but one example of the important role that Jewish traders and manufacturers played in Iran's economy during this period. Although their modest appearance allowed some foreign travelers to see them as impoverished and vulnerable, it has been shown that they were in fact quite important in financing domestic and long-distance trade.[9]

One clue to understanding the nature of tensions that possibly contributed to forced conversions may have to do with the duality of implementing *dhimmi* rights and *jezya* taxation policies toward indigenous non-Muslims, as distinct from newly arrived non-Muslims. There was a discrepancy with regard to the Armenian merchants of New Julfa who were granted privileges and protections that exceeded those customary under *dhimmi* laws. The taxes collected from them were treated as crown revenue (*khassa*) and went directly into the royal treasury. Given the status of the Farahabad Jews and the Safavids' granting of tax exemptions to encourage manufacturing and trade, it is probable that the same distinctions existed between the Jewish merchants and silk manufacturers and indigenous Jews elsewhere. This might have been at the root of the forced conversions that came into full force later under Shah 'Abbas II (r. 1642–66).[10] According to della Valle, many Christians in the Mazandaran region converted to Islam rather than repay the loans made to them by the shah. It is possible that a number of Jews also underwent similar conversions.[11]

The events leading to the nominal mass conversion of the Jews of Farahabad was triggered by the murder of Abu'l-Hasan Lari. He was a Jewish convert to Islam who reportedly obtained a fatwa from the ulama for the enforcement of a dress code and other restrictive measures against Jews—possibly as means of blackmailing his former coreligionists.[12] Using the fatwa, Lari tried to enforce the discriminatory *dhimmi* dress code in a number of cities with sizable Jewish communities. Instead of giving in to the pressure, and in a sign of communal solidarity against an outside intruder, the Jewish leaders of Farahabad conspired to murder Lari. His murder was instigated by the influential merchant and community leader Elezar (Lalezar) and was carried out by a group of Jews around 1620.[13] The Jewish leaders of Farahabad were apparently close to the shah and saw themselves as holding the honorary status of Shahsevan (Friend of the Shah), a royal guard military corps formed by 'Abbas I to counter the influence of the more established Qezelbash tribal leaders.

The mass conversion of the community that followed the murder can be seen as a form of legal maneuvering to protect a privileged community from severe punishment and provide the authorities with

a rationale for discounting the crime. Given the Jews' political standing in the newly founded city, it is highly unlikely that they were under
pressure to publicly demonstrate their faith in Islam. A few years later,
under Shah Safi (r. 1629–42), the community reverted to Judaism.[14]
This incident demonstrates the complexity of the conversion process.
Even though indigenous Jews at times became the victims of abuse and
discriminatory rulings by the increasingly powerful ulama, privileged
communities with royal connections such as the one in Farahabad
could use conversion (in this case, temporary conversion) as a means of
escaping severe punishment.

Another layer of complexity in the process of conversion can be
observed in the wave of persecutions in Isfahan around the same time
(1620) that led to a group acceptance of Islam. In this telling example, the course of mass conversion was initiated by internal conflict
among the leaders of the Jewish community, as a result of which one
disgruntled Jewish leader converted to Islam. According to Jewish
sources, he was accused of embezzling communal funds, subsequently
converted to Islam, and then accused other Jewish leaders of using
black magic against the shah. Alarmed by this reputed magical power,
the shah ordered that all Jewish texts containing material relating to
magic be collected and destroyed.[15] According to a contemporary Jewish source, *Ketab-e Anusi*, the shah ignored the advice of the prominent
Shi'i legal scholar, Shaykh Baha' al-Dini 'Amele, who at the behest of
Jewish leaders interceded with the shah and advocated the conversion
of the Zoroastrian community.[16] The shah reportedly resorted instead
to scare tactics to intimidate the Jews into converting by throwing some
of them in front of a pack of wild hounds. In this way some 75 Jews
were forced to convert.[17]

Other than the conventional assumption that explains the shah's
behavior as a reflection of his belief (common at the time) in the power
of magic, it may be that he had other considerations relating to the
Jew's economic presence in the Isfahan market. Perhaps it is not a
coincidence that during the same period (1621) some Armenians other
than those residing in Julfa were also pressured to convert to Islam. It
has been argued that these developments were related to the deteriora-
tion of relations with European powers, and that part of Shah 'Abbas's
strategy was to use Christians and Jews as leverage in his dealings with
Europe.[18] The entire affair of the Armenian forced conversions was

called off when the shah realized the economic consequences of his action after the Armenian merchants ordered back a caravan of silk that was on its way to Europe.[19]

A few years later in 1625, the entire Jewish community in Isfahan converted to Islam upon the order of Shah 'Abbas I and remained nominally Muslim until his death in 1629. While the *Ketab-e Anusi* reports a dispute over tax collection (presumably the *jizya*) as the basis of the shah's decision, it is unlikely that the astute ruler would erratically make such a decision without regard for its outcome. We can only speculate about the motives behind his order as being a possible resolution of the inconsistencies and complications caused by the dual systems of taxation, one for newly arrived merchants such as those in Farahabad and another for indigenous Jews. Here conversion may have been used as a ploy to circumvent a complex situation concerning taxation. But not all conversions seem to have been based on greed or pragmatism.

The most widespread cases of the persecution and forced conversion of Jews and Christians in the Safavid period took place under Shah 'Abbas II (r. 1642–66). In the beginning, according to one Western traveler report in 1644, he was tolerant to all religions. According to Tavernier, "Persians give full liberty of conscience of whatsoever religion they be."[20] Beginning in 1656, however, a series of persecutions led to the forced conversion of various Jewish communities. The most extreme case was in Isfahan, where the Jews at first resisted conversion and consequently were forced to leave the city. They were also threatened with having their houses expropriated. According to the Safavid chronicle *'Abbas-nameh*, financial incentives such as forgiving past-due taxes and the payment of two *tomans* per household were offered at the time of conversion "for the tranquility of each person." Perhaps as an additional incentive to the community, and after much negotiation, a much larger payment in the amount of 5,000 *tomans* was reportedly made to the leader of the community from the funds of a religious endowment (*waqf*).[21] The new converts in Isfahan were under severe scrutiny to observe Islamic rites. After a convert informer reported wine-drinking by new converts, he was killed in a gruesome group murder.[22]

A number of other Jewish communities also suffered persecution during this period. Some, such as those in Kashan and Hamadan, went through a number of conversions and re-conversions and a process of "education" by the ulama, but a majority finally reverted to their ancient faith. Others, such as the Jews of Farahabad who had nominally accepted Islam under ʿAbbas I in the 1620s but had reverted to Judaism a few years later, resisted conversion even under the pressure of torture. Unlike earlier instances, perhaps in this case the terms of conversion required stricter public observance of Islam. In Hamadan, the Jews ended up refunding the financial incentive they had received from the governor at the time of their "conversion" and returned to Judaism.[23]

Various explanations have been given for the entire conversion campaign under ʿAbbas II in the 1650s. A Safavid chronicle cites the refusal by two Jews to observe dress codes meant to identify them, such that "Muslims could not avoid being infected by [their] impurity."[24] A Jewish source, *Ketab-e Anusi*, blames the fanaticism of the Grand Vazir Mohammad Beg Eʿtemad al-Dowleh, himself reportedly a Christian convert to Islam—perhaps with a dark history of confiscating his relatives' property—as the main instigator of the persecutions. Whatever the motives, the effort to force conversions largely remained an administrative initiative and never gained the support of prominent ulama. Mulla Mohsen Feyz Kashani, the celebrated theologian and philosopher-mystic of the period, opposed the campaign. Even the head of the religious administration, the holder of the office of *sadr*, was at best indifferent to forced conversion on the grounds that it violated the Shariʿah. Ironically, the campaign took place at a time of economic prosperity and peace with Iran's neighbors. None of the observers was able to point to a specific economic or political motive for this dark episode in Safavid history. The process of mass conversion and re-conversion finally came to an end after it became clear that the Jews were adamant in adhering to their faith and their communal loyalties.

The above cases are instructive examples of how a substantial Jewish community with ancient roots and significant economic presence gradually lost its social status and was subjected to waves of persecution and forced conversion. We can attribute this social demotion at least in part to the community's lack of protection beyond the *dhimmi* guarantees now frequently violated. Unlike the Armenians, who could rely on their economic clout and trade connections with European powers, the unprotected Jews may indeed have been an easy target of persecution. The arrival of European missionaries, such as Spanish Jesuits with

strong memories of the Inquisition and of the forced conversions of
Jews and Muslims, may have also transmitted into the Iranian environment elements of European anti-Semitism.

There are no clear motives for forced conversions based on financial
incentives. Moreover, detrimental effects on the Safavid economy can be
documented. As Matthee has shown, Jewish participation in financing
trade fell drastically in the mid-seventeenth century. Muslim financiers
who were restricted by Shiʻi rules against usury could not have filled the
vacuum that occurred as a result. Banian (Gujarati Hindu) financiers
and money-changers increasingly took on the critical task of financing
the trade ventures that were indispensable to Iran's commerce.[25] Here
we can observe an example of state intervention with consequences
that went far beyond its narrow religious objectives. The haphazard
persecution of Jews continued under the late Safavid rulers and gave
rise, especially under Shah Sultan Hosein (r. 1694–1722), to a sense of
insecurity among indigenous entrepreneurs, thus hindering the accumulation of capital in the Iranian economy and effectively directing its
flow outside of Iran.

Neither Jews nor Christians were the most persecuted religious
group in Safavid Iran, however. As noted above, Buddhists, who did not
enjoy any of the protections guaranteed to the *dhimmi* by the Shariʻa,
were much more frequently subject to abuse by tax collectors and governors.[26] However, to further place the condition of non-Muslims in
Safavid Iran into the proper context, one has only to consider the condition of Jews in Europe during the early modern period to see that
"until comparatively modern times, Christian Europe neither prized
nor practiced tolerance itself, and was not greatly offended by its
absence."[27]

At times, the forces of religious conformity were strengthened when
they were tied to political objectives. The rise of the Safavids and the
ascendancy of Shiʻism as a means of political legitimacy created a new
politicized dimension to relations with non-Muslims. The bizarre and
mostly fruitless attempts made under Safavid rule to forcibly convert
Jews in large numbers by providing them with financial incentives and
exerting social pressure on them demonstrate the resilience of Jewish
religious convictions at times of increasing pressure toward conformity.

The Enigma of Identity in Qajar Iran

Iran in the first half of the nineteenth century experienced the early challenges of modernity and Western technological dominance through the painful shock of military defeat. The loss of territory to Tsarist Russia was accompanied by the heavy economic burden of war reparations. The defeat of Iran's Herat campaign in 1838 and British involvement in it demonstrated how vulnerable Iran was, even to a remote Western power with a colonial presence on its southern borders. That Iran's attempted military reforms were no match for Western military might was a further sign of its structural weakness. At times the humiliation of defeat by superior European powers found expression in the relegation of a fringe group to the position of a domestic "Other." If the military superiority of Western opponents was unsettling, the defenseless non-Muslims with their stigma of "impurity" and their reputed connection with the foreign enemy were a convenient target for displacing anger and frustration. The fact that some among the Jewish elite were economically privileged made it even easier to justify such aggression.

It is important to acknowledge that the nineteenth century in Iran was a fertile ground for conversions and a period of considerable religious fluidity. Faced with the challenges of modernity, humbled by Western economic and military dominance, and disillusioned by manifestations of social and political stagnation, the people of Iran were compelled to face a profound identity crisis. For many, religious conversion became a means of dealing with this crisis and with deeper socio-economic changes the country was experiencing. The messianic Babi movement, for example, attracted a large number of followers, including entire communities, who strove to forge a new identity. The increasingly powerful Shi'i clerical establishment and its attempt to monopolize the country's religious life caused many to be attracted to a variety of Sufi orders which offered an alternative to the conformist approach of orthodox Shi'ism. The appearance of Christian missionaries, although their contact with the Muslim majority was limited, introduced new debates and challenges to religious discourse.

As we will discuss below, in Mashhad local politics and international forces beyond the control of the Jews forced them to convert to Islam in 1839. But elsewhere during the nineteenth century, a few privileged Jewish individuals converted to Islam voluntarily to their great advantage. As ambitious Jews who maintained close contacts in the ruling class, they represent the opposite end of the conversion spectrum. For those Jews with exceptional abilities, those pursuing political ambitions, or even for those with a desire for economic advancement, joining mainstream Shi'ism was an almost inescapable path. Needless to say, their experience of immediate advancement to the ruling classes is by no means representative of that of a common convert. Their experiences can only tell us about a very special type of mobility limited to those with exceptional abilities and court connections.

Aqa Esma'il Jadid al-Islam Pishkhedmatbashi (royal servant) (d. 1875?) converted to Islam at a young age "by the royal intercession" (beh dast-e shah) of no less than Fath 'Ali Shah (1772–1834).

As a convert with few or no political ties, he became a trusted confidant under three Qajar shahs and kept his position for over a period of more than forty years. As execution of Grand Viziers by Qajar shahs was a common occurrence, behind the scene confidants such as Aqa Esma'il served as important sources for political and administrative continuity. He was known for his honesty and loyalty to the throne, and he completed a number of critical royal missions with competence.[28]

Aqa Esma'il's family only grew in influence at the Qajar court. His son, Aqa Reza 'Akkasbashi (1843–89), also known as Eqbal al-Saltaneh, held high-ranking positions including command of the royal armory. He is known as a scholar and as Iran's first professional photographer. He learned the trade from a French photographer around 1859. His artistic accomplishments are an example of how innovation and modernity were often associated with conversion. His younger brother 'Ali Naqi Hakim ul-Mamalek studied medicine and philosophy in France and served as a royal physician. But in typical Qajar fashion, he was assigned a number of high-ranking administrative positions and provincial governorships. He is known as an educator, a compassionate philanthropist, and as a skilled statesman able to "quench [Naser al-din Shah's] wrath." The family's rise to power was not unlike the families of Amir Kabir and Amin al-Sultan both of whom rose to the highest rank of Grand Vazir from modest positions as court servants.[29]

An example of a lesser known but influential political figure of the early twentieth century is Esma'il Khan Mo'azed ul-Molk (d. 1918?). He was the son of Hakim Nasir, an influential Jewish physician and convert (also known as Nasir al-Atebba).[30] Soon after his conversion, Esma'il Khan rose in the ranks of the Qajar administration in the 1910s and held critical positions, including Kermanshah's foreign office agent (*kargozar*), deputy finance minister, and deputy to the second *majles* (parliament) in the 'Etedaliyyun (moderate) faction. His role as a de facto governor of Kermanshah during the First World War was critical in the negotiations with various occupying armies. His job was further complicated by the rise of competing centers of Iranian authority and the formation of the pro-German Iranian government in exile (*komiteh-ye defa'-e melli*). He was murdered during the last months of the war, a victim of his pro-British and pro-Russian sentiments during a volatile time of grave insecurity.[31]

Even though pejorative references to a Jewish past survive in the writings of their contemporaries, high-status converts were relatively free from the stigma of "new-Muslim" identification. However such elite conversions, which resulted in immediate entry to the ruling class, were rare and were restricted to a special group of highly talented, well educated Jews, such as the family of Iran's celebrated scholar and statesman of the Mongol period, Rashid al-Din Fazlullah.

The Mashhad Episode of 1839

As discussed above, the forced conversions of entire communities of Jews did take place in Safavid Iran. Yet most conversions were initiated by a royal decree and were generally short-lived. The case of the mass conversion of Jews in Mashhad in 1839,[32] on the other hand, is a landmark in the religious history of the period. Mashhad is by far the most significant case of forced conversion in modern Iran, not only for its size (thousands reportedly converted to Islam), but also for the circumstances that led to the mass conversion. The incident presents an unusual example of mob violence that resulted, first in the nominal acceptance of Islam by the whole Jewish community, followed by the maintenance of a double identity that endured for at least a century.

The circumstances that led to the riots and the complex economic and political factors that instigated it deserve close examination. The consequences of Great Power rivalries, changes in the economic status of some Jews, the pressures created by a renegade Qajar army, local elite rivalries, the local administration's ineptitude, and possibly imported European anti-Semitic ideas all had their part in shaping this painful episode. Of equal significance was the emergence on the Mashhad horizon of an Usuli *mojtahed* clique with an interventionist and conformist perspective. The unique characteristics of Mashhad's Jewish community—its internal divisions, its combination of economic prosperity and political vulnerability, and its cultural distinctions—also played a role in the course of events. The Jewish community's resistance to forced conversion in turn entrenched the Mashhadi Jewish identity and not surprisingly terminated earlier attempts at religious dialogue, which had been in motion prior to this incident.

As far as can be ascertained, the history of the Jewish community in Mashhad was relatively short, dating back only to the reign of Nader Shah Afshar (r. 1736–47) who, despite his later anti-clerical sentiments, established his new capital in the major shrine city of Mashhad, initiated urban improvements, and restored the shrine of the Eighth Shiʻi Imam Reza in the heart of the pilgrimage city. Nader is believed to have brought some Jews to Mashhad from Gilan with the intention of using the cash from his campaigns—perhaps following Shah ʻAbbas's model—to make Mashhad a center of silk production and trade.[33] One can speculate that the Gilani Jews in question were probably imported from the Farahabad émigré Jewish community, about whom no further references can be found in the post-Safavid sources.[34] The fact that they were involved in the silk trade of ʻAbbas's time and considered themselves as part of the Safavid elite, may have persuaded Nader to employ them as reliable agents for the commercial revival of his reconstituted Safavid empire. In 1746, again following ʻAbbas's model, Nader employed Jewish agents in sensitive positions. After eliminating his guard corps at the fortress of Kalat near Mashhad, where much of the treasure from his Indian campaign was hoarded, he brought in Jewish administrators, presumably from Qazvin.[35]

The favorable economic conditions enjoyed by the Jews attracted other Jews, including those from Kashan and Lar, to join the Mashhad community. A famine in Yazd in 1770 gave rise to an even larger wave of Jewish immigration. By the 1830s, the Mashhad community had reached an estimated 2,400 individuals or 400 households.[36] In the absence of a Jewish neighborhood in Mashhad, and in consideration for the shrine city's requirement to observe Shiʻi rules of "ritual purity," the Jews were placed in the neighborhood adjoining *Eʻidgah* (the festival arena) formerly occupied by a Zoroastrian community. The latter community's mysterious mass departure, presumably to India, happened soon after Nader's return from the subcontinent and may have been part of the forced migrations that were common in this period. The Zoroastrian bathhouse and temple were thus converted into a Jewish bath and synagogue.

The Jews soon began to play an important economic role as traders at a time when British woolen textiles, among other commodities, were introduced into the region.[37] They were also involved in the trade in "antiquities," jewelry, leather, and sheepskins purchased from the Turkomans in the vicinity. The British favored dealing with the Jews and later supported them politically. Unlike their Armenian counterparts, the Jews had no ties to Russia. After the Russian advances in Central Asia in the 1860s, however, the Jews of Mashhad benefited from the preferential treatment that their Central Asian counterparts received from the Russian authorities. The Jews of Khorasan, using their contacts with Jews and Sunni Turkmans in Central Asia, also played an important role in financing the thriving Khorasan trade with Central Asia and Russia. They were favored for their mediational function between Shi'i Khorasan and Sunni Turkestan.[38] Dealing with diverse communities naturally engendered among the Mashhad Jews a cosmopolitan character that was essential to their commercial success.

By all accounts, the Jews of Mashhad were among the most affluent of the Jews in Iran, and perhaps the only ones involved in long-distance trade. They were part of a regional trade network that expanded not only throughout Khorasan but had connections with Jewish communities in greater Khorasan, Turkestan, and the outer regions of Central Asia. As non-Muslims, they were at times in the advantageous position of conducting trade between various rival sectarian and ethnic groups. Through the ancient silk route, they exported textiles and spices to Bukhara and Khiva and imported furs from Bukhara.[39]

The Turkoman slave trade, which supplied Persian peasants, townsmen, and women of Khorasan to the slave markets of Khiva and Bukhara, and sometimes returned them to their relatives after collecting a ransom, was one of the major sources of insecurity in the Khorasan region. According to Rev. Joseph Wolff, an eccentric Jewish convert to Protestantism who was then serving as a missionary educator in Khorasan, "the Jews of Sarakhs and Khiva [were] suspected by

the Persians of assisting the Turkomauns in getting slaves."[40] Yet there
is no evidence that the Mashhad Jews were involved in this trade, even
though on one occasion, according to the British officer and spy Arthur
Conolly, a beggar (*fakeer, faqir*) grabbed a Jewish man by the beard in
Mashhad and accused him of having sold him into slavery.[41]

Notwithstanding the economic advantages of living in Mashhad,
its proximity to a Muslim shrine entailed certain restrictions for Jews.
A meticulous observation of Shi'i rules, for example, forced them to
wear the customary patch, a humiliating reminder of their segregation. In spite of such practices, however, there was also a good deal of
interaction between Jews and Muslims, including Sufis and enlightened
members of the local ulama who accepted the Jews into their circles
and were willing to disregard the laws of ritual "impurity."

After the assassination of Nader Shah in 1747 deprived the Jews
of their main source of protection, they turned for political support
to the British traders and the Sunni Turkomen tribes with whom
they continued to have cordial relations.[42] The Jewish role in assisting
British agents was crucial in the region extending from Khorasan to
Herat and the Central Asian cities of Samarqand and Bukhara. A
network of Jews throughout the region acted as banking connections,
trading contacts, and sources for British intelligence. Since Europeans,
like other non-Muslims, were considered ritually "impure" and were
not permitted to stay in Muslim homes or use Muslim public baths,
and in the absence of any indigenous Christians, Jews took on the roles
of housing providers, guides, and negotiators. As financiers, their role
was also vital for the British who, for security reasons, could not carry
around large sums of cash.

In addition to financing British agents in the early decades of the nineteenth century, affluent Mashhadi Jews, as they were known, on occasion
even acted as guarantors of the British currency. In the mid-1830s when
the governor of Herat, fearing British economic monopolies, ordered
a ban on British currency and precipitated its drastic devaluation,
Mulla Mehdi, a leader of Mashhad's Jewish community, quickly arrived
in Herat to stabilize the value of British vis-à-vis Russian currency.[43]
Holding the title of *vaqaye'-negar* (chronicler) of Mashhad, Mulla Mehdi
along with two other Jewish agents took on an important intelligence-
gathering mission in the region. Some Jewish merchants in Herat also
dealt in arms and ammunition on behalf of the British.

The Aftermath of the Herat Campaign

The forced conversion of the Mashhad Jews in 1839 coincided with a period of political crisis in Khorasan and the first Anglo-Iranian confrontation over Herat. The British connection with Mashhadi Jewish leaders, and their collaboration in arms dealing and intelligence gathering, is noteworthy in the context of imperial British interest in Herat and Iran's desperate efforts to secure its eastern borders. Mohammad Shah's (r. 1834–48) two-year long siege of Herat to enforce what he saw as Iran's legitimate claim to the area came to a humiliating end in September 1838—just months before the forced conversions in Mashhad—after the British, in a classic case of gunboat diplomacy, landed troops on the Persian Gulf island of Khark.[44]

Like the attempts a few years earlier under the governorship of Crown Prince 'Abbas Mirza (d. 1833) to secure Khorasan's borders against domestic rebellions and Turkoman raids, this campaign too became a source of social and economic stress for the region's population. The villagers bore the burden of providing food and conscripts for the army. Returning from Herat, the shah's defeated and starving troops are reported to have plundered the villages en route to Mashhad.[45] More affluent elements of the population in the urban centers were often saddled with the campaign's financial burden. Concerned with future British advances, the shah decided to garrison some of the plundering army in Mashhad for possible future campaigns, hence putting even more stress on the region's economy.[46]

Among the demands made on the urban population was the requirement for households to board the troops—presumably in the absence of adequate garrison accommodations. Wolff reports that as early as 1831, upon the arrival of the crown prince's modernized Army (*nezam-e jadid*) of Azerbaijan with a number of European officers, Jewish families were asked to lodge the regiment's mostly non-Muslim or newly converted officers whose ritual "purity" must have been suspect at best. The Jews tried to present an "outward appearance of poverty,"[47] and they must have been uncomfortable with their unwanted and presumably arrogant guests. Yet Wolff criticizes the Jews for not realizing that "if the officers were not with them, the common soldier would commit mischief among them."[48] Given the affluence of many Jewish tradesmen and the rumors of treasures they kept in their homes, one can only speculate about what the officers saw or how they may have been tempted to loot the possessions of their hosts.

Forced Conversions

The riots that led to the mass conversion of Mashhad's Jews took place on March 27, 1839 (10th Muharram 1255 AH), on the day of 'Ashura. This holy day commemorates the martyrdom of Imam Hosein and is often accompanied by expressions of high religious fervor, and occasionally by acts of violence.[49] On that day in 1839, the entire Jewish community was forced to accept Islam following anti-Jewish riots during which 32 to 35 Jews were reportedly killed.[50]

Aside from the usual discrepancies in detail, the sources are in agreement over the supposed course of events that led to the outbreak of anti-Jewish violence.[51] Most Jewish and Persian Qajar accounts report that the killing of a dog which was intended to remedy a Jewish woman's skin disease was seen as a gesture meant to ridicule the Imam's martyrdom on its anniversary. Under such a provocation, the mourning crowd reacted with spontaneous violence. One Persian source even makes the bizarre claim that Jewish children held up the dog's head on a pole and sang profanities, this on a day when Jews were always terrified of the possibility of attacks by volatile crowds.

Most secondary accounts take for granted some version of this story as being responsible for provoking the riots.[52] However, the only suggestion of any evidence of potentially offensive behavior by Jews toward Muslims during an Islamic celebration may have been related to drinking. According to Conolly, who attended a wedding party in Mashhad's Jewish neighborhood in 1830, liquor (*'araq*) was consumed in "immoderate amounts" and the participants were making enough noise to draw the attention of the *darugheh* (sheriff), who asked them to be more considerate during the "Mohammadan festival," hoping at the same time to avail himself of the corrupting liquor.[53]

Public disrespect toward Muslim saints in a holy city on the most celebrated Shi'i holy day would be hard to imagine. In fact, in Qajar Iran, allegations of the victims' misconduct were familiar pretexts for premeditated attacks on rival or minority groups.[54] The accusation has the familiar tone of the European blood libel that was used to instigate many instances of anti-Semitic persecution. One can speculate that if such ideas were not already in circulation in nineteenth-century Iran, they may have been introduced or encouraged by European officers garrisoned in Mashhad at the time. At least, the question merits further investigation.

The supposed insult was most likely staged at the time of the Shi'i mourning ceremonies, when large crowds, including pilgrims from neighboring villages as well as soldiers in transit with whom the Jews had no relations, could easily be excited and manipulated. There is evidence that the riots were not a spontaneous reaction by zealous and out-of-control mourners—although some of them may have joined in the looting—but rather were the result of a premeditated scheme. On the eve of the riots, Mirza-ye Askari (d. 1863), the Imam Jom'ah (a leading member of the ulama designated by the shah to lead Friday prayers and deliver the Friday sermon) of Mashhad, warned one of his Jewish friends of imminent danger and instructed him to leave his home and stay with Muslim families. Askari's Jewish friend had reportedly converted to Islam but had kept his new faith secret.[55]

Although no clear evidence exists to incriminate any of the collaborators, tracing those who benefited from this incident may provide clues to the identity and motives of the perpetrators. Among those who were aware of the imminent plot we can identify some underpaid and disgruntled officers whose rank and file reportedly started the riots. The governor-general of Khorasan, Allahyar Khan Asef al-Dowleh,[56] also gave his approval. Some high-ranking ulama were aware that riots were planned but were unable or unwilling to do anything to stop them. Other local notables may have helped save the lives of some of the victims.

Some six months after Mohammad Shah's defeated army had arrived in Mashhad, "the soldiers of the garrison" reportedly initiated the violence when they "hurried to the Jews' quarter, pillaged it and killed several of the wretched inhabitants."[57] The "Triumphant Regiments" (asaker-e mansureh), whose record did not match their glorified title, were a product of the military reforms initiated by the reformer Prince 'Abbas Mirza (1789–1833).

One of the regiments in question was almost certainly the Bahadoran, which consisted mostly of Russian deserters and native Assyrian Christian recruits. This regiment was headed by Sam Khan Ilkhani (also known as Sam Khan Urus), a Russian deserter of Armenian origin who had defected to Iran during the second Russo-Persian war of 1826–27, and was a convert to Islam.[58]

After the defeat of the reformed army in war with Russia, the Bahadoran regiment had accompanied 'Abbas Mirza to Khorasan in 1831, and remained there after his death in order to exert control over the unruly region. Three years earlier, the provincial government had lost control of Mashhad for six months in 1828 when the rebel Mohammad Khan Qara'i pillaged the city and extorted money from its inhabitants.[59] Although the Bahadoran regiment was initially effective in returning order to the region, it was underfunded and poorly disciplined and proved to be a major burden on the city and the surrounding villages.

Some years after the forced conversions in Mashhad, at the outset of the secessionist Salar rebellion in 1848, we find the same disenfranchised regiment fighting the "people of Mashhad," possibly over demands for payment. During the course of a full-scale battle, some 700 lives were lost, including those of key figures such as the chief of police, the influential Qajar governor, and the custodian of the Shrine of Imam Reza.[60]

As tsarist officers, Sam Khan and his subordinates in the Baduran regiment may well have been exposed to the rising anti-Semitic sentiments that were widespread in early nineteenth-century Russia. Having taken part in the failed Herat campaign, the defeated regiment may have seen the Jews as a logical scapegoat, particularly if their ties to the British were known.

Governor Asef al-Dowleh's inaction in the 1839 Mashhad riots may be an indication of his tacit approval or possible active role in the riots. According to one source, he may have gone along with the plan in a desperate move to ease the pressure of the rebellious demands from the troops.[61] More tangible and substantial than the property taken from Jewish homes was the merchandise of Jewish traders that was confiscated by the authorities. The goods in question were substantial enough to require the intervention of the shah's emissary, who bypassed the governor and returned them to the Jews after their conversion.[62] We can safely assume that the confiscation of such substantial wealth could not have occurred without the governor's approval.

The role of the young Imam Jom'ah Mirza-ye Askari in the episode remains enigmatic, however. The fact that he had prior knowledge of the forthcoming riots may indicate his possible participation in the plot. His close ties to Sam Khan, for which he was later imprisoned by the rebel governor Salar, may further implicate him in this affair.[63] Moreover, he reportedly took possession of some of the Jewish property, which he was later obliged to return following the intervention of the royal emissary. The Imam Jom'ah and other ulama and notables are also reported to have "seized and married the prettiest of the Jewesses."[64] This was a familiar bonus for the ulama and the notables who played a role in such affairs. Other Jewish women are reported to have been sold into slavery, possibly to the thriving Central Asian slave market. If we were to assign a humanitarian motive to the Imam Jom'ah, it is plausible that he was indeed trying to protect some Jewish women from slavery.

The influential Hajji Mirza Musa Khan (d.1846), a half brother of the notable Chief Minister Mirza Abolqasem Qa'em-Maqam (who had been slain by Mohammad Shah in 1835), was a major player in the complex scene of Mashhad shrine politics. As one of the few surviving members of a clan of high-level administrators, Musa Khan had in effect left the field of court politics and taken the influential position of *motewalli-bashi*, trustee of the Shrine of Imam Reza, in Mashhad in 1831.[65] This position was a powerful and independent one that often brought him into conflict with the state-appointed governor and the Imam Jom'ah over control of the shrine's vast endowment and the disposition of religious taxes.

It is possible that the forced conversion of the Jews was an unintended consequence of a plan to placate a starving army that, unlike the traditional army, had no roots in the area or connections to the city's social fabric. The Jews of Mashhad were in a position of economic advantage, but as non-Muslims they were politically weak. As such, they were drafted to bear the heavy burden of housing and feeding the regiments officers that no other segment of Mashhad society was willing to carry.

In the absence of protection from state authorities, the only other force formidable enough to stand up to the officers and their allies and offer protection against total destruction turned out to be the trustee of the Shrine of Imam Reza. Musa Khan's decision to extend protection to the Jews, aside from its humanitarian aspect, may well have had political implications. As an experienced official, he must have been mindful of the value of the allegiance of a sizable community who as "new converts" would be dependent upon his favor. In counterposition to the Imam Jom'ah's conspiracy to confiscate Jewish assets, Musa Khan's move was an astute maneuver to undermine the attempted confiscation. Such protection could only be provided in the physical setting of the shrine, where non-Muslims could enter only after having converted to Islam. In the final analysis, we may observe, the pernicious chain of events strengthened the hand of one religious authority supported by the central government against another religious authority representing a new interventionist attitude among the ulama and at the expense of a helpless community.

As in most mass conversions, the decision to convert to Islam was made by the community leaders who were trying to end the anti-Jewish violence. The Chief Rabbi of Mashhad, a certain Mulla Davud Cohan, was reportedly the first to convert. Having sought protection from the influential trustee of the Shi'i shrine, he uttered "the illustrious *shahada*," after which all the Jews are reported to have "attained the true religion of Islam."[66] In the aftermath of the riots, some within the Jewish community genuinely accepted Islam and began a new life as "new Muslims" (*jadid al-Islam*).[67] Others migrated to the Central Asian communities of Bokhara and Samarqand where they were able to practice Judaism more freely under Sunni rule. Yet others (perhaps a majority) while accepting Islam, maintained a dual identity by practicing Judaism in secret for an entire century until they were able to return to their ancestral religion during the Pahlavi period.[68]

As far as the history of the Mashhad conversions is concerned, it is highly likely that a protracted course of events was telescoped by the sources into a single day, and not without reason. The presentation of the events which are supposed to have taken place in the midst of the mourning processions of 'Ashura during a single day is a powerful dramatic device. The deadly rioting, the looting, and the taking of Jewish women were reportedly followed within hours by the appearance of the entire Jewish community (i.e., the heads of some 400 households) at Hajji Musa's house to utter their testimonial and seek protection. This may well demonstrate how a complex and lengthy episode involving many actors and events can be constructed as an instantaneous act of irrational mass frenzy.

Besieged by a sense of guilt and shame after their conversions, many Jews' first reaction was one of self-blame. "Our sins allowed the Muslims to use a false pretext and armed mobs to suddenly attack us," wrote one victim, weeks after the attack. Yearning for deliverance by an external force, he wrote: "Now we have no hope other than the grace of the Almighty, the coming of the Messiah, or the arrival of the British to keep us alive, treat us compassionately, and save us from the exiles of Ishmael."[69]

Ironically, the forced conversions interrupted the flickers of harmonious assimilation and religious dialogue that had developed in Mashhad. Although some Jews sincerely accepted Islam, most continued to secretly observe Judaism, a unique case in the history of Iranian Jewry in the Qajar period. Even those who had voluntarily converted to Islam were forced to tolerate the burden of the stigma of their past. Some children of converts, however, had a different view of the experience of their fathers. 'Azizullah Jazzab, whose family was among the Jewish converts to Islam and who was raised as a Muslim, reverted to Judaism after he learned of his ancestral faith. He then completely reversed the direction of assimilation that his father had initiated and began to practice a strictly orthodox form of Judaism.[70] Later, he converted to the Baha'i faith.

Remarkably, most new converts managed to secretly practice Jewish rites despite a great deal of pressure from the ulama, including prohibition of any type of animal slaughter by the converts (to prevent the observance of Kosher laws) and strict requirements to attend the mosque on a regular basis. Children were required to attend Qur'an classes. Such harsh strictures were not without their reasons, of course, since most conversions were not genuine. But the ulama's insistence on strict conformity to Islamic practice indicates a deep urge to control. Whatever the immediate causes and historical circumstances were in this case, they offer us a glimpse of an emerging cultural pattern.

Jewish Sufis and Secret Converts

It is hard to imagine that the Jews would have succumbed to pressure to become Muslims without any kind of cultural precedent. In fact, prior to 1839, conversion to Islam among the Jews of Mashhad was not unheard of, and cases of secret conversions and double identities were reported.[71] Moreover, Mashhad enjoyed an unusually high level of interaction between Jews and Muslims. In particular, some Jews had close links to local Sufi orders. The "Jewish Sufis," as Wolff calls them, were most likely attracted to an alternative view of Islam which was not concerned primarily with the Shari'ah and its preoccupation with ritual "impurity." According to Wolff, the Sufis of Mashhad were antinomians who disregarded the Shari'ah. They believed that salvation was secured by becoming absorbed in the divine being, a condition that separated the seeker from all evil, thus allowing him to violate any religious law.[72] This apparently enabled the Sufis in Mashhad to ignore the "ritual impurity" of the Jews and, like the Baha'is a half-century later, accept them as equals.

Wolff states that some Sufis of Mashhad, aside from believing in 124,000 prophets and seeing prophetic attributes in their own Sufi leaders, even disregarded dietary restrictions such as the prohibition against eating pork. He also reports that public demonstrations of Sufi sacrilege toward sacred symbols of Shi'ism included defecating in the holy shrine and burning the Qur'an. But, it is possible that such outrageous charges were merely the usual accusations brought against people with non-conformist views.

Mystical and literary texts such as Rumi's *Masnavi* and Hafez's *divan* were transcribed into Judeo-Persian and must have been read by literate Jews and recited to the others. Subscribing to the esoteric aspect of religion common in Sufi thought, enthusiastic Jews could justify their secret appreciation of Islam. It has been suggested that some Jewish laymen read the Qur'an and found common ground between Islam and Judaism through the biblical stories (*qisas*) shared by the two traditions.

A good deal of religious curiosity seems to have existed in Mashhad at the time. In one instance in 1831, Crown Prince 'Abbas Mirza invited the Christian missionary Wolff to debate the Jews. There was also a degree of social intercourse between the Jews—some with secret identities—and enlightened ulama such as Hedayatullah Askari, father of the aforementioned Mirza Askari. He held regular gatherings with Jews at his house and supposedly debated them cordially.[73] Hedayatullah Askari reportedly attended to the needs of the Jews and even built a separate school for them where he could interact with them free of the strict rules of "impurity."[74] The father's latitude was in contrast to the rigidity of his son, Mirza Askari, who entertained "contempt for European learning" in favor of traditional Islamic knowledge.[75] Such a contrast between father and son can be attributed to the spread of legalistic Usuli Shi'ism in Khorasan in this period.

One Jewish community leader who had secretly converted to Islam around 1827, through discussions with Hedayatullah Askari, reportedly taught Persian mystical texts to a select group of students after lessons on the Jewish religion.[76] Another Mashhad Jewish figure, the noted poet Malamed Simantub (d. 1830?), was responsible for multi-lingual literary and scholarly works and also engaged in debates with the Shi'i ulama.[77] A certain Mulla Benjamin, a rabbi convert originally from Yazd, translated the Qur'an into Judeo-Persian and, according to Wolff, performed a pilgrimage to Mecca.[78]

Although there appear to have been distinct class divisions among the Jews of Mashhad, it is not clear how those divisions played into con-version patterns, for Jews of every social level were attracted to Islam. According to Wolff, who mostly associated with affluent Jews during his visit in 1831, the Yazdi Jews who immigrated to Mashhad during the 1770s, some thirty years after a majority of the city's Jewish immigrants had arrived, were considered "unclean, dishonest and [were] despised by the rest of the Israel." Wolff also reports that the Jews of Mashhad did not even intermarry with those of Yazd "on account of their bad character."[79] Hence it is difficult to conclude that the level of religious interaction between Jews and Muslims was a function of their social class. Yet we know that some among the leadership of the Jewish com-munity, including the assistant to the chief rabbi (dayyan), were attracted to Sufism and almost certainly had accepted the validity of Islam.

The forced conversions in Mashhad can be understood as the con-vergence of two prevailing developments in early nineteenth-century Iran. The rise of a more conformist and legalistic Shi'ism coincided with the social disruptions caused by Iran's response to the early manifestations of modernity and European hegemony. Both factors contributed to the outbreak of the riots and the mass conversions that followed. This incident also had major disruptive consequences for the process of assimilation and interfaith dialogue among Jews and Muslims.

3

EMERGENCE OF THE
BAHA'I ALTERNATIVE

The Baha'i religion was established in nineteenth-century Iran and grew to become a world religion in the twentieth century.[1] The predecessor of the Baha'i religion was the Babi movement founded in 1844 by Sayyed 'Ali Mohammad Shirazi, a charismatic young merchant from Shiraz with moderate exposure to traditional Islamic education. He came to be known as the Bab, at first claiming to be an intermediary to the Hidden Imam (qa'im). Later he claimed to be that promised messianic figure himself who, according to conventional Shi'i belief, had been in hiding for a millennium and whose long awaited "Return" would end all injustice in the world. Although the Bab spent the last years of his life persecuted and imprisoned, the new Babi movement attracted thousands of followers throughout Iran from all social classes, including members of the lower- and middle-ranking ulama and their followers, women, merchants, and peasants, as well as urban commoners. By the time of his execution in 1850, the Bab's message had evolved into a major force, partly due to the activities of his radical followers, such as the woman poet Qurrat ul-'Ayn.[2] The new movement eventually called for the abrogation of the Shari'ah and an end to the Islamic dispensation.[3]

The Babi movement, with its radical declaration of the coming of a new age, was partly a religious response to Iran's social and cultural crises and to the challenges posed by early manifestations of Western modernity. Despite its many esoteric and at times peculiar teachings and ascetic practices, its main message was forward-looking, in part inspired by the ancient Iranian concept of cyclical renewal and religious vitality expressed as the messianic notion of "Return." Unlike other contemporary Islamic revivalist movements that sought religious reform through the reinterpretation of Islam or by calling for a return to a primal "true Islam," Babism called for a revival of the essence of religion, a sweeping break with the past, an end to Islamic practices, and a fundamental paradigm shift that was made imperative by the coming of the promised Messiah.

The rapid growth of the Babi movement was also partly a culmination of the strong messianic currents of mid-nineteenth-century Iran, expressed in popular Sufism with its heightened sense of expectation of the advent of a savior. These currents had deep roots in salient developments within Shi'ism during the eighteenth century when, after the destructive Afghan invasion and prior to the emergence of the Qajars as a new unifying force, Iran suffered through periods of instability, civil war, and the disruption of central authority.

The resulting vacuum in legal and political authority helped foster the authority of the urban notables, particularly the Shi'i ulama. By the middle of the nineteenth century, a new class of high-ranking ulama had emerged, some with enormous wealth and vigorous political influence, who at times challenged the authority of the central government. The privileges of these high-ranking ulama in turn created significant tensions among the less advantaged lower ranks where many saw the rise of a *mojtahed* (recognized jurist) elite as a betrayal of moral leadership. Parallel to this development was the growing dominance of the Usuli school, which elevated the *fatwa* (legal opinion) of the *mojtahed* as the primary element in the theory and practice of Islamic jurisprudence.[4]

Even more relevant to the emergence of the Babi movement was the rise of the Shaykhi school of Shi'ism which sought to reinterpret and rationalize the notion of the presumed "occultation" of the Hidden Imam through the presence of a "perfect Shi'i," or single individual, who during each given era served as an intermediary to the Hidden Imam. Aside from Shaykhism's ideological contribution to the Babi humanization of the promised savior, Shaykhi converts to Babism, indeed entire communities of Shaykhi converts, formed the nucleus of the new movement and fostered its rapid growth in the early years.[5]

In addition to threatening the legitimacy of the powerful Shi'i religious establishment, the Bab's claims posed an indirect challenge to the authority of the state. The Babi movement rapidly grew more radical, and by 1848 many of the Bab's followers were interpreting his declaration of the return of the promised Qa'im, the messianic figure in hiding, and the advent of a new era as justification for the abrogation of Islamic Shari'ah. The Babis also viewed the high-ranking ulama as a corrupt and abusive establishment that deserved to be eradicated. Some followers even saw part of their mission as an inevitable confrontation with the Qajar state. Their dual attack on the state and the clerical establishment led to violent confrontations, armed resistance, and subsequently to the general persecution of the Bab's followers. After the attempted assassination of Naser al-Din Shah (r. 1848–96) by a group of Babis in 1852, this persecution reached its climax in the gruesome mass killings of Babis in Tehran and elsewhere. Thus was the movement suppressed and forced underground through an effective alliance of the two divided sources of authority, i.e., the state and the clergy.

In the months before his impending death, the Bab forbade his followers from opposing any person who might claim to be his successor, the messianic manifestation he had foretold in his writings. This gave rise to a variety of claims to succession and what may be characterized as a "democratization of religious charisma." Eventually, the Babis in Iran had to choose between the two sons of a court official who soon became the main contenders for leadership. Mirza Hosein 'Ali Nuri, entitled Baha (the Light) by the Bab and later known as Baha'u'llah, was recognized as the actual leader of the community. His younger half-brother, Mirza Yahya Nuri (1830–1912), entitled in his teens by the Bab as Sobh-e Azal (Morning of Eternity), was also alluded to by the Bab as the leader of the Babi community. Baha'u'llah managed to capture the loyalty of a large majority of Babis in Iran, mainly through his visionary, non-violent transformation of the original Babi message, especially after 1868, when a decisive break occurred between the two brothers.

For many Azali partisans who found a sense of communal solidarity in their allegiance to the mostly isolated Sobh-e Azal, the defeat of Babi militancy gave rise to more radical, even agnostic tendencies, including a total rejection of their Islamic heritage, and the search for a new nationalist identity that was articulated in a call for political agitation and revolution. Azali Babis, who preferred to maintain the public guise of mainstream Shi'is, played a vital role in the Constitutional Revolution (1905–11), especially in its early phase.[6] Despite their anti-clerical tendencies, the Babis were not responsible for the execution of the leading anti-constitutionalist high ranking cleric (*mojtahed*) of Tehran, Shaykh Fazlullah Nuri, in the aftermath of the 1909 civil war. Even though a number of the ulama continued to support the revolution while others persisted in opposition, the execution of Nuri can be seen as a milestone, a daunting fulfillment of Babi anti-clerical aspirations and a bleak symbol of the transition to an alternative secular Iran that emerged over the following seventy years.

For a majority of the Babis, the movement's messianic tendencies found expression in the freshly defined moral vision that later came to be known as the Baha'i faith. Under the leadership of Baha'u'llah, who claimed to be the messianic fulfillment of the prophecies of all earlier religions, a post-messianic order emerged that in time broke away from the cultural bounds of Islam and, during a formative century, underwent substantial evolution of its own.

As a Babi leader, Baha'u'llah was imprisoned in 1852, but soon exiled to Baghdad, the provincial capital of Ottoman Iraq, where he abandoned the bitterly divided Babi community and spent two years in seclusion away from his followers among the Sufis of Kurdistan. From Baghdad, due to the Iranian officials' fear of Babi agitation, the Ottomans further exiled him to other Ottoman cities more distant from Iran, first to Istanbul (1863) and then to Edirne (1863–68). In Edirne, he made a more explicit claim to divine manifestation breaking entirely from Sobh-e Azal, who had shared his exile.

In his letters to Muslim and European monarchs in 1868, Baha'u'llah articulated a new moral faith with an inclusive social message of non-violence, universal peace, and a universal *lingua franca* (to be learned with vernacular languages). He praised constitutional monarchy, called for an international collective security order, and denounced the rise and dominance of military ambitions in the West. He also advocated public welfare and reduced taxation through reduction of military expenditure and war efforts.[7] Through a stream of letters to his followers known as "tablets" (*alvah*), he maintained continuous contact with the Babi (and later Baha'i) communities of Iran including some Jewish converts whom he addressed as "descendents of Abraham" (*abna-'e Khalil*), thereby ascribing to them a common ancestry with Muslims and Christians. A network of emissaries and itinerant advocates (*moballeghin*) propagated his ideas and engaged in debates with the lay-men and the clergy.

Baha'u'llah's break with his younger half-brother was a defining moment in an often bitter relationship between the respective followers of the two leaders, even as they were exiled to ever more remote Otto-man territories. Baha'u'llah and most of his companions were sent to the garrison city of 'Akka in Palestine, while Azal was exiled to Famagusta in Cyprus. After a period of harsh confinement, Baha'u'llah gradually came to enjoy more freedom and was able to receive many visitors, including believers from Iran.

Most notable among the changes Baha'u'llah introduced was a call to end Babi militancy, violence, and opposition to the state, even though he was not always able to control his followers' unruly behavior. Baha'u'llah's repeated calls for "complete obedience" to governmental authority further distanced the movement from the earlier militant and anti-Qajar positions of many Babis.[8] Yet despite these drastic changes, a significant portion of the intellectual foundations of the Baha'i faith were laid down by the Babi notion of revival in a "new age" and by the call for an end to the old practices of the Shari'ah. Early Babi mass conversions throughout Iran were vital to the Baha'i community's social base and its rapid expansion, starting in the 1860s.[9]

Besides Babi ideas, Baha'u'llah was influenced by nineteenth-century Persian Sufism and the ideas of the European Enlightenment to which he was exposed through contact with Ottoman intellectuals. His *Ketab-e Aqdas* (Most Holy Book, 1873) outlines religious laws and prac-tices, perhaps in response to what many followers expected of a formal religion. It advocates progressive ideas such as compulsory education and emphasizes the education of girls. The book also contains more traditional or conventional laws, such as a complicated inheritance law. This approach to inheritance reflected the Shi'i environment in which it originated and simply modified an esoteric Babi text; Baha'u'llah later discarded it. Among the new laws relevant to the condition of the Jews of Iran was his call for the elimination of religious and racial prejudice and a complete rejection of the idea of "ritual impurity" (*nejasat*).[10]

Baha'u'llah appointed his eldest son 'Abbas Effendi (1844–1921), later known by the title of 'Abdu'l-Baha (servant of Baha), as his suc-cessor. 'Abdu'l-Baha's ministry was one of growth and community development. The new faith grew not only among Muslims, Jews, and Zoroastrians in Iran but also in already established communities in places such as India and Egypt. More significantly for the future development of Bahaism, important gains were made in Europe and America. 'Abdu'l-Baha further developed Baha'i social and political ideas and made a conscious effort to extricate the new religion from its status as a Shi'i sect, promoting it as a world religion. His progressive ideas, outlined as early as 1875, included the elimination of racial and gender inequalities, the lessening of economic disparities, the promotion of public education, and world peace. These ideas, which he proclaimed in missionary journeys to Europe and the United States (1911–13) as Baha'i principles, were considered radical even by Western standards. His call for racial equality in the United States and his insistence on racially integrated meetings was the subject of some controversy and received much attention. It was during 'Abdu'l-Baha's ministry that many Jews in Iran converted to the Baha'i faith. Much of the expansion of the Baha'i community can be attributed to his skills in community organization. He maintained personal communications with his followers through thousands of "tablets" (letters) in his own hand addressed to Baha'is, new converts, and sympathizers.[11]

Many of the ideas and practices relating to the Baha'i nonparticipation in politics, which are rooted in the writings of Baha'u'llah, were further developed during the ministry of 'Abdu'l-Baha. During the early phase of the Constitutional Revolution, he seems to have been impressed by the movement's progressive ideas. In a tablet presumably written in 1908, and published in 1911 in response to accusations that the Baha'is were anti-constitutionalists, 'Abdu'l-Baha referred to the Constitutional Revolution and the 1908 Young Turk Revolution in the Ottoman Empire as having shaken the "foundations of despotic rule (*estebdad*)" and having brought about the downfall of "tyranny and injustice (*zolm va jowr*)." In another tablet, he encouraged Baha'is to participate in the elections to the Constitutional Assembly (*majles*) and by "all possible means" to elect Baha'i leaders (*ayadi*, "Hands of the Cause") to that body.[12]

In the following years, however, 'Abdu'l-Baha's enthusiasm seems to have turned into anxiety, possibly over the active revolutionary role of the Azali Babis for whom he had a particular distrust. Perhaps even more significant was his concern over Baha'is becoming associated with the revolution and thereby becoming victims of persecution in the midst of revolutionary upheavals and later civil war. The afore-mentioned Nuri's references to the Constitutional Movement as being anti-Islamic and led by Babis and other materialists and heretics, would no doubt have been cause for serious alarm on the part of 'Abdu'l-Baha, whose memory of the 1903 massacre of Baha'is in Yazd was very much alive.[13] It is in this context that his repeated warnings against partici-pation in politics, which he expressed in increasingly strong language, should be understood.[14]

Although the question of the origins of Baha'i non-participation in politics needs further investigation, it would only be reasonable to assume that 'Abdu'l-Baha's warnings were in part a reaction to various groups of Baha'is in Iran, evidently on both sides of the conflict, who apparently insisted on taking an active role in the upheavals. In a later tablet, presumably addressed to a Baha'i supporter of Mohammad 'Ali Shah, 'Abdu'l-Baha praised the institution of monarchy but strongly prohibited any political activity by his followers. Such prohibitions were also an attempt to counter charges of anti-constitutionalist sentiments that were directed toward the Baha'i community.[15]

Partly as a result of such criticisms, the Baha'is became more reso-lute in enforcing the doctrine of non-participation in politics in official activities, and Baha'i sources have generally avoided partisanship and political activism. Among Baha'i activists who ignored this prohibi-tion, Ehsanullah Khan Dustdar (1883–1938?), a Marxist revolutionary leader and co-founder of the short-lived Soviet Socialist Republic of Iran, is worthy of note. Other less prominent Baha'i revolutionaries who challenged state authority during the post-World War I period have been left out of the conventional historical narratives. The fact that they often concealed or abandoned their Baha'i associations does not resolve the questions raised by this rather complex part of Iran's history. The Shi'i practice of *taqiyya* (dissimulation of faith) may have found a new political dimension during this period.[16]

'Abdu'l-Baha's grandson and successor, the young Western-educated Shoghi Effendi Rabbani (1897–1957), was known as the Guardian of the Baha'i faith (*vali-ye amrullah*). His leadership was initially challenged by members of his own extended family and by others who considered his style too bureaucratic and his vision too Western. Besides further expansion, his main focus was to institutionalize and internationalize the religion through the establishment of an "Administrative Order" built on a hierarchical network of local and national elected councils, termed "Spiritual Assemblies." As part of his effort to further expand the domain of the faith, he produced compelling English translations of many Baha'i scriptures. He referred to his ministry in the development of the faith as "the era of independence" (*esteglal*), a time that demanded a more disciplined commitment from his followers. He discouraged multiple religious identities, such as those adopted by many Jewish Baha'i converts. [17] Since 1963, the international Baha'i community has been under the leadership of a body known as the Universal House of Justice (*bayt al-adl 'azam*), consisting of nine men elected every five years in a multi-level, secret-ballot election without nominations or campaigns.

The first century of Baha'i history saw dramatic changes under various charismatic leaders. Under the leadership of Baha'u'llah, the Bab's messianic message was further liberated from the confines of Shi'i Islam and inspired a reformist movement with strong Iranian and mystical influences. 'Abdu'l-Baha further developed the faith's social ideas and made a concerted effort to expand its reach beyond the Islamic sphere by propagating it in Asia and the West. Shoghi Effendi envisioned an organized global religion, one that was influenced by twentieth-century ideas of systematic planning and centralized bureaucratic institutions. The dynamism of the faith, its initial flexibility and its ability to redefine itself account for much of its success during its formative period when it faced much opposition and persecution.

The Iranian Baha'i Community

Notwithstanding its reliance on charismatic leadership, Iran's Baha'i community from the beginning had a life of its own. In the 1880s, following the conversion of a number of prominent Shi'i ulama, such as Abul-Fazl Golpaygani, a leading scholar of his day, the Baha'is fully articulated their message and justified their faith based on a hermeneutic reading of past scripture, including Jewish scripture.[18] Golpaygani was perhaps the most notable of the prominent Shi'i ulama who became Baha'i leaders. His wide range of contemporary knowledge, his command of logic, his ascetic modesty and his warm personality greatly appealed to a wide range of "seekers" and "contenders." Rayhan Rayhani, whose autobiography provides an important case study of Jewish conversion to the Baha'i faith, states that on two occasions when Golpaygani visited Kashan to debate with the Jewish rabbis, they proved unable to meet his challenge. Even if his assessment might be attributed to a convert's enthusiasm, the debates indicate an unusual command of biblical arguments on the part of Golpaygani.

The Baha'is also enjoyed an increasing organizational advantage. Beginning in the 1870s, a new group of Baha'i leaders, which included a number of enlightened ulama converts, initiated a new direction in organization and social activism.[18] Through the establishment of institutions such as the Councils of Deliberation (*majles-e showr*), which later became the elected bodies known as Spiritual Assemblies (*mahfel-e rowhani*), and the appointment of a national body known as the Hands of the Cause of God (*ayadi-ye amrullah*), the Baha'i community became increasingly well organized. A separate appointed office (*amin-e huquq-ullah*) was responsible for collecting a voluntary religious tax to support community expenditures. The figure of the full-time itinerant teacher (*moballegh*) who made regular visits to Baha'i communities in urban and rural areas was instrumental in the expansion of missionary activities and the education of lay Baha'is.

By the time of Mozaffar al-Din Shah (r. 1896–1906), an era of relative liberalization, the Baha'is who saw themselves as "the party of God" (*hezbu'llah*) had the organizational means in place to advance what they saw as a divinely inspired cause (*amru'llah*). After a half-century of efforts to erase their inherited image as subversive opponents of Qajar rule, the Baha'is were no longer identified with anarchism and political agitation—at least in the eyes of the new Qajar ruling elites—while many among the educated public increasingly came to see Baha'is as representing progressive ideas and offering a reform-minded alternative to traditional religion.[20]

As precursors of reformist activism, Baha'is played an important role in Iran's modern education movement. As early as 1883, Persian Baha'i expatriates in Ashkhabad established the first Baha'i schools for boys and girls. Iran's first Baha'i school was established in Tehran in 1897— just prior to the beginning of Iran's modern school movement—by the Baha'i reformist and scholar Adib Taleqani (1848–1919). Formally recognized in 1889, Tarbiyat (Arabic, training and nurturing), the boys' school in Tehran, like a number of others throughout the country, was known for its Baha'i association and its high academic standards.[21] As an important step toward outreach and social activism, Baha'is established schools (including girls' schools) in a number of other Baha'i population centers, mostly through local initiatives and with encouragement from 'Abdu'l-Baha. In the post-Constitutional era of invigorating reform, schools were the bastions of modernity and a target of tensions instigated by traditionalist elements (see Chapter Eight).

Localized charitable foundations (*sanduq-e khayriyeh*), collected donations so that the foundation's income could support charitable causes and Baha'i public institutions. In a letter originally addressed to Yerevan Baha'is, 'Abdu'l-Baha promoted the idea, encouraged broad participation and stressed the importance of local initiative and local control. Hamadan's Baha'i charitable foundation was founded around 1901. Some of the proceeds from this foundation were used for the novel project of a public library—another innovation of the Muzaffari period. The Ta'id public library (*qara'at-khaneh-ye Ta'id*) reportedly contained some four thousand volumes in four languages and was one of the first efforts to set up a secular public library. Yet the authorities closed it down within years of its establishment, apparently because they regarded it as subversive.[22] This library may have predated a similar public library in Tabriz founded by a group of constitutionalists around 1906, which soon became a center of revolutionary activity.[23]

Contacts with Baha'i communities in the West helped advance a modern agenda. The establishment in 1910 of the Persian-American Educational Society by American Baha'is in Chicago with the goal of providing educational, medical, and technical assistance to Iran went far beyond any earlier Baha'i educational effort.[24] American Baha'i women volunteers joined their co-religionists in Iran to establish education for women (first in Hamadan in 1908, and then in Tehran in 1911) [see Plate 9]. Baha'i meetings for "Advancement of Women" (*taraqqi-ye nesvan*) [see Plate 16] were conducted with programs similar to those of the *mahfel* (reserved for men) and were important steps towards encouraging women's agency and social engagement.[25]

Another important conduit for modernity was communication and exchange with large communities of Iranian Baha'is in foreign cities. A number of Baha'i communities in Russia, Egypt, India, Palestine, and central Asia, mostly formed of Iranian Baha'i immigrants, maintained close contact with Iran and were an important channel for transplanting modernity. In this way, Baha'is found a support system that facilitated education, business and trade, cultural exchange, and the publication of Baha'i scriptures.[26] Starting in the 1880s, a large number of Baha'is migrated to territories newly fallen under Russian rule. There, they were exposed to new Western ideas and movements, including the October Bolshevik Revolution. Eventually, these Western-educated, Iranian Baha'is were forced to return to Iran under Stalin's purges during the 1930s, and their return had a modernizing influence on the Baha'i community.

Those who took the critical step of changing a fundamental aspect of their identities through conversion were more apt to undertake experiments in novel endeavors and professions. Historically, many innovations came from fringe groups with nonconformist identities who used them as a means of subverting the hegemony of the dominant and often oppressive traditionalists. A break with convention was most prominent in the fields of theology, literature, philosophy, and art but also in areas such as handicrafts.

As an expression of their modern outlook, some Baha'is chose new professions. One such profession, frowned upon by the Shi'i ulama for its association with imagery, was photography, which was embraced by non-Muslims such as Baha'is who taught the trade to their coreligionists as a novel and artistic profession. One of Iran's pioneer photographers and its first known filmmaker was Mirza Ebrahim Khan 'Akkas-bashi (1874–1915), son of an accomplished Baha'i painter Mirza Ahmad (b. 1848). Ebrahim Khan, who was later given the title of Mosavver Rahmani (the divine illustrator) by 'Abdul-Baha, was Naser al-Din Shah's court photographer and later during the Muzzafari period around the turn of the century began his first experimentation as a cameraman.[27] Other Baha'i artists practiced their trades in the provinces, such as Mirza Hasan Chehreh-negar (d. 1913?), a leading early photographer in Shiraz.[28] A certain Mirza Saleh in Hamadan was another early photographer who taught the trade to his friend Sayyed Asadullah Qomi, a cobbler with poetic talent turned Baha'i teacher. Amateur photographers around the turn of the century who were more obscure became important catalysts for urban change.[29]

Among Baha'i artists whose conversions inspired artistic innovation was Mirza 'Ataullah Khan 'Ata'i, son of Mirza Mahmud Naraqi, whose family had early Babi roots, and a grandson of the renowned Mulla Ahmad Naraqi. He received the title of Sani' al-Soltan from Naser al-Din Shah who was impressed by his artistic abilities. An accomplished painter and a leading student of the celebrated painter Kamal al-Mulk, he was also a pioneer sculptor. In addition to his artistic work, he held the prominent position of the chief treasurer of customs.[30]

Music was another field frowned upon by the traditionalist ulama. Musicians were often stigmatized and many had to hide their artistic interests from outsiders—even their own families. In contrast, the value of music and the role of musicians were praised in the Baha'i scriptures. This was reinforced by the important role music played within the Baha'i meetings, in the "chanting" of prayers (*talavat-e ayat*) and group singing of poetry, an innovation inspired by the musical tradition within Sufi circles. It can be argued that the Baha'is provided an alternative and at times complementary channel to the Sufi meeting houses (*khaneqah*), by providing a support group for those whose artistic interests would have otherwise remained suppressed by the forces of tradition.

The link between artistic expression and a modern religion becomes more evident from a list of Baha'is, both converts and sympathizers, who made contributions in the field of Persian music. The celebrated Mirza 'Abdullah (1843–1918) was a court virtuoso and a major figure during Iran's musical revival of the late nineteenth century. He is widely credited for having a major role in organizing the repertoire of classical music into canonized modes and melodic movements known as the *radif*, which is associated with his name.[31] Though probably a secret Baha'i convert, Mirza 'Abdullah maintained contacts with the Baha'i community, performed in Baha'i meetings, and was the recipient of some correspondence from 'Abdu'l-Baha.

Among early promoters of Iran's national music, including its ethnic and folkloric components, the composer and founder of Iran's National Orchestra, 'Ali Muhammad Khadem-Misaq is worthy of note [see Plate 15]. His father Mirza Mehdi converted to Islam from Judaism in Qom and became a *zurkhaneh* (lit., house of strength) musician and Shahnameh orator before eventually becoming a Baha'i.[32]

Hosayn Sanjari (d. 1942), who became a Baha'i, was a skilled Tar player. His son Heshmat Sanjari (1918–95) was one of Iran's accomplished composers of contemporary classical music and a conductor of Tehran's Symphony Orchestra (1960–71). Aminullah Hosayn (b. 1907) was another accomplished Western-music composer of the oriental style who was raised in a Baha'i family in Russian Ashkhabad. His work is an example of the successful amalgamation of Eastern and Western musical influences.

Many Baha'i artists thrived during the post-Constitutional period (1910–1925), a time of cultural flourishing. This period was arguably the Baha'i movement's most critical period of community growth, second only to its expansion at the beginning of the Babi revolution. However, some of these artists grew distant from the Baha'i community as a secular alternative became more accessible during the Pahlavi period. Their distance from the community notwithstanding, much of their sense of creativity and innovation can be attributed to the conversion experienced within their families—a transformational experience with consequences that often lasted over generations. Despite these impressive contributions to the cultural history of Iran, the Baha'i affiliations of many artists and intellectuals have been discounted or outright denied by their relatives in an attempt to thwart the stigma of belonging to a persecuted religion. Conversely, the Baha'i community has often shied away from claiming artists and intellectuals with political associations or uncertain commitments to the hardening boundaries of religious membership.[33]

Post-constitutional Expansion

During the dynamic years of the constitutional period (1905–11), the Baha'is benefited from a generally heightened sense of intellectual curiosity and openness toward new ideas on the part of the intelligentsia. For Iran's minorities, assimilation was a logical correlation of the Constitutional Revolution, with its anti-clerical and secular tendencies and its calls for equal rights for all citizens, national integration, and modern education. More than ever, the foundations of traditional religion as the bulwark of personal identity were shaken. The mosque and the ulama, as the ghetto and the rabbis, were no longer the exclusive determinants of one's place in society. But unlike the secular constitutionalist ideology, the Baha'i message was not merely articulated around a social reform program and a political agenda. Rather, it claimed the power to reinvigorate Iranian society by reviving its most basic foundation, namely its religion.

The Constitutional Revolution promised protection under the rule of law and an end to multiple and unpredictable sources of coercive authority. The constitution also promised, and to a limited extent

delivered, a greater degree of security for non-Muslims. Although
protections under the constitution were only extended to "recognized
(*rasmi*) religious minorities" such as Jews and Christians, Baha'is also
benefited from the establishment of a more secularized legal system
and a rationalized system of government based on the rule of law.

The large number of Baha'i conversions during the post-
constitutional period (1906–25) can in part be explained by the weakness of alternative ideologies. Prior to the 1930s, the nationalist, the
leftist, and (in the case of the Jews) the Zionist ideology had not fully
developed in Iran, while the Baha'i message of indigenous religious
renewal and social reform was fully articulated and increasingly well
organized. Together with their sympathizers, those with more discreet
and distant associations with the Baha'is, urban converts formed a visible segment of the population that was more educated than ordinary
Iranians and more interested in the modern education of their children.
According to a non-Baha'i observer, as many as one thousand children
performed in a Baha'i holiday celebration in Tehran in 1921.[34]

The Baha'i rural population also grew. As Rayhani indicates, "there
was not a single Baha'i" in Aran, a village near Kashan known as a center of Sufi activity, while he was living there in 1900. Within decades
it became a thriving center of Baha'i life. Although demographically
small, the Baha'is represented a new urban, educated population that
increasingly found itself in harmony with the demands of a secularizing society.

The rapid rate of expansion boosted the community's level of self-
assurance. The new sense of confidence was partly generated by finding new allies among the elite. Although the majority of Baha'is were
impoverished and socially disadvantaged, a number of influential figures were also attracted to the new faith, starting in the Mozaffari period
and especially after the Constitutional Revolution. According to one
British observer, the Baha'is boasted that their faith would soon become
"Iran's next state religion."[35] Given the rapid rate of Baha'i growth
among sectors of the intelligentsia around the turn of the century, it is
conceivable that some Baha'is might entertain such expectations.

In any case, the Baha'i success story—the growth of the community
between the 1880s and the 1930s—is all the more remarkable considering the strength and cruelty of its opposition. At its very inception
the community was subject to a venomous propaganda campaign

launched by the Shi'i establishment. Having taken the drastic step of breaking with Islam and believing in a revelation that appeared after Prophet Mohammad, "the seal of the prophets." the Babis, and later the Baha'is, earned the implacable enmity of the ulama. To the familiar accusations used against heretical groups, generally known as *abaheh,* such as engaging in wife-sharing orgies, dealings in sorcery, using tea as a potion to spellbind potential converts, and even possessing hidden demonic horns and a pointed tail, were added more modern and politically charged accusations. These included serving as the agents of one or another colonial power, supposedly in order to undermine Iran's religious and national solidarity. These charges were strengthened by the Baha'i refusal to participate in political activities, which was often seen as pro-monarchist during the Constitutional Revolution and later under Pahlavi rule, and by the greater receptivity of educated Baha'is to Western ways. Nevertheless, like other entrenched myths, such as the anti-Jewish attitudes embedded in the Iranian psyche, the anti-Baha'i mindset—more nuanced, perhaps, but still present in the writings of some secular intellectuals—has shown remarkable resilience.[36]

For a variety of reasons, by the 1950s, Iran's Baha'i community had lost much of its innovative vigor as advocates of an indigenous modernity and could not match its previous impressive growth of the post-constitutional period. In the post-World War II period of relative political freedoms, the Baha'is became more inward looking and less engaged with new ideas and trends articulated by the left and by nationalist intellectuals. That Baha'is lost their edge as a proponent of modernity may also be in part attributed to the preeminence of state-sponsored secular nationalism, a powerful mode of modernity which now defined Iran's new national narrative. Parallel currents to this state-sponsored agenda were a growing leftist movement and a reformulated fundamentalist discourse. These new alternatives were supported by a range of ulama and by intellectuals with a variety of leftist and Islamic tendencies and influences.

An increasingly organized anti-Baha'i movement led by the ulama and other traditionalist elements managed to adapt to the new post-war political environment. After losing much of their authority during decades of disciplined secularization under Reza Shah (1925–41), the newly revived ulama once again managed to gain legitimacy and authority. In 1955, the ulama under the leadership of Ayatollah

Borujerdi succeeded in gaining the active support of the regime to start an anti-Baha'i campaign.[37] New organizations exclusively dedicated to anti-Baha'i activities emerged, along with a network of dedicated volunteers and trained debaters who adopted new techniques to oppose Baha'i propagation.[38]

By mid-century, Baha'is in Iran had not articulated a reinterpretation of their message that could encompass the dominant leftist or modernist global discourse. Anti-Baha'i propaganda transformed itself to suit the post-war anti-colonial mood, now denouncing the Baha'i community, not as religious heretics, but as an imagined political "internal Other." This put an end to mass Baha'i conversions. Even individual conversions were slowed to a trickle.

4

NEW FORMS OF CONVERSION

In the latter part of the nineteenth century, a new trend in Jewish conversions began to emerge. While sporadic conversions to Islam continued, Jews in significant numbers converted to other religions, especially the Baha'i faith, and to a lesser extent Christianity. These conversions represented a revival of the age-old but mostly dormant trend toward cultural assimilation. They also reveal a new purpose in conversion, which now served as a vehicle for assimilation to modernity. Here the primary interest of the converts was no longer to accrue the benefits of conformity to the state religion, but to find meaning through a broader and more inclusive identity that transcended the confines of traditional communities and Shi'i exclusivism.

Although reliable statistics are hard to find, a number of foreign observers have made estimates about the number of Jewish Baha'i converts during this period. According to Ephraim Neumark, there were an estimated two million Baha'is in Iran in 1884, including "many Jews." Some fifty years later, the Jewish scholar Dr. Abraham J. Brower estimated the number of Jewish converts in the mid-1930s to be "thousands and perhaps ten thousand of Jews." He reports the number of converts in the mid-1930s to be "around a quarter of the Jews of Hamadan," while he estimates the Jewish population of Hamadan at the time to be 8,000. He also reports that as many as 700 Jews in Tehran converted to the Baha'i faith. These figures at first may seem inflated, yet given the fluidity and range of Jewish-Baha'i identity in this period, from sympathizers to propagators, these estimates may not be unreasonable. The British diplomat Lord Curzon's estimates in the 1880s, prior to the early-twentieth-century wave of conversions, are perhaps more representative of converts who openly confessed their

Baha'i convictions. His figures for Kashan, Hamadan, and Tehran estimate 50, 100, and 150 Jewish families respectively. He also reports that as much as 75 per cent of the Golpayegan Jewish population have "formally joined the Bahai movement and their numbers have since increased considerably," which would amount to a mass conversion among the Jews of that area.[1]

Conversion and Multiple Identities

Baha'i conversion must be seen in the larger context of the fluidity of religious identities in Iran during the second half of the nineteenth century. In the Iranian environment, where public and private spheres were traditionally kept separated from each other, it was not unusual for one to have multiple religious identities even after a conversion. Nor was it unusual for various members of an extended family to convert to different religions.[2] Yet unlike earlier incidents of collective conversion to Islam, conversions to the Baha'i faith were grounded in individual convictions and private experiences.

The 1840s witnessed a great number of conversions of Muslims to the Babi religion that transformed the identities of individuals and at times communities. Beginning in the 1870s, Jews and Zoroastrians along with a few Armenians converted or became sympathetic to the Baha'i religion, whose main body of followers consisted of Muslim converts.[3] At a time when it was illegal in Iran to conduct missionary activity among Muslims, American and European missionaries were able to attract a sizable albeit smaller number of Jewish converts and sympathizers to Christianity. Some Muslims and Jews were attracted to various forms of Sufism, and even to materialist agnostic beliefs.[4] In a world where religion was the primary form of identity, the adoption of new religions can be seen as a reflection of profound underlying social changes.

While conversion to Islam, Christianity, and the Baha'i faith was not unusual among Jews in the latter quarter of the nineteenth century, there is at least one reported instance of mass conversion to Judaism. In the 1890s, the inhabitants of the Russian village of Pirvolni, near the Iran border town of Astara, who were presumably Shi'is, converted *en masse* to Judaism for reasons that are not entirely clear. All we know is that they joined a group of privileged "mountain Jews" who benefited from a higher social status. Reportedly, these converts to Judaism did not face any opposition from the Russian authorities who typically opposed religious conversions.[5]

For converts like Rayhan Rayhani or Aqajan Shakeri, who came from modest backgrounds, and even the more privileged Hafezis, life around the turn of the century was deeply affected by war and revolution, famine and hardship, economic decline, political uncertainty, and the weakening of central authority. Under such circumstance, faith became one of the few anchors of personal stability and comfort available.

Overwhelming social challenges tended to reinforce religious convictions. Through the new doctrine claiming the fulfillment of Jewish messianic expectations, many found an avenue by which to integrate themselves into the Iranian national narrative. This took them out of the Jewish ghetto and beyond the limits of their impoverished and marginalized community. European-style schools opened new horizons and introduced doubts about traditional norms and values. The search for a new identity was negotiated in a climate of Christian missionary preaching, Sufi discourse, and Baha'i advocacy. The adoption of new religious identities in conditions of crisis and turmoil can thus be seen as a reflection of the challenges brought forth by conflicting modes of modernity.

New market forces enhanced internal immigration, especially among younger Jews. Hamadan, a center of Jewish conversion, enjoyed a booming economy during the last quarter of the nineteenth century as a result of the growing Baghdad trade. It attracted a wide variety of migrants from other Jewish communities throughout Iran. It also attracted a community of affluent and Westernized Iraqi Jews. Immigration entailed new occupations and work environments and a departure from traditional limitations guarded by ancient communities. More significantly, immigration meant a breakdown of the ghetto, both geographically and mentally. Unlike in Tehran and Kashan, Jews in Hamadan were less restricted in their choice of neighborhoods and were more dispersed throughout the city. This meant less communal control and a more cosmopolitan self-awareness.

Conversion and Messianism

Besides being a period of questioning traditional religious conventions, the nineteenth century witnessed an acceleration of ancient Jewish and Shi'i messianic expectations. According to the Christian missionary

Henry Stern, who visited Iran in the 1850s, the prominent Jewish physician Hakim Harun of Kashan confessed that "Christian salvation was in perfect harmony with the Scripture, and far superior to the fanciful system of Rabbinism." Stern further claims that Harun assured him that many of the Jews of Kashan "will as intensely love Christ and his Gospel, as they formerly rejected the one and despised the other."[6] As discussed in Chapter Five, a number of Hakim Harun's family members converted to Islam and the Baha'i faith. Even if one discounts the enthusiasm of the Christian reporter, these statements may point to the strengthening of a deep-rooted sense of messianic expectation among the Jews. One indication of the presence of messianic memory in Kashan during this period was the customary practice of Jews going to their rooftops on the Sabbath to pray for the capacity to recognize the Messiah at the time of his advent.[7]

Babi scriptures, as well as a number of Sufi and popular figures, placed much emphasis on the importance of the year 1260 or 1261 AH, which coincided with a millennium (according to lunar years) after the passing of the Eleventh Imam and the occultation of the Twelfth in 260 AH/873–874 CE. According to an early Babi source, "Christians, Europeans, Mandaeans (Sabaeans), Zoroastrians, and Jews as well as Ni'matullahis, Isma'ilis, and Zaydis all acknowledged the importance of the year sixty-one [1845]" as the anticipated date of the return of the promised Messiah, with Jews specifying the month of Rabi' al-Awwal of that year.[8] It is not unlikely that the coming of the year 5600 (1840) of the Jewish calendar awakened a sense of millennial anticipation in many Jews. In fact, the preoccupation among Jews with "dating" the coming of the messiah became so commonplace that rabbis had to ban the practice. As in other instances in Jewish (and Islamic) history, the clerical establishment stood against any specific calculation of the timing of the messianic advent.[9]

Yet the longing for an imminent end to oppression continued. As noted in Chapter Two, prior to the forced conversions in Mashhad in 1839, some Jews there had voluntarily yet secretly converted to Islam.

As early as the middle of the nineteenth century, an interfaith dialogue was already in process. Part of that dialogue was a commentary titled "A Response to Jewish Questions." In contrast to the prevailing adversarial tone of most of the anti-Jewish literature of this period, its tone and content was reportedly mild, having been written by converts to Islam. Starting in the late 1870s, Hamadan became a center for Jewish conversion to Christianity, Islam, and the Baha'i faith, a process that may be seen as a continuation of an earlier interfaith dialogue.[10]

The early nineteenth century was also a period of rising messianic fervor in Iran and in the Caucasus. Mosheh Mizrahi, a prophetic figure who referred to himself as Messiah ben David, along with his brother, who was named by him Messiah ben Yosef, proclaimed his claims in his book. Originally from Shirvan in the Caucasus, Mosheh Mizrahi traveled extensively in Caucasia, the Ottoman Empire, and far into Iran. He reports having had visionary dreams. Influenced by Kabalistic thought, he promised the imminence of the time of redemption (geulah) and an end to Jewish troubles during the month of Adar of the year TaQ'aD (beginning February 21, 1814). The Prophet Elijah was expected to reveal to the Messiah Mosheh Mizrahi various deep secrets. The completion of his book, so Mosheh Mizrahi argued, would bring about the final redemption. Later he postponed the date of redemption to the year TaR (1840), which coincided with a number of other messianic expectations.[11]

An unknown number of Jews in Tehran also converted to Islam in the 1870s, following the lead of a single Jewish rabbi.[12] Other rabbis such as Rayhani's relative encouraged their followers to convert to Islam if the Messiah did not appear by the impending date of 1884. Rayahni witnessed the conversion of the family of Mulla Rabi-Eshaq, "the most learned rabbi in Tehran." During one Passover feast when he hosted an elaborate dinner, he was asked: "Honored Rabbi, when will the Messiah come?" He replied: "If he doesn't come by hatarmad, [5644/1884][13] you can all go and become Muslims on my account."

Rayhani continues:

His brother Mulla 'Abdu'l-'Aziz was a devout and learned man but had many superstitions (mohumat). He taught the Torah to the youth and was known among Jews for his piety. He waited until the year 5644, and then he went to Hajji Mulla 'Ali Kani [the leading Shi'i cleric of Tehran] and converted to Islam. He afterwards used to carry his now-deceased brother's books on his back, teaching the Jews in the Jewish quarter about Jesus and arguing the truth of the Prophet Muhammad.[14]

Rayhani's own "final" conversion dates to that same year. The significance of 1884 in instilling messianic fervor is further highlighted by the case of a mass migration of Shirazi Jews to Palestine during that year. One motive is said to have been the desire to escape persecution, a familiar pattern in the history of Shiraz's Jews. Perhaps more remarkable is that the migrants reportedly saw their difficult journey from Shiraz to Palestine by sea via Bushehr as a means of precipitating an end to Jewish Exile (*galut*) and of accelerating the arrival of the Messiah.[15]

Even conversion to Christianity did not completely put an end to messianic fervor. Around the turn of the twentieth century, these tendencies were reflected in the messianic claims made by a certain Hakim Musa, a son-in-law of Aqa Hayyem Lalezar, an early Baha'i who later became a Christian missionary. Musa studied Western medicine in Hamadan's American missionary hospital and was one of Hamadan's reputable physicians. His claim to be "the forerunner to the Jewish Messiah" does not seem to have attracted much attention.[16]

Conversion and Social Change

This fascinating phenomenon of messianic expectation and religious ambiguity, which many Jews experienced in the 1870s and 1880s, coincided with a number of social and economic changes that occurred within a relatively short period of time and had a lasting effect on Iranian society. The growth in population throughout the nineteenth century was accompanied by increased contact with the West in the form of improved communications, notably print and telegraph, and a dramatic rise in the volume of foreign trade. Contact with Western powers also brought military defeat, diplomatic humiliation, monetary collapse, and financial dependency. The recurrence of devastating famines and the visitations of worldwide epidemics only intensified the crisis. As in many other parts of the world, Iran's once-thriving textile production and trade suffered the onslaught of cheap industrial-age European goods and experienced a marked decline. Iran's economy became more dependent on global trends, including recessions and currency devaluations. Military defeats and the loss of territory in the face of Russian expansionism and British colonialism brought home the painful realization of European economic and technological superiority and highlighted the inadequacies of the Qajar regime and its state organization.[17] These and other factors helped to undermine Muslims' sense of confidence and even their faith in the authority of Islam as the superior religion.[18] For many Iranians, their main preoccupation became how to confront what they viewed as their overwhelming political, economic, military, and even intellectual backwardness. This meant questioning traditions and conventions and experimenting with unconventional identities.

Yet economic change in nineteenth-century Iran also included more constructive processes. The introduction of European manufactured products expanded the domestic market, increased demand for some of Iran's products, such as carpets and high-quality textiles, and facilitated the emergence of a national economy by the time of the 1905 Constitutional Revolution. Many members of the Jewish community, even those with little capital, benefited from these conditions by forming trading partnerships. These organized branches in places like Rasht, a silk production and distribution center in the densely populated north; Hamadan, an emporium for the Basra trade in the Persian Gulf; Arak, an emerging trade center where Jews enjoyed much freedom in the bazaar; and Sanandaj and other Kurdish towns, which were markets for Kashan silk products.

Migration and the Weakening of Communal Ties

The expansion of trade and the decline of local economies like that of Kashan meant that a growing number of younger Jews, many still in their teens, left their ancient communities for towns with small Jewish communities or none at all. In such circumstances, they experienced new work environments and new kinds of emotional stress. Difficulties finding access to kosher food, which was essential to Jewish identity, became another source of anxiety, while prohibition on the use of public baths due to concerns over Shi'i laws of ritual purity meant isolation and hardship. The social isolation of young migrants with weakened family and community bonds was a significant factor in their attraction to Baha'i functions. Baha'i gatherings offered not only hospitality but a universal message of tolerance and equality with Baha'is of Muslim origin who would otherwise have considered them "impure" and avoided close interaction with them. Some Baha'i gatherings held in Seneh in Kurdestan on Saturday afternoons, for example, attracted Jewish enthusiasts and thus became a cause of concern for the agents of the Alliance Israélite Universelle, an organization dedicated to the education and emancipation of oppressed Jewish communities.[19]

Concerned with the Baha'i successes, the Alliance agent in Hamadan tried to discourage Jews from attending Baha'i meetings and even tried to disband the gatherings by puting pressure on the local authorities. He even demanded that his superiors in Tehran pressure the governor of Hamadan to administer corporal punishment (the bastinado) to the new converts. He also tried witout much success to stop the rabbis from presiding over marriages involving converts. The rabbis' economic interests in conducting marriage ceremonies trumped pressure from the Alliance, however. In fact, many traditionalist Jews opposed the Alliance, accusing them of teaching students "non-Jewish material.[20] Nevertheless, some Jews continued to convert and, when elected to Baha'i community councils (*mahfel-e rowhani*), became recognized community leaders.

The Gender Factor

In contrast to the Jewish men of Kashan, Jewish women there—who remained in their hometowns, stayed at home, and were not exposed to education, to the new economy, or to the evolving structure of the workforce—did not generally convert. Rayhani describes his first wife as "the only Jewish Baha'i woman in Kashan" and reports that she was harassed by other Jewish women. Through her memoirs, we know of at least one other early female Baha'i of Muslim background in Kashan, an educated woman who had taught in Baha'u'llah's household in 'Akka.[21] Outside of Kashan, Jewish women with more education did convert in significant numbers.

A number of the Jewish women of Hamadan are reported to have became dedicated Baha'is. According to Isabella Bird, a Christian British woman who visited Hamadan around 1890: "Some of the Jewish women, who have become *Babis,* ask to have the New Testament read to them in the hope of hearing something which they may use in the propagation of their new faith." It is plausible that the women Bird refers to also included the literate Babi women of the merchant and land-owning Naraqi family, some of whom had an interest in scholarship and had become followers of Tahereh Qurratul-'Ayn.[22]

Strains and Social Insentives

Yedidia Shofet, a contemporary rabbi from Kashan, attributes the Jews' attraction to the Babi/Baha'i religion to a variety of familiar factors such as the expressions of acceptance and "kindness" by Baha'i leaders and scholars (many of whom were formerly members of the ulama and still wore clerical attire) and the Jews' lack of a "deep knowledge" of Judaism. The latter may be a reflection of the condescending views of some Western observers towards Persian Jews. He also cites more mundane motives such as the willingness of Baha'i landlords in Hamadan to accept lower rent from young Jewish migrants.[23]

Another critical account, of Baha'i efforts to convert Jews in Arak, is significant in that it stresses not only Jewish "ignorance" and "simple-mindedness," but also divisions among Jewish rabbis as contributing factors to the Baha'i success in attracting young Jewish migrants. This description of Mirza Aqa Khan Qae'm-Maqam, an influential local Baha'i landowner who offered an open invitation to his home and who personally welcomed young Jewish guests, echoes similar accounts by other authors for whom conversion somehow parallels "deception."[24] The above observations of factors contributing to the process of conversion may fit sociological models developed by a combination of "strain" and "social influence" theories. Strain theory argues that religion is "a way to transcend and transvalue" deprivation by offering a form of "private status" to compensate for discrimination in the secular world. Social influence theory holds that people are socially free to join a new religion when they lack ties to their own religious community. Once they form bonds with members of a new community, they are attracted to the new religion. As socially underprivileged individuals with weak community bonds, many vulnerable migrants became "socially free" to join a new religion, while the Baha'i community's acceptance of Jews as equals provided the necessary "strong social relations" with the new community.[25] Much of this sociological discourse is based on the European experience, where Jews converted to Christianity as a matter of social advancement or professional necessity. A well-known example is that of early nineteenth-century (1790s to 1870s) England, where conversion of Jews to Christianity was a widespread and institutionalized part of a nation-building project involving thousands of Jews.[26] However, an examination of the intellectual, cultural, and religious dimensions of conversion in

Islam reveals a more nuanced process involving complex dynamics that shape religious identity.

The cultural and intellectual dimensions of Jewish conversion in Iran, one can argue, were at least as significant as social factors. The Baha'i message introduced young migrants to a whole new set of ideas and debates, such as ethnic and gender equality, religious tolerance, the importance of education, world peace, and economic justice. Through attendance at Baha'i schools, or contact with the more literate members of the community, some Jewish converts became well versed in Arabic and Islamic literature. Rooted in Persian mysticism and inspired by its literary heritage, Baha'i texts were a vital link to Persian high culture for Jewish converts who were generally deprived of an education in Persian and had become isolated from it. In fact, Persian language and literature served as vital catalysts to unify Iran's diverse population at a time of greater socio-cultural integration. Becoming a Baha'i, one might argue, was a way for people to abandon parochial traditional divisions and embrace this common culture while maintaining family and social loyalties to their own communities.[27]

What can be characterized as a Baha'i cultural language developed and was communicated in Baha'i meetings (*mahfel*). Held on a regular basis in private homes or Baha'i centers, and at times attended by "seekers," the *mahfel* program included group musical recitations of prayers and poems, the reading of Baha'i texts in Persian and Arabic, the discussion of polemical arguments grounded in the fulfillment of the prophecies of the Hebrew Bible, missionary experiences, and conversion accounts.[28] The repeated sharing of such accounts and anecdotes reinforced the oral tradition and may in part account for the lucidity and rich detail of accounts such as those by Rayhani and Shakeri. It may also shed light on the Baha'i preoccupation with engaging in religious debate (*tabligh*), whereby they challenged traditional religious views and expounded their own.

The new Baha'i cultural language can also be credited with promoting an interest in Persian poetry and producing a great number of Baha'i poets of various qualities. Like other sectors of Iranian society, Baha'is too were engaged in writing poetry. These included Babi and Baha'i women—most notably the formally educated Tahereh Qurrat al-'Ayn, the haphazardly educated Rayhani (who became known as *Rayhan-e sha'er*, Rayhan the Poet), and the celebrated semi-literate poet Mohammad-'Ali Isfahani, better known as Salmani. These poems received a broad Baha'i audience as part of group musical sing-alongs—part of a new leisure culture which also included informal social gatherings, and novelties such as outdoor picnics and comedy performances. Cultural distinctness also found expression in calligraphy, especially through the artistic illustration of Baha'i texts, and in Persian classical music that was adopted for chanting Baha'i prayers (*alvah va monajat*) inspired by tunes also used for the mystical chants of the Sufis and the Jewish songs of the synagogue.

The new Baha'i persona, especially at the turn of the twentieth century, was manifested in modern attire and dress code, in standardized Persian vernacular free from provincial and communal vocabulary and intonations, and in an emphasis on personal health and hygiene. These were in compliance with the emerging modern Iranian identity that stressed national homogeneity and an aversion to signs of a parochial past. In the early 1920s when Iranians had to embrace a new identity by choosing a family name, Baha'is chose surnames that specifically indicated their religious convictions.[29] On occasion, even ordinary symbolic expressions of modernity, such as refusal to conform to the customary practice of shaving one's hair, caused strong reactions from clerics and traditionalists and pushed individuals seeking a modern image toward conversion.

The Baha'i Message

Yet for many, it was the novelty of the Baha'i religious message that had the greatest appeal. In the latter part of the nineteenth century, the Baha'is were among the first to introduce a new discourse into Iran's otherwise conservative Islamic environment. What may be seen as an indigenous response to modernity stressed the need for the renewal of religion, the unity of humanity, social and political equality, ethnic and gender harmony, and the acceptance of religious minorities. In a society where identities were primarily religious or ethnic, a new faith that called for rationality and the equality of all races and creeds proved attractive to an emerging cosmopolitan class in search of alternatives to traditional identities. The Baha'i message recognized and attempted to come to terms with the increasingly pervasive presence of modernity. Its all-inclusive approach to past religions accepted the validity of all past prophets as "manifestations" (*zohur*) of the Divine

Truth whose mission was to renew the "Covenant" (*'ahd*) of God with humanity. Baha'u'llah's proclamation of the "coming of the New Era" (*zohur-e dawr-e badi'*) created a sense of messianic urgency in the minds of underprivileged Jews seeking salvation and escape from their persecuted past.

As such, conversion can be seen as a reconciliation of new faith with the fundamentals of deeply held Jewish convictions. Jewish beliefs and practices were seen in a new light, rejecting those now believed to be extraneous traditions and "superstitions" that had developed over the centuries under the dominance of clerical authority. As discussed in Chapter One, this purist view, which depreciated the rabbinic tradition and instead held up the Torah as the primordial source of religious inspiration, had deep roots among Iranian Jews, perhaps through the influence of the anti-rabbinic Karaite movement. However, the break with rabbinic tradition was more extensively developed in Baha'i texts that reintroduced the old Perso-Shi'i notion of the renewal of the age, the coming of the "New Era," and the advent of a new "Manifestation." The non-literal and metaphorical Baha'i reading of holy texts, a familiar theme in the Persian mystical tradition, appealed to the emerging rationalist trends influenced by modernity.[30]

Many Baha'i values were compatible with a fluid religious identity. A non-dogmatic, time-based, and relative approach to religious truth allowed wide latitude for interpretation of the message. In fact, Baha'i texts de-emphasize the idea of an absolute and all-encompassing deity, emphasizing instead the founder's role as a "Manifestation of God," and even as the incarnation of the deity, thus giving the Divine a human dimension. The "Manifestation," the "non-God" as described by Alessandro Bausani, is a departure from the conventional image of a Judeo-Islamic transcendent God. The "Manifestation" is seen as a human's sole avenue for finding "traces" in an eternal journey for transcendence and a mirror by which the believer may arrive at "moments of consciousness," when only blurred clues to understanding of a Higher Being may be realized.[31] No degree of ritual or piety can insure salvation, and no degree of seeming transgression can permanently deprive one of such rare "moments."[32]

The Baha'i concept of "Manifestation" resonates with the ancient Zoroastrian God as guide and companion (*raz*), discussed in Chapter One. This unorthodox mindset was preserved and sustained in the Sufi

tradition but became increasingly dormant under pressure from forces
of legalistic religion, especially after the dominance of legalistic Shi'ism
in the early nineteenth century. Baha'u'llah revitalized this earlier
notion while rejecting Sufi pantheism, exclusive individualistic knowledge of God, as well as almost all forms of dogma. Equally important
was what seemed to be a conscious effort to minimize ritual obligations
and Shari'ah-style laws.

A humanized deity in the person of the promised Messiah was a
source of inspiration to some converts. After a great deal of struggle with
a poorly transcribed Arabic passage from the writings of Baha'u'llah,
the young Rayhani was exhilarated by reading: "This is the day when
the unborn God has been born." The writings of Baha'u'llah, with
their declaration of the advent of a Messiah who would put an end to
people's misery, had deep appeal for many. His acceptance of all earlier
religions as aspects of one and the same truth allowed for the accom-
modation of multiple religious convictions.

Joining a Persecuted Faith

Notwithstanding these intellectual, cultural, and socio-economic
explanations, the conversion of Jews to the Baha'i faith raises the question of why an already persecuted minority would choose to join a new
religion that was subject to even harsher persecution, rather than seek
the relative security of conversion to Islam. Here is a paradox that begs
for an answer.

Disenfranchised converts such as Rayhani, a peddler traveling on foot
throughout the countryside, would have had no status or connections
outside of the Jewish community and little protection in the erratic,
unruly conditions of nineteenth-century Iran. In such a hostile environment, where the murder of an infidel could be justified as religiously
sanctioned or permissible, becoming a Baha'i could only increase the
potential for humiliation and add the risk of anti-Baha'i persecution
to an already precarious existence. Cutting ties with the Jewish community (as required by Islam) entailed much stigma and loss. A tenuous
quasi-Muslim recognition as a "new convert" (*jadid ul-Islam*), with all
of its derogatory connotations, could not have been regarded as much
of a bargain. In one case during the early years of the constitutional
period when anti-Jewish riots marked an early outcome of the revolution, a police bureaucrat refused to accept Rayhani's word that he was

a Muslim and asked to see proper "papers" supposedly given to him by one of the ulama to certify his belief in Islam.[33] Such humiliating practices may explain why many younger Jews chose to accept the risk of persecution in return for becoming an equal member of a movement that saw itself as the fulfillment of the prophecies of all religions and on the cutting edge of modernity.

In this sense, the Jewish converts can be seen as the classic "subaltern," clearly placed outside of any "hegemonic power structure," a doubly oppressed minority within a minority.[34] As such, they participated in shaping both Jewish and Muslim identity. Just as the Jews, as a minority, helped reinforce the Muslim majority's Islamic identity, the Jewish Baha'is served the role of the "Other" for both Jews and Muslims, thus helping to buttress the identities of both.

Yet as subalterns, the Jewish Baha'is, like Mashhad's Jewish converts to Islam, played a critical subversive role and defied their assigned position as a disenfranchised and socially excluded minority (see Chapter Two). The Mashhad converts had resisted oppression and the hegemonic authority of Shi'i majority through a nominal conversion to Islam, while secretly practicing Judaism. The Baha'i converts, on the other hand, embraced a new religion which (while accepting the validity of Islam) challenged the fundamental doctrine of the "finality of divine revelation" (*khatamiyyat*)—one of Islam's claims to superiority. In both instances, the subalterns in effect undermined the authority of the dominant hegemonic culture.

Few choices were available to those seeking to rise above the confines of the Jewish ghetto. A superficial declaration of belief in Islam by uttering the confession of faith (*shahada*) was rather common, either in forced conversions (as shown in Chapters Two and Eight), or under other coercive pressures built into the Shi'i legal system. For example, a nominal conversion to Islam at the time of the death of a relative could protect the assets of an affluent family against the claims of other, convert family members, who under Shi'i law could otherwise lay claim to the entirety of the family's assets.[35]

For those who had nominally converted to Islam under pressure but secretly practiced Judaism and avoided intermarriage with Muslims, a sense of isolation from the Muslims was compounded by their mostly self-imposed estrangement from other Jews.[36] In contrast, the Baha'is in theory, and to a reasonable extent in practice, accepted Jewish converts as equal members. Nevertheless, putting into practice the Baha'i ideas of racial unity was not always an easy task, as age-old anti-Jewish prejudices at times proved to be resilient.[37] Conversion to the Baha'i faith following a prior coversion to Islam can be seen as an expression of a trend among those who were seeking new alternatives but who were ill at ease with the second-class appellation of *jadid ul-Islam*.[38] The privileged Hafezi family of Hamadan, who were (Jewish) Baha'is *prior* to formally accepting Islam, were easily assimilated as Muslims, but they still felt an intellectual urge to remain Baha'is.

Obviously, not all conversions from Judaism to Islam were forced or nominal. Yet even devout converts to Islam were not always accepted as equals, and some convert communities were burdened by the demeaning title of *jadid ul-Islam* for generations. Although discrimination against converts of whatever background is contrary to the principles of Islam, distrust of Jewish converts nevertheless persisted. Kashan's community of Jewish converts, who had presumably been strict observers of Islam since the Safavid period, was stigmatized as *jadid ul-Islam* for centuries.[39] Indeed, as far back as the early years of the Islamic era, the stigma of a convert's lingering Jewish identity sometimes persisted beyond death, and cases of shaming a public figure for his alleged history of conversion occur to this day.[40] As discussed in Chapter One, this may explain the tendency of many converts to conceal information about their past and to seek a new environment, often through migration, in order to obliterate their previous identity.

A more recent case of a public figure being attacked for a family history of conversion can be seen in the "accusations" made against 'Abbas Amir-Entezam, Deputy Prime Minister under the provisional government of Mehdi Bazargan in 1979, for being a "recent Muslim." Mr. Amir-Entezam denied the "charges" and stated that his father was buried in the Muslim cemetery.[41] Similar allegations have been made against a whole host of post revolutionary political figures with solid "Islamic credentials." Like Baha'is, new-Muslims of Jewish origin are supposedly inherently seditious and subversive, with an agenda to cause harm to Islam. The notion evokes the familiar stigmas anchored in a dark part of the Iranian psyche where age-old anti-Jewish suspicions and hatreds persist.

Accepting Multiple Identities

In contrast to Muslims, the Baha'is (at least initially) tolerated fluid or flexible religious identities. The adoption of a Baha'i identity did not necessitate abandoning deep-rooted social ties involving many kinship, marriage, and business relationships. Most early Jewish converts continued to attend Sabbath services and observe the rituals of Yom Kippur. Rayhani's account even provides examples of converts, especially those in clerical positions, who together with their numerous "followers," reclaimed their Jewish identities after having converted to the Baha'i faith.[42] Marriages between Baha'i families of divergent backgrounds (Jewish/Muslim) did not occur in Kashan until around 1929, although they gradually became common.[43] For a short while Jewish Baha'is even ran a kosher butchery in competition with the one run by the rabbis.[44] In Tehran, Jewish Baha'is had their own Baha'i Spiritual Assemblies for some years before 'Abdu'l-Baha put an end to the practice. In a letter from "the Spiritual Assembly of Israelitish Baha'is" of Tehran in 1903 addressed to the "Christian Baha'is of Chicago," the Baha'i converts expressed their solidarity with the American believers by quoting biblical passages as proof of their new religious conviction.[45] Baha'i tolerance of dual identities allowed for a wide range of believers and sympathizers, ranging from ardent propagandists and active community leaders to those who, in line with the Shi'i practice of dissimulation of faith (*taqiya*) and esoteric (*bateni*) identity, remained discreet about their faith and maintained distant ties to the community of believers.

The environment of fluidity notwithstanding, there was also considerable interaction between Muslim and Jewish Baha'is. One revealing example is evident in the diaries of Mirza Mehdi Ekhvan al-Safa [see Plate 18] (d. 1919), a self-educated itinerate Baha'i teacher of modest background who was in Hamadan during the Constitutional period (1906–07).[46] A detailed account of his daily activities includes a report on participation in social events and functions held in homes of Jewish and Muslim Baha'is. Such functions included introductory and advance study classes, religious debates with prospective "seekers," meetings to urge new believers to make financial contributions (*hoququllah*), and consultation on community affairs, including resolution of business disputes and school administration.[47]

Several decades on, beginning in the 1930s, the multiple identities and loose associations which had been key elements in the growth of the Baha'i movement were challenged by an increasingly well defined and institutionalized form of religious identity. This process of consolidation and bureaucratization, which was influenced by prevailing Western trends, made it more difficult to sustain multiple religious identities. Even though many continued to maintain their association with other religious communities, the tendency toward centralization produced a more tightly knit Baha'i community in which membership in other religious communities and attendance at mosque and synagogue services were no longer considered acceptable.[48] This transition in the development of Iran's Baha'i community was accompanied by an equally significant process of institutionalization which placed elected administrative bodies much more firmly in control of religion and daily life. Through these institutions, new rules for formal "enrollment" (tasjil) were established (although many Baha'is were never enrolled) and Baha'i laws such as those relating to marriage, the prohibition against working on Baha'i holidays, and even occasional temporary travel restrictions were more vigorously enforced.[49] These developments coincided with and may in part explain the decline in the rate of growth of the Iranian Baha'i community by the 1950s

The story of Jewish conversions in nineteenth-century Iran highlights the convergence of a number of distinct processes at a time of rapid historical change and rising challenges, including most notably the advent of modernity and national integration. At a time of high messianic expectations among the Jews, a new faith promising tolerance and equality inspired a sense of optimism and the expectation of an end to age-old prejudice and discrimination. Its acceptance of multiple affiliations allowed for fluidity in religious identity and provided the necessary space to negotiate conversion in new environments. The Baha'i faith was in harmony with a more Iranian identity. Its deep indigenous roots tapped into cultural reservoirs shared by Iranian Jews. It also had elements of a modern religion: its universalistic outlook was inclusive of all races and ethnic groups; its emphasis on "Progressive Revelation" gave believers much latitude to reinterpret and redefine doctrine, thereby hindering the crystallization of dogma; and its emphasis on the harmony of science and religion provided justification for a modern, rational mindset.

5

UNCERTAINTY AND CONVICTION: EARLY EXAMPLES OF CONVERSION

The Baha'i message of tolerance and acceptance of the followers of all religions as equal believers was attractive to many Jews. However, conversion among the Jews was concentrated in certain communities and absent from others. This may be attributed to the roles certain Jewish communities played in rapidly changing trade centers, such as Hamadan in the late nineteenth century. These changes were accompanied by the introduction of new messianic themes by Christian missionaries and Baha'i teachers. In contrast, Jewish communities in Isfahan, for instance, were less exposed to new economic forces and more restricted in their interactions with non-Muslims.[1] Other communities, such as the Jews of Kashan, though equally restricted by traditional norms, were under pressure to move to places such as Hamadan in search of work. This migration exposed Kashan to new ideas, broader horizons, and a more modern outlook, mostly through the movement of young men.

Even though most conversions to the Baha'i faith among Jews took place during 'Abdu'l-Baha's ministry (1892–1921), the earliest Jewish encounter with the Babi/Baha'i religions goes back to the earliest years of the Babi movement. In 1847, the notable woman Babi leader Tahereh Qurrat al-'Ayn stayed briefly at the house of the Jewish physician Elezar (d. 1881) in Hamadan, before his father expressed concern over possible trouble. He feared that the association of a rebellious Muslim woman with a Jewish family might lead to anti-Jewish riots.[2] Although Elezar never openly confessed his belief, his Babi sympathies later found expression through at least one of his associates who was more suited to change and openly confessed his Baha'i belief.

The circumstances of many early conversions to the Baha'i faith cannot be determined with certainty. The earliest known Jewish Babi convert in Tehran, according to Baha'i sources, was a physician whose name, Hakim Masih (*mashiah*, i.e., Messiah), may suggest an earlier conversion to Christianity or Islam. The fact that two of his sons confessed to Christianity and Islam further supports this possibility.[3] Originally from Khwansar, near Golpaygan, an ancient Jewish center and later a center of Babi mass conversion, he first became a sympathizer in 1848, when he attended Tahereh's debates with Shi'i scholars in Baghdad. In 1861, Hakim Masih openly confessed his Babi beliefs along with his wealthy brother and court physician Haqnazar (Islamicized form of the Hebrew Ezekiel). He came into contact with the new religion through the Babi (and later Baha'i) leader Mulla Sadeq Moqaddas while attending to sick Babi prisoners in Tehran's notorious dungeon (*Siahchal*, black pit) for some two months. His conversion demonstrates an early ecumenical attitude, at least on the part of some Babi leaders, which saw the Babi mission going beyond the boundaries of Islam.[4] By 1880, according to Curzon, there were 150 Jewish Baha'is in Tehran. Yet despite this early expansion, Tehran, which was becoming a center of economic growth and immigration, was not the most active center of early Jewish conversions.[5] This may in part be attributed to the concentration of the community in the Jewish quarter (*mahalleh*) where strong communal and traditional bonds discouraged change.

The Hakim Nur Mahmud Family

The highly educated and influential Jewish family of Nur Mahmud (d. 1317/1899–90) in Tehran was well connected and included a number of court physicians with ambiguous religious loyalties. Hakim Nur Mahmud himself was a Jew, but seems to have secretly converted to Islam. He was the most well-known son of the Hakim Harun of Kashan, an affluent physician and local dignitary with a large progeny. Hakim Nur Mahmud's complex religious affiliations and his disposal toward the acceptance of new ideas was typical of the Harun family: some of the extended family converted to the Baha'i faith while others became Muslims [see back cover photo].

The Baha'i religion was introduced to the family around 1879 by Hakim Aqajan and Rahim Khan Hafez al-Sehha, two early Jewish converts—physicians from Hamadan—who traveled to Tehran and stayed with Hakim Nur Mahmud. (For more on Rahim Khan, see Chapter Eight.) Though Nur Mahmud never openly confessed Baha'i beliefs, a number of his relatives became sympathizers and prominent Baha'is.[6] It is possible that internal disputes within the extended family influenced the pattern of conversions.

Among Nur Mahmud's relatives, was his notable nephew and son-in-law, the influential physician 'Aqiba (1858–1912), later known as Mirza Khalil. After his conversion to Islam, he became a Baha'i through prolonged discussion with Rayhan Rayhani, then a young convert form Kashan who befriended him in the 1870s when they both lived in Tehran in the house of Nur Mahmud. (For more on Rayhani, see Chapter Six.) Khalil's conversion story is fascinating, spanning two generations, involving multiple religious convictions, and including marriage and inheritance disputes. These family tensions can be traced back at least a generation earlier to Khalil's father, Ebrahim, a son of the aforementioned Hakim Harun Kashani.

Ebrahim initially converted to Islam in Hamadan and was thereafter shunned by the family and denied a share in his father's estate. This was contrary to Islamic law as practiced in nineteenth-century Iran, under which a convert to Islam might legally lay claim to the entire family inheritance, cutting off all Jewish relatives without recourse. One can surmise that such a complete reversal of prevailing practice would only have been possible if Ebrahim's brothers, including Hakim Nur Mahmud, had likewise converted to Islam and asserted their own claims to the paternal estate.

Here we can infer a nominal, and perhaps covert, conversion to Islam employed as a legal strategy to protect the economic interests of privileged family members. The fact that this practice was tolerated by both the Shi'i ulama and the rabbis is by itself remarkable. The flexible application of Shi'i law made it possible, especially among privileged and influential sectors of the Jewish community, to use nominal conversion as a legal maneuver without incurring the usual demands on converts to publicly observe such Islamic edicts as attendance at the mosque or strict observance of laws of "impurity," particularly with reference to their Jewish relatives. Despite these nominal conversions, it is important to note that the Nur Mahmud family maintained its prominence in the Jewish community. In later years, some of its members even served as Jewish representatives in the Constitutional Assembly (*majles*).

As blood ties were rarely broken over financial disputes, Khalil, who like his father Ebrahim was known as a Muslim convert, became the medical apprentice of his uncle Nur Mahmud and lived in his home in Tehran in the 1870s. However, old tensions resurfaced when Khalil made a bid for the hand of Nur Mahmud's daughter generically called Khanom (lit., lady). Her family opposed the marriage, possibly because of Khalil's dire financial situation and the prospect of his future claims against the family's substantial assets under Muslim law. The family's concern might also have been related to the rivalry between Ayyub, Khanom's brother, and Khalil, her suitor. Rayhani reports that: "They even tried to marry her off to a Muslim, but she would not consent."[7]

Consequently, Khalil and his bride-to-be eloped and took sanctuary in the royal stables, a rare and dramatic move that among other things demonstrated her independence.[8] While in the royal sanctuary, the privileged young Jewish woman and her poor cousin Khalil, now a Muslim, got married. In an intriguing drama of remarkable fluidity, the couple was married in both Muslim and Jewish wedding ceremonies. Khalil's conversion to Islam and abrupt marriage were able to overcome objections of Khanom's family. However, Islamic law does not normally allow Muslims to marry in Jewish ceremonies. One can only speculate about the circumstances of the two ceremonies, one performed by a Jewish rabbi and the other by a Shi'i cleric, and the officials' different understandings of the couple's complex identities. The incident conveys a picture of blurred religious confessions, tolerated by clerics of both communities when the interests of a privileged family were at stake.

These events are also noteworthy for the role played by women and their alliances. Ayyub's second wife, Tavus, according to one source, helped to arrange the elopement of her husband's sister. This proved to be a hazardous adventure, which led to Tavus's banishment from her home and subsequent divorce by her intractable husband. Nonetheless, it is clear that women at times were willing and able to subvert patriarchal power relations, even if they paid a high price for their actions.[9] Khalil's wife, Khanom, asserted her independence by refusing to abandon observance of Jewish kosher laws for a few years after her marriage. Even Ayyub's own death, reportedly the result of his first wife giving him the wrong medication, may be seen by a skeptic as a case of spouse's foul play.[10]

Just as Mirza Ayyub had anticipated, Khalil later put forward a legal claim related to the family inheritance, perhaps indirectly to compensate for his father's disinheritance. Mirza Khalil also tried to discredit Mirza Ayyub, his cousin and brother-in-law, who was a Baha'i sympathizer (or perhaps a secret convert), by alleging that he was a Babi. To counteract Khalil's campaign, the influential Ayyub called on one of his own Baha'i connections—while maintaining the support of Jewish leaders—and eventually managed to turn the tables on Mirza Khalil. Some time around 1890, Mirza Ayyub with the help of "the deputy minister of foreign affairs (who was a Baha'i) and the Russian trade representative" managed to have Mirza Khalil thrown in jail, possibly on charges of blasphemy.[11] Mirza Khalil's friend Rayhani paid him visits in jail, bringing him food and giving presents to his guards in tacit exchange for more lenient treatment of the prisoner. It was during this time that Rayhani and Khalil engaged in a long-running debate over religion that ironically resulted in Khalil's Baha'i conversion.[12]

Rayhani was also instrumental in securing Mirza Khalil's release from prison. Equipped with a sense of self-confidence unusual for a person of his status, Rayhani sent a number of petitions to government officials and even made a personal appeal to the celebrated statesman Mirza 'Ali Khan Amin al-Dowleh. His initial approaches brought an intimidating response, presumably from the deputy minister in question who threatened: "You are sending too many petitions. I am going to put you in Anbar Prison and have all your teeth pulled out."[13] But the eventual positive outcome—as well as the threatening initial reply—demonstrate that, contrary to the stereotype, even a man of little wealth and no privilege such as Rayhani could demand a certain degree of access to the Qajar administration. Ironically, Rayhani's efforts were aimed at countering Russian diplomatic authority interceding on behalf of a Baha'i sympathizer and leading to imprisonment of a future Baha'i.

After Khalil's release, he became active in the Baha'i community, wrote a commentary in Judeo-Persian on Baha'i biblical proofs, visited Baha'u'llah in Palestine, and joined one of Tehran's first Baha'i administrative councils.[14] At the same time, he retained his prominence in the

Jewish community, at least until 1906 when he ran as an unsuccessful candidate to represent the community in the Constitutional Assembly. He and his wife Khanom, through the services of the prominent Baha'i scholar and Shi'i legal expert Sadr al-Sodur, were able to recover the substantial sum of 5,000 *tomans* as a result of their claim to her share of the family estate.[15] Their case was based on the legal argument that Khanom, now presented as a Muslim convert, was not subject to the Jewish custom of denying married women all right to any share of their father's inheritance.

The Nur Mahmud family demonstrates how a privileged family with multiple religious identities might continue to practice Jewish rituals and maintain a position of leadership within the Jewish community. Adopting at least the pretense of Islamic conversion was almost a prerequisite for avoiding the Shi'i fetish of "impurity" and establishing social ties with the Muslim elite, including court connections. The family's Baha'i sympathies can be seen as a vehicle for coming to terms with modernity and taking part in Iran's intellectual discourse. Yet the freedom to negotiate these seemingly conflicting identities was, for the most part, available only to the sophisticated and influential Jewish elite. For commoners, conversion to Islam usually meant a complete break with their community, the loss of communal protection, forfeit of economic benefits, and (among Muslims) suffering the stigma of being a "new convert."

The various branches of Nur Mahmud's extended family evolved to represent different facets of their multiple convictions. Over time, these identities were further defined. Khalil became a leading Baha'i propagator, responsible for a number of conversions among Tehran's Jews.[16] Within one generation, after the establishment of a secular Pahlavi state, many family members with Baha'i leanings shed their multiple religious confessions to become full-fledged Baha'is. Khalil's children were highly educated and assumed a pronounced modern outlook as committed Baha'is. Those within the extended family who opted for a cosmopolitan identity in exchange for traditional values and normative beliefs found novel opportunities. They gave up the traditional family practice of medicine and attained high administrative positions, mostly in technical fields.

On the other hand, the disputes over inheritance between Khalil and his cousins and in-laws led to a lasting rift within the family that even

Baha'u'llah's indirect intervention could not mend. This family feud may explain Ayyub's eventual distance from the Baha'i community.[17] His side of the family remained more committed to their leadership position in the Jewish community, serving as representatives to the *majles* during the Pahlavi period. Still other members of the extended family, all descendents of the acclaimed Hakim Harun Kashani, became committed and practicing Muslims.[18]

Faith and Social Position

Family disputes over inheritance often became a central, at times even an absurd, part of many conversions. Mirza Nasir and his father, Rabi', lived in Hamadan around the turn of the century. Both father and son were Jewish converts to Islam, but they were known for their bad relations, such that there were even rumors that Mirza Nasir may have been responsible for his father's sudden death. In order to validate his claim to sole ownership of all the family assets, Mirza Nasir reportedly spent the substantial sum of 200–300 tomans (40–60 pounds sterling) "to get a judgment from the ulama to prove that his father was not a true Muslim and to prevent his father's burial in the Muslim cemetery." This posthumous reversal (from Islam back to Judaism) of the father's conversion defies many conventional understandings of interfaith relations.[19]

If a return to Judaism from Islam could be costly, at least the postmortem reversal of a Baha'i identity was easier to accomplish. A more recent example of reclaiming a Jewish identity driven by power relations and economic interests can be observed in the burial of the Jewish Baha'i convert Hajji 'Aziz 'Alaqban of Hamadan in 1935 [see Plate 19]. He had made a small fortune in the Baghdad trade and had accumulated a sizable landed interest. During his funeral procession, some 200 Jews and Baha'is are said to have set out to accompany his remains to the Baha'i cemetery. However, in a pre-arranged move by his sons, the procession was suddenly redirected midway to the Jewish cemetery, where he was buried. This allowed Hajji Aziz's sons to exclude their married sisters entirely from the family inheritance. They posthumously returned their father to the status of a conventional Jew in order to serve their own economic interests. Ironically, it was his affluence and success that helped to deny him his chosen modern identity of a Baha'i.

Years of litigation on behalf of Hajji Aziz's daughters proved ineffective because, in matters related to the inheritance of Jews and (by extension) to the inheritance rights of the "unrecognized" Baha'i community, the Pahlavi judicial system favored the traditional practices of Jewish law.[20] This is one example of how modernity restricted the rights of women by favoring a simplified reading of Jewish law that disinherited daughters. The new legal systems left out many nuances of the traditional system that had given women room for legal maneuvering. For example, during the nineteenth century, well-to-do Jewish women, such as the aforementioned Khanom, on occasion converted to Islam in order to claim a part of their family's wealth as provided for under Shari'ah law.

Another case of the interplay between financial disputes and conversion is provided by the family of Aqa Refu'a in Hamadan. After his first wife, Sara, did not bear him any sons, Aqa Refu'a married his second wife, Khatun, who gave birth to Mehdi. However, soon after Sara also gave birth to a son, named Ha'im. The half brothers engaged in a typical competition over family assets. In a creative move (presumably to exclude his first wife and his younger son), Aqa Refu'a transferred all his assets to his favored son, the elder Mehdi. To counter his father's legal actions, the younger Ha'im, who was an apothecary (*'attar*) by occupation, and later his mother, Sara, converted to Islam. They sought the protection of the influential Kababian family in whose presence they pronounced their confession of faith (*shahada*). To further establish ties to the Muslim elite, Hai'm (now known by his Islamicized name Habibullah) terminated an engagement to a young woman from a Jewish Baha'i family and married into the devout Kababian family.

Nevertheless, the dispute over the transfer of family assets to Mehdi turned out to be a lengthy battle. It is possible that Mehdi also converted to Islam in a move to equalize his legal standing. Some years later, however, after the death of their father and the settlement of their finances, the two half brothers became close. Mehdi, now known as Hajji Mehdi [Arjomand] (1870–1941), became a prominent scholar and Baha'i author. He was literate in Persian and Arabic and was well versed in Jewish and Christian scripture. He was also an affluent craftsman who ran a silver retrieving shop. As a result of his friendly association, his brother, Habibullah, became a Baha'i sympathizer, if not a convert.[21]

Habibullah's Baha'i sympathies became so well known that his wife and her family obtained a decree from the Imam Jom'ah of Hamadan annulling his marriage on grounds of Habibullah being an apostate. Having lost his family, Habibullah moved to Tehran and became an active Baha'i and a successful physician with the official title of Shams al-Hokama. He later went to Palestine to visit 'Abdu'l-Baha. He even took custody of his son and sent him to Tehran's Dar al-Fonun college where he studied medicine and became an accomplished physician. Habibullah is yet another example of converts to Islam who gave up the benefits of Muslim identity (and in his case remained part of a powerful family) in favor of commitment to a new faith that was more compatible with their modern inclinations and more accepting of them as Jewish converts. This case also demonstrates how, despite severe consequences mandated in the Shari'ah for apostasy, in practice religious convictions often shifted with relative ease.

Yet managing the multi-confessional labyrinth was not without its hazards. 'Azizullah was the favored son of Da'i Rubin, an early Jewish-Baha'i convert with a Christian past and close Judeo-Muslim relatives. 'Azizullah's "outstanding intelligence" helped him master Persian and French at Hamadan's Alliance school. He first became an apprentice to a pharmacist but "escaped" to Tehran for unknown reasons. He later worked for a merchant in Rasht where he "suffered immensely." Discouraged from pursuing traditional occupations, he took a job as an interpreter to a Baha'i who was traveling to Europe. On the way there, he met 'Abdu'l-Baha in Egypt in 1908. [22]

Upon his return from Europe, 'Azizullah's education and family connections landed him a prestigious job in Iran's newly formed modern tax office. He gradually rose to the prominent rank of regional tax auditor assigned to Qazvin, where he "kept a Muslim appearance." For a convert hesitant to associate with other Muslims, living in a new city must have been a very lonely experience. Despite the warnings of his relatives, but perhaps because of his social isolation, 'Azizullah invited his parents to live with him and his family in Qazvin. However, after two years the parents were forced to return to Hamadan. Their cultural differences were obvious enough to shatter the family's Islamic disguise and expose their Jewish heritage. Soon his associates accused him of financial misconduct, reportedly a result of religious intolerance. These charges led to loss of his job, imprisonment for two months, and payment of a 1,500 *toman* fine. 'Azizullah subsequently made his way to Tehran to engage in trade. Like many other converts of his time, he struggled with the demands of earning a livelihood within the modern sectors of society. His traditional ties, his inability to break with his Jewish past and adopt a secular self, as well as his dependence on his extended family rendered him unfit for the role of a modern civil servant supported solely by his own nuclear family.[23]

'Azizullah, The Modern Tailor

Among Tehran's less privileged converts was a certain Eshaq, later named 'Azizullah (1873–1950), son of Mulla Daniel, a literate Jewish peddler of meager means from Tehran. 'Azizullah left behind his memoirs as recorded by his son, an incomplete version of which has been published.[24] As a traditionalist, Mulla Daniel had even opposed the Alliance Israelite school because its curriculum included non-Jewish material.[25] Eshaq despised his family's poverty, his low social status, the miserable and unsanitary conditions of the Jewish ghetto, and the humiliation the Jews suffered for their "ritual impurity." He became a tailor, an unconventional choice for Jews of his time, yet a conscious first step toward social mobility. His experiment with a new religious identity as a "semi-Baha'i" who frequented Tehran's Sufi circles (known for their tolerance of non-Muslims), finally led to full acceptance of the Baha'i religion around the turn of the century. To him, the Baha'i message instilled a sense of optimism in that it prophesized a future of advancement and progress for the Jews.[26]

Eshaq's final break with the Jewish community came, not over religious disagreements, but through a more symbolic gesture of break with tradition. His professional success and his association with the Baha'is, including some from more privileged groups, had made him more mindful of his attire and hygiene. What was truly objectionable to traditionalist Jews and led to his eventual estrangement from the Jewish community was his refusal to conform to the customary practice of shaving his head and growing facial hair. Shaving the head was prohibited by Baha'u'llah in the Ketab-e Aqdas (Most Holy Book), but it was also a statement of commitment to modernity on the part of converts. In another context in 1887, Jewish leaders of Hamadan, offended by Jewish-Baha'i men growing their hair, had used physical force to shave their heads.[27] Here we can observe how the traditional system's intolerance towards any public expressions of nonconformity could force those with the slightest noncompliance to traditional norms to search for new and more tolerant communities.

Hamadan Converts and a New Economy

Hamadan was perhaps the most important center of early Jewish Baha'i conversions at the turn of the century. Hamadan was also a Babi/Baha'i center going back to the early years of the movement and the visit of the Babi leader Tahereh Qorrat al-'Ayn. She was able to attract a network of enthusiastic Muslim followers, including learned women of the nobility.[28] These women's networks, mostly centered on relatives of the Babi and Baha'i merchants, were unusually well educated and worked to "support and promote the faith among other women."[29] Among learned Babi women of Hamadan, Sakineh Khanom (d. 1917?), wife of the Baha'i merchant Sayyed Ahmad Naraqi, was—according to one source— "among the women geniuses of her age." She reportedly had extensive knowledge of Babi and Baha'i history, as well as of Arabic and Persian literature.[30]

The earliest known cases of Jewish conversion in Hamadan go back to two unnamed Jewish brothers who encountered a Babi merchant, Hajji Mohammad Baqer Nabil-e Mosafer (traveler). They reportedly were impressed by his piety and integrity and were eventually converted to the Babi or Baha'i faith—but probably maintained an Islamic public persona. When a Jewish convert to Islam openly cursed the new faith, one of the brothers got into an argument with him, and the two were taken to the Hamadan governor. There, the Babi man accused his opponent of being a false Muslim and cited his own (Babi or Baha'i) conviction as proof of his genuine belief in Islam. The Hamadan ulama, who were dismayed by the two brothers' acceptance of Islam through Babi channels, banished them both from Hamadan in 1866, with encouragement from the local rabbis. The brothers may be one of many examples of Babis and Baha'is who for variety of reasons were lost to history.[31]

Aside from such isolated cases of Jewish conversion, and prior to the widespread conversion of Jews in the 1880s, there was a sizable community of at least twenty Babi-Baha'is in Hamadan including two women believers in the 1870s.[32] By 1881, a group of twelve Baha'is and a Babi, mostly merchants and shopkeepers, were arrested and persecuted. This incident points to a sizable, mostly underground community in Hamadan.[33] Such concentration may have been related to Tahereh Qorrat al-'Ayn's early efforts and Hamadan's proximity to Baghdad, where Baha'u'llah had lived (1853–1863). Hamadan was also a relatively safe haven for the Babis and Baha'is because of the protection extended to them by the influential landowners and Babi-Baha'i sympathizers, the Qaragozlu family.

Among Hamadan's Babi and Baha'i notables were the Naraqi family. They were descendants of a prominent ulama and merchant family originally from Naraq, near Kashan, and descendants of the notable Shi'i theologian Mulla Ahmad Naraqi (d. 1828). A number of Mulla Ahmad's grandsons became Babis, and later Azalis, while at least in some cases their descendants accepted Baha'u'llah's claims and became devoted Baha'is. They played an instrumental role in introducing their faith to the Jewish community of Hamadan.[34]

The well-known physician Hakim Aqajan [see Plate 3] (d. 1298/1881) is the first believer of Jewish origin in Hamadan about whom some details are known.[35] Aqajan was reportedly first attracted to Babis and Baha'is in 1877, when he was invited to treat a patient in the Naraqi household. According to these accounts, the young Hakim Aqajan was impressed by the family's expressions of respect towards him, their disregard for laws of purity, and their willingness to share food with him. The family's sympathetic attitude did not change even after Aqajan gave their patient the wrong medication. Though medical mishaps were common in a traditional setting, a case of medical malpractice could nevertheless create great risk for a Jewish physician.[36] Moved by the Naraqi's leniency and tolerance, Aqajan reportedly inquired about their beliefs. Their discussions initiated a dialogue that resulted in his eventual conversion of the Babi/Baha'i religion and also led to the conversion of his cousin, the influential physician Hakim Rahamim (1844–1942), later known as Rahim Khan Hafez al-Sehheh, who became an active Baha'i and community leader.[37] Another cousin of Hakim Aqajan, Aqa Hayyem Lalezar, a watchmaker "of meager means," also became a Baha'i but soon recanted his conviction and became a Christian missionary.[38] Such identity swings were not unusual and the early Jewish converts often belonged to multiple religious communities.

The conversion of the two physicians was a turning point in the spread of the Baha'i message among the Jews of Hamadan. However, the growth of the Baha'i faith in Hamadan in the late 1870s and the 1880s was intertwined with the expansion of Christianity, which shared its message of the coming of a promised messiah.

As early as the 1820s, the eccentric English missionary Joseph Wolff (1795–1862), a Jewish convert to Christianity, preached among the Jews of Hamadan with no tangible success. Other English preachers and itinerate distributors of the Bible in Hebrew also traveled to Hamadan preaching the gospel. Their initial failure to attract converts may in part be explained by their general lack of interest in and confusion over Iran's languages, cultures, and customs. Their negative attitude toward Jews and Muslims can be gauged in the following passage:

> The evils of their [the Jews'] social position have, as may be inferred, affected their moral character . . . The people who breathe the impure atmosphere of Mohametanism, and their own system of belief is not the most refined and pure, should be tainted with all the vices and crimes which so long have polluted this fair and fertile land and changed it into a den of sin . . .[39]

Later, the American Presbyterians were more successful in attracting the Jews of Hamadan. Presbyterian Mission work started in 1877 among Hamadan Catholic Armenians and later among the Jews with considerable initial success attracting some thirty, mostly young Jewish converts—though a majority of them seem to have become Baha'is soon after.[40] The Presbyterian success was owed to such men as James Hawkes (1853–1932), the author of the substantive Persian dictionary of the Bible and the founder (in 1884) of Hamadan's boys school.[41] In addition to schools, American missionaries established Hamadan's first Western-style hospital where a number of young aspiring Jewish physicians were attracted to the opportunities presented by a Western medical education.

However, the mass conversion of Hamadan Jews to Christianity owes its success in part to a process of Jewish-Muslim interfaith dialogue in the mid 1870s. According to Jacob Latka, of the London Society for Promotion of Christianity Among the Jews, who visited Hamadan in 1881–82, interest in Christianity was first instigated among the Jews through debates with Muslims:

> Some six years ago [1875] a party of influential Jews and Moslems used to gather at Hezkiel Hyim's house, for the purpose of discussing divers topics of learning. They soon touched on religion, and

the Moslems referred to the degraded condition of the Jews and to their own superiority in proof that their own religion must be superior to that of the Jews. This they argued from the righteousness of God. Hezkiel Hyim was struck by this argument; but then, the thought occurred to him, Christianity must by the same reasoning be much superior to Moham- medanism, inasmuch as Christian nations are much superior to Mohammedan nations.[42]

Hezkiel Haim may well be the aforementioned Aqa Hayyem Lalezar, Hakim Aqajan's cousin who was among the minority of converts who remained Christians. One can only speculate about the identity of the tolerant "influential Muslims" who disregarded Shi'i impurity laws and whether they were the same members of the Naraqi family who intro- duced Aqajan to the Baha'i faith.

Conversions to Christianity paralleled early conversions to the Baha'i faith, and to a large extent they facilitated Baha'i development. Hamadan's rapid Baha'i expansion may in part be explained by the activities of the Presbyterian mission in Hamadan that prepared the ground—especially among younger Jews—awakening their messi- anic longings. Perhaps as important as their messianic preaching, the Christian missionaries played a significant role in the transformation of Jewish converts by providing an intermediate community, before a Baha'i community could be formed. Baha'is attended Sunday church services and sent their children to the American Presbyterian mission school before Qajar authorities closed it down temporarily.[43] Yet at the same time, the Christian converts reportedly held regular "secret meet- ings" to discuss Baha'i teachings. These were followed by regular visits by Baha'i itinerate teachers, equipped with biblical arguments, who helped sharpen the debate. By the mid-1880s most Jewish Christian converts and sympathizers had become Baha'is, a development that may be attributed to the Baha'i organizational advantage and their indigenous modern message.[44]

The conversions of Hakim Aqajan and his cousin, Rahamim, are a case in point. When they accepted the Baha'i message, both men were perceived, at least by the missionaries, as leading and devout Chris- tians. According to one missionary account, Aqajan had been baptized and as a result had faced opposition from the rabbis.[45]

Aqajan's funeral, moreover, illustrates this ambiguity. It also points to the significance of burial and the location of the burial site in determining how the various communities the deceased associated with posthumously attempt to settle a convert's complex identity. Agajan's funeral was held in the Jewish cemetery and was attended by 300 mourners, apparently of different faiths, including many multi-confessionals. The initial opposition by Jewish leaders to his burial there, presumably on grounds that he was no longer a Jew, was overcome through the intervention of notable Baha'is (a'yan) who apparently did not see a contradiction between his Jewish identity and his Baha'i conviction, not to mention his Christian loyalties. The Jewish rabbis' "fear of skirmishes with dedicated Baha'i youth" persuaded them to cave in.[46] Adding to the complexities of the funeral, Sham'un; a Nestorian priest, now a Presbyterian missionary, delivered a sermon testifying to Aqajan's Christian conviction.[47]

According to one source, Hakim Aqajan made a deathbed confession of his faith in Christ, asking the Nestorian missionary "not to neglect his children."[48] It should be noted that missionary accounts had a distinct interest in presenting a positive picture of converts to their Western readership. Nevertheless, Hakim Aqaqjan represents an early example of Hamadan Jews exploring alternative religious communities. His openness to both the Baha'i and Protestant Christian messages is indicative of a new, universal outlook and a general inclination toward breaking past traditional religious and communal boundaries.

Nonetheless, faith in Christianity was often accompanied by material rewards. In the absence of modern schools and with the failure of the traditional school (maktab) system—at least in Hamadan's Jewish community[49]—one important incentive for Jews to participate in church services was the opportunity for their children to attend missionary schools and to learn English. Moreover, many missionaries were equipped with quality medical knowledge and were able to teach Jewish physicians Western medical practices, including surgical procedures. Many oppressed and mistreated Jews also saw the missionaries as sources of political influence and protection. According to one missionary, many converts had the "expectation of political and secular advantage, hoping to receive protection against the extortion of Mohammedans [and] wished the American mission to furnish them with schools."[50]

According to one Baha'i source, Jewish converts affiliated with the Christian missions in order to receive protection from the missionaries after their commitment to the Baha'i faith. Such protection from the Western missionaries may have been seen as essential at a time when many Qajar authorities still considered Babis (and by extension Baha'is) as dangerous agitators and were particularly hostile towards them. According to this interpretation, Christian conversion was used as a cover for Baha'i conversion.[51]

However, expectations of protection from Western missionaries did not last long in the face of the governor's indiscriminate and abusive attitude towards all non-Muslims. On one occasion, in September 1881, a group of young Jewish converts accompanied by one of the missionaries took the unusual step of going on a camping trip to the Alvand mountains near Hamadan. As a result of a complaint by Jewish elders, the youth were arrested on the pretext that they had entered sacred Muslim grounds. The governor imprisoned and bastinadoed the new Christians, but released them after payment of a heavy fine. He also imprisoned and bastinadoed the community's pastor, Sham'un. Confidant of Western support, Sham'un filed a complaint through diplomatic channels on behalf of the Christians. But he was released through the intercession of the influential Jewish Baha'i physician Hakim Rahamim. Facing possible execution, he immediately fled to the village of Sherevin where he sought protection from the landowning Qaragozlu family who were friendly to the Baha'is and had close ties with Hakim Rahamim.[52]

In spite of attacks from Jewish leaders and hostile officials, the number of the Christian-Baha'i converts continued to grow. Within two years of Aqajan's conversion (1877–79), with the help of other itinerate Baha'i teachers (*moballegh*), Aqajan and Rahim Khan were able to attract some 50 Jews to join the Baha'is of Hamadan. This number is curiously close to the number of Jews reported as converts to Christianity in missionary accounts of the same period.[53] This may suggest a group conversion among Jews in Hamadan, adopting Christianity in conjunction with the Baha'i faith. In fact conversion to Christianity soon became a stepping-stone to other Baha'i conversions, and later to Muslim conversions.

The development of the Presbyterian Church in Hamadan, and the Jewish conversions to Christianity that it accomplished, was only one aspect of a larger social process that included the amalgamation of religious convictions at a time of impending change. The Presbyterians established themselves in 1875, and by 1877, James Howkes established the first missionary school in a house he rented from a certain Jewish merchant named Rubin. After two years, the school was moved to another location (the house of Hakim Aqajan) to make room for a Baha'i "House of Worship" (*mashreq al-azkar*) which, according to Hafezi, Rubin offered to the Baha'i community "for two years at no charge."[54]

It is not clear how Rubin's house was transformed from a Presbyterian church to a Baha'i meeting place. Hafezi claims that for a while, Hawkes was invited to the House of Worship to preach, "as a matter of expedience (*maslahat*) . . . until its Baha'i [identity] was uncovered (*baha'iyyat 'alani shod*) and the missionaries were "dismissed" (*'ozreshan khasteh shod*). However, it is likely that the picture was not as clear as Hafezi's condescending report portrays it. The overlap of Jewish, Christian, and Baha'i schools, meetings, and preaching may have continued at least for a few more years.

The break between Baha'i and Christian confessions came about gradually and was not finalized till 1887, when the prominent Baha'i scholar Abul-Fazl Golpaygani debated Christian ministers in Hamadan. It was through the instrument of similar debates that Golpaygani had helped articulate the standard Baha'i biblical arguments and proofs.[55] Discussions between Baha'is and missionaries continued with regular weekly debates lasting some eighteen months. The principals were a Jewish Baha'i scholar, Hajji Mehdi Arjomand (see Chapters Seven and Eight), and American missionary, Dr. George W. Holmes (d. 1910). A summary of these debates became the basis for a published book of Baha'i argumentation. According to Hafezi, these debates put an end to interfaith dialogue, as the missionaries chose to avoid encounters with Baha'i teachers after that.[56]

Abul-Fazl Golpaygani's second visit to Hamadan (1889/90) can be seen as a turning point. During his three month stay, his impressive personality and sharp debating skills were responsible for a significant number of conversions of people from a range of religious and class backgrounds. Apart from the Jewish converts, a number of the nobility and high-ranking administrators also became attracted. Among them was Mohammad Mehdi Mirza Mu'ayyad al-Saltaneh, a scholar with

Shaykhi leanings whose meeting with Abul-Fazl was facilitated by a
Jewish convert who was his business associate. His nephew, Mohammad Hosayn Mirza, also a Baha'i, was a provincial chief telegraph
officer who later became an official in the court of Ahmad Shah with
the title Mu'ayyad al-Mulk.[57]

The Presbyterian loss of membership to the Baha'is may be in
part explained by the converts' desire to come to terms with Islam.
The Baha'i attitude toward Islam was a major doctrinal and spiritual
innovation, which allowed Jews to accept the validity of the Prophet
Mohammad without repudiating their Jewish heritage. Such a moral
arrangement allowed the converts to preserve their family and community ties. In many instances, accepting Christianity was a first step—and
a critical one—in this process of religious exploration. Conversion to
Christianity or to Islam thus necessarily unsettled powerful, traditional
communal bonds and, in many instances, prepared the way for an
almost simultaneous Baha'i conversion.

Conflict and Socioeconomic Divisions

What started as a movement of reform and inclusiveness within the
Jewish community was soon pushed back by defenders of tradition. The
Jewish leaders remained insistent on strict observance of the details of
Jewish ritual practice, especially the Sabbath and Kosher laws. The traditionalist rabbis saw their role as protectors of Jewish traditions above
all and would not tolerate deviations. They repeatedly defined Baha'is
as being outside of the acceptable boundaries of Judaism. More liberal
Jews were critical of this approach and saw it as a narrow definition of
religion. Such distaste may well explain why so many converts were
willing to endure stigmatization and persecution to uphold their commitment to their new faith.

The dramatic success of the two Baha'i physicians In Hamadan
during the late 1870s led to tensions within the Jewish community.
Some of these tensions may be explained by old professional rivalries
among Hamadan physicians that can be traced back over generations.
Beginning in the mid-nineteenth century, a new group of Jewish physicians, many with knowledge of written Persian, had challenged their
more traditional colleagues who claimed an inherited right to the profession. Many of those who converted to Christianity and to the Baha'i
faith seem to have come from within this same group of new, aspiring
physicians.[58]

Yet the sources of division and estrangement, even within extended families, were not limited to Baha'i conversions. Jews also struggled against the Christians. One Jewish zealot formally complained to the governor against his own relative, a Christian convert, and reportedly went so far as to threaten: "We must crucify Christ once again."[59] In one instance in 1884, Jewish elders in Hamadan who opposed modern missionary schools wrote to the "Commission for Investigation of Grievances" in Tehran requesting the government's help to prevent Western (*farangi*) educators from teaching Jewish youth and asking to "leave them to their own religion."[60]

On occasion, confrontations were tainted with malice. Tensions against Baha'i converts of Hamadan appeared early on in 1877, when Jewish leaders complained to the governor that one of the converts, a certain Hajji Yari (d. 1918/19), had insulted the Jews by denigrating their beliefs and customs as superstitions. This early complaint points to older tensions and professional rivalries among physicians within the community that predated the Baha'i conversions. A crowd of Jews gathered in the town's main square and their numbers reportedly grew to a thousand after urban street crowds joined them, ready to engage in collective action that might result in looting. As the main ingredients of an anti-Babi pogrom were being formed, the Baha'is became particularly alarmed when Jewish leaders rejected their offer to resolve their differences without involving the Muslims. Perhaps as a sign of desperation and fear of rioting mobs, Rahamim tried to deflect the attack by turning the tables against the vulnerable accusers. He repeated a familiar European imported charge of blood liable against the Jewish community.[61] Once the Jewish leaders witnessed the excitement within the pliant crowd, they feared for their own security and dispersed. This confusion led to street fighting reminiscent of Babi skirmishes.

In a debate in front of the governor, the Jewish elders accused the young Baha'i converts of "wearing new-style (*pashne-nakhab*) shoes, eating the [non-kosher] bazaar meat, and refusing to shave their heads (*zolf migozarand*)." The governor is reported to have taken offence at the implication that Muslim-slaughtered meat was ritually impure and ruled that such "baseless charges" should not be the cause of public disturbance. The affair came to an end with the usual payment of a fine supposedly for causing public disorder.[62]

When their appeal to the Qajar governors proved ineffective, the rabbis tried to counter the conversion movement within the Jewish

community using their monopoly over rites and rituals and Jewish public spaces. The use of the Jewish bathhouse by the converts thus became
a point of contention. To counter the ban of the rabbis, the converts
tried using the political leverage of the missionaries. In response to a
petition by American missionaries to Tehran around 1878, the chief
minister Hosayn Khan Mushir al-Dowleh, confirmed the right of Jews
to convert to Christianity (and of course to Islam). However, he also
upheld the right of the Jewish rabbis to deny use of their bathhouses to
non-Jews. As the petition failed to accomplish its objective, the converts
threatened to abandon the Presbyterians and join the church run by the
British Church Missionary Society.[63]

Tensions with the Jews of Hamadan increased as Baha'i conversions
accelerated. Perhaps in reaction to Abul-Fazl's successes, a new wave
of persecution occurred around 1881. As with earlier measures against
converts to Christianity, the governor responded to the complaints of
Jewish leaders by arresting a number of Baha'is. As usual, they were
released upon payment of a fine.[64] The Jews repeated complaints to
the government, mostly related to Baha'i consumption of non-kosher
food. The Baha'is defended themselves by pointing out that they were
consuming lawful Muslim food that Jews considered impure. Such
arguments were particularly effective with Muslim authorities. In one
instance in 1890, in front of the Hamadan council of twelve notables
and merchants responsible for settling local disputes, the Jewish elders
threatened to sever all ties with Jewish Baha'i converts unless they
agreed to conform to Jewish practices. Baha'is responded by accusing
the rabbis of distorting the laws of the Torah and making innovations
contrary to scripture. This was a familiar Baha'i line of argument that
sought to discard the entire rabbinic tradition.[65]

Religious divisions within Hamadan's stratified Jewish community
may well have been fueled by economic factors. According to Aqajan Shakeri, a Baha'i convert of humble background, Hamadan's
Jews in the nineteenth century were a community of mostly poverty
stricken, underprivileged laborers engaged in menial jobs (see Chapter
Seven). Besides trade, which often proved tenuous and in any case did
not flourish until the end of the century, one of the only avenues of
mobility for Hamadan Jews was the practice of medicine. All other
avenues to social mobility were closed to non-Muslims. Monopolized
as a hereditary profession within a few Jewish families, traditional Jew-

ish physicians had for centuries served most of the medical needs of Hamadan and its surroundings.

In the last quarter of the nineteenth century, however, traditional physicians (*hakim*) were challenged by a new group of younger physicians, some equipped with Western medical training. According to one source, Rahamim (later known as Hafez al-Sehheh) and physicians like him gained good reputations with the public and the ruling classes for their medical skills and better treatment of patients. This meant higher fees for their services: one-half *qeran* to one *qeran* per visit. This was twenty to forty times the income of a day laborer, such as Shakeri's father. At one point around 1873, the prominent physician Rahamim's wealth (which substantially increased in the later decades) was estimated by his son at a staggering one thousand *tomans*. On another occasion in 1896, he is reported to have earned 600 *tomans*, plus gifts and expenses, for an extended visit to Poshtkuh, 200 miles southwest of Hamadan, to treat a major land-owner's eye ailment. Even discounting for Yuhanna Hafezi's possible overstatement of his father's wealth and status, his account confirms the picture of a changing and substantially stratified Jewish community. A few well-known physicians, such as Rahamim, connected with privileged classes, governors, and local landowners to earn substantial salaries. Their services were rewarded not just by fees and gifts but with access to power and influence. Some even became intimate with the households of provincial elites.[66] Naturally, because of wealth and access, the new physicians gained a position of leadership within their own community. Much of the divisions and tensions within the Jewish community can be explained in this context.

Another contributing factor to the community's disturbed equilibrium were the pressures exerted by Western agencies such as the Alliance Israélite Universelle, a French secular organization devoted to the advancement of education among disadvantaged Jews. Alliance Israélite was focused on modernizing ancient Jewish societies, such as the Jews of Iran, so that they would be immune to conversion. Particularly conscious of the potent power of modernity to subvert the traditional practices of religion, like those of the Persian Jews, the Alliance offered a modern version of Jewish identity. Nonetheless, the Alliance agent in Hamadan struggled against Baha'is. He expressed frustration over the willingness of Jewish rabbis to perform marriage ceremonies between converts and Jews. He saw this as incentive for

further conversion. The same agent urged the Jewish elders to demand
action (i.e., the bastinado) from the governor if Jewish law was violated by converts. He held the governor responsible for the enforcement
of clerical rulings related to religious laws, since this was a mainstay
of social control and therefore part of the governor's duties.[67] This
kind of collaboration between Jewish elders and greedy (or financially
pressed) governors eager to collect fines seems to have become a recur-
rent pattern around the turn of the century.

Contribution of The Jewish Baha'is

Despite traditionalist opposition, many Jews continued to convert,
became recognized as Baha'is, and were elected to Baha'i Spiritual
Assemblies (*mahfel rowhani*, local leadership councils). As propagators
they helped introduce the Baha'i faith even to Muslims and some
members of the ulama. A notable example was Hajji Sayyed Ahmad
Sadr ul-'Ulama (1868–1907), titled by 'Abdu'l-Baha as Sadr al-Sodur,
a member of a leading ulama family of Hamadan, and later a leading
Baha'i scholar and teacher. He learned about the Baha'i faith around
1898 through his Jewish-Baha'i physician.[68] As Jewish converts, their
contribution to Baha'i scholarship was limited to a few treatises on
Torah prophecies and polemical discourse with Jews. However, as later
generations of Jewish Baha'is became more assimilated, their contributions to scholarship on the Baha'i religion became more significant.[69]

Jewish converts who persevered in their faith made other important
contributions to the Baha'i community. Beginning in the 1920s, many
Jewish converts experienced substantial social mobility and economic
advancement, often using community networking in what amounted
to a form of "ethnic economy." Some even sought and received guidance from 'Abdu'l-Baha on how to start their businesses.[70] Others were
philanthropists and became known as major donors to the Baha'i community.[71]

A number of (mostly second-generation) Jewish Baha'is benefited
from the high level of education they received in modern (including Baha'i) schools and joined the growing educated middle class of
the Pahlavi period [see Plate 17]. Many advanced in business and as
professionals. One leading Baha'i, a highly respected professor of medicine, Manuchehr Hakim (1910–81) was murdered in his Tehran office
allegedly for his Baha'i activities.[72] Among other Baha'is from Jewish

background who gave their lives solely for their religious belief during the post revolutionary period were two brothers and prominent businessmen, Eskandar and Jalal 'Azizi.[73]

Many used their education to become successful professional entrepreneurs.[74] A few became leading innovators and industrialists, important agents of modernity, and major contributors to Iran's economy and industry. One notable innovator and industrialist, Khalil Arjomand (d. 1944), an engineering professor, founded Arj Industries (1937) and was responsible for introducing the manufacture of a number of vital industrial products to Iran. Habib Sabet, was a well-known industrialist and mega-entrepreneur whose ventures included establishment of Iran's first television stations (1959).[75]

The conversion of a substantial number of Jews to a persecuted minority religion was a unique phenomenon in Islamic Iran, if not the entire Muslim world. They added color to an already diverse community of Baha'is, including a few Qajar notables, physicians, radical revolutionaries, and eccentrics—but mostly the poor and disadvantaged. Within a relatively short time, as their faith evolved from a popular messianic antiestablishment movement to a highly institutionalized religious organization, their experience in the Baha'i community included elements of change and continuity. Early Jewish Baha'i converts maintained patterns of economic activity similar to those of their Jewish relatives. As they became more assimilated and adopted a more mainstream Iranian identity, they tended to become more educated than Jewish counterparts and their social mobility more geared towards professional occupations.[76]

6

RAYHAN RAYHANI:
A PEDDLER LIVING THROUGH
CRITICAL TIMES

Rayhan Rayhani's autobiography (*khaterat*) was written as a tes-timony of faith: the story of a religious journey in a changing environment [see Plate 4]. It is the life of an ordinary Iranian Jew cop-ing with modernity through indigenous assimilation rather than resort to European ideologies—whether nationalist, Marxist, or Zionist. It is also a remarkable record of social and communal life at a criti-cal juncture in Iran's modern history. Its candid language and richly detailed narrative offer a unique window into the ideals and the think-ing of common men and women in a traditional yet evolving culture.

As a member of a marginalized sector of society branded as ritually "impure" by Shi'i law, Rayhani illustrates the often invisible experi-ence of the "Other," who carried the burden of being "unwanted." His account is a refreshing view of history from below. It tells the story of commoners who struggled to survive in a harsh environment of insta-bility, war, and economic decline and who struggled for improvement in spite of overwhelming traditional obstacles. The fascinating picture he draws of the undercurrents of life in Iran challenges conventional notions of rigid social and religious barriers. His testimony gives insight into a life wherein, as a matter of survival, identities had to be both resilient and negotiable.

Rayhani's memoirs are an account of Baha'i conversion through the eyes of a man with modest self-education, but acute powers of observa-tion. His personal and mostly straightforward account, written toward the end of his long life, provides us with glimpses of his search for a new identity. His story reflects the complexity of the conversion process and the interaction between a range of factors including Iran's social and political transformation, from the late Qajar period through the Constitutional Revolution and the rise of Pahlavi rule. For Baha'is, this was a period that began with messianic expectations and fluid beliefs, and ended with doctrinal and communal consolidation. Rayhani started out as what can be called a "Judeo-Sufi" Baha'i and ended up with a mainstream Baha'i identity, a notion defined during his lifetime. Conversion meant increased communal tensions and persecution, but also new opportunities for assimilation during a time of increasing national integration. Moreover, Rayhani's life story is an account of the difficulties faced by an itinerant clothier and retailer in an era marred by famine, sharp economic dislocation, and insecurity.

Rayhani first wrote his memoirs in Judeo-Persian (Persian in Hebrew script) in 1938, and soon thereafter in Persian script. He received support and guidance from the prominent Baha'i scholar and historian Fazel Mazandarani. Rayhani's son, Na'im, commissioned his father's autobiography and even paid him a meager fee. Employing an anecdotal style, the author's wide coverage and extended time frame, his remarkable memory of people, places, and events, his sympathetic and yet direct approach, and above all his radically transformed worldview, provide valuable insight into the history of the common people in Iran.[1] His own intellectual development, from an unprivileged Jewish orphan with little education to the propagator of a new religion skilled in Jewish and Islamic polemics, as well as his interest in composing poetry, represents the rise of a new group of Jewish converts with increased levels of assimilation into Perso-Islamic culture.

Rayhani's account gives voice to the life of a marginalized and "invisible" religious community from an insider's perspective at a time of dynamic change and active debate. He expresses his own views and experiences in an informal style. As a convert, Rayhani was able to transcend religious and ethnic boundaries, gaining distance from and critical perspective on them. As an active participant in the debate over religious renewal, his insight is invaluable.

Rayhani's work is for the most part a frank and uncensored account, relatively free of the "authoritative" omissions of some later Baha'i sources.[2] The information he provides about organic relationships between influential Baha'i merchants and local *luti*s (bazaar ruffians),

such as Nayeb Hosein, for example, offers a rare view of symbiotic relations between a rising merchant class and traditional urban elements.
Nevertheless, he is relatively silent with respect to political developments in the Constitutional movement. This raises the question of
whether he was uninformed about the activities of his fellow believers
or chose to ignore them to comply with the prevailing Baha'i position
that demanded non-participation in politics and frowned on all political
discussion. Such communal strictures were particularly stressed during
the period when he wrote his memoirs, as discussed in Chapter Three.

Yet despite such omissions, we detect in Rayhani's account a man of
remarkable individuality whose religious transformation, and particularly his experience of conversion, gave him a new voice, a new view of
himself, and a new perspective on the changing world around him—a
voice that otherwise would have remained inaudible. His very wish to
share his autobiography with posterity—symbolized by his son—speaks
of a modern self-awareness that comes through naturally with all its
roughness and raw sincerity. Such an autobiographical project would
have seldom occurred to the ordinary men and women of his time.

Childhood and Early Life

Rayhan Rayhani was born in 1859, to a modest Jewish family of Kashan.
An oasis on the edge of Iran's Great Desert, Kashan is an ancient city
with an old Jewish community. It had been home to many outstanding
artists and intellectuals, including prominent Jewish poets, historians,
and musicians.[3] It was also a center for the manufacture and trade
of carpets and textiles.[4] During the early decades of the nineteenth
century, Kashan had a thriving textile industry whose workforce was
divided along ethnic and gender lines. The sorting of raw silk thread
was done by Jewish women, while Jewish men, of whom Rayhani was
an example, played an important part as shopkeepers, peddlers, and
traders of silk [see Plate 13]. However, major forces of change in the
latter part of the nineteenth century made life more difficult for many.
Economic crises intensified; famines and epidemics took thousands of
lives and left thousands of families (such as the Rayhani's) distressed
and without income or protection. Rayhani's father seems to have been
a victim of the fourth cholera pandemic (1865–71), which peaked in
Iran in 1871, one of several outbreaks in nineteenth-century Iran. The
epidemics were especially devastating in the south where as many as
10 or 20 per cent of the population perished.

What is perhaps more significant than Rayhani's hometown is his experience in Tehran. As a ten-year-old orphan, he was forced to leave Kashan on the back of a mule, riding as ballast on one side of a saddlebag against the meager merchandise of his uncle. Life in Tehran exposed Rayhani to realities beyond the sphere of Kashan's Jewish ghetto with its physical, social, and psychological isolation. This change in environment meant less family protection but also more independence, thus posing new challenges that could not be answered by the traditional worldview within which Rayhani had been raised. As a teenager during the famine of 1871, he encountered British diplomats and American missionaries who helped him get through those difficult days. As a result of these encounters, he seems to have become more sympathetic to Christian ideas.[5]

He was also exposed to the revival of messianic yearnings among Iranian Jews during these years. His faith must have been disturbed when a relative of his, a Jewish rabbi whom he had come to trust, gave explicit directions that unless the Jewish Messiah (*mashiah*) returned by a certain date, then, "on my account, convert to Islam" (*mosalman beshavid begardan-e man*). This was by no means an isolated case, as Jews of Iran had long resorted to messianic hopes at times of social and economic crisis.

During this same period, Rayhani seems to have come to terms with accepting (or at least being sympathetic to Islam) although he does not elaborate on how this came to pass. Belief in Mohammad as a prophet of God seems to have become sufficiently widespread among young Jews for the Chief Rabbi of Tehran to declare in a sermon that Jews with such beliefs were born of "illegitimate seed" (*tokhm-e haram*). Rayhani was deeply shaken by this warning: "I began to cry," he writes, "because I knew that I believed in Mohammad as a prophet of God— and I had convinced others of his prophethood as well. Had I made a mistake? My heart was in turmoil." Overwhelmed by this burden of guilt and the possibility of being a fatherless child, he tells us that he found comfort only in the story of Jesus, which he learned from Christian missionaries. [6]

Later in life, Rayhani conducted his business in the villages and townships in the vicinity of Kashan; many of which, such as Aran and Bidgol, were Sufi strongholds. As Rayhani came into contact with the Sufis, he seems to have at least become sympathetic toward them. The reverence he held for his contemporary Ne'matallahi Sufis of Gonabad had a lasting influence in him, even after his Baha'i conversion.[7]

While in his teens during the 1870s, Rayhani lived in Tehran for several years and encountered a variety of intellectual challenges. Living at the home of the prominent physician Hakim Nur Mahmud, son of Hakim Harun, he witnessed the daily life of an educated, socially assimilated, affluent, and well-connected Jewish family originally from Kashan. While literacy among Jews was rare at that time and limited to Judeo-Persian, Nur Mahmud's family prided itself on its accomplishments in the fields of traditional Islamic medicine, Arabic language, Persian literature, and calligraphy.[8] The family's interaction with the Qajar court and Muslim notables, one can assume, would have been impossible without at least a nominal acceptance of Islam.[9] The multi-ethnic culture of Nur Mahmud's household helped to overcome many parochial barriers and gave the young Rayhani a more modern outlook on life.

Ambivalence and Conversion

Around 1878 Rayhani was first introduced to the debate over the coming of a new religion. Two early Baha'is from Hamadan, the aforementioned Hakim Aqajan and Hakim Rahamim (Rahim) Hafez al-Sehheh, who were both educated physicians, arrived at Nur Mahmud's house hoping to convert him to the new faith. Even though Nur Mahmud himself never confessed Baha'i beliefs, a number of his sons and a daughter either became converts or close sympathizers. For those who became Baha'is, such as Mirza Khalil, a new intellectual discourse, which stressed the common divine origin of all religions, allowed Baha'i converts sufficient latitude to reconcile with Islam, while continuing to practice Jewish rituals and maintain their positions of prominence and leadership within the Jewish community.

Sitting behind a closed door, Rayhani carefully listened to the all-night debate between the Baha'is and the enlightened Hakim Nur Mahmud held "on condition that no one else present should say a word." The Baha'is presented new, rational, and yet metaphorical, interpretations of biblical texts that raised fundamental questions in Rayhani's mind. He was so agitated by their arguments over Jewish prophecies and their dismissal of rabbinical authority that, by the morning, he was ready to physically attack the Baha'is. He later engaged Hakim Aqajan in debate but found no satisfying answers for his questions:

"Do you make weekly sacrifices to God on the Sabbath and on the other holy days [as required by Jewish law]?" [Aqajan challenged him.]

"We have no Cohen, no temple," I replied [meaning, it is not possible to observe this biblical injunction, therefore the verse is not binding on Jews today].

"Did God himself send you a message and say, 'I have excused you'? Is it not necessary for a new messenger of God to come and say, 'It's all over, God excuses you'? Otherwise, according to the holy book, all Jews who violate the law of the Torah are 'unclean.'"

"Give me two days to respond," I replied.

"You can have two months," he said.[10]

This was the beginning of what Rayhani later saw as five "years of desperate confusion" (*ayyam-e sargardani*). These were the years when he intensely struggled to root out contradictions and inconsistencies in his beliefs, which he later characterized as "fallacies and superstitions" (*khorafat va mowhumat*).

It was also during this period of uncertainty that much of Rayhani's religious identity was reshaped, often through painful experience. As he sought out Baha'is in Tehran, and later in Kashan, he encountered a range of believers—some with profound convictions, others eccentric and colorful. He observed the death of a drug-addicted Baha'i calligrapher whose job of transcribing Baha'i scriptures for a living was insufficient to support his opium habit and who died in poverty, much of his art work going to waste.[11] He met a self-described "drunken failure" whose shame prevented him from associating with other Baha'is.[12] He had the unnerving experience of staying overnight in the home of a Baha'i ascetic who wept all night long and whose behavior others accepted as that of a man who was simply "in love," presumably with his new faith.[13] He encountered an unscrupulous believer who took his money and taught him a lesson about the shady dealings of certain Baha'i pretenders. He even got a taste of the ways of the famous Baha'i leader Jamal Borujerdi who, according to Rayhani, was in the habit of exploiting other Baha'is; and he met some of his poor and disillusioned victims who had renounced the Baha'i religion to become atheists.[14] The range of Rayhani's contacts points to a community of essentially marginal and broken individuals who are mostly forgotten or left out of later Baha'i accounts. Baha'i texts written in later decades pass over the misfits to present the Baha'i archetypal image of educated and successful men and women.

Rayhani's bleakest experiences were his witness to the public execution of Babis and Baha'is who died for their faith. As a child, he witnessed a Babi execution (*Babi-koshi*)—a common scene on Qajar Iran's landscape—when he encountered the bloody remains of an elderly Babi man lying next to the bodies of two youths in Kashan's main square. He overheard women talking about the victims having been accused of and executed for participating in a local rebellion. Many years later the imagery remained with him as one of his earliest memories:

> One day when I was seven years old, I was going home for lunch with my schoolmates. As we passed the Government House in Kashan's main square, we saw three corpses. Four or five women walked by and one of them said to the others: "Those two were killed for joining the rebel Shah Mirza, but that one is the Shaykh of Mazgan; he was killed for becoming a Babi."
>
> I guess the first two were fifteen or sixteen years old—I can't say exactly now. The shaykh had prepared himself by performing his ablutions, washing his hands and feet and saying his prayers, before the executioner cut his throat.[15]

Much later, Rayhani witnessed the public execution in Tehran of the Babi-Baha'i leader Mulla 'Ali-Jan Mazandarani, a thirty-eight-year-old mulla who had obtained the highest rank of *mojtahed* before he became a Babi. Mazandarani returned to his hometown of Mahforujak in Mazandaran to take a leadership position and converted the whole village to the new religion. An alliance between local clergy and provincial authorities led to his execution on June 26, 1883. In Rayhani's moving account of the execution, he describes the pandemonium in the town square. After the event, the executioner made his customary rounds in the bazaar to extort donations from the shopkeepers, including the young Rayhani himself. These poignant memories must have impressed upon him the risks associated with converting to the new religion.[16]

Nevertheless, none of these disturbing experiences quenched Rayhani's thirst or diminished his determination to encounter more

Baha'is. Perhaps he was desperately struggling to come to terms with the troubling questions that must have preoccupied him: his fear of not recognizing the Messiah, his desire to make sense of the various religious traditions to which he was being exposed, and the unanswered questions about Jewish law posed to him by the Baha'i advocates.

Finally, his agonizing period of uncertainty came to an end after a revealing dream Rayhani had around 1883. This was the year his rabbi had indicated when he said, "On my account, convert to Islam." The dream, a familiar experience in the autobiographical narratives of converts, marked a spiritual milestone in his life. Through this means, he seems to have confirmed his new Baha'i identity to himself and authenticated it to others. Here we can observe the beginning of a new stage in Rayhani's religious transformation, one that continued to preoccupy him some forty years later, when he wrote his memoirs:

> Suffice it to say that when I awoke I felt as if I had been reborn with a new soul. It seemed that my body had changed too. Or if my body remained the same, my mind had certainly been transformed. I instantly shed all of my superstitions. It was as if a new world had opened before my eyes.[17]

Beyond the transformational dream, however, Rayhani's conversion seems to have been the logical outcome of his ongoing debate over Baha'i topics with a certain Hajji Elyahu Kashani. Although he does not elaborate on the nature of their debates and disagreements immediately prior to his "complete" conversion, one can surmise that their discussions centered on Baha'u'llah's messianic claims. By the 1880s, there were radically different views among Baha'is about Baha'u'llah's spiritual station, ranging from the belief that he was merely the leader of the Babi community to believing him to be the person proclaimed by the Bab as "He whom God shall manifest" (*man-yozhurullah*), or a new "manifestation of God" (*mazhar-e zuhur*), or even the embodiment of the Godhead himself.

Pious Thieves

The enigmatic Hajji Elyahu who played a central role in Rayhani's conversion and whom he describes as "the most skillful and accomplished" professional thief in Kashan before his conversion was yet another eccentric character who curiously held a position of leadership in Kashan's Jewish community.[18] According to Rayhani:

He headed a clan of some forty Shirazi Jews who had moved to Kashan. They were Jewish sayyeds[19] pretending to be moneychangers. They would approach Muslim pilgrims on the road and offer to buy their [silver] coins. Then they would steal as much as they could, for they considered stealing from gentiles to be lawful. [Even though] they looked down on the Jews of Kashan, they gradually became the community's recognized leaders (*kadkhoda va ra'is*).[20]

As an early Baha'i convert, Hajji Elyahu traveled to Palestine, presumably during the lifetime of Baha'u'llah, to pay homage to him in 'Akka. There he admitted to 'Abdu'l-Baha that he was devoid of any useful skills, as in his previous life he was but a common thief. On 'Abdu'l-Baha's recommendation, he served for a while as a guide to some European travelers who came to visit 'Abdu'l-Baha. Hajji Elyahu stayed a year with them in India and earned a substantial sum, which, according to Rayhani, he spent on "a lavish wedding feast and expensive parties." His continuous monetary demands on leading Baha'i figures (supposedly for his services as an itinerant Baha'i teacher) present an image that is far from the norms of Baha'i morality. His demands on Rayhani, who had to care for him when he was ill, "and his gluttonous servant" who "spent eighteen days at my house and didn't give me a penny," were a heavy burden on the struggling peddler. Hajji Elyahu later moved to Egypt where he fades into oblivion.[21]

Despite his weaknesses, Hajji Elyahu was a rather successful Baha'i propagator. It appears that in the 1880s and 1890s many Jewish converts went through a two-tiered conversion process. Teachers such as Hajji Elyahu mainly argued the validity of Christ and left the next stage of conversion to other Baha'i teachers more familiar with Islamic scriptures. As a result of his activities, Hajji Elyahu suffered much hardship at the hands of Tehran's Jewish traditionalists. He was even considered "ritually impure" (*nesekh*) by other Jews. On one occasion around 1894, a religious debate with Jewish contenders led to a dispute and a subsequent gang attack "with the intention of killing him."[22]

Earlier in life, Rayhani had known other aggressive thieves, including his own relative whom he saw as "a very pious and God-fearing man," one who "gave to the poor as much as he could," but who considered Muslims to be "infidels" with "no religion" and therefore felt justified in stealing from them and abusing them. After his conversion, Rayhani found a way to heal the "wound" he carried in his heart as a result of observing this uncle take advantage of a Muslim peasant. He cites the Jewish leaders' twisted reading of the scripture as being responsible for misleading the community: "Taking of the possessions of all the nations of the world is permissible. They [the Jewish leaders] consider it more permissible than their mother's milk." Whereas, Rayhani observes, the Torah merely says, "When you fight (*jihad*) against those who worship images, take their belongings [as booty]."[23]

The picture Rayhani draws of nineteenth-century Kashan—a town known for its conservatism—is one of predominantly polarized and belligerent communal relations between Jews and Muslims. Some Jews did not hesitate to cheat and steal from vulnerable Muslims, while Muslims often abused and humiliated Jews, especially the disadvantaged. Mobs occasionally engaged in anti-Jewish riots. Both sides distrusted one another and remained apart. Yet both sides justified their behavior on religious grounds: Muslims generally considered Jews inferior and "impure," while many Jews saw Muslims as infidels (*guim*) deserving of deception.

Such hostility may have played a role in the high level of violence towards itinerant Jewish peddlers that Rayhani describes. But such negative attitudes cannot be solely explained as stemming from anti-Jewish sentiments. Peddlers after all provided a necessary service to isolated villages and traditionalist ulama, often the instigators of anti-Jewish violence, were less present in the countryside. It is possible that peddlers were resented as outsiders who might disturb the delicate balance of a small, isolated community. The resentment could have had a gender dimension. If Rayhani's close relationship with the women of Mehrabad village, in the Arak region, is any indication, it may well explain the hostility of village men toward Jewish peddlers. The "Jewish peddler" may have become stereotyped as a result of years of mutual distrust. The fact that some Jews, including Rayhani's relatives, made profits by exchanging fabric and household items for antiquities and old coins of greater value may also have fueled resentments.

However, the full picture of Muslim-Jewish relations was complex, as the two communities also engaged in substantial mutual economic activity. Beneath the surface there was also a good deal of congeniality, especially between Jewish retailers and their Muslim clients, and especially the women. There were also instances when Muslims extended compassion to Jews and defended them when wronged and deprived, although Rayhani tends to overlook them.[24]

It can be argued that the polarization of the two communities was, to an extent, a reflection of the increasing power of the clerical establishment. In the latter part of the nineteenth century, Iran's Shi'i ulama had reached a high point of political and legal authority. Many of them possessed enormous wealth and maintained their own private armies. And while Rayhani held the rabbis responsible for misleading the Jews, some Shi'i ulama instigated anti-Jewish feelings and even organized riots on occasion.

As a child, Rayhani experienced contemptuous attitudes toward the Jews. Early in life he learned lessons in submissiveness. He was taught the need to show respect whenever he passed a Shi'i cleric—even though, according to Rayhani, the cleric would often respond "as one would to a dog." On one occasion when he greeted a certain mulla without prostrating himself, while he was standing the cleric pushed the tip of his cane against his chest such that he fell back into a pile of manure.[25]

Even as late as 1920, Rayhani witnessed the deadly threats and public humiliation meted out to a "wealthy Jew" in Kashan named Morad who had protested against traditional acts of discrimination based on "ritual impurity." A young mulla named Sayyed Ahmad, who was probably trying to impress his followers, ordered them to set Morad on fire in the middle of the bazaar. Morad's life was saved only after other Jews used their connections with the cleric's agents, presumably the *lutis*, paying off some of them and giving "a lot of money" to the cleric himself.[26]

Curious Rebels of Arak

In contrast to the situation in Kashan, clerical authority in communities like Arak was more tolerant of Jews and social relations less constrained by traditional discriminatory norms. The usual humiliations were distinctly absent, and there were no anti-Jewish riots. Instead, there was an amiable sense of coexistence between the two communities. In the mid-1880s, soon after his conversion, Rayhani went to the town of Soltanabad (later known as Arak) some 150 kilometers northwest

of Kashan. Arak was a thriving trade center with a growing carpet
manufacturing sector. Its flourishing economy was based on the export
of carpets to Europe. As a young city, established around 1800 near a
Qajar military camp, Arak deviated from many traditional conventions, notably the prohibition against Jewish merchants trading in the
main bazaar. The wealthiest man in town and the largest landowner
was the influential chief *mojtahed*, Hajji Aqa Mohsen Araqi (Araki), a
pragmatic cleric and businessman who maintained good relations with
the Jewish migrants living and working in his bazaar properties. These
conditions attracted a growing number of young Jewish entrepreneurs.
This made Arak a growing center for the conversion of young Jews to
the Baha'i faith.

Yet Arak was also an unruly region with many disputes over land.[27]
There were cases of the state appropriating properties in neighboring
villages. Mohammad Shah's minister, Hajji Mirza Aqasi, confiscated
land from the estate of the Qa'em-Maqam family in Farahan and the
surrounding areas. These properties were still being disputed by members of the late minister's extended family decades after his execution.[28]
When Rayhani arrived in one of these villages—possibly one that was
involved in the dispute—he aroused a good deal of interest among
rebellious landowners. They seem to have had contact with other
Baha'is and were curious about the new religion. Nevertheless, they
were nonplussed by the anomaly Rayhani presented as a "Babi Jew,"
a contradictory persona that confounded the prevailing stereotypes of
the cowardly Jew and the militant Babi.

For unknown reasons, Rayhani's arrival provoked outright hostility from one of the rebels, who attacked him physically. We can only
speculate about why. As suggested by the line of questioning the village
chief later put to Rayhani in private conversation, the attack may have
been a response to familiar rumors of sexual transgression commonly
attributed to the Baha'is. Rayhani's explanation of this incident is
sketchy and perhaps even intentionally blurred. Significantly, it was the
women—one of whom was known to Rayhani and whom he describes
as an *'aref* (enlightened; a seeker of the true path)—who took the risk
of staging a medical emergency during a tense confrontation and managed to save his life. Although he does not elaborate on the nature of
his acquaintance with the *'aref*, it is consistent with the common pattern
of Muslim women feeling relatively comfortable with Jewish peddlers

and shop keepers who, as a marginalized group, were less threatening to them than other men.[29] Rayhani's story provides us with an important example of how women in the countryside in the 1880s might hold sympathies or loyalties independent of their male relatives.

Things settled down after Rayhani's angry adversary was sent on an emergency mission, and he joined the family for dinner. His new-found self-perception as a Muslim, itself being an inclusive part of his new Baha'i identity, allowed him the courage to disregard age-old and strictly observed Jewish dietary restrictions. He thus ignored the modest yogurt and bread prepared specially for him and started to eat from the meat dish provided for his host's extended family. Stunned by this inconceivable breach of custom that made the dish "unclean," the rest of the family watched with disappointment as Rayhani finished the meal by himself. His disregard for the "ritual impurity" of Jews, a cornerstone of Jewish-Muslim relations, demonstrates a remarkable sense of self-confidence stemming from his new identity.

Debates and Confrontations

In the following years, Rayhani's enthusiasm for his new faith entailed discussion and debate with fellow Jews. Most notable among those he helped "direct" (to the Baha'i faith) was the aforementioned influential Mirza Khalil 'Aqiba (see Chapter Five). As an enthusiastic convert, Rayhani became an outspoken advocate of a messianic message and the metaphoric biblical arguments of the new faith. This approach challenged the conventional literal reading of biblical prophecies, such as the resurrection of the dead. Other points of debate centered on issues which the Baha'is saw as rabbinic innovations, such as elaborate dietary laws and the use of wine as a necessary component of Jewish rituals.[30] Extreme dietary proscriptions—for example, that "even a needle in the body of an animal makes it forbidden (haram)," and that "if someone eats meat that was slaughtered by Muslims, he is rejected, impure (najes), and no longer Jewish"—were seen as a departure from scripture by rabbis who, according to Rayhani, "set aside the commandments of Moses and spread their own words."

Such provocative arguments at times led to confrontations with the Jewish rabbis, whom Rayhani considered hypocrites and demagogues with little intellectual substance. The rabbis, on the other hand, saw themselves as the defenders of tradition and the guardians of religious and ethnic boundaries, and the Baha'is as "young light-weights," among whom there was "not a single older person" and who were the source of division within the community. In fact, there was a significant generational component to conversions during this period.

One can argue that Jewish Baha'i conversion at times represented a way for young, liberated men to reject Jewish clerical authority. Like Rayhani, many young Jews who had left the ghetto to seek new economic opportunities or who had been educated in European-style schools were dissatisfied with the leadership of traditionalist rabbis. Such views seem to have been widespread among Jews and were not limited to converts. Rayhani cites other examples such as the "well educated" man who "all his life refused to be called a rabbi (*mulla*) because he scorned the title." This was consistent with the growing anti-clerical trend that became more widespread during the Constitutional Revolution.[31]

The examples of injustice that Rayhani recounts are intended to demonstrate a certain similarity between the rule of the Jewish rabbis and that of their Shi'i counterparts. He cites the case of a poor, unmarried, immigrant woman, with no family or community ties to protect her, who was accused of buying (less expensive?) non-Kosher meat. Rayhani was present when the rabbi administered corporal punishment:

> They put her in a lightweight sack and beat her with sticks. When she cried out in pain, the rabbi said, "Beat her." Those present were laughing . . .[32]

On another occasion Rayhani's elderly uncle spent a night in the cold outside the city walls because the rabbi's strict enforcement of Sabbath rules even prohibited entry into city gates. Such rigid enforcement of Jewish law can in part be explained by the Shi'i ulama's backing of the rabbis. According to Rayhani, the ulama admonished the Jews: "Either convert to Islam or obey your own clergy." In a society that relied on religion for the maintenance of social control, such tactics became increasingly prevalent.

The rabbis' authority was undermined by effective Baha'i missionary activities, causing further tension. Rayhani was one of the first Jewish converts in Kashan. As increasing numbers of mostly younger, male Jews converted, the community elders came to see the promoters of the

Baha'i message as a threat. Nevertheless, they showed considerable tolerance toward the new converts, so long as they observed Jewish ritual practices and conformed to public norms. However, open expressions of the Baha'i non-literal reading of Jewish scripture and claims of the advent of the Messiah by the more outspoken converts such as Rayhani gave rise to increasing apprehension. Public defiance of Jewish laws and practices, especially non-observance of the Sabbath, crossed the line of tolerance and were unacceptable.

On occasion, the rabbis and elders were successful in curbing the spread of the new religion. Rayhani recounts the story of Mulla Solayman (d. 1932), a popular rabbi who, during the debates with Abul-Fazl Golpaygani in Kashan (1888/89), "became a Baha'i and brought along his seven or eight hundred followers." A year later, Rayhani reports, "there were anti-Baha'i persecutions and Mulla Solayman and his followers became Jewish [again]." It is worth noting that unlike most ex-converts, Mulla Solayman remained somewhat sympathetic to the new religion and "did not preach against the Baha'is". He also maintained close ties with his Baha'i relatives.[33]

Rayhani does not give any details about the persecutions that forced Mulla Solayman and his followers to return to Judaism. Nor do other Baha'i sources make any mention of mass reversions to Jewish identity by "follower" converts.[34] Yet we know of other cases of persecution involving members of Mulla Solayman's family during the same period, initiated by Jewish elders and carried out by the governor of Kashan. Tensions led to violence when two of Mulla Solayman's brothers were arrested and tortured around 1900. Mulla Musa (Musheh) was an outspoken Baha'i who publicly proclaimed the coming of the promised savior. More significantly, he was the first convert to publicly defy Jewish law by opening his shop on the Sabbath. The Jewish elders demanded that the governor enforce their rulings, including the death sentence in accordance with the law of the Torah.[35] Mulla Musa was arrested, imprisoned, and beaten, but eventually he was freed upon the intercession of his relatives. He left Kashan to live in Lahijan where he was murdered in 1905, on the eve of the Constitutional Revolution, apparently by an anti-Baha'i gang. Mulla Musa is considered to be the first Jewish convert who paid with his life for openly advocating his beliefs.[36] His brother Mulla Rabi' was also arrested by the governor of Kashan and severely beaten in 1903. He died in Tehran in 1910, reportedly as a result of the injuries he received in Kashan.[37]

These rising tensions with the rabbis and the increasing persecutions of this period help to explain why Rayhani chose to take refuge in the nearby village of Aran after a confrontation with Jewish elders in Kashan:

> When I went to Kashan and got married in 1890, I had expenses to pay and yet I couldn't work there. I couldn't endure the vicious hostility of the anti-Baha'is. Every day they would say, "Let's go to the mulla's house and curse [i.e., curse Baha'i sanctities]."[38]

Yet even in the small village of Aran where most people "were still unaware of what a Baha'i was," he was not immune from harassment by Jewish clothiers who made trouble for him by spreading word that "Rayhan was a Babi."

However, not all of efforts to hinder conversion to the new religion were successful. When a group of ten young men converted in Kashan around the turn of the century, concerned Jewish elders tried to frighten them and to "get them to recant their faith so that others might not become Baha'is." To this end, "they gave money to the governor of Kashan and [promised] that he would be able to collect [fines] from the Baha'is too."[39] Six of the new converts were imprisoned allegedly for having "renounced their religion and cursed their prophet." Rayhani, accompanied by another Jewish convert, Hakim Faraj (1856–1906), came to the young men's defense.[40] Hakim Faraj, who became a Baha'i during the debate between Abul-Fazl Golpaygani and the Kashan Jews around 1888/89, also had a colorful past. He had become a Christian, reportedly at the urging of his father who on his deathbed asked him to investigate the validity of Jesus. Later on, he became a Muslim and a Sufi before becoming a Baha'i.[41] Rayhani and Hakim Faraj demanded that the responsible Jewish petitioners be brought to the governor's house to state the basis for their accusation.

Instead, at the urging of the rabbis, the governor ordered Rayhani himself put in jail.[42] This led to appeals to the authorities in Tehran similar to those Rayhani had undertaken a few years earlier to free Mirza Khalil. Rayhani's wife sent a telegram to Mirza Khalil who spent a hundred *tomans* appealing to the authorities in Tehran. He succeeded in obtaining seven telegrams from various officials sent to the governor, including a decree from Chief Minister Moshir al-Dowleh ordering the release of the converts. Outraged, the governor reluctantly agreed to free the prisoners, who had not publicly violated any laws, and to settle for a much smaller "fine." The amount was negotiated through the governor's guards, who apparently served as intermediaries for extorting money from the prisoners. As a way of asserting their faith, the young Baha'i converts insisted on paying no more than 19 *tomans* each in fines.[43]

The governor justified his imprisonment of the young converts on the grounds that he was defending the Jewish religion. "If this trend continues," he wrote to the chief minister, "it will not be long before the entire Jewish population becomes Baha'is." According to Rayhani, when Moshir al-Dawleh read the governor's telegram, he said: "This man says the Jewish religion will gradually be lost. To hell with the loss!"[44]

Later, after the release of the prisoners, a telegram from Mozaffar al-Din Shah ordering the release of the prisoners arrived. Mohammad Karvansara was one of the few influential Baha'is in Kashan. He was bold enough to insist that a reluctant Rayhani should deliver the telegram to the governor and demand a refund of the fine.[45] In what turned out to be an imprudent move, Rayhani was persuaded to make his demand and present the shah's telegram on the first day of Now-Ruz, an occasion when the governor customarily received gifts from the shah and the town's notables, including the Jewish leadership. Already embarrassed by the reaction from Tehran and irritated by his inability to collect substantial fines, the governor's swift and harsh reaction may have been a bid to reassert his authority. The immediate public beating Rayhani received may have been partly intended to impress the Jewish leaders present who, after all, had gotten very little for their money. But when Rayhani protested his treatment, and in despair cried out his faith in the prophet of Islam and all the Shi'i imams, the governor's guards immediately stopped the beating, perhaps mindful of the proscription against abusing a Muslim convert. Rayhani was finally released after the influential chief of the telegraph office (an Armenian Baha'i convert or sympathizer, according to Rayhani) intervened to warn the governor of the consequences of abusing the messenger who had delivered the shah's decree.

This incident took place following a period of liberalization under Mozaffar al-Din Shah, which enabled the Baha'is to marshal the courage to stand up to the capricious behavior of the governor. As Rayhani puts it, "This whole affair went fairly smoothly, since it happened under the reign of Mozaffar al-Din Shah. If it had happened before his time, it would have been a disaster."

Although the most conspicuous reactions to Baha'i conversions came from Kashan's Jewish elders, on at least one occasion the Baha'is had to deal with the other extreme of the Jewish religious spectrum, namely the atheist Jews. Rayhani informs us of Haqnazar, a Jewish merchant in the nearby village of Aran, who was hostile to Islam but accepted the Baha'i faith—until he came to Tehran, where he came under the influence of "some Jews who had forsaken their belief in God." He was cast out of the Jewish community because of his expressions of atheism. "Gradually he weakened, his business suffered, and ultimately he was destroyed."[46] The business losses that Rayhani refers to might be attributed to the fact that when the rabbis declared someone an infidel, all financial obligations of Jews to that person could be voided. His case demonstrates the vulnerability of the secular option in a society based on religious and ethnic divisions. It also points to the significance of a multi-layered identity in the absence of a non-religious option.[47]

Merchants and Notables

Notwithstanding the pressures and persecutions associated with conversion, becoming a Baha'i was not devoid of social advantage. As a Baha'i, Rayhani regarded himself as an equal and accepted member of a diverse community that included not only peasants and urban laborers, craftsmen, peddlers, and shopkeepers but also landowners, local notables, and affluent merchants. Other influential figures, such as the chief of the telegraph office and Kashan's sheriff (*darugheh*), were loosely connected to the Baha'i community or could be counted among a growing number of Baha'is whose identity was at best informal and at times completely secret. When Rayhani was in trouble with the local governor, he seems to have benefited from his contacts with the Baha'i telegraph chief who provided vital access to the central government.

On one occasion in 1903, when Rayhani was the victim of mistaken identity at his home in Kashan's Jewish quarter, his imminent arrest turned into a "memorable" conversation that lasted all night, as he and the *darugheh* discussed, over cups of tea, "Baha'i subjects [such as] the discipline and education of children."[48] The fact that a local official was having tea in a Jewish home, in complete disregard of the

laws and conventions of ritual impurity, had important symbolic significance. One might reasonably assume that, on that night, Rayhani
proudly saw himself as a member of a movement through which he had
acquired self-esteem and a new identity that was much less constrained
by the social and intellectual confines of the ghetto. Such associations,
especially with members of the Qajar ruling elite, were made possible
through the Baha'i community. These encounters, otherwise inconceivable for a Jewish peddler, must have given Rayhani a perception of
security in a hostile environment.

Rayhani's encounter with the Qajar notable Mehdi Khan Ghaffari
(1865–1917), also known as Qa'em-Maqam and later as Vazir Homayun, offers insight into the conversion of a Qajar elite figure. Mehdi
Khan was the youngest and most prominent son of the celebrated
statesman and diplomat Farrokh Khan Ghaffari Amin al-Dowleh.[49]
The Ghaffari family was perhaps the most influential family in Kashan,
well known for the number of statesmen, artists, and scholars it produced. Mehdi Khan's first court appointment was under Naser al-Din
Shah, whom he served as a personal secretary. He maintained a position of influence under Mozaffar al-Din Shah, and during the reign of
Mohammad 'Ali Shah, he headed several ministries and held a number of governorships. He became a Baha'i in 1909, when he was the
governor of Arak, and in 1910 he went to meet 'Abdu'l-Baha, first in
Alexandria and later in Paris. He spent three months in Alexandria and
"saw God with [his] own eyes," as he later described it to Rayhani.

Rayhani met Mehdi Khan while he was living on his property in the
vicinity of Kashan, where Mehdi Khan spent the last years of his life
and according to Rayhani showed particular interest in Baha'i mystical
themes. He donated his house in the village of Vadeqan near Kashan
to serve as a Baha'i school and later a Baha'i center. His Baha'i association has been omitted from histories of the Ghaffari family. This
is consistent with the demands of Iranian historiography during the
period, which omitted or censored all mention of Babi and Baha'i presence. Sanitized Baha'i sources are also mostly silent about him, and
remain silent as well as about a number of other Qajar notables with
Baha'i associations, perhaps in an attempt to minimize association with
political figures.

Opponents of Mehdi Khan Vazir Homayun have criticized him for
his corruption and his close association with Chief Minister Atabak.

He has also been ridiculed as a "court clown."[50] Other sources testify to his literary sophistication, and his dedication to reform and devotion to modern education.[51] Yet he may be best remembered for his instrumental role in persuading Mozaffar al-Din Shah to sign the Constitution during the last days of his life.[52] His eagerness to spend time with the poor and semi-educated Rayhani, whose company he apparently enjoyed, is an indication of a remarkable friendship in a Baha'i setting.[53]

Through his association with the Baha'i community, Rayhani came to know some of the leading merchants of Kashan, among them the influential Hajji Mohammad Hosein Lotf-e Kashani who later gained the title of Amin al-Tojjar as head of the *majles-e tejarat* (merchants council).[54] His Baha'i identity, which Rayhani claims he held openly, does not seem to have been a barrier to obtaining this position, demonstrating once again how economic imperatives might trump religious prejudices in Qajar society.

Just as privileged Jewish converts at times benefited from their new religious identity, so did privileged Baha'is occasionally overcome their enemies. In 1885/86, Hajji Mohammad Hosein came under attack by his rival merchants and their ulama allies for having traveled to 'Akka to pay tribute to Baha'u'llah.[55] They "removed Hajji Mohammad Hosein's turban from his head in the bazaar and [publicly] humiliated him." However, Hajji Mohammad Hosein soon afterwards "went to Tehran, spent 3,000 *tomans*, obtained the title of Amin al-Tojjar, and came back to Kashan."[56] According to one source, Naser al-Din Shah even rebuked Mulla Habibullah and banished him from Kashan, possibly as a result of Hajji Mohammad Hosein's complaints.[57]

Hajji Mohammad Hosein served as the chairman of Kashan's Baha'i Spiritual Assembly, of which Rayhani was a member. This body oversaw the affairs of the Baha'i community, including supervising "teaching" (*tabliq*) committees, mediating marriage and divorce disputes, and even, according to Rayhani, recommending marriage prospects and finding business opportunities. The Assembly originally consisted of nineteen (later reduced to nine) individuals of various economic backgrounds. Rayhani assures us that members of the Assembly exercised considerable respect toward one another and that "there was freedom of opinion within the Assembly and [Hajji Mohammad Hosein] spoke with the utmost courtesy." He also observes, however, that "no one dared to question what he did or say anything to him about his own affairs."

Nevertheless, the underprivileged Rayhani found enough courage to raise sensitive questions about the future of Hajji Mohammad Hosein's estate: "You have no children and no Baha'i inheritors. Life is nothing to depend on and this worldly position is ultimately of no use. Think of something useful to do." The affluent merchant met his death before he could make any such decision, however. The government appropriated much of his estate, and some of his Baha'i writings and illuminated manuscripts were destroyed.[58]

Other appropriations and abuse took place during the lifetimes of some merchants. The early years of Mozaffar al-Din Shah's reign (1896–1907) were marred by fiscal problems and abuses of power, including the persecution of non-Muslims by the prince-governors and some of the Shi'i ulama. According to Rayhani, Kashan's governor, sometime around 1903, sent for five brother merchants who lived in the vicinity of Kashan and for five other "men of means, and kept them waiting under the hot summer sun in their sheepskin coats." He demanded that they each pay 100 *tomans* for their release. The notables, all of whom "wore turbans" took protective sanctuary (*bast*) in a shrine near Aran:

> The governor and five of his men walked right into the shrine, tore off the men's turbans, tied their hands together and brought them back to Kashan on foot. They marched them through the bazaar in a line with their hands tied to each other. The governor got their money, but how much I do not know.[59]

This incident is an example of the governor's disregard for the sanctity of the *bast*. More significantly, it is an example of the much less common abuse of the generally respected members of the merchant class. Abuses of merchants by the financially strapped state during this period are known to have contributed to the Constitutional Revolution of 1905.[60]

Baha'i Persecutions

The above episode coincided with the 1903 massacre of Baha'is in Yazd. During the same year, Rayhani witnessed the initial planning stages of a foiled anti-Baha'i pogrom in Kashan. The ulama of Kashan are reported to have initiated the following exchange with the governor, asking:

> "Why are you attacking the Muslims? They killed the Baha'is in Yazd and plundered their property. You should arrest the Baha'is and seize their property too, since taking their property is permitted [by Shi'i law]."
>
> To which the governor responded. "You are trying to start an uproar in our peaceful town."[61]

From his early childhood, Rayhani had witnessed violent attacks against Babis and Baha'is. Religious antipathy and association with past Babi militancy made life especially dangerous for Babis and Baha'is, who were often victimized by spontaneous collective violence that could be instigated with very little effort. Rayhani refers to "routine persecution" during the holy month of Ramadan and the mourning month of Moharram, when Babis and Baha'is were often targeted by mob violence or subjected to public humiliations. Religious emotions ran high during these dramatic periods of mourning, self-flagellation, and passion plays. These emotions were acted out toward the "self," as well as against the "Other" through anti-minority violence. An oppressed populace might easily displace their anger and frustration by directing it toward a stigmatized minority. This was part of an almost accepted pattern of social behavior, similar to urban factional infighting between the Haydari and Nemati factions. The authorities either tolerated or were unable to control factional violence and attacks on disadvantaged non-Muslims.

In particular, at times of economic weakness, territorial loss, and political humiliation, Iran's fringe groups were easy targets for the increasingly frustrated majority who were impressed by the might and progress of European encroachers. The image of the latter was frequently embellished by the exaggeration of their role in Iran's politics as alleged in various conspiracy theories. Rayhani recounts that this pattern of misdirecting anger against the oppressor was even replicated by idle Jews who, deprived of their musical entertainment during the month of Moharram, sought the help of another subaltern, a wandering Dervish, to engage in a substitute diversion at the expense of the even more oppressed Baha'is.

Dervish Qasem of Kashan who was friendly with the Jews and wrote poems for them for ten *shahi*s . . . took a coffin, put a live man inside it and marched across town behind it with his [Sufi] battle axe on his shoulder, singing poems insulting the Baha'is. A mob was clapping and dancing before and behind the coffin as it traveled from one city gate to another.[62]

Aside from "routine" incidents directed against Baha'is, there were premeditated persecutions that often had at least the blessing of the ulama or local landowners. There were a variety of agendas and objectives involved: a governor seeking economic gain; a younger, lower-ranking member of the ulama in search of stature and recognition; or a more powerful member of the ulama asserting his authority against his rivals, possibly with an eye toward confiscating the victim's assets.

Jews and Baha'is shared the predicament of being the occasional victims of persecution, especially during periods of instability. One abhorrent outbreak of anti-Jewish persecution in Tehran which took place "at the beginning of the constitutional period [1905–1909], before constitutional laws and order were in place," was triggered by a certain Sadr ul-Ulama, who according to Rayhani handled much of Tehran's judicial business.[63]

When Rayhani was staying with his relative Aqajan, he witnessed a premeditated staging of this persecution by a group of *luti*s and a woman collaborator. She was ostensibly visiting a Jewish midwife who ran a practice from Aqajan's house when she suddenly started screaming accusing "four tough Jews" of sexually molesting her. A large crowd (some two thousand according to Rayhani) soon gathered and within hours "a few Jews had been injured and some of their houses had been looted." By day's end, even though several sentries were posted around the Jewish quarter, the situation became more chaotic as "the guards were behaving worse than the offenders." Over the next seventeen days "even with the guards there, the crowds periodically attacked the Jews, beat them up and pillaged their property." Aqajan Majzub was a convert to Islam who later became a Baha'i. During the riots he managed to gain protection by paying the guards and by attending to them. He also had friendly relations with Sadr ul-Ulama who apologized to him, saying, "Aqajan, was that you? They [the trouble makers] did not realize it was your house." The openness of undisguised negotiations with the trouble-making Sadr ul-Ulama and possible payment of a bribe, demonstrates the fragile nature of life during periods of social and political crisis and the complicated finesse that was required to negotiate one's safety.

Harassment, Revolution, and the Reign of Chaos

As discussed in Chapter Three, the extent of the involvement of the Baha'is and their sympathizers in the Constitutional Revolution is a matter that calls for further investigation.[64] Though Rayhani is silent about the constitutionalists in Kashan, he does recount his interaction with a Baha'i who later became an active proponent of the Constitutional movement. The *darugheh* whom he identifies as a Baha'i was almost certainly Pahlavan Mohammad Aqa Pilband, a renowned athlete and valiant *luti* who later joined the ranks of the constitutionalists and was murdered by Nayeb Hosein's son during the counter-revolutionary years (1908–09).[65] Rayhani does not mention the *darugheh*'s revolutionary activities, and this figure is absent in other Baha'i narratives. This may indicate that he had only a loose association with the Bahai's, or that he later broke with them perhaps over his political activities. Another notable activist, curiously absent from Rayhani's account, was Khavari Kashani, known as Fakhr al-Va'ezin (1854–1914), an eloquent preacher, a poet, and an influential journalist. He dedicated his illustrated rhymed treatise against drug use (*afyun*) to his son. (Use of opium was prohibited by the Bab and Baha'u'llah.) His association with Baha'is is known to us only from a poem he wrote in praise of 'Abdu'l-Baha.[66]

During the late period of Qajar rule (1896–1925), and before Rayhani finally migrated to Tehran, he worked as a shopkeeper and peddler (presumably of fabrics and haberdashery), traveling primarily and extensively in the vicinity of Kashan but also through many other regions of Iran. His detailed account of his endeavors as a peddler in the face of exploiting government officials, banditry, and the breakdown of law and order demonstrates the insurmountable obstacles to the economic advancement within the merchant classes. Despite widespread hopes for justice and equality, the Constitutional Revolution failed to bring about security or major economic improvements.

Rayhani's perilous adventures in the countryside in pursuit of a meager income also illustrate the serious obstacles to the formation of a respected central authority and the accumulation of small and large merchant wealth, in particular the insecurity of means of transport, and the increasingly belligerent actions of the governors and local landowners. An example of the latter is Arbab Aqa Baba of Mashkan (Mashkun), a local chief who became a Baha'i, but who nevertheless persisted in his traditional role as the peasants' oppressor. Even though "he had all the village affairs under his control," his behavior was such that "all the village landowners and peasants [including his sons-in-law] were against him." He had to flee to Tehran on the eve of a rebellion in the village, only to return with a decree assuring him of the governor's protection.

His unpopularity seems to have reflected negatively on his new faith, for despite all the efforts of Baha'i teachers, "not one person" in the village became a Baha'i. His story demonstrates that expansion of the Baha'i faith in Iran's countryside—particularly in villages and townships where Bahai's became a predominate majority—was not simply a result of the conversion of the landowners, though this might be an important influence. Much more important in mass conversions in the countryside was the conversion of trusted local religious leaders.

During the decade after the civil war of 1908, Rayhani witnessed the spread of rebels and bandits to whom the weak central government often resorted to establish a pretense of law and order. In an atmosphere of overlapping and contradictory secular and religious legal authorities, civil and criminal laws were not enforced. It was in these circumstances that Nayeb Hosein's gang of local rebels rose to power in Kashan, and many small landowners and farmers in the surrounding villages were subject to the whim of these vicious and capricious bandits. Among the victims were Baha'is whom Rayhani had gotten to know during his years of traveling in the countryside. Prior to the turn of the century, Nayeb Hosein had been a *luti* chieftain in Kashan, with all the usual connections to merchants and notables and was a familiar type in Iran's urban scene.

However, the role of the *lutis* as a valiant local militia began to break down during the constitutional period, when anti-constitutionalist officials hired Nayeb Hosein and his gang as their private army. According to Rayhani, it was during this period that Baha'is distanced themselves from Nayeb Hosein and discouraged his participation in their gatherings. His sons, including the eldest and leading son Mashallah Khan (Sardar), seem to have moved away from their sympathy for the

Baha'is and gravitated toward Sufi leaders. Rayhani tells us that prior to Nayeb's final arrest, leading to his execution in 1920, a truce with the Sufi-inclined *mojtahed* Habibullah led to the division of Kashan into two sectors, ruled by the two contending forces, and that the *mojtahed*'s forces were even more cruel than the brutal followers of Nayeb:

> Mulla Habibullah gathered together a few *lutis* and gave each one a title, such as "Courage of the Shari'a" (*Shoja' al-shari'ah*), "Lion of the Shari'ah" (*Zayqam al-shari'ah*), and "Illumination of the Shari'ah" (*Sho'a al-shari'ah*).[67] They walked around town boasting. Right after that, Nayeb Hosein rebelled and came back to Kashan to kill the mulla's men. The mulla's eldest son Mehdi met with Nayeb's son Mashallah and they entered into a pact [to divide the city]. Mehdi would take [the area around] the Isfahan Gate and Mashallah [would take the area] outside Dowlat Gate (*dar-vazeh dowlat*). People were less fearful when they were summoned by Nayeb, because they were frightened to death by the mulla. If one of his men came to take them to the mulla, they would rather die. This is what the people of Kashan had to live with until Nayeb's affair came to an end. Then, the mullas and the *mojtaheds* multiplied.[68]

Rayhani's account demonstrates how the post-constitutional civil war became an instrument for infighting among local urban groups and for suffering locals had to endure at the hands of both sides of the struggle.

During World War I, when central authority in Iran was on the verge of complete breakdown, Nayeb and his gang captured Kashan's state armory and took control of the entire region extending from Qom to Isfahan. They were responsible for many atrocities, including mass rapes and indiscriminate killings, especially in the countryside. Their control of Iran's main roads caused a complete disruption of trade and manu-facturing in the Kashan region.[69] Rayhani faced desperate conditions and could barely feed his family. His connections in the countryside and his profession as a peddler allowed him to trade in enough food to save them from starving.[70]

But Nayeb Hosein was only one of a number of outlaws and bandits who rose to dominate the countryside during the chaotic years of the war, when central government authority broke down and the economy was devastated. Iran now faced extreme conditions: insecurity, political instability, famine, foreign occupation, and vulnerability at all levels of society. These conditions provide a context for the widespread popular support for a centralizing state under Reza Shah Pahlavi (1925–1941).

Rayhani does not share much about his experiences after he finally moved to Tehran. Perhaps he did not feel his position in Tehran's Baha'i community of the 1930s was as significant as his prominent position in Kashan's community. A new class of younger Baha'i leaders was emerging, some of whom were the children of Persian Baha'is who had immigrated to Russia in the late nineteenth century, received Western-style education, and had been deported back to Iran during the years of Stalinist terror. Their vision of the community was based on a mission to broaden the Baha'i message through a hierarchical and institutionalized structure that was less reliant on personalities. Just as they aspired to present a flawless public image of the community, their production of history was also sanitized, based as it was on "authoritative" narratives that minimized or excluded the less savory details found in accounts such as Rayhani's. In this respect, Rayhani offers a voice from the past, when community life centered on individual relationships, identities were negotiable, and the historical narrative had not yet been canonized.

7

AQAJAN SHAKERI:
MISERIES OF A JEWISH LIFE

The memoirs of Aqajan Shakeri (1884–1964) are a first-hand, narrative account of the new opportunities, and the obstacles to economic advancement, that emerged in Iran during a period of rapid socio-economic and political change at the end of the nineteenth century. The document is a detailed description by a layman of the common deprivations and social discrimination that many Iranians, including Jews and Baha'is, faced during this time. New opportunities allowed a few to overcome the dire economic conditions of a restrictive past, but others were forced to continue their bitter struggle with poverty and despair. As such, Shakeri's memoirs reflect the challenges and complexities of a society undergoing rapid social changes, changes that endangered traditional relationships.

Like Rayhani's account of his life, Shakeri's autobiography has many layers of significance. It is a rare account written by a commoner that defines a unique, modern "self." The individuality that emerges from the experience of writing one's memoirs is at variance with traditional forms of self-definition based on religious, ethnic, or geographic group identity.[1] Few of Shakeri's contemporaries would have seen their life experiences as a matter of interest to others. Yet for a number of Jewish converts, writing became an instrument for finding voice and individuality. In their memoirs, they found meaning in defining a new "self" shaped by a modern and ecumenical religious identity.

Shakeri's urge for self-expression was urgent enough for him to threaten his offspring with the withdrawal of his blessings from them if his memoirs were not published. He even assigned a part of his meager assets to cover the cost of their publication.[2] However, a number of obstacles, including the author's raw and traditional style, his divergence from the middle-class sensibilities of his offspring, and the contradictions his account offers to an orthodox and sanitized Baha'i history, in the end defeated the publication of this document.

Shakeri's self-stated purpose was the conventional passing on of "warnings and advice to the new generation." He wrote a pious memoir. Occasional material successes are only worthy of note for their transience, while moments of true exuberance and lasting meaning only come through a sense of brotherhood and the "joy of fraternity" among other Baha'is. Though at times preachy and self-serving, his record is nevertheless a remarkably bold testimony to a life of economic hardship and uncertainty.

One may find Shakeri's view of the Hamadan Jewish community excessively negative and its miseries exaggerated. During the last quarter of the nineteenth century, many Jews from other parts of Iran migrated to Hamadan to take advantage of the city's thriving trade and economic growth. Yet Shakeri remembers his early life among the Hamadani Jews as an experience of disadvantage and exclusion from the city's growing prosperity. Possibly, his account may reflect sharp inequalities within the Jewish community itself. He may also have been influenced by traditionalist Baha'i historical notions, common in the 1950s, which blamed the victims of discrimination for having rejected the prophets of God and their religions. He remarks: "Our fathers having strayed by rejecting Prophet Mohammad were also punished by God with great vigor." Nevertheless, despite their obvious biases, views from below such as those of Rayhani and Shakeri are of great interest. If nothing else, they balance the often idealistic view of Jewish life commonly found in later narratives that reflect the community's socio-economic rise and its tendency to forget past degradations (see Introduction).

Shakeris' relatively long (265 pages, including appendices) memoir was written over a number of years and was compiled over ten months in 1960–61 when the author was in his mid-seventies. The raw style and his poor handwriting are characteristic of the writings of many of his self-educated contemporaries. The text was transcribed in the 1980s for legibility and with some annotation explaining the local Hamadani dialect (see Introduction and Note 2 above).

Plate 1. Aqajan Shakeri of Hamadan (1884-1964).
See p. 149.

Plate 2. Yuhanna Khan Hafezi (1870-1951).
See p. 173.

Plate 3. Hakim Aqajan, first Baha'i convert in
Hamadan (d. 1880). See p. 106.

Plate 4. Rayhan Rayhani.
(Photo courtesy of the Rayhani family)

Plate 5. Hakim Ilya (Elyahu), father of Hakim Rahamim Hafez al-Sehheh at center. See p. 175

Plate 6. Hakim Rahamim Hafez al-Sehheh (seated at center) with his household. His son Yuhanna is seated to his right c 1922. See p. 175.

Plate 7. Yuhanna Khan Hafezi seated at right with other family members. See page 173.

Plate 8. From left Yuhanna Khan Hafezi, Hajji `Abd ul-Hasan Ardakani (Hajji Amin), Shalom Farid. See p. 173.

Plate 9. A gathering of Kashan Baha'is on the occasion of a visit by the American Keith Ransom-Kehler (center) in 1932. See p. 121.

Plate 10. A group of Hamadan Jews c 1899. See p. 164. (Photo courtesy of Iraj Shamsian)

Plate 11. Faculty and students at the Hamadan Alliance School where French language and culture was emphasized. See p. 202. (Photo courtesy of Faryar Nikbakhat)

Plate 12. Students of Hamadan Ta'id School (est.1908) in 1915 with headmaster Monsieur André, seated at the center. His western style clothing, the uniforms, the flag, emblems and the portrait of the education minister display a modern vision. See p. 202.

Plate 13. A group of Kashan Jews and students of the city's first Jewish school, Madreseh Aqa Yequtiyel (est. 1911) in the 1920 s. See p. 121.

Plate 14. Vahdat-e Bashr Baha'i school (*Hadiqeh Vahdat*) Kashan, 1927.

Plate 15. Ali Mohammad Khadem-Misaq (standing at center) conductor of the first Baha'i orchestra Tehran, 1940 s. See p. 72.

Plate 16. Baha'i women of Hamadan in a gathering of "Advancement of Women" (*Taraqqi-ye Nesvan*), 1936. See p. 70.

Plate 17. A group of Rasht Baha'is (c 1932) including physicians, merchants, scholars, Baha'i teachers, lawyers, land owners and farmers. See p. 116.

Plate 18. Itinerate Baha'i teacher Mirza Mehdi Ekhvan al-Safa. See p. 92.

Plate 19. 'Aziz 'Alaqband of Hamadan (d 1935). See p. 101.

Childhood and Family Life

Aqajan Shakeri [see Plate 1] was born into a poor but observant Jewish family in Hamadan. His father Ibrahim (1835–1907) was renamed Ebi in childhood at the time of a life-threatening illness, in a traditional desperate effort to elude evil spirits. Though Ebi married young, his first two wives died without bearing children. His third wife bore him seven children by the time he had reached "an old age" (his early 50s), five of whom survived. The dire living conditions, lack of sanitation, hunger, and even starvation that Shakeri bitterly recalls were common among Iran's impoverished classes and point to a rarely explored class stratification among the Jews of Hamadan, known for their relative affluence and cosmopolitan outlook by the 1890s.[3]

The Shakeri family shared the miseries of many impoverished Iranians of their time, suffering from the poor state of medicine:

Except for my [younger] sister Sara, we all came down with scalp ringworm (*kachali*). As a remedy, they put sap on canvas (*zeft-e karbasi*) [and applied it] to the skull. After a week the bath attendant would pull it off along with all the hair, and blood would come gushing out. We died and came back to life under the attendant's hands. Our other misfortune was typhoid fever. We all came down with it, one after another. Lacking proper medicines, we each suffered for months, before the next child got sick.[4]

Even though modern medicine was available in Hamadan in the 1880s, thanks to the efforts of American missionaries, home treatment for relatively simple ailments could lead to major complications:

Two months after my sister Ribqa [1892–1957] came down with typhoid fever, a blister grew on her lower lip. My father called for Faraj the surgeon who sliced open her lip, disfiguring her permanently. My mother's only relative and advisor, her sister Morvarid, went to the American Protestant Hospital. A woman [a nurse] came to our house, examined her and said the surgery should not have been done. For the next two months, she brought her medicine, hot water, toys, and money for food, until she was well. Later, my mother sent my sister to a more affluent family as a housekeeping apprentice, and there she became a Baha'i. When she came home to visit, we would curse the Baha'is and ridicule her. But she prayed for us.[5]

As apprentices, probably with little or no salary, less advantaged Jewish girls like Ribqa could enjoy better living conditions while learning homemaking skills. This practice was also common among the Jews of Kashan, where teen-age girls (*dasi*) learned homemaking and crafts such as silk sorting from more experienced women.[6] Ribqa later married a Jewish man but divorced him soon after. Her daughter was a teacher at Hamadan's Baha'i school.

Shakeri's mother Mihel had lost her parents and two young brothers at an early age, a fact that may explain her marriage to an older man. Her frequent weeping and wailing only increased the misery of her children.[7] Yet it was poor Jewish women such as Mihel, the most powerless in society, who were the first to open themselves to the forces of social change. Morvarid's openness to modern medicine and Ribqa's conversion in the face of family opposition and abuse point to an intriguing pattern whereby the most powerless were willing to give modernity a chance.

Prior to the development of Hamadan as a trade center (beginning in the 1860s but fully developed in the 1890s), Shakeri's father ran a meager business in partnership with his brother, who sent him merchandise from Baghdad. These imports included linen shrouds, which he reportedly sold at cost as a community service. The use of inexpensive fabric was required by the rabbis for burial, perhaps in an attempt to provide equality in death for all Jews at a time of widening social gaps. According to Shakeri, his father's financial condition declined drastically after he made a vow to give up all his modest possessions if he could have children. This may have served as a convenient rationalization for the family's years of brutal poverty, however. Ebi's business failures were evidently the result of his own mismanagement and indifference to financial affairs. Despite his wife's protests, for example, he reportedly took no action when merchants with whom he shared his shop stole his merchandise.

Ebi's financial problems were compounded by legal entanglements when he had to defend himself against a suit brought by his nephew, Mehdi, who as a convert to Islam had a legal advantage. Mehdi made a claim for losses in the collapse of his father's and uncle's joint venture and "employed Zandi, a ruthless government agent (*farrash*), to harass Ebi." Shakeri's father, in turn, took sanctuary (*bast*) at the home of the influential mujtahed Hajji Aqa Mohammad Qazi, and declared bankruptcy (*eflas biroun avard*). Nevertheless, he was forced to go to jail. In the end, a group of "well-wisher merchants examined the accounts and negotiated the sum of 48 *tomans*" to cover the debt. Ebi paid off his debt to his nephew with a loan on his inherited home. He later gradually repaid the loan using his wife's income and the salaries his children earned through their apprenticeships. Penniless, he would wander around all day, walking "ten to twenty kilometers a day, with no lunch," working odd jobs supposedly as a laborer, and earning a meager ten *shahis* (one pence). He would spend nine *shahis* on some two kilos of bread, which was often all his family had to eat.[8] This is yet another example of how conversion to Islam might give the Muslim convert the upper hand in any financial dispute.

The family's financial misfortunes are a testimony to the precarious nature of economic affairs in Iran during the latter part of the nineteenth century. Western economic dominance, now in full force, had led to the collapse of important manufacturing sectors. Cheap European manufactures, especially textiles, flooded the markets. Perhaps even more significant than the impact of the industrial revolution was the heavy burden of inflation fed by a vicious cycle of currency devaluation and export of precious metals. Extreme inflation made it profitable to export the silver contained in the country's coinage. In his youth around the turn of the century, Shakeri worked as an apprentice in a silver rendering shop and played a small part in the export of silver.[9]

Extreme poverty often led to tensions within the family. Much of the heavy financial burden was borne by the women and children who had no control over their circumstances. As the family's main breadwinner, Shakeri's mother Mihel had, in addition to her household chores, two or three jobs: peeling almonds, sorting silk, and weaving textiles. She would arrive home late at night, usually after her husband did, both of them tired and stressed. Often a scene of family strife and physical abuse would result: "When my father kindly asked for a drink of water, she demanded money to make dinner. He offered the one *shahi* he had and a fight would begin, she pulling his white beard and he grabbing her by the hair, causing us much grief and anguish."[10] Pervasive domestic strife may also point to changing gender roles. Women were increasingly shouldering the household expenses, yet gaining little authority or respect and facing more tension at home from husbands frustrated by their failure to fulfill the traditional male role.

Despite his chronic financial problems, Shakeri's father Ebi, like his pious ancestors, faithfully performed his religious duties. Not having the means to make his own wine, for years he performed his Sabbath prayers by soaking a few raisins in water, then squeezing them into a cup, and this he would hand around to his family.

> One year, despite his wife's disapproval, he sold a [copper] pot to buy grapes which he then put in a large clay jar he had inherited, and pounded them with a stick all day to make wine. Once the wine was fermented, he took it out of the damp cellar. He sealed it and stored it in a very large glass container in our main room.

Ebi's wine-making enterprise turned into yet another disaster, however. One October Sabbath night when, "using our mother's wages," the family had the luxury of a meat dish. Shakeri pouted over not getting enough meat. In a defiant mood, he protested by swinging the meat-pounder (*gousht-koub*) around the room until, "[as if] an angel aimed it exactly," the flying mace hit the glass jar at its very bottom, shattered it and spilled its entire contents, over a hundred liters of wine, on the floor:

> . . . over the carpet, the bedding, and out through the doors and windows. My father, mother, and brother jumped at me, yelling and screaming, hitting me and pulling my hair out. We had no bedding to sleep on, and they howled like dogs all night, while I was broken and in pieces.[11]

The Shakeris' struggle with poverty was not uncommon, and at least one of their Jewish neighbors suffered similar misfortunes. This was Mehdi, his wife Makhmal, and their daughter Tala, whose "beauty, chastity, and sweet voice can hardly be described":

> Yet because she was poor, no one would marry her. It was customary for young men to marry into families of some means. The engagement [customarily] took seven or eight months, during which the young man had to be invited for dinner every Saturday night. One day Tala complained to her father at lunch: "We are tired of having bread for every meal." Aggravated, Mehdi said to Tala, "Give me the dish, and I will get you some yogurt." (Yogurt was two *shahis* for two kilos.) The family sat waiting and he didn't

come back. They looked everywhere and could not find him. The night passed and he did not return. Eventually, they held mourning ceremonies, thinking he must have been killed. Three years later, he came back. "What kind of yogurt was this?," they asked him. (He became known as Yogurt Mehdi.) "I had no money, and I was so embarrassed that I went to Russia." In those days, people from all parts of Iran went to Russia to bring back some money.[12]

Shakeri's brother-in-law, Hatan, six months after marrying his disfigured sister Ribqa, left her and was not heard from for twelve years. He returned starving and distraught during the famine of 1917–1918. His wife rejected him, even though her family agreed to support him.[13] These vanishing men demonstrate the breakdown of the traditional male role as the family breadwinner in the face of increasing economic strain. Their disappearances may be explained as desperate efforts to escape humiliation, as well as desperate bids for a better future. Their absence, and that of thousands of men who were known to be working abroad, meant more family responsibility for mothers and daughters, although this did not always become a source of women's empowerment.

Even though Ebi had inherited the inferior half of a family house, his living conditions never improved. Lack of direct sunlight was a serious problem during Hamadan's long cold winters. Shakeri recounts having suffered from extreme cold—on the Sabbath especially, since the family was dependent on a Muslim woman to start their fire. Their main source of water was a house yard well which was particularly unsanitary due to Hamadan's porous soil conditions and the well's proximity to "a toilet on one side and a trash-filled garden on the other, making its water filthy and bitter . . . causing us numerous illnesses." Jews were often denied access to better quality spring water because of their supposed impurity and were forced to take their drinking water from polluted sources. This was the direct cause of the children's typhoid fever and other diseases. The overcrowded Jewish bathhouse, "with insufficient water and a filthy bath pool," which in any case the Shakeris could afford no more than once every three weeks, increased their vulnerability to disease.[14]

A Failed Education

Traditional education often proved to be an additional burden on children and family. When Shakeri was six years old, he and his brother had a short-lived experience of schooling in the traditional Jewish *maktab*.[15] The family's dire finances did not allow for tuition and other related expenses. "On the other hand, our father did not have the money to pay the teacher the two *shahi* a week. Nor did we have the money for a mat or a sheep skin to sit on and a clay brassier to keep us warm."[16]

The blind and reputedly "illiterate" Mulla Ya'qub and his son Mulla Musheh ran a school of some 60 students. Their heavy-handed use of collective punishment as a means of discipline and an instrument of instruction was not uncommon within the traditional system and was practiced across religious lines:

> The teacher had devised a clever strategy to frighten the pupils and make them follow his orders. He had by his side three or four long wet twigs, and he would lift all of the kids' feet one by one and hit us hard until we all had tears in our eyes. My brother and I were so hurt by being punished without having done anything wrong that one day we came home, stored a pile of stones on our rooftop, and started stoning the teacher's house across the alley from us.[17]

This act of vengeance by the two brothers marked their departure from the oppressive, traditional *maktab* and foreshadowed the demise of the traditional educational system soon to be replaced by modern schools. The decayed nature of the traditional system in this period also contrasts with the education of earlier generations, including Shakeri's own grandfather Davud, who reportedly wrote poetry imploring the Messiah to return. He transcribed the fourteenth-century Jewish poet Shahin Shirazi's rendition of the Torah into Persian poetry. Within that same decade, American Presbyterian missionaries started a small school and by 1900, Hamadan's Alliance Israelite School would become a major agent of change for the Jewish community.[18]

If lack of supplies and cruelty in the classroom were not sufficient impediments, the difficult and distasteful chores the students were required to perform for the teacher put an end to any desire for schooling. One such chore involved having students "walk a long way to the Jewish butcher's shop to bring back blood in broken clay jars, getting beaten on the way and having stones thrown at us by Muslim kids."

The father and son who ran the school used animal blood, for its magical properties, or perhaps to save on the cost of ink, for their profitable talisman-writing enterprise. These magical objects were "scribbled amulets" written in an abstract style that "they claimed the ghosts (*jenn*) wrote during the night in a malady-healing script (*khatt-e ahou*)." Reportedly, Muslims were faithful customers and, judging by the volume of blood used, they were particularly taken in by the powers of these Jewish soothsayers.

Exclusion and Violence

The picture Shakeri draws of Jewish-Muslim relations in Hamadan underscores social inferiority and segregation through the traditional mechanism of ritual "impurity." The Jews had enjoyed greater prosperity during the early modern period, but by the late nineteenth century they had been pushed into the lowest ranks of society. Aside from fortune telling, according to Shakeri, the Jews of Hamadan worked as peddlers and sewage cleaners.[19] Many peddlers (*chorchi*, derogatory) who sold their wares to the surrounding towns and villages were, according to Shakeri, away from home for an entire year, returning only during the Jewish festival of Passover ('*aid-e fatir*). In the countryside, "the children threw stones at them and incited stray dogs to attack them."[20] At times, Shakeri's depiction seems extreme:

> One time when two peddlers, who had divided up some villages between them, mistakenly showed up in the same village on the same day, the villagers beat them, saying, "The country is in chaos when two Jew-boys come to our village on the same day." A peddler named Tamir had shortness of breath, and they buried him alive. . . .[21]
>
> My father used to say that whenever there was a heavy snow, the Muslims forced the Jews to clear the snow from their rooftops. God is my witness how much I myself suffered at their hands and how they beat me. [22]

Another example of the social exclusion of Jews, a product of the Shi'i laws of ritual impurity, was the prohibition on the use of the public baths. This was a serious problem for itinerant Jewish merchants and peddlers in the countryside. When Aqa Khodadad could not make ends meet in Hamadan, he moved to a nearby village. But he faced

grave consequences when, having no place else to wash himself, he
secretly used the village public bath in the middle of the night. Shakeri
recounts: "They attacked him and wanted to kill him, saying, 'You polluted our bath.' He had no choice but to become a Muslim, and even
though he had a wife and children in Hamadan, they forced him to
marry a coarse (*nakareh*) woman." Shakeri seems to have been much
more concerned about the forced marriage than he was about Khodadad's forced (and nominal) conversion to Islam.[23]

As discriminatory and socially restrictive as the laws of impurity were
for the Jews, they were remarkably reciprocal. Both Muslims and Jews
considered each other impure. "If a Muslim's body touched [any large
container] of wine or vinegar, the Jews considered it impure (*nasakh*),"
writes Shakeri.[24] This became a source of resentment for the dominant
Shi'is who felt that they alone were entitled to draw the lines of social
exclusivity.

At one point, Shakeri recounts a gruesome story of the murder of
Aqa Haym Sion, a Jewish peddler in Malayer who was from Isfahan.
Shakeri had warned Aqa Haym about the dangers of going to the
Arak region, which was known for its unruly inhabitants. He had even
insisted on settling their accounts prior to Haym's departure. At the
Turgir fortress, Aqa Haym made the mistake of unintentionally reveal-
ing his Jewish convictions when he turned down the community meal
he was offered and instead asked for boiled potatoes. Shakeri writes:
"They choked him to death using wool carpet yarns. Broke his skull
and pealed off the skin from his face."

The hosts' violent behavior may be indicative of increasing hostility
toward Jewish peddlers, who provided an important service in a predominantly rural society, but who may well have been blamed for the
rampant inflation of the Muzaffari period (1896–1906). Aqa Haym's
fate also points to the hazards of an out-of-control countryside where
many independent areas persisted.[25]

Judging by Shakeri's account, violence, including domestic violence,
seems to have been an inescapable part of Jewish life. Shakeri keenly
observes the association between domestic violence and the humiliation that many men endured outside (and arguably inside) the home:

The Israelite brethren's other misfortune was that they drank wine
and spirits on the Sabbath on top of much heavy food prepared
the day before. They got drunk, threw up, had hangovers (*kho-*

mar mishodand), remembered the miseries they suffered during the week, became enraged and started to beat their defenseless wives. Having no other protectors, some wives took refuge with Muslims and had no choice but to become Muslims. If that happened, the [Jewish] family held mourning ceremonies for them, as if they were no longer alive. [26]

Here we can observe how a good deal of gender oppression seems to have come from within the family and the community and was augmented by external elements of discrimination and social humiliation. The women who sought protection by converting to Islam as a last resort present a different genre of forced conversion, compelled not by Muslims, but rather by internal family violence. Though we cannot be sure of the prevalence of this phenomenon, it does illustrate another domestic avenue of conversion to Islam, which is usually mostly attributed to external pressures and persecution.[27] It also demonstrates how conversion could serve as an instrument for change in a variety of situations.

In Malayer, Shakeri met a broken young Jewish man who worked for a meager salary as a servant in the home of a Jewish physician. One night he opened up and, according to Shakeri, confessed to nothing less than murdering his wife for no particular reason:

> "A few years back, when I had recently married, I got angry one day, took my wife to the room and started to beat her with a chain. The more she pleaded with me, the harder I beat her. She went to sleep, and the next day she died. She had no relatives or defenders."
> "Had she done anything wrong?" I asked.
> "No," he replied.
> "Then why did you beat the poor defenseless woman?"
> "I just got angry," he replied.[28]

Yet aggression was not limited to domestic violence and was often visible outside the family boundaries. Shakeri relates the account of the deep enmity between his mother and her Jewish neighbors who "were at each other's throats every day and wounded each other in the face."[29] These scenes, provided in the memoir in intimate and personal detail by a keen and daring observer, illustrate a common but less discussed dimension of oppressive and violent relations, namely neighborhood disputes.

Conversion and Tribulations of Faith

Though proud of his pious Jewish ancestors, as a convert to the Baha'i religion, with a positivist rational viewpoint, Shakeri came to be critical of what he considered extreme traditionalism and superstition:

> One Yom Kippur evening, when many oil-burning lights were lit in the synagogue in memory of the lost ones, suddenly the wind blew and the curtain around the pulpit caught fire. The congregation (*morid*) said, "This is the house of God, the fire will go out on its own." The pulpit caught on fire and soon the whole wooden building was in flames. The Muslims came to help, and the water carriers (*saqqa*) [brought water], but they could not put out the flames. It's a long story, 36 great Torahs were burned, each one worth 700 *tomans* at the time.[30]

Early in life, subconscious questioning of this kind of religious fatalism, spurred on by challenges from positivistic Baha'is, gave Shakeri a strong desire to study and defend his ancestral faith. The urge to become literate in Persian was not so much a conscious desire for social mobility as it was a desire to study the scripture (*tafsir*, *fazel-khawni*) in Persian translation. As a young adult, Shakeri learned to read and write Persian from his younger sister Sara. She must have played a significant indirect role in his conversion, although curiously, he does not elaborate on this. Almost certainly a Christian convert or sympathizer, Sara had attended the Presbyterian missionary school in Hamadan. She was knowledgeable in medicine and specialized in eye ailments.[31] At this point in his life, when Shakeri's traditional belief in Judaism was being undermined by the "relentless" challenges of the Baha'is and their calls for debate, and perhaps exposure to Christian missionaries, Shakeri felt obliged to respond by writing his own polemical treatises. This effort, along with the study of Baha'i scriptures and discussions with Baha'i teachers, eventually led to his conversion.

Shakeri's conversion was in effect the culmination of discussions and debates with Baha'is over a three-and-a-half year period. "During the first six months I had, to an extent, accepted Baha'u'llah as a messenger of God. But accepting the prophets Mohammad and Jesus was difficult because I had read a number of polemics against Islam and Christianity." At times Shakeri criticized the rabbis for what he saw as their ignorance of the Torah and the Commentaries (*tafsir*).[32] On one occasion, anguished by his doubts, Shakeri could not stop crying when special prayers for the coming of the Messiah were being recited in the synagogue, and he asked the rabbi to translate the prayers into Persian.[33]

Shakeri's extended and tormented uncertainties gradually came to an end when he was around twenty-six years old. At that time he and his brother openly confessed their new conviction in their synagogue and were subsequently expelled. Curiously, this important development in the conversion process; as well as the role played by his sister, the educated Christian sympathizer (or convert), Sara; and the family's first Baha'i convert, Ribqa, are left out of his otherwise detailed memoirs.[34] Perhaps, this omission can be explained as the result of reconstructing memory at an advanced age, or his hesitation to give credit to the women in his life, or perhaps as part the author's subconscious amnesia concerning the ambivalence and oscillation that surrounded his conversion.

Despite these omissions, Shakeri was surprisingly open at the time of his conversion about his resentments toward his painful past and his determination to leave it behind. His declaration of faith took an unusually angry form, aimed at physically removing himself from the space he associated with loss and deprivation:

I sold my antique prayer ambulate (*asbab namaz, tefillin*?) and came home. In the middle of the night, water started to drip on my head from a leak in the roof. I woke up and pulled the blanket over my head. The rotten wool got into my mouth. I got up and hit the window so hard that all the neighbors woke up. . . . In the morning after my mother and brothers left for work, I took a hammer, a sugar-loaf hacker, and smashed the plaster, broke all the doors and windows, threw the furniture outside, and demolished the steps leading to the house. I took out all the pain and suffering I had endured on that house. Then I went to the bazaar and put the house up for sale. When my mother and brothers showed up in the evening, there was no way to enter the house.[35]

The family was eventually able to take out a loan and relocate to a more decent home.

Making Ends Meet

Shakeri's angry reaction may be partly explained by the frustrations he experienced at work. At age twelve, he and his older brother Rahim were forced to take demanding and usually abusive jobs as a house-boy and an apprentice to a merchant, respectively. In addition to the assurance of regular meals, the benefits of Shakeri's job were mostly educational, as the starting salary of "one *toman* per year plus a pair of shoes and socks" was negligible. At age twenty, after some years spent gaining experience, Shakeri refused a very attractive offer from a previous master and Baha'i teacher, partly out of fear of pressure to become a Baha'i. Instead he took a less desirable position as an appren-tice to his cousin. "You had better be content if you want [to remain in] the Israelite ways," his cousin warned him.[36] Yet even as an expe-rienced assistant to a merchant, he had to endure humiliation from his abusive boss and relative. This was in addition to the stones thrown at them and the verbal taunts and abuse of neighborhood children who made a game of harassing Jews.

There were, however, also protectors of the mostly defenseless Jews. Shakeri reports receiving protection from a chivalrous *luti*, who showed much hostility toward Shakeri's cousin and superior, but who consid-ered protecting the disadvantaged Jews to be part of his *luti* code of honor. This sense of fellowship between the persecuted and the tradi-tional protectors of the weak may point to a universal resentment of exploitation by the wealthy.[37]

Working as an apprentice to a merchant or as a peddler often involved traveling to small towns where there was no Jewish community. This meant complete isolation and hardship, without access to "kosher meat, no companions, and no bathhouses." Being deprived of the services of the bath attendant meant that the customary necessity of shaving one's (usually infected) head by the unskilled became especially painful, "as though each hair were being pulled out one by one." Dietary restric-tions were yet another problem: "Yogurt and boiled eggs were all we could eat." When Shakeri bought some cooked beets from the bazaar, his Jewish roommates criticized him for having violated kosher laws by consuming a food cooked in a non-kosher pot.[38]

Forces of Change

The post-constitutional period was a time of increasing national integration, expansion of the national economy, and the spread of a secular
and rationalist alternative to traditional life. It was in this context
that the breakdown of ritual traditions seemed inevitable. Traditional
limitations ultimately could not withstand the forces of change and
modernity. Observance of Kosher laws became exceedingly difficult
for migrant merchants. This was also a time when a nationalist discourse and the call for a united Iranian identity weakened communal
boundaries.

Shakeri's conversion in his mid-twenties coincided with the considerable improvement of his economic situation, which he accomplished
through ties to other Baha'is. Though his affluence was short-lived, it
was an important influence in shaping his modern identity and facilitated his socialization into a new community. After fourteen years of
"miserable" apprenticeships, and in partnership with his brother and
two Baha'is of some means, he started a rather successful wholesale textile business in Hamadan's bazaar around 1910. The business earned a
substantial profit during the first year of operation:

> I put in 70 *tomans*, my brother Haym put in 100 *tomans*, and [my
> previous boss in the silver shop Mehdi] Arjomand and Mirza Aqa
> Jan together put in 300 *tomans*...We had good credit and we worked
> with 7,000–8,000 *tomans* worth of merchandise. Business was good
> and by the year's end we made 800 *tomans* [160 pounds].[39]

By turn of the twentieth century, a number of global and national
factors were contributing to a substantial increase in the import of
inexpensive European textiles. The opening of the Suez Canal in the
1860s, together with the advent of the steamship, meant a shorter
transport route from Europe. The credit market improved and tar-
iffs were rationalized. As subjects of the British Empire, Iraqi Jewish
merchants in Hamadan had economic and legal advantages as well as
close ties with Bombay and Europe—and they provided the vital trade
links. On the national level, post-constitutional freedoms provided new
legal protections and reduced archaic restrictions on Jews engaged in
business.[40]

Shakeri and his partners saw themselves as having a novel approach
to conducting business according to what might be characterized as a

new puritan work ethic. This they understood as an expression of their faith and a Baha'i business code (*hesab-e amri*). Many small merchants who engaged in joint trading ventures lacked the necessary education, experience, and even the basic accounting skills required to conduct business in the new economy. This often led to protracted squabbling over how the books were kept. Perhaps as a result of internal disagreements or a fluctuating market, Shakeri and his partners dissolved the partnership by holding a single meeting with the determination to agree on all accounts after saying Baha'i prayers. Business disputes among Baha'is were occasionally resolved by the Baha'i Spiritual Assembly (*mahfel-e rowhani*), then an appointed body of Baha'i leaders, which had considerable authority among believers including that of levying fines.[41]

Yet Shakeri cannot be regarded as fully modern in his orientation. His ideas about business success lacked any concept of reinvestment, a crucial element of capitalist practice. He still had one foot in his traditional community, and he continued to respect and fulfill his traditional obligations to relatives and to the Jewish community. These commitments prevented him from focusing his resources on the accumulation of wealth and the expansion of his business. Shakeri blames his financial failure on the mismanagement of household expenditures and conspicuous consumption, including numerous elaborate ceremonies and parties related to his marriage.[42]

Struggling with Tradition

At age 36, soon after his first successes in commerce, Shakeri had to bear the heavy burden of an elaborate engagement and wedding. The festivities included a number of customary but expensive ceremonies in which dozens of poor, uninvited guests had to be fed. No doubt, the bride's demand for such wedding displays was extreme. Such demands would vary depending on the perceived wealth of the prospective husband. Although the heavy cost, especially at the onset of World War I, may have satisfied Shakeri's traditional obligations to share his wealth with his community, it also severely drained his newly acquired capital. In this respect, his modernity can be seen as incomplete. Though at one level he believed he had overcome what he regarded as "superstition and ignorance" (even though at times he castigates himself for reverting to tradition), his social life was still embedded in traditional obligations.

Favorable economic conditions, a puritan work ethic, and access to capital through a new network of coreligionists could not withstand daunting political upheavals. Shakeri's partnership came to an end during the political turmoil resulting from Mohammad 'Ali Shah's 1908 campaign and the establishment of the "Minor Despotism." As Shakeri relates: "Things were getting chaotic and our store was about to be looted." One of the anti-constitutionalists' main objectives was to eradicate any signs of change associated with modernity. "They [forcibly] shaved people's heads and tore their [Western-style] suits."[43]

In addition to political instability and a lack of security, severe market oscillations were a major hindrance to entrepreneurial development. During the turbulent mid-teen years (1911–15), Shakeri ran a textile shop in Malayer. He and his brothers were attracted by Malayer's favorable conditions, in part the product of a growing local economy fueled by carpet manufacturing and export. Yet they soon suffered from a pre-World War I "trade war," caused by an oversupply of Western textiles, and a severe recession which brought them to the verge of bankruptcy. With the onset of war came a complete reversal: an end to the recession and a fourfold increase in the price of textiles, which enabled them to liquidate their assets (for the substantial sum of 3,000 *tomans*), close up shop, and return to Hamadan.[44]

Shakeri's troubled road to economic advancement was made possible by post-constitutional freedoms, new economic opportunities, and the growth of a national economy. Yet repeated political disruptions became impediments to development. Like Shakeri, many small merchants suffered from the post-Constitutional civil war and the counter-revolution (1910); followed by foreign occupation, famine and the chaos of World War I. This was followed by a global depression in the late 1920s and 1930s. These overwhelming obstacles can shed light on the question of why many merchants like Shakeri, despite their modern business ethics, their initial economic advancement, and their access to capital ultimately suffered from unremitting deprivation and poverty, especially in the inter-war period.

Modern Crises

In many instances, the transition from traditional to modern means of livelihood could prove difficult, even fatal. One case of frustrated economic advancement was that of Aqa Solayman, son of Baba Musheh, an early Baha'i in Hamadan. Solayman and his brothers worked in the family business as apothecaries (*'attar*), but found limited opportunities for advancement, since their education was limited to Judeo-Persian. After their father's death, Solayman and his brothers started an import business through Baghdad and Tabriz; but "like many other merchants" they failed and lost their entire investment. Solayman, whose sons had also failed in similar ventures, died from depression (*maraz-e deqq*) in 1914.[45]

Shakeri's numerous ventures with his brothers in Malayer and Hamadan in the wholesale and retail business of textiles, though at times somewhat successful, eventually led to bankruptcy around 1921. For Shakeri this was the ultimate shame, a reminder of his father's past and a betrayal of his Baha'i image and work ethic.[46] Yet other more structural forces were also at play. As Hamadan's economy suffered from a shift in trade routes from Basra to the Persian Gulf ports in the 1940s, Shakeri, like many other small merchants, left his family behind to take up residence in Tehran. There he took on a low-salary apprentice job "worse than being an errand boy . . . working day and night including Fridays" for a Jewish Baha'i antique exporter to the United States.[47]

Though by no means a consistent beneficiary of the city's prosperity, Shakeri witnessed Hamadan's rapid economic expansion and the new social mobility within the Jewish community during the 1920s. Business contacts in Baghdad, though they did not prove profitable for Shakeri's father, were now a source of instant wealth. Owing to a number of regional factors, Hamadan around the turn of the century became Iran's center for British textile distribution. Through their Iraqi Jewish contacts, a number of Hamadan Jews and Jewish Baha'is were at the center of a lucrative trade [see Plate 10]. Shakeri could later remark: "The Israelite brethren all became importers, wholesalers, brokers and clothiers, etc. They prospered and [many] bought large properties with running water from Muslims in Hamadan and [estates] in surrounding villages." [48]

The Trials of Faith

Just as Shakeri struggled for economic survival during troubled times, he also had to deal with the formidable challenges of preserving his new faith. Prior to his migration to Tehran, Shakeri spent many years in the small community of Malayer. Although initially it was a relatively free environment for Baha'is, by 1911 when Shakeri arrived there the community had become inactive after persecutions and the murder of two prominent Baha'is a few months earlier. Malayer may be an example of how vulnerable small Baha'i communities were in the face of the rise of traditionalist elements during the anti-constitutional period.[49]

Isolated and concerned with losing his enthusiasm, as some others evidently had, Shakeri asked a Baha'i friend and teacher for guidance and prayers. "The only way not to have your faith quenched is by teaching it," replied his friend.[50] For many early Baha'is, engagement in religious debate and conversion of others to their faith, was a means to reassure themselves in their beliefs as much as it was a way to convince others. A vital connection with the wider international Baha'i community was made through a subscription to the Baha'i periodical, *Najm-e Bakhtar* (*Star of the West*), which Shakeri shared in secret with other Malayer Baha'is. The bilingual publication mailed to Iran from the United States was a new window onto a growing international community. It reinforced Shakeri's cosmopolitan identity and helped the isolated believer identify himself with a growing movement, with followers in places in Europe and America that most Iranians had never heard of.[51]

Anxiety over keeping his faith and also over possibly becoming the target of new persecutions was paradoxically accompanied by a sense of empowerment. For reasons Shakeri does not explain, the small group of Malayer Baha'is came to enjoy a good deal of local influence. One can speculate that by the late 1910s the Baha'is were better educated and played an important part in the post-Constitutional state building efforts such as the establishment of the gendarmerie.[52] The development of these power relations further complicated inter-communal relations with the Jews. On the one hand, there was a good deal of positive interaction based on common interests. For example, as non-Muslims were not allowed in the public baths, Shakeri and another Jewish convert established a new Jewish bathhouse and used the proceeds to pay the salary of a rabbi whom they hired from a nearby community to perform Jewish ritual slaughter.[53]

On another occasion, Shakeri was instrumental in retrieving the body of the aforementioned peddler Aqa Haym Sion who had been murdered in the hazardous countryside of Arak. Shakeri learned about the incident from an unidentified source. Since the few Jews in Malayer were afraid to venture into the area, he and a group of five other Baha'is volunteered to take on the dangerous task of retrieving the corpse for proper burial—an essential necessity for the salvation of the deceased, according to Jewish belief. Empowered by their new social standing, Shakeri and his friends received help from the head of the Malayer gendarmerie, who was an influential coreligionist. He gave them a letter addressed to his counterpart in Khondab without whose help entering into the unruly area would have been too risky. After traveling on foot to Khondab, the friendly gendarme officer gave them horses and accompanied them with his men in a challenging search to find the grave:

> They had dug a shallow grave in the middle of the night. Unable to see in the dark, they had left his feet sticking out. . . . His donkey was meandering around with some of his merchandise (fabric) draping from it. As soon as his son Yuhanna saw the grave, he said, "These are my father's shoes." The officer said, "You must bury him here, as he was killed eighteen days ago." But I said, "he is Jewish and his family wants to visit his grave and to say prayers for him." We pulled the corpse from under the dirt, and they brought a ladder to carry the corpse on a mule, We got to Khondab late at night. There, we left the corpse in the mosque. But soon people complained saying: "Your corpse has polluted our mosque." Immediately, we sent men to move it. The village elders were very hospitable to us [in spite of Shakeri's Jewish association and perhaps because of the his connection to the officer]. Eventually we managed to bring the corpse to Malayer. But we suffered immensely, as human-corpse stench is worse than that of any animal."[54]

Shakeri's extaordinary efforts to ensure the proper observance of Jewish burial practice may be an indication of how committed he remained to the force of tradition. Yet despite these services, he nonetheless had belligerent confrontations with the "Israelite brethren." In one instance, months of religious arguments with a few contentious Jews led to insults against Baha'i holy figures and a confrontation that nearly turned violent, although the two sides made peace shortly afterwards.[55]

Despite these occasional tensions, at times Shakeri was able to take on the role of community arbiter. When Aqa Ebrahim Kashi divorced his wife by paying the appropriate fee to a certain rabbi, Mulla Ebrahim

Haym, Shakeri was called in to mend the family dispute. He rejected the grounds for divorce, the wife's supposed inability to bear a son, and claimed that the true reason had more to do with Aqa Ebrahim becoming wealthy and his desire to marry a more qualified woman. "What is the fault of this poor estranged woman?" Shakeri claims to have said. He then, using his persuasion skills, managed to reverse the divorce on the condition that the wife would become pregnant with a son within a year. He claims to have saved the marriage by making a vow to Baha'u'llah for him to provide the unhappy couple with a male offspring. When their son was born, they oddly named him Nurullah.[56]

This sense of bold engagement was not limited to relations with Malayer's small Jewish community. In the absence of Baha'i institutions, Shakeri and his friend felt the need to take charge of the affairs of the small Baha'i community as well. On one occasion in the village of Uzman in the 1910s, where many had converted, including the main land owner, Shakeri reports collecting a fine of one *toman* for disobedience of Baha'i prohibitions on participation in politics (*khatay-e amri*). He then used the fine to feed a gathering of nine Baha'is. "What a memorable night. . . . There were nine of us chanting prayers and singing songs from Baha'i poets and classical Persian poetry, and everyone said, 'That was the best meal we ever had.'" [57]

Yet Shakeri had his own share of faith-related trials and anxieties. At a critical point in his life, during the late 1920s, he seems to have been gravely concerned about the possible consequences of his association with coreligionists who had criticized Shoghi Effendi's leadership. If Shakeri himself never subscribed to such critical views, his anxieties may have stemmed from his fear of incurring guilt by association. Fearing that Shoghi Effendi might excommunicate him from the Baha'i community, and as an assertion of loyalty, Shakeri and two other Baha'is took a group photograph to send to the Baha'i leader. On the back was written a single plea: to be treated "not with justice but with mercy."[58]

This kind of demanding view of the individual by Baha'i institutions may be seen as the beginning of the kind of institutional authority that increasingly became characteristic of Baha'i life. For example, Shakeri appears to be more puritanical and judgmental than Rayhani. This might be explained in part by Rayhani belonging to an earlier community of Babis and Baha'is, less engaged with piety and matters of law and authority and more interested in personal relationships and connections. On one occasion in Malayer, Shakeri, who disapproved of Aqa Ebrahim Kashi's multi-confessional activities, being "Jew, Christian, or Baha'i at different times," demanded that he cut his young son Nurullah's long hair, which he had allowed to grow as part of a Sufi vow.[59] Shakeri was also critical of some Baha'is for having utilitarian purposes for associating with the Baha'i community and questioned their loyalty to the faith. [60]

Conversion and Empowerment

At times, association with the Qajar elite was a source of empowerment to converts such as Shakeri. Among the Qajar Baha'i elite, Shakeri mentions Hamadan's governor Gholam Reza Khan Ehtesham al-Dowleh, son-in-law of Mozaffar al-Din Shah and son of Zayn al-Abedin Khan Qaragozlu (known as Amir-Afkham), the prominent governor of the Hamadan region known for his enormous wealth. The family's association with the Babis and later the Bahai's, mostly through the women, goes back to their relationship with the early Babi woman leader Tahereh. Ehtesham al-Dowleh helped defend Hamadan's Baha'i center after it was threatened by a mob in 1909.[61] Like Mehdi Khan Ghaffari in Kashan, Ehtesham al-Dowleh represents the post-constitutional Qajar elite in decline. Some of these were attracted to the Baha'is, possibly as more moderate advocates of modernity and as an alternative to the radical constitutionalists who were influenced by the Azalis.

Less celebrated, but often more useful, were the converts' connections with scattered centers of urban power such as the *luti* elements. In the absence of a modern police force, governors at times hired the local *lutis* as their agents, partly as means of placating them. In Hamadan around 1915, Shakeri and his Baha'i friends had close relations with a certain Nayeb Mirza, a leading *luti* leader, a government agent (*farrash*) and, according to Shakeri, "a close friend of Reza Khan [Mirpang, later Pahlavi]." On occasion he protected Shakeri's friends. When the Jewish elders filed the usual complaints with the authorities against them, along with payment of a bribe, Nayeb Mirza intervened. He became a Baha'i through Shakeri's efforts and soon after destroyed all the alcohol in his home, though he later went back to drinking. Later on, according to Shakeri, Nayeb Mirza was wrongfully convicted for the murder of an innocent bystander in a typical *luti* street fight and was executed around 1918. The incident can be seen as a sign of the end of urban unruliness during the pre-Pahlavi phase of central authority development.[62]

Just as significant as the converts' ties to the declining *lutis* and Qajar aristocracy were their connections to the modern security forces. On one occasion in Malayer, around the time of the 1918 famine, influential Baha'is within the newly formed gendarmerie helped to release Shakeri's associates who ran a bakery and had gotten into a fight with a gendarmerie official during a supposed bread riot.[63] These cross-cutting ties to various centers of urban power were crucial for the Baha'is' survival, being a small and marginalized minority with many enemies.[64]

The Baha'i Community

Economic opportunities in Hamadan coincided with an escalating rate of Baha'i conversion and, according to Shakeri, increasing tension and estrangement between the Baha'i and the Jewish communities. After the Baha'i assembly, in an attempt to foreclose the option of multiple religious identities among their new converts, required them to open shop on the Sabbath, the rabbis refused them the use of the Jewish bath and the Jewish cemetery. The Baha'i response was to establish their own bath and their own cemetery.[65] After the rabbis stopped performing wedding ceremonies for converts, the Baha'is began performing their own ceremonies, and there was no fee required for a cleric. One new convert even offered to perform free circumcisions on newborn boys.[66]

A sense of empowerment was reinforced through the Baha'is' vibrant community life in Hamadan. In addition to regular Friday morning meetings for prayers and socialization at the Baha'i center, there were Saturday afternoon meetings for "seekers," where discussion of prophecies and reading of the scripture often led to conversions. Organized efforts to raise funds to support Baha'i teachers started relatively early in the twentieth century.

Baha'i community life also included a fair amount of entertainment, leisure, and personal bonding. A taste for the outdoors cultivated through organized hiking trips to the countryside was an expression of a modern outlook. A favorite activity in such outings was group singing of Baha'i poems and prayers. Persian music, poetry, and stories, often instilled a sense of fraternity in the enjoyment of these new forms of entertainment. Prior to the advent of the gramophone and the radio, there were few opportunities available to listen to music outside of synagogue chants. Shakeri repeatedly recounts the exhilarating and "unique" experiences he had in Baha'i meetings as he traveled throughout the region. In addition to Baha'i principles and writings, moralistic and anecdotal themes from Persian literature and fables were often heard in speeches and discussions. Sometimes an itinerant teacher would take on the role of entertaining the congregants. Shakeri describes an instance in the village of Amzajerd where 150 people were singing and greeting a Baha'i teacher, who in turn treated them to the unusual experience of what amounted to a comedy performance. He told funny stories that caused "men and women to laugh for half an hour."[67] This must have been a novel experience in a setting dominated by Iranian Shi'i culture, where the most common reason for gathering (outside of mosque attendance) was to perform a mourning ceremony.

Life as a convert entailed many novelties and new experiences that made the risk of harassment and persecution more tolerable. In 1934, when enhanced security and improved roads had greatly facilitated domestic travel, Shakeri undertook his first extended visit as a tourist to Tehran and Mazandaran. This modern experience was made easier by a network of Baha'i families in small towns and villages who warmly received him in their homes. In Tehran he was invited and fed by no less than 20 Baha'i households, and he recounts his experience of attending large meetings as "a glimpse of heaven." In Mazandaran he visited and stayed with a network of Jewish Baha'i physicians whose conversions had facilitated their residence in towns and villages where there were no Jewish communities.[68]

A Troubled Marriage

Shakeri's exposure to modernity had little effect on his conduct in family matters as he contracted a traditional marriage that was characteristic of the time. When he returned to Hamadan from Malayer in 1915, a few years after his conversion, he had accumulated enough wealth to have a respectable wedding. At the age of 30 or 36, he married a 13-year-old girl, whom he reports as having been presented to him as a 15-year-old. Her mother, Tuti, was a young widow who had married a widower with a teen-aged son who was Shakeri's friend. The girl therefore had to be married off, since it would have been considered indecent for the young step-brother and -sister to live together in the newly formed household. Both Shakeri and his bride were supposedly drawn into the marriage against their wills:

> I was tricked. The girl had not yet even reached puberty and had no knowledge or instruction in the Baha'i faith. She wanted a young, good-looking, tie-wearing man and had no interest in marrying me. My mistake was that I did not send anyone to investigate her. During the 90-day engagement period, I did not dare to have much contact with her or to get to know her.[69]

Shakeri does not admit to any of his own possible fantasies that may have made such a young girl attractive to him.

Familiar complaints about the expenses and difficulties of the wedding ceremonies were compounded when, on the wedding night, the marriage was not consummated. The young bride, who had registered her displeasure by spilling ink on the marriage contract, "ran away to her mother's house [and hid in the] coal storage room in her wedding gown." She was slapped in the face by a male cousin, and soon after developed an hysterical condition. All remedies proved ineffective and only further drained Shakeri's finances. These included seeking the assistance of a Muslim soothsayer, which Shakeri describes as a "stupid mistake." Soon after the wedding, Shakeri went back to Malayer, temporarily leaving his child bride with his mother in Hamadan and arranging for the girl to continue her schooling.[70] The two finally came together but had a troubled relationship, even though for several years Shakeri lived in Malayer, away from his family.

Eventually his tormented marriage came to an end, presumably in part due to his inability to provide sufficiently for his wife, and to her lack of interest in the Baha'i faith. Shakeri does not go into details of how his wife of seventeen years managed to divorce him and to remarry. However, his description of running into his six children, aged 3 to 16, on a roadside in Tehran after they had been "dropped off" by their mother is one of the more moving parts of his memoirs. Virtually homeless and penniless, and having been denied help even from the Baha'i assembly, he was at one of the lowest points in his life. His sole protection at this time came from a Baha'i family who provided him with food and shelter. Later, for a number of years he struggled to support his children on his own and with the help of his twelve-year-old daughter who took on the household chores.

Like Rayhani and many of his compatriots, Shakeri never completely recovered from his economic downfall and could never adjust to the new national economy that was centered in Tehran. Both Rayhani and Shakeri lacked essential economic skills, such as a proper education, sufficient capital, and overseas business contacts, to engage in the increasingly profitable and sophisticated import-export trade. In Tehran he worked for an antique dealer exporting to New York, a serious loss of status. He complains bitterly about mistreatment by his employer. One of Shakeri's few remaining options was to become a real estate agent, a difficult calling in which he never succeeded. During his last years in Tehran, Shakeri had to settle for a less desirable occupation as a construction supervisor.

Shakeri represents a turn-of-the-century convert who was caught between forces of change and tradition. Intellectually he felt liberated by his conversion from what he saw as outmoded beliefs and practices. He was also socialized into a community with a more cosmopolitan outlook and with a diverse membership. Yet in many ways he remained a traditional man. His transitional predicament was one cause for the failure of his marriage. Moreover, by the time of his arrival in Tehran in the late 1930s, at a time of state-sponsored secularism, his version of modernity—lacking Western education, access to capital and freedom from tradition—had little currency and had already lost much of its value.

8

THE HAFEZ AL-SEHHEH FAMILY:
PRIVILEGES AND PERILS
OF CONVERSION

The last decades of the nineteenth century may be understood as an interim phase in the emergence of Iranian modernity. Change from within, as well as an increase in contacts with the West, presented serious challenges to traditional communal bonds of solidarity. At the same time, such developments created the social space that allowed certain individuals to negotiate new, alternative, multi-layered identities. The period also saw an increase in religious innovation and a loosening of stringent communal boundaries, which opened the door to increased interreligious interactions. By the beginning of the twentieth century, however, the changes introduced by state-sponsored secularization had, at least partially, reversed these religious ambiguities. State action helped revive and reinforce Jewish and Baha'i communal boundaries and re-polarize religious communities.[1]

Yuhanna Khan Hafezi (1870–1951) has written a long and detailed account of his family history and Hamadan's non-Muslim communities [see Plates 2, 6, 7, and 8]. Also known as Yahya, he was the son of the family patriarch Hakim Rahamim (1844–1942), later known as Mirza Rahim Khan Hafez al-Sehheh (superintendent of public health). Yuhanna Khan was educated in the American school in Hamadan in the mid-1880s. Later on as a young man, he accompanied his father to Baghdad where they lived for an extended time and where Rahamim carried on a successful medical practice. During the late Ottoman period, and later in the 1920s during the British Mandate, Baghdad was being transformed from a traditional provincial capital into a cosmopolitan regional center.

Unlike most Jews of his time, Yuhanna Khan was as literate in Persian as he was in his traditional, communal Judeo-Persian. He was also competent in English and familiar with Arabic. His broad cultural abilities gave him a sophisticated worldview that was rare among his peers. Like a number of his family members, he became a leading physician, but he was also a successful businessman. His family was well connected to the Hamadan landed notables and Qajar officials, as family physicians and business associates. Yuhanna's attention to detail, his remarkable memory, his informed insight, and his relative openness make his memoir a unique source for social, economic, and religious history in the Hamadan region. Unlike the accounts of the self-educated and underprivileged Rayhani and Shakeri, he was able to chronicle the story of a wealthy and influential family's accomplishments, perils, and challenges as they sought to negotiate multiple identities in a rapidly changing nation.

Sufis, Philosophers, and Physicians

Yuhanna Khan's father, Hakim Rahamim (Rahim Khan Hafez al-Sehheh), was probably the most influential Jewish convert of Hamadan. His long life (1844–1942) coincides with the rise and fall of Hamadan as an important trade center, the rise of a new religion, and the advent of a secularizing modern state. His life also personifies a new age of interwoven identities and a wide spectrum of social change. Hakim Rahamim's family connections were as important a factor in his success as were his personal abilities. His family was prominent among a small group of relatively well-to-do Jewish physicians in Hamadan who almost monopolized the profession within the region.

Hakim Rahamim's grandfather, Mushe (or Mu'iz), also known as Falsafi Sufi (philosopher mystic), appears to have been a highly educated "free thinker" (azad-andish) and mystic. He reportedly even held a Sufi circle (khaneqah) in his home, in addition to sponsoring one of Hamadan's Jewish synagogues.[2] Such an acceptance of different religious practices—perhaps all supporting an underlying common set of beliefs—can find deep roots in Iranian Sufism. The Rahamim family's openness to multiple religions may well be explained by their participation in Sufi orders going back to the early decades of the nineteenth century.[3]

Rahimim's grandfather, Mushe, was a goldsmith (*zargar*) and money changer (*sarraf*). He was imprisoned and nearly killed for dealing in a stolen, presumably jeweled, "royal cap" belonging to the crown prince, 'Abbas Mirza.[4] After his release from prison, Mushe abandoned previous metal work and studied medicine. He started practice: first in Nahavand and later in Hamadan. In Hamadan, he was reportedly the object of the "jealousy" of other Jewish physicians. His remarkable change of profession presumably was the result of a pledge that he would never engage in his previous occupation. Medicine was one of the few professional alternatives open to a Jew, though it turned out to be no less hazardous. Reportedly, he died as a result of injuries he suffered after he was beaten by the relatives of a patient who died.[5]

Hakim Rahamim's father, Elyahu, son of Mushe, was orphaned at thirteen [see Plate 5]. He worked first as an apprentice under a Jewish physician, but left his job and managed to receive an education in Persian from a learned Muslim apothecary (*'attar*). He then used his knowledge of Persian and Arabic to study various medical texts.[6] Elyahu's practice in Hamadan gradually developed a favorable reputation. While still in his twenties, he reportedly became one of Hamadan's leading physicians, serving "the notables (*a'yan*), the aristocrats (*ashraf*), and the ulama" of the city.

Learning to read Persian (as opposed to Judeo-Persian) was unusual among Iran's Jews, who were generally forbidden to study Persian and Arabic or to apprentice with Muslims for reasons relating to religious "impurity." One plausible explanation for his ability to overcome this restriction may be found in the family's Sufi connections, and possibly even an informal conversion to Islam.[7] In any event, contrary to the conventional view that assumes strict ethnic segregation, sometimes close ties developed during the mid-nineteenth century between members of different religions.

Rahamim's relatives on his mother's side were also participants in interfaith dialogue and various intellectual debates. His mother, Tamar, was the daughter of a certain Mulla Elyahu, one of Hamadan's leading rabbis (not to be confused with the aforementioned Elyahu). Mulla Elyahu's elder son, Ela'zar Hain ben Elyahu (also known as Mulla Lazar, Persianized as Lalehzar), at one time a leader among Hamadan's Jews, was well versed in Persian, Jewish, and Islamic learning and took an interest in the Babi debates. As a man of learning and a secret convert to the Babi religion (or at least a sympathizer), he briefly hosted the Babi woman leader Tahereh Qorrat al-ʿAyn when she arrived in Hamadan in April 1847. Perhaps as a result of his various intellectual interests, or his prominent position of leadership, other Jewish elders later lodged complaints on two occasions against him with the shah based on unspecified charges of "encroachments or crimes" (*taʿadiyyat ya jaraʾem*).[8] As a result, Elaʿzar was forced to leave Hamadan and take sanctuary in Tehran. But he was able to return after the intercession of the influential Jewish court physician Hakim Yazqel (Haqq Nazar), a Babi convert or sympathizer (see Chapter Five).[9] According to Netzer, in Elaʿzar's surviving papers, his writings on ecumenical themes suggest that he "was involved with the [Babis and] Bahaʾis."[10]

Two years later in the mid-1850s, when similar complaints were made, Mulla Elaʿzar was forced to leave for the capital for a second time, where he took sanctuary with the French legation. This was at the time when Joseph Arthur Gobineau was responsible for the legation. The renowned French philosopher and historian had a keen interest in Iran's religion and culture and was the author of two works on the subject. His *Religions et philosophies dans l'Asie Centrale* extensively discusses the emergence of the Babi movement.[11] Using his connection with the French diplomat Gobineau, Elaʿzar presented his case to the shah. In a royal audience, he reportedly impressed the shah with his learned remarks and gained his release on the condition that he not return to his hometown of Hamadan. While in Tehran, Elaʿzar remained in close contact with Gobineau and with the cultured Parsi Zoroastrian representative in Tehran, Manakji Limji Hushang Hateria (Manakji Saheb).

Elaʿzar's collaboration with Gobineau is highly significant since it resulted in a new edition of a translation of one of Descartes' pivotal works, perhaps the first modern Persian translation of classical Western philosophy. As Gobineau recalls:

> It is mostly in the light of this [Mulla Sadra's] school that I trans-
> lated into Persian, with the help of a learned rabbi, Mulla Lalezar
> Hamadani, Descartes' *Discourse on Method*. Naser al-Din Shah
> dared to order its publication.[12]

The remark about the daring action of the shah most likely refers to the destruction of an earlier translation of the same work. A translation of *Discourse on Method* was first published in 1853 (1270 AH) a couple of years before Gobineau's arrival in Iran in 1855. (He resided in Iran between 1855 and 1861, and again between 1861 and 1863.) The book was reportedly "burned," most likely as the result of a fatwa of the ulama, presumably because it was considered subversive. If so, the ulama's response to Decartes was in keeping with the reaction of their seventeenth-century Catholic counterparts who strongly opposed Descartes' rational approach to religion and political authority.[13]

Ela'zar's role in this project is remarkable in a number of ways. It demonstrates his linguistic abilities in Persian and in French, which may well have been self taught. This is further demonstrated by his ability to collaborate with Gobineau on the publication of theoretical texts.[14] An even more important part of his career, unnoticed by most scholars, was his subversive role in resisting injustice and discrimination against subaltern Jews and nonconformists. His role in introducing what may be considered the genesis of a secular discourse underlines his contribution to the emergence of Iranian modernity. Ela'zar's subversive activities may well have been energized by his Babi leanings and by radical figures such as Tahereh Qorrat al-'Ayn.

The Patriarch's Early Career

It was within this family culture of learning and interfaith exchange that the young Rahamim, son of Elyahu and nephew of Ela'zar, would become an important link between the family's past and its new Baha'i affiliation. He received his education in Persian and Arabic from a tutor at home. He was reportedly especially well versed in Persian literature and mystical texts, many of which he had memorized. He later studied medicine with a certain Hajji Mirza 'Ali Qoli, using medical texts which were kept in his family library. Rahamim's lose association with a Muslim tutor indicates the family's extended interaction with people outside of the Jewish environment. Such avenues of learning, which were unavailable to other Jewish physicians of Hamadan, gave Rahamim a considerable advantage in his practice and led to increasing tensions with Hamadan's traditional physicians.

Rahamim's career got a boost around 1873, when he was invited to the northwest Ardebil region. He stayed there for three months to care for Sayf al-Molk, a close associate of Crown Prince Mozaffar al-Din Mirza. Impressed by Rahamim's skills, Sayf al-Molk invited him and his physician cousin, the aforementioned Hakim Aqajan, to Tabriz and introduced them to the crown prince, who offered his full support and encouraged them to stay and to start a practice there. Rahamim's son, Yuhanna Khan, claims that his father was unhappy with the severe discriminatory rules against the Jews which were enforced in Tabriz, the lack of a Jewish community and the difficulties he found in observing Jewish kosher laws. According to his son, such considerations forced the religious physician to return to Hamadan. However, according to Mazandarani, he in fact converted to Islam while in Tabriz, under circumstances unknown to us, and "became known as *jadid* [*al-Islam*]."[14] If this is in fact the case, it is possible that Hakim Rahamim may have later become disillusioned with his decision. In most instances, conversions to Islam did not eliminate the deep-rooted stigma attached to Jewish ancestry that most Muslims held. This might help explain Rahamim's search for a new community and his attraction to Christianity and to the Baha'i faith a few years later.

Even if Rahamim's association with the Tabriz royal entourage may have been soured by ethnic isolation and religious intolerance, such association significantly boosted his status and advanced his career. According to Yuhanna Khan, local landed notables of the Hamadan region "exclusively" sought his medical services, a considerable advancement for a 29-year-old physician who now demanded handsome fees. This allowed him to join an elite propertied class, a rarity in any case, but especially among the mostly impoverished Jews of Hamadan.[15]

Sometime around 1877, Hakim Rahamim and his cousin and associate Hakim Aqajan seem to have converted to Christianity at the onset of the evangelical activities of American Presbyterians in Hamadan, and may have been a cover for his Baha'i conversion. Curiously, their conversion to the Baha'i faith seems to have taken place almost simultaneously. Later in 1892, during the anti-Jewish persecutions, Rahamim's religious affiliations were supplemented by a conversion to Islam (or perhaps a reaffirmation of an earlier Tabriz conversion, now openly professed). Such a complex identity reflects the assortment of religious options suddenly available in Iran at the end of the nineteenth century—from American-style evangelism, to indigenous reformist Bahaism, and even more radical secular materialism. If conversion to Islam continued to promise only a lukewarm acceptance by the dominant Muslim community, the Christians and the Baha'is offered an enthusiastic welcome to converts. Their new interpretations of the Jewish sacred scriptures raised questions about what converts now saw as superstitious and outmoded traditional beliefs. Once the rationalist Pandora's box was opened, people like Rahamim could raise similar questions about traditional Christian beliefs, such as the doctrine of Holy Trinity. These were familiar questions traditionally raised by Muslim critics. They were now used by the Baha'is to attract Jewish converts in the Christian Church, who had taken an initial step towards finding an alternative to Judaism.

Ambition and Advancement

Around 1879–80, the new convert Rahamim, together with his cousin Hakim Aqajan, traveled to Tehran to expand their client base among Tehran's elite. They knew they could rely on the help of the notable physician Nur Mahmud, whose family had a history of friendship to their own (which would later lead to intermarriage). According to Rayhani, the two Hamadan physicians were on a mission to propagate the Baha'i faith to the family of Nur Mahmud.[16] In any case, the Hamadan physicians were able to expand their connections in Tehran beyond the provincial circles they had frequented.

In this respect, Rahamim's connections as a family physician with Hamadan's aristocracy turned out to be particularly helpful. The land owning Hesam al-Molk, of the powerful Qaragozlu family of western Iran, was among Iran's most affluent individuals at the time. Despite its power and influence, the Qaragozlu family had long-standing sympathies toward the Babi and (later) Baha'i religions. The women of the family had been particularly amiable to the new message ever since they had given refuge to Tahereh Qurrat al-'Ayn on their estate in 1847. The family also had marriage ties with Moshir al-Dowleh, with whom at times they interceded on behalf of the Baha'is. This connection later turned out to be of benefit to Hakim Rahamim in his dealings with the Grand Vizier and other members of the Qajar establishment.[17]

While Hakim Rahamim was in Tehran, and as part of a continuing conflict, Jewish elders from Hamadan and Tehran lodged a complaint with the grand vizier, Hosayn Khan Moshir al-Dowleh, charging that: "Hakim Rahamim and a few other Jews have become Babis and are violating the Jewish laws. They touch fire on the Sabbath and ride [mules?]…"[18] In response to Moshir al-Dowleh's inquiries, however,

Hakim Rahamim reportedly avoided discussion of his Baha'i conviction by professing Judaism and to have stated that he and others were merely investigating the Christian faith, just as they were obligated to investigate Islam. It is possible that he even went further and reaffirmed his previously adopted Muslim identity. After some scrutiny, the issue was settled with Moshir al-Dowleh's enlightened recommendation to Hakim Rahamim that: "You should keep your beliefs to yourself."[19] The incident demonstrates a change of attitude by more moderate Qajar officials towards those accused of Baha'i affiliation. By the 1880s, the Baha'i rejection of political violence as a means of reform was becoming better known to some within the Qajar ruling elite.

Remarkably, Hakim Rahamim's strategy and the peaceful resolution of the complaint provided new professional opportunities for the astute physician. Being an eye surgeon (*kahhal*), Hakim Rahamim's plan was to expand his practice in the capital. But soon after his encounter with the grand vizier, Hakim Rahamim faced yet another complaint, this time from Muslim physicians of Tehran, who might have felt threatened by the competition. In response to charges that he had defamed the reputation of one of Tehran's physicians, Hakim Rahamim had to defend his professional qualifications by answering to an add-hoc jury of Tehran's prominent physicians. The examination was adjudicated by none other than the notable Minister of Sciences, Prince Ali-Qoli Mirza E'tezad al-Saltaneh.[20] Hakim Rahamim's impressive performance reportedly gained him a formal certificate to practice (*tasdiq-nameh*) throughout the country, a source of envy even for his host, the celebrated Nur Mahmud.[21] Rahamim's superior medical knowledge may in part be explained by his earlier exposure to modern medicine through contact with the American missionary doctors.[22] As a convert to Christianity, Rahamim could well have received training in Western medicine, a substantial advantage among Hamadan's competitive physicians.

Hakim Rahamim spent most of the 1880s in Baghdad managing a lucrative medical practice.[23] Initially he faced opposition form the city's other Persian Jewish physicians. He was contemplating leaving Baghdad when he consulted a maverick group of Babi-Baha'is who reportedly bullied his enemies into submission.[24] Later, he occasionally returned to Hamadan with lavish displays of his wealth, including Arabian horses. On one occasion, Rahamim visited Hamadan with a concubine in his company, but he soon had to return her to Baghdad to put and end to protests staged against him on account of a non-Muslim owning a Muslim slave.[25]

During Hakim Rahamim's stay in Baghdad, his multi-layered identity found yet another dimension when he and his son Ya'qub became Ottoman subjects, in order to protect against accusations of being Babis and for their material well-being.[26] Ottoman citizenship meant additional protections, especially for non-Muslims, given the capitulatory rights for foreign subjects imposed by European powers on Qajar Iran. Foremost among these rights was general immunity from the jurisdiction of the Qajar judiciary, which was often administered by provincial governors or by the ulama's Shari'ah courts. Instead, judicial matters for all foreign subjects, Ottomans included, were handled through the foreign ministry and by Ottoman consular authorities.[27]

Conversion to Islam

Hakim Rahamim may be an exceptionally successful example of an aspiring Jewish physician who made use of multiple, layered identities to counter disadvantages and to cross-communal boundaries. It is tempting to dismiss his various conversions as purely utilitarian, even cynical. Yet central to his embrace of modernity were his evolving personal convictions and beliefs in the new faiths. These became an indispensable intellectual dimension of his transition, an anchor to modernity without which his adoption of modern ways would have been much more difficult if not impossible to achieve. Leaving behind tradition, by definition, entailed the need to question religion. The acceptance of a new messiah, therefore, provided a potent faith-based mechanism that allowed him to break away from old practices and ancient ingrained beliefs without discarding religion altogether.

In 1892, Hakim Rahamim, now in his forties, declared himself a Muslim. This was a perilous time for the Jews of Hamadan who experienced a new wave of persecution. The exact nature of Rahamim's circumstances during this period, as reported by his son Yuhanna, is not entirely clear. Nor is the sequence of events leading to his conversion explained. However, his open acceptance of Islam may be seen as yet another phase in his social adjustment and intellectual development.

As mentioned, other sources date Hakim Rahamim's conversion to Islam to a much earlier date during his stay in Tabriz in the 1870s.

His son's account marks his extended stay in the countryside, as physician to the Qaragozlu family, as his first steps toward the acceptance of Islam. Yuhanna suggests that the new surroundings gave his father a new incentive to declare his belief in Islam, presumably to eliminate social restrictions relating to ritual "impurity." Nevertheless, it is remarkable that he could adopt yet another religious identity given his earlier acceptance of Christianity and the Baha'i faith.

Yet the timing of Rahamim's conversion to Islam provides clues to more immediate causes for such a decision. September 1892 was a time of severe persecution for the Jews of Hamadan who were presented with the undesirable choice of either accepting Islam or conforming to strict medieval Islamic rules of subordination for non-Muslims.[28] Such laws governing the non-Muslims (*ahl-e dhimmah*) had periodically become a source of difficulty for the Jews. These laws had roots in Islamic medieval times but were further developed in the seventeenth century by the renowned Shi'i cleric Mulla Mohammad Baqer Majlesi (1616–98). His decrees came at the height of Shi'i clerical influence and coincide with the arrival of Catholic and Jesuit missionaries in Iran, many with anti-Semitic views common in seventeenth-century Europe.[29] The most humiliating among the long list of new prohibitions and compulsions introduced in this period was the requirement that Jews wear a patch.[30] By the nineteenth century, though some restrictions were still enforced, the more severe laws had been mostly forgotten.

According to Hafezi, these renewed restrictions imposed on the Jews of Hamadan in 1872 were subject to the ephemeral nature of Qajar society and only lasted for a year. It is possible that Hafezi understated the length and severity of anti-Jewish persecutions. However, given the short-term motives of the perpetuators of the anti-Jewish campaign in Hamadan, the loose nature of the anti-Jewish coalition, and the difficulty of enforcing any new rules under a fragile and powerless local government, his assessment does not seem farfetched.[31]

Open conversion to Islam, however, would have helped Hakim Rahamim (now known by the Islamic version of his name, 'Abd al-Rahim, or Rahim) overcome a number of day-to-day obstacles relating to matters of ritual purity, especially at a time of heightened pressure on the Jews. For a physician who had to attend to patients in isolated locations inhospitable to Jews, conversion to Islam was not solely a step towards assimilation, but arguably a necessary step for gaining equality before the Shari'ah legal system.

Legal and economic necessities went hand in hand with intellectual needs. For Baha'i converts who accepted Islam, the intellectual path to Muslim beliefs had already been paved. As a Baha'i, Rahamim reportedly gradually came to question the necessity of maintaining a Jewish public persona. He stated to his son: "I wanted to save myself and my family from this stigma [of being a Jew] . . . [and] as [Baha'is] we had no objection to the validity of Islam and the prophet Muhammad."[32] On the other hand, for a physician of Rahamim's stature, an open Baha'i identity could result in serious professional harm and would have been extremely risky, if not impossible to sustain. Adoption of a Muslim persona, therefore, became the rational extension of a long process of negotiating religious identities.

Persecution and Mass Conversion

Such material advantages notwithstanding, it was the dynamic of the 1892 persecution episode that triggered Rahamim's formal acceptance of Islam. These occurrences are best seen within the context of Hamadan's disorderly, even rebellious, political environment throughout the 1890s. The success of the 1890–91 Tobacco Rebellion led to a distinct increase in the influence of the ulama, while causing a decline in central and provincial authority. This, in turn, led to the expansion of the power of the landed aristocracy, with their chronic land disputes and infighting. These conditions became fertile ground for the ulama to gain power by taking sides in disputes, acting as judges in property cases, and by becoming key players in the urban violence when land disputes on occasion spilled over into fighting between city quarters.[33]

One leading player in the increasingly complex local politics of Hamadan was Mulla 'Abdullah Borujerdi (d. October 16, 1896), a leading local mujtahed also known as Akhund-e Mulla 'Abdullah. Originally from Borujerd, he established a base in Hamadan in the 1880s. His personal appeal and outward expressions of piety, including enforcement of a strict ban on the public use of opium, won him a large following.[34] His connections with local land owning families, the local *lutis*, and Tehran's high-ranking ulama gave him the confidence to assert his influence in Hamadan. By 1888, he was confident enough to take on the city's Shaykhi faction, declaring them nonbelievers (*mortad*) and ritually impure—thus refusing them the use of the main mosque.

This turned out to be a miscalculation, however. The governor of the city, the celebrated 'Abdul-Hosain Mirza Farmanfarma, with the support of the chief minister Mirza Yusof Mostowfi al-Mamalek, arranged for Mulla 'Abdullah's banishment to Tehran, where he was detained for two years. His return to Hamadan was arranged through Tehran's ulama, who interceded on his behalf with Qajar officials.[35]

Upon his return to Hamadan around 1890, Mulla 'Abdullah naturally sought to rebuild his former influence. It is plausible to see this entire episode of Jewish persecution in Hamadan as an opportunity for Mulla 'Abdullah to once again exercise broad authority by exploiting rising anti-Jewish sentiment. Perhaps because of deteriorating urban conditions, the improved economic status of some Jews in Hamadan was the source of considerable resentment among the general public. Moreover, Mulla 'Abdullah may have foreseen the important advantage he could gain from forced conversion of Jews. By bringing under his own influence a growing number of affluent Jews, such as Hakim Rahamim, he could collect religious taxes from them in return for extending legal protection and political advantage.

Be that as it may, the immediate circumstances leading to the outbreak of this wave of anti-Jewish violence cannot be delineated with certainty. According to one account, the abduction of a young Jewish girl and her conversion to Islam, followed by her change of mind, her desire to recant Islam, and her wish to return to her family may have caused the uproar. As mentioned above, it was not unusual for destitute Jewish women and victims of domestic abuse to flee their homes and convert to Islam.[36]

Hafezi, on the other hand, attributes the outbreak of Jewish persecution to a group of drunken Jews, including a Jewish musician, on their way home from Hamadan's countryside, who supposedly bullied two Muslim laborers into dancing for them. Ironically, it was common for Jewish peddlers to be humiliated by Muslims in this same fashion. Some of the followers of Mulla 'Abdullah who witnessed the incident reported it to him and it was seen as a general insult to the Muslim community by Jews. The next day, Mulla 'Abdullah ordered the offending Jews to be bastinadoed, delivered them to the governor for further punishment, and demanded enforcement of the medieval laws against the Jews.[37] According to a newly discovered Judeo-Persian document, Mulla 'Abdullah's fury also included an attack on Baha'is of Muslim origin "all of whom" reportedly "went into hiding." The source also reports that Jewish Baha'is converted to Islam but refused to "curse" Baha'u'llah even after they were tortured.[38]

Beyond their immediate causes, such incidents of Jewish persecution often had deeper social roots. Interestingly, Hafezi reports there were rising public tensions against Jews months before the issuance of the anti-Jewish edict. Such resentments mostly stemmed from the rise in the social and economic status of the Jews. As stated by Rahamim's son, the Muslims were complaining that: "The Jews are getting too bold, their appearance is not distinguishable form Muslims. They ride horses and wear fine (*fakher*) clothing, to the point that Muslims who do not know them precede in greeting them [with *salam 'alaikum*]." Yuhanna also points out that the Muslims were especially hostile to him and his older brother Ya'qub for their conspicuous displays of wealth: towards Yuhanna "for riding horses [and] towards my brother for having servants accompany him in the manner of nobles. On occasion, when Ya'qub went hunting, he even showed off his [precious] guns and hounds."[39] In a meeting with the Jewish leaders, Mulla 'Abdullah complained about the fine attire worn by wealthy Jews and threatened persecution if they did not agree to some restrictions.[40]

This unease with Jewish wealth, referred to as "boldness," may be seen as an expression of anxiety over even occasional challenges to the customary role of the Jews in Iran as the destitute "Other," expected to act as the subordinate to the dominant Muslim "self." This psychological dimension of persecution is seldom discussed in the Western sources or in conventional Persian accounts of the period, which mostly stress the ethnic and religious significance of the events.[41]

In an attempt to resist the new Jewish-patch rules, a few dozen Jewish men who seem to have been among the more affluent, took refuge (*bast*) at the city's telegraph office and sent appeals to Tehran and to European authorities through the Alliance Israélite administrators in Baghdad.[42] Mulla 'Abdullah ordered his own followers to close the bazaar on the following day and to stage their own counter-protest (*bast*) at the telegraph office, sending counter-appeals to the shah presumably complaining of Jewish disrespect towards Muslims and demanding strict enforcement of medieval Shi'i rules. Subsequently, a large crowd of some five thousand of 'Abdullah's supporters surrounded the telegraph house. The crowds intimidated the guards, threatening to "takeover and plunder the office, and to kill the Jews" who had taken refuge inside. The telegraph officer, Mirza Asadullah Hamadani, who happened to be a Shaykhi, and whose community had already been victimized by Mulla 'Abdullah, soon found himself a target of sectarian hostility by the aggressive crowd. Fearful and defenseless, he was unable to provide further protection to the Jews.[43]

While in the telegraph office, some thirty or forty Jews, in a desperate move to end a life-threatening situation, converted to Islam. They left their sanctuary and asked for protection in the house of Mulla 'Abdullah. On the way, some managed to flee to their homes while others were brought before Mulla 'Abdullah. Mindful of prohibitions against forced conversions, Mulla 'Abdullah promised them his protection and allowed them to return home. He also invited them to carefully consider their decision to profess Islam. After some back and forth, about twenty Jews converted. In addition to adopting Islamic names, they were ordered by 'Abdullah to take an "Islamicizing ritual immersion" (*ghosl-e eslamiyyat*) and were given regular instruction and training in Islamic obligations, such as prayers.[44]

In addition to Hakim Rahim and his son Yuhanna, who accepted Islam while in the village of Sheverin, the residence of the Qaragozlu notables, and his older son Ya'qub, who later converted at Mulla 'Abdullah's house, Yuhanna lists the names of some of the Jews who converted under duress during this episode, including many of his own relatives:

> Hakim Musa 'Amu, known as Mirza Musa [Ehteshami, whose family later became Christians]; Aqa Mashiyah Hajji Lalezar, who became Mirza Mehdi [Lalehzari]; Hakim Yari, who became Mirza Taher [Hakim Rahim's son-in-law, who was later known as Taher Baher. His son became a prominent Baha'i gynecologist, but was later expelled from the Baha'i community]; Yari, who became Mehdi; Ebrahim Hazqiya, who became Mirza Ebrahim; his son, [also] Hazqiya, who became Yahya; Khodadad Aqa Yahuda, who became Mirza Khodadad-e Jadid; Mirza Ya'qub 'Alaqband, along with his sons; Eliya Dallal, who became Mirza 'Ali, together with his two sons, Ebrahim and Eshaq; Aqajan Aqa 'Ezria, who became Mirza 'Ali; 'Aziz Dallal, who became Mirza 'Aziz; Morad Jarrah (surgeon), who became Mirza Morad Jarrah; his son Rabi', our house servant, who remained Rabi'; Nisan Gabra'il, who became Nasir [who received "tablets" from Baha'u'llah, mar-

ried a Muslim woman and went to Karbela for pilgrimage. His son, Yusof, married Hakim Rahim's daughter, Dina, and was a devout Baha'i. Yusof had two sons—Habib, a Baha'i physician, and Gholam-Hosain, a Muslim military officer. Yusof's daughter, Farahangiz, was a Baha'i]; Morad Zargar (goldsmith); and a few others whose names I can't recall.[45]

Despite the terrifying circumstances of the conversions and the humiliating acts of coercion, in due course some converts reverted back to Judaism under pressure from family members. Others remained nominal Muslims and seem to have found comfort in a relative improvement in their social standing, even joining the circle of Mulla 'Abdullah himself that was among the city's most influential groups. Some affluent Jews, such as Hakim Rahim and his two sons, Ya'qub and Yuhanna (Yahya), who frequented local notable circles, were warmly received with feasts given by Mulla 'Abdullah's prominent followers celebrating their conversion to Islam, perhaps because of their social standing.[46]

Yet in general, most Jews of Hamadan never considered conversion. They, above all, could not abide violating the kosher dietary laws. Their only choice, if they wanted to escape the humiliating patch (other than staying home) was to leave town "for a while" and continue a Jewish life in places like Tehran. For women whose relatives converted to Islam, the experience of accepting Islam was particularly painful, since they were generally more observant of the laws and practices of Judaism, especially concerning the preparation of food. Yet at least in the case of the Hafezi family, the women were finally persuaded to accept Islam a few months after the men.

For the vast majority of mostly disadvantaged Jews who maintained their ancestral faith, the painful reality of wearing a patch for all males over the age of ten became inevitable. Even an attempt by Jewish physicians to obtain an exemption was denied. Although the anti-Jewish prohibitions only lasted a year, after which they faded out in the complexities of local politics, "the miseries of the Jews only worsened by the day." This was not the case for many who maintained a Muslim identity, at least on the surface.[47]

For the relatively few who remained Muslims, one of the more important advantages they enjoyed was arguably their new equality before the Shari'ah legal system. Conversion to Islam was also a source of social support and legal protection. As converts, they became devotees (*maradeh*, pl. *morid*) of Mulla 'Abdullah, who certified their conversion, to whom they now paid religious taxes, and whose opinion they could rely on in commercial and property disputes. Such an arrangement offered important legal standing and access to a prominent religious authority. These were crucial requirements for an upwardly mobile group of Jews and Jewish Baha'is with a considerable interest in commerce and land ownership.

According to the Presbyterian missionary James Hawkes, the conversions to Islam after the anti-Jewish persecutions in Hamadan generated some interest in Christianity, a year or so later—though he gives no figures on the number of converts.[48] It is possible that those who had already distanced themselves from Judaism by converting to Islam now became more willing to consider other religions as well, including Christianity and the Baha'i faith.

Among the poor Jewish men who converted to Islam during this episode was a certain Mirza Eshaq, son of Ebrahim. His half brother, Gholam-Hosain, also became a Muslim and, like many other converts to Islam, subsequently a Baha'i. He was a house servant and a textile repairman, with a talent for music. He studied various instruments with masters in Tehran and occasionally worked as a professional musician. He even traveled to Palestine to visit 'Abdu'l-Baha, accompanied by a Baha'i vocalist. In Iran, when he was invited to perform at "reveling festivities," he reportedly at times used such occasions to spread the Baha'i message.[49]

Mulla 'Abdullah and Power Politics

Mulla 'Abdullah's colorful career points to the many complexities of the religious and political culture of Iran in the 1890s. By the end of 1892, after the implementation of his anti-Jewish restrictions, 'Abdullah's influence was at a new height: a reported 20,000 followers prostrated behind him in prayer. Yet such influence had its own hazards, as it naturally attracted the hostility of other ulama. Among his rivals was a certain Haji Aqa Mohammad, whose main source of income was reportedly to "find pretexts to extort money from the Jews."[50] The conversions now deprived him of income, and he blamed Mulla 'Abdullah for giving the Jews his protection in return for their loyalty and outward subordination.

In the meantime, the Jews of Hamadan had appealed to the British government, and the diplomatic pressures that resulted forced the shah to reprimand Mulla 'Abdullah. Demanding an end to harassment of the Jews, the shah ordered him to Tehran and replaced the governor with Prince Jahansuz Mirza. The defiant Mulla 'Abdullah sought immunity by moving to the residence of the Ottoman consular representative and repudiated the new governor by issuing competing and conflicting edicts in land disputes and criminal cases.[51]

Tensions reached a new height when Mulla 'Abdullah, now involved in local land disputes, took the unusually bold step of calling for the governor's expulsion. After a couple of days of the Akhund's absence from daily prayers, his followers took notice of his signals, closed the bazaar, and joined in demonstrations leading to violence and mayhem in front of the governor's house. Desperate and defenseless in the face of the large, aggressive crowds, Jahansuz Mirza fled the city. The mob then attacked the governor's house and looted his entire property. His futile attempt to reoccupy the office he had dearly paid for was blocked by forceful public opposition.[52]

Humiliated by this obvious loss of provincial control, the central government was caught between the rising power of ulama and local landowners and foreign pressure to protect the Jews. Its response is indicative of the increasing weakness of central authority. Unable to raise troops to put down the urban revolt or to arrest the rebellious cleric, the chief minister, Amin al-Sultan, engineered the support of the ulama of Najaf to reprimand him. Afterwards, the landowners who supported him were called to Tehran where they were briefly imprisoned. Mulla 'Abdullah, perhaps in response to the Najaf appeal, chose to go to the capital—ostensibly to make his case to the shah for his innocence and the innocence of the landowners in the ongoing rebellion. His departure marked the beginning of the end of the anti-Jewish prohibitions.[53]

Regardless of Mulla 'Abdullah's role in the embarrassing affair, the shah was content to keep him in Tehran, away from trouble, while punishing the defiant landowners.[54] In the capital, however, the cunning Mulla 'Abdullah found a large following in the city's main mosque and became a contestant in Tehran's urban political skirmishes by taking part in a dispute between two leading *mujtaheds* of Tehran, Mirza Hasan Ashtiyani and his old friend and covert Azali leader, Mirza

Hadi Dowlatabadi.[55] According to Hafezi, Mulla 'Abdullah himself had Azali-Babi affiliations. This is a remarkable allegation, given the fact that other sources have portrayed him as an unyielding anti-Babi figure.[56] However, if true, he would not be the only Shi'i cleric with alleged Azali association around the turn of the century who was responsible for anti-Jewish persecutions.[57]

Alarmed by Mulla 'Abdullah's rising influence and slick political maneuvering, the shah followed the advise of the Tehran ulama, sent him gifts, and asked that he return to Hamadan. A crowd of well-wishers, reportedly in the thousands, celebrated his triumphant return to Hamadan. But the presence of the troublesome Mulla in Hamadan accentuated ulama rivalries and urban factional fighting. He disrupted the city's life by repeatedly instigating the closure of the bazaar and by refusing to lead the Friday prayers.[58]

Such an environment of factional hostility and weakened central authority typically made conditions ripe for anti-Jewish violence. Ironically, it was the direct intervention of Mulla 'Abdullah himself that prevented another potential disaster. In one instance, some of the mulla's enemies reportedly infiltrated his followers with the intention of starting another anti-Jewish riot. He personally intervened to calm the excited crowds reportedly by standing on a rooftop next to the Jewish neighborhood, holding the Quran in his hand. In doing so, he averted accusations of instigating a riot while at the same time trying to bring Jews under his protection and control.[59]

Among Jews and new-Muslims with close ties to Mulla 'Abdullah, Hakim Rahim and his family were some of the most notable. The astute cleric must have been aware of the family's multiple identities as Jews, Muslims, and Baha'is. But he was willing to overlook this for practical reasons. To him political allegiance trumped his clients' desires to venture beyond mainstream Shi'ism, so long as they maintained an Islamic appearance.

The Next Generation

Rahim's son, Yuhanna (1870–1951) also known as Yahya Khan Hafezi, besides being an accomplished physician, a successful businessman, and an investor, also had a keen sense of history. His extensive family and community network and his openness about his family's multiplicity of religious convictions allowed him to draw an exceptionally full picture of those whose lives were transformed by conversion. As a physician and an entrepreneur, his account contains important information on the social and economic life of Hamadan. He had a successful medical practice, but also made substantial profits from running a pharmacy which dispensed some Western medicine. He was also skilled in construction and undertook a number of building projects.[60]

As a child, together with his older brother Ya'qub, he attended various traditional Jewish *maktab*s and tutorials, but like the Shakeri brothers, he and his brother also did not long survive the traditional education system. They were pulled out of the *maktab* after suffering severe corporal punishment, which caused serious injuries and kept one of them in bed for three months. Afterwards, presumably as Christians, they were admitted to Hamadan's newly established and more gentle American missionary school. Attendance at the school would probably have involved instruction in Christian beliefs and doctrines and participation in Christian Sunday services.[61]

When the time came for the two brothers to find wives, tradition came into conflict with modern values. One of the family's major fears was the possibility of claims on family wealth in case of divorce. Had they married into Muslim families, they could face legal dangers, especially if their in-laws were to denounce them as crypto-Jews. To avoid such complications, in 1895 the family picked an eleven-year-old (Jewish) Baha'i cousin for the 25-year-old Yuhanna (Yahya). Yuhanna admits to the violation of Baha'i age limits, but states that such laws were not widely known or practiced.[62] However, as converts to Islam, the family's public observance of the Shi'i rules of ritual cleanliness restricted their association with Jews and Jewish Baha'is. To solve this problem, they had to seek the help of the Mulla 'Abdullah to sanction this union between two Jewish Baha'is. The mulla, now a friend of the family and presumably a recipient of financial benefits as a result of that friendship, offered to arrange a marriage with "any number of Hamadan's elite [Muslim] families." The Hafezis argued that the two cousins were not only in love, but that the bride was willing to accept Islam—though she was being restrained by her family. The family's resistance was because they would not be allowed to have contact with their daughter if she were to become a Muslim.

In a clever move to engage Mulla 'Abdullah's support and convince him to give his blessing for a marriage to a non-Muslim family, the

Hafezis requested his assistance in convincing the bride's family to consent to the marriage. He did so by assuring them that visiting their Muslim relatives would be acceptable, as long as the Shi'i laws of "ritual cleansing" were observed, after each visit. In this case, "cleansing" involved the purification of whichever place they visited.[63] Such rituals would have required "cleaning" all objects the Jews touched by ritual "immersion" (*kor dadan*). All polluted non-washable areas would have to be purified, presumably through some creative method designed by the inventive and friendly *mujtahed*.

Yuhanna's older brother, the flamboyant Ya'qub, following his family's wishes, married "down," into a family of modest means, with a complicated identity profile similar to his own. He chose a spouse from one of the Jewish families that had converted to Islam during the "patching" persecutions a few years earlier, "but who were in principle Baha'is."[64]

However, not all Shi'i clerics were so amiable to the needs of converts. One form of discrimination against Jewish converts to Islam was the arbitrary prohibition of burial in both Jewish and Muslim cemeteries. In one instance around 1903, according to Hafezi, a certain new convert, Mirza Nabi, traveled from Rasht to arrange for a Jewish marriage ceremony for his daughter in Hamadan. This led to a public protest by Jews who objected to a Jewish man marrying a Muslim convert's daughter. When the rabbis boycotted the ceremony, the wedding was cancelled. The affair caused Mirza Nabi much distress, leading to his death soon after. Barred from Jewish and Muslim cemeteries, his corpse remained unburied at his home in a chest, which served as a temporary coffin. The ultimate fate of the homeless corpse is unknown.[65]

Hafezi also reports the case of Mirza Eshaq, brother of the aforementioned Hajji Mehdi (later known as Arjomand), who became a Muslim and later a Baha'i (see Chapter Seven). When he died in 1905, during Hamadan's cholera epidemic, he was more fortunate than Mirza Nabi, since his relatives managed to bury him in the Muslim cemetery "with much difficulty" (implying a larger than usual fee to allow the burial).[66]

The Jewish and Shi'i clergy sought to delineate clear lines of religious identity by asserting their authority over burial rites. But they were not always successful. At times converts found ways around strict religious demands. For example, the leaders of the small, new-convert community of Hamadan purchased a property for a "private cemetery," perhaps an abandoned cemetery from bygone times. But when remains of older graves were found on the property, the charge of destroying graves of Muslims by Baha'is was raised, a charge which could have easily led to persecution had it not been for Rahim Khan's close connections with the city's ulama and other notables.

According to Yuhanna Khan, his father's allies included the deputies of the new governor 'Abbas Mirza Sardar-Lashgar (son of the celebrated 'Abd al-Hosein Mirza Farmanfarma), who were Baha'is or had Baha'i sympathies. More important was the support of Hajji Shaykh Baqer, son of Aqa Shaykh Ja'far, a low-level *mujtahed* from the village of Bahar who became Hamadan's leading *mujtahed* after the passing of Mulla 'Abdullah in 1896, and later a supporter of the Constitution. Hajji Shaykh Baqer was also a ruthless enforcer of the Shari'ah. When the government refused to administer capital punishment on a convicted felon, a police officer, he took it upon himself to act as the executioner. Nevertheless, according to Hafezi, he was not hostile to Baha'is and is even reported to have read 'Abdu'l-Baha's writings.[67]

Ya'qub's Misfortunes

Despite restrictions on new converts, the case of Mirza Ya'qub, son of Rahamim, presents a rare example of a convert's rise in social status and the dangers that such status might include. The Hafezi family's influence, privilege, and social status could not, in the end prevent a classic tragedy and their own near devastation. Their conversion to Islam, their ties to an influential cleric, their friendship and business ties to the landed aristocracy, even the capitulatory protections of the Ottoman government, could not save them from loosing a son and most of their belongings at the hands of a capricious strongman and royal agent.

Rahamim's eldest son, Ya'qub (1868–96), was the favored son of the family. After overcoming a troubled youth, he found his way into the circles of the local nobility. He had a taste for material pleasures, hunting, and revelry. According to his brother, infatuated by connections with the local elite, Ya'qub became increasingly boisterous and arrogant, unusual and dangerous for a new-Muslim. To avoid trouble, the family had to send him away from the "corrupting influences" of his friends and associates.[68]

Upon his return to Hamadan in his mid-twenties, the impulsive Ya'qub had become a devoted Baha'i. In one instance, when a Jewish child in the American missionary school shouted religious insults at his Baha'i schoolmates, Ya'qub first warned the parent, then arrogantly beat him in public.[69] Since Ya'qub was an Ottoman subject, the assaulted party complained to Baba Khan, the foreign ministry agent (*kargozar*), a young and as yet unestablished newcomer to city's complex political scene. Baba Khan's attempt to detain the influential Ya'qub was thwarted by the Ottoman agent and other local notables allied with Ya'qub and only lead to Baba Khan's embarrassment.[70]

In due course, Baba Khan himself, like many of Hamadan's local elite, joined Ya'qub's network; he spent "days and nights" at his home and "abided by his wishes." Yet continued tensions eventually led to a confrontation. According to Hafezi, a couple of "morally corrupt" *lutis*, Hasan Abdal and Taqi Qahvehchi, now employed as Baba Khan's agents (*farrash*), attempted to assault a Jewish woman but were stopped by Aqa Solayman Zargar, a Jewish Baha'i and the woman's relative. Frustrated, the *lutis* complained to their master, accusing Solayman of verbally insulting Baba Khan. A few days later, after "excessive drinking," Baba Khan brought in the helpless Solayman and ordered him to be bastinadoed by the two *luti* agents. While Solayman was being beaten, Ya'qub and his friends inadvertently arrived at the scene to pay Baba Khan a visit and were confronted by the scene of Solayman's torture.[71]

Determined to teach Baba Khan a lesson, Ya'qub reported the incident to Solyaman's relatives. The family was willing to forgo of the case, but upon Ya'qub's insistence they were persuaded to lodge a complaint with the governor, 'Abd al-Samad Mirza'Ezz al-Dowleh, Naser al-Din Shah's step-brother. The governor who had "substantially gained from the Jews and other non-Muslims," probably by extorting informal taxes from them, resented Baba Khan's meddling in their affairs. With encouragement from Ya'qub, he strongly rebuked the drunken Baba Khan and dispatched a report to Tehran. Baba Khan's plea for reconciliation with the Jewish elders, who themselves were "fearful of Ya'qub," was ineffective, and the affair led to his swift dismissal.

Baba Khan's case is an example of a mid-level Qajar administrator trying to push the limits of his authority too far, within the complex scene of local politics. In effect, he attempted to expand his control beyond foreign nationals protected by capitulatory laws, to include the protection of Jews and Christians, which was increasingly demanded by European powers. Yet in familiar style, instead of making such protection a real concern, he tried to exploit non-Muslims for his own benefit.

Baba Khan's behavior illustrates an exploitive pattern typical of the era. An earlier *kargozar* in Hamadan meddling in Jewish and Baha'i affairs is reported around 1891. After a Jewish rabbi, Mulla Rabi', complained about the Baha'is refusal to comply with the Jewish practice of shaving their head, the *kargozar* took it upon himself to arrest the Baha'i youth, tie their hands, and forcibly shave them. His motive may have been simply to enforce Jewish law or a bid to assert control over the Jewish community. Astonished by the forcefulness of the protests of another Baha'i who confronted him, he ordered his men to beat him. Baha'is complained to the governor, Ahmad Mirza 'Azod al-Dowleh, and to the foreign office in Tehran about this unfair punishment by an unauthorized agent. The *kargozar* tried to persuade the Baha'i plaintiffs to drop their claims against him, but they persisted and he was dismissed.[72]

The Baba Khan affair demonstrates how political influence tied to economic advancement could trump religious disadvange. But influence had even more to do with the ability to manipulate the haphazard and multi-layered system of Qajar administration. These complexities made a rather frail provincial administration vulnerable to attack by the likes of Ya'qub. Yet soon, Ya'qub himself became a victim of capricious rule and paid for it with his life. To compensate for their weaknesses, governors and state officials occasionally tried to demonstrate their power through arbitrary and oppressive actions usually towards those at the bottom of the social hierarchy. But at times, even the rich and privileged, such as Ya'qub himself, suffered at their hands.

Mozaffar al-Din Shah's assent to the throne (r. 1896–1906) offered an opportunity for a showdown of authority, especially in troubled regions like Hamadan. To quell unrest there, the shah appointed one of his most influential statesmen to bring calm to the region. Amir Nezam Garrusi (1820–1900) was the shah's close associate and his chief administrator (*pishkar*) during his long residence in Tabriz as the crown prince. Amir Nezam was a peculiar combination of a refined literary scholar and a ruthlessness military commander. He typically had *carte blanche* to use violence when he felt it necessary to demonstrate royal might.[73]

Amir Nezam's arrival in Hamadan on a royal mission to settle tribal disputes coincided with disturbances instigated by the luti factions associated with the two rival *mujtaheds*, Mulla 'Abdullah and Hajji Aqa Muhammad Qazi. The *lutis* in Aqa Mohammad's entourage mostly:

> . . . hung around the house of Aqa Mohammad [near the Jewish quarter] harassing the Jews in order to earn income for the Aqa [Mohammad Qazi]. They also took a share [of the loot] for themselves. They knew what went on in the Jews' homes better than they did themselves. They caused trouble for any one whom they disliked. The Jews, who were scared of them, paid them whatever they asked. They also entered the houses of Jews which were located away from Muslim view, for some revelry. They demanded payment on behalf of the Aqa in a number of ways, including extortion money for any Jewish home in the neighborhood repaired or added on to; payment at weddings; fees to register home purchases; fees for the settlement of business disputes; fees to declare bankruptcy and to settle bankruptcy claims. The Aqa even started to harass Muslims, causing them much trouble."[74]

According to Hafezi, Mirza Ya'qub became the victim of a conspiracy concocted by Aqa Muhammad, who had lost much of his influence to the immensely popular Mulla 'Abdullah. Aqa Mohammad's band of *lutis* accused Ya'qub of having abducted a married woman to have sexual relations with her. Apparently, the accusations were made public after Mirza Ya'qub refused to pay the *lutis* extortion money. Though we can not be certain about Mirza Ya'qub's innocence, similar accusations of sexual misconduct were familiar pretexts in Qajar times for extortion or the instigation of riots. As a result, Aqa Mohammad reported the alleged abduction to Amir Nezam, calling Mirza Ya'qub a Jewish Babi and threatening to cause grave disturbance if swift action was not taken by the governor. One may detect deep-rooted tensions in Aqa Mohammad's aggressive tone. This may have been caused by his loss of control over the Hafezi family, who were now under the protection of his rival Mulla 'Abdullah.

Mirza Ya'qub was arrested on September 18, 1896. Given Amir Nezam's extraordinary power, neither Mulla 'Abdullah nor the Ottoman representative in Hamadan was willing or able to protect him.

Shortly after the arrest, by the orders of the Amir, Ya'qub was brought to the citadel where the Amir resided and was summarily executed—despite pleas from the Hamadan governor, Prince E'tezad al-Saltaneh. Following his execution, government soldiers were sent off to take possession of Ya'qub's horses in the stables of the Hafezi home. When they arrived, they also took some of the house's furniture. This gave the public the impression that the Hafezi house was not being protected any longer.

In a typical Qajar era riot, the house and the family-owned pharmacy were entirely looted, and part of the house was set on fire. The women of the household managed to save some of their possessions by throwing them into the yards of their friendly Muslim neighbors. But they were soon forced to abandon their properties after being threatened with a mass murder. Word of the looting soon spread to the countryside, but by the time the rural crowds arrived, the house was in ruins. The frustrated crowd then attacked the houses of neighboring Jews. It was only after the neighbors sent pleas for help that soldiers arrived from the citadel and restored relative calm. Nevertheless, looting continued for days, and even the doors and some of the bricks of the Hafezi home were carried off. Despite their local influence, social tensions caused by the success of a Jewish family may well have persisted even after their conversion to Islam. The association of the Hafezis with the Baha'i faith placed the family at even greater risk.[75]

Soon after, Amir Nezam came to realize the extent of the family's influence and their capitulatory protections. Mulla 'Abdullah was enraged and threatened to retaliate against him. Realizing that his actions might have grave consequences, the Amir ordered the return of all looted property to the Hafezi family, though only a few items were actually retrieved. Finally, the Amir was relieved to leave the area when he received a new assignment from Tehran to root out yet another rebellion in Kurdistan, where the lives of the shah's own daughter and son-in-law were at risk.[76]

The Hafezi affair was soon placed beyond the authority of local officials and was elevated to a diplomatic affair. The Ottoman minister, Manif Pasha, who in 1896 happened to be in Tehran to attend the aborted fiftieth anniversary of Naser al-Din Shah's rule, but who instead participated in the shah's funeral and the new shah's coronation ceremonies, lodged a complaint with the chief minister, Amin al-Sultan.

This created an excellent opportunity for the Amin al-Sultan to attack his adversary Amir Nezam, who was widely known to be a contender for the position of chief minister. In response, Amir Nezam defended his decision for the summary execution of Ya'qub but denied having any part in the subsequent looting, which he attributed the victim's "Babi" association.[77]

In fact, Mirza Ya'qub's execution and the subsequent looting of his family's house and business were devastating blows to the family's social status and caused financial loss that brought them to the brink of bankruptcy.[78] Mirza Ya'qub's father, Hakim Rahim, who was absent from Hamadan at the time of his son's execution, moved to Tehran and for months tried to pursue litigation for his losses, lobbying the Ottoman ambassador and Iran's high ranking officials. Hakim Rahim even began a medical practice in Tehran to support himself while awaiting the outcome of his case.

Yuhanna Khan recounts the sad fates of many of the culprits in his brother's death in a rather fatalistic, moral tone in his memoirs, as if the perpetrators were paying for their crimes. What comes through in his account is a stark picture of the decline, within a decade, of the old Qajar establishment and the advent of the Constitutional Revolution. He lists numerous sons of Qajar notables, wealthy *mujtaheds* and their powerful *luti* gangs who ended up with loss of status, trapped in drug and alcohol addiction, and in poverty. Only a handful managed to adjust to the demands and realities of the rising centralized state.[79]

The Hafezi family disaster turned into a relative advantage when the affair finally came to an end in 1897, with the intervention of the new chief minister, 'Ali Khan Amin al-Dowleh. The shah awarded Hakim Rahim the prestigious title of Hafez al-Sehheh (administrator of public health), along with a sizable annual stipend of 500 *tomans*. No description of the duties of the title is known.[80] This settlement was made possible mostly because the family members were Ottoman subjects. The extended legal case also helped the Hafezi family to establish new contacts at higher levels of the royal court.

In the meantime, to compensate for their losses, the family increased its involvement in Hamadan's thriving textile trade at the turn of the century, and then more intensely in the aftermath of the Constitutional Revolution. In a pattern of occupational diversity, Yuhanna Khan— now less active as a physician—together with his brother-in-law Mirza

Taher, entered into partnership with two Jewish merchants, at first only as agents of textile imports to Tehran earning a commission. Making use of their adventageous position as Muslim converts while maintaining Jewish business connections, the Hafezis then expanded their trade and improved their position from agents of textile sellers to direct dealers. They co-opted some of their Jewish competitors by making them partners in their enterprise, and rationalized their business through a division of labor and by forming a formal partnership (*sherkat*).[81]

Jewish and Baha'i merchants in Hamadan, with their partners in Tehran, "gradually dominated" (*motedarrejan karha beh dast yahud oftad*) the textile trade. Ironically, their disadvantage within the Shi'i legal system turned into a major advantage. Iraqi Jews in Hamadan, who controlled European trade connections through Baghdad, favored working with Jews, not so much out of religious solidarity but rather for practical business reasons. Unlike their Muslim counterparts, Jewish merchants had no protectors among the ulama who could manipulate the Muslim legal system. They could not easily use bankruptcy, for example, to avoid payment of their debts.

If Jewish merchants in Hamadan found advantage in global changes, they were nevertheless adversely affected by the old discrimination against their partners in Tehran. Unlike Hamadan, the discriminatory practices that prevented the Jews (and Jewish Baha'is) from having businesses in the bazaar's main thoroughfare and other important places of business persisted in Tehran. One notable exception was the Amir caravansary where most Jews and Baha'i traders, including Yuhanna Khan's partners, conducted business. Resenting the dominance of the Jewish merchants even in the Amir caravansary, their Muslim competitors closed shop and sought the assistance of the ulama to ban them. In 1899, the ulama issued a decree affirming the ban. The Jews were thus harassed and barred from entering the bazaar with the ulama's support and the tacit approval of the new chief minister Amin al-Sultan. This was a source of grave concern for their Hamadan partners, who had substantial stakes in Tehran.[82]

Fearing another financial disaster, Yuhanna Khan made an emergency trip to Tehran to collect the partnership's debts. During his extended stay, claiming an Islamic identity, he effectively took over the business from his Jewish partners, now banned from business. He also connected with a network of Jewish converts to Islam, including mer-

chants and officials, with whom he spent his leisure time. During the
Shi'i mourning holidays of Arba'in in Shemiran (near Tehran), they
attended mourning ceremonies during the day and followed that up by
drinking at the home of a Muslim employee at night. Even Yuhanna
Khan noticed the audacity of his predicament and reminisced about
the grave consequences that could have resulted from "Jewish-born
[converts] drinking in a Muslim home during mourning holidays."[83]

Even though the partnership withstood external attacks, it could not
bear familiar internal disagreements among the partners. Their written
contract and their efforts in consulting with elders were no match for the
confusion that resulted from poor accounting practices. In this respect,
the convert to Islam was no different in his traditional mindset from his
Jewish partners. In 1902, one dispute between Yuhanna and his Baha'i
partners was settled through the Baha'i assembly, a designated body of
Baha'i notables that attended the affairs of the community. On another
occasion, a dispute was settled with the help of one of the Hamadan
ulama, Aqa Muhammad Baqer, who was perhaps more capable in
financial matters.[84] This indicates a good deal of pragmatism on the
part of all parties, at least in business dealings.

Community Life

Throughout the 1880s and 1890s the Baha'i community in Hamadan experienced considerable growth, especially among Jewish youth.
Because of the political influence of a number of Baha'i physicians,
there was relatively less opposition from the Jewish elders than there
had been elsewhere, in communities like Kashan. Since most Baha'is
were Jewish converts, prayer meetings were held on Saturdays. The
Baha'i assembly was in charge of the community's affairs. After the
looting incident of the Hafezi family household in 1896, the Hamadan
Baha'i community went into shock and temporarily ceased all activities. But it soon recovered during the early reign of Muzaffar al-Din
Shah, a period of relative toleration. Circumstances changed with the
opening of the Alliance Israélite school in 1900. One of Alliance's
main missions was to stop the conversion of Jewish youth to the Baha'i
faith. The Alliance administrators gained capitulatory privileges
through the French consulate to extend their influence to protect the
Jews. They encouraged Jewish elders in Hamadan to isolate the Jewish
Baha'i converts by denying them their services.

In 1902 property for a new Baha'i center (*hazirat al-qods*) was purchased, and the building was completed a year later through community
effort.[85] In 1904, perhaps as a result of what was seen by the cash-
strapped governor Salar al-Dowleh, son of Naser al-Din Shah, as a
challenge to Baha'i affluence, "a few" Baha'is were arrested and jailed
on trumped up charges of "disturbing order." They were ordered to
pay a two-thousand-*toman* fine. The Baha'is refused to pay, and through
intermediaries, the demand was diminished. Even the Iraqi Jews, who
were concerned about the debts the Baha'is owed them, became
involved in the negotiations. After the prisoners were released on bail,
a number of Baha'is took sanctuary in the telegraph office in a daring
display of unity. Their petitions to the shah and the chief minister, 'Ayn
al-Dowleh, used an audacious tone that foreshadowed the discourse of
the later constitutional period. Demanding their rights as citizens, they
stated:

> We are the subjects (*ra'iyyat*) of this government. If you do not
> accept us as such, we are willing to emigrate *en masse* out of this
> country. But we shall not stand for having our livelihood (*sarmayeh*)
> taken away from us with a different excuse each day. We no longer
> have any fear of your threats and are willing to die for our inde-
> pendence (*esteghlal*) [from our oppressors]. We will not leave till we
> get satisfaction from this government."[86]

As a result, all charges against the Baha'is were dropped at the order
of the shah. In response, after consultation with other leaders, one of
the Baha'is sent Salar al-Dowleh a letter of gratitude using a concilia-
tory tone, along with a valuable gift that reportedly won his favor. As a
result of the episode, according to Yuhanna Khan, the Baha'i community gained relative freedom and a more favorable reputation. Even if
Yuhanna Khan exaggerated the revolutionary tone of the Baha'i petition, the conduct of Baha'is can be considered a departure from their
more cautious behavior during the Naseri period when they typically
relied on personal connections and outside assistance.

Despite some cooperation on matters of common interest, religious
differences often interfered with good relations between Jews and Baha'is
and led to communal tension. Even more important than the separation of the cemeteries, the establishment of modern schools marked the
beginning of serious divisions between the two communities. Baha'is

participated in fund-raising efforts for the opening of the Alliance Israé-lite school in 1900.[87] The oddly unified opposition of the Shi'i ulama and the Jewish rabbis against the Alliance was ineffective in the face of the support rendered by the French government.

Perhaps in a move to appease the rabbis, though uncharacteristic of the Alliance's secular agenda, all students at the school were required to observe Jewish rituals and perform prayers at the synagogue [see Plate 11]. When the Baha'i assembly's request for an exemption for the Baha'i students was rejected, the Baha'is pulled out their children and started their own makeshift school. The Muzaffari era (1896–1906), it should be noted, was an age of educational initiatives and opening of new schools. Having lost a "majority" of the student body, according to Yuhanna Khan, the Alliance school reportedly came to a standstill and complained to the governor, Zafar al-Saltaneh.[88] This placed the Baha'i converts in a precarious position, as they were legally unable to assert their independence from the Jewish community. Instead, they cautioned the Jewish elders about the potential consequences of religious debates before the governor, warning them that disclosing "Jewish beliefs and practices that are in conflict with Islam" might turn Zafar al-Saltaneh's anger against them. In the end, the school officials conceded and the Baha'i students returned to school.[89]

Nevertheless, tensions continued and reportedly increased in 1908, with the arrival of a new principal. This coincided with Baha'i efforts to establish a number of schools throughout the country. A substantial sum of 2,000 *tomans* was raised from "thirty or forty reputable Baha'i mer-chants," and in September, Hamadan's Ta'id (divine blessing) School opened [see Plate 12]. The Mohebat (bounty) girls school, established in 1909, hired a number of educated Baha'i women as teachers and administrators.[90] Initially, the teachers were mostly Alliance graduates from convert families, though gradually the new schools benefited from a number of educated Baha'i men and women teachers.

In the post-Constitutional era of invigorating reform, both Baha'i and Jewish schools were diligent advocates of modern education. In a Now-Ruz parade in 1913, in front of the government office, the students of rival schools marched in step to the music of school bands, with slogans, cheers, uniforms, and banners. The parade was an impressive display of modern symbols and a demonstration of state support for modern schools of diverse religious affiliations. The Baha'i teachers' public speeches in Persian and Arabic, as well as Alliance teachers' speeches in French, demonstrated a new voice and became a step towards public recognition for both Jews and Baha'is.[91]

Each school represented a different approach to modern life. The Alliance school, following a Western educational pattern, emphasized French language and culture, a vital tool in a commercial center such as Hamadan. The Ta'id School's strong program in Persian, Arabic, and bookkeeping reflected its orientation towards indigenous modernity and cultural assimilation. In 1913, under the French educated Iranian who adopted the name Monsieur André, the Ta'id School received formal recognition from the Ministry of Education. The officials reportedly went so far as to publicly declare it "an example for all [modern] schools."[92]

Conclusion

To sum up, a privileged few of Hamadan's Jewish community took advantage of concurrent historical processes at the end of the nineteenth century to advance their social status and to navigate a labyrinth of multiple religious identities. Many disenfranchised and stigmatized Jews also managed to substantially improve their lot. A number of major patterns may be observed in the lifetime of the author, Yuhanna Khan Hafezi. Within a generation (1880–96), the Hafezi family improved their economic standing by accumulating capital through a successful medical practice, then investing in Hamadan's thriving textile market of European industrial products. Their assets were diversified, as they also engaged in construction and opened a pharmacy. Their success came after unfettering the bonds of their traditional religion. Their association with the American Presbyterian missionaries allowed them to receive medical training, a vital link for professional success. Their Christian connection became an early avenue for Western-style education for their children, giving them a significant edge in their future professional and business careers.

As privileged converts to Islam, the Hafezis gained new social status and even managed to circumvent much of the stigma associated with being "new-Muslims." Becoming Muslim also reinforced their political ties to influential clerics to whom they gave their allegiance and from whom they received support. As physicians, they formed political and business ties with their influential clients, including aristocratic families.

Professional and language skills allowed them to establish themselves in the Ottoman Empire, from which they obtained capitulatory protections and advantages. This was an additional means of protection for navigating the chaotic world of Qajar provincial politics.

On the surface, the Hafezi family's multiplicity of identities may seem self-serving, even unprincipled, and an easy path to social and economic advancement. Yet this view overlooks a crucial dimension fundamental to social change. In a society that publicly labeled individuals and restricted their social positions based on their religion; a multiplicity of religious identities became a necessity. Where secularism was non-existent or, at best, in its infancy; and where unconventional thinking was hardly tolerated; few options existed for those bold enough to seek independence from age-old, traditional conventions.

In the case of the Hafezi family, adopting Jewish, Christian, Muslim, and Baha'i identities may be seen as means of "deconstructing" organized religion and rejecting its legalistic, clerical establishment. Accepting the essential unity of all religions, as outlined in the Baha'i message, was a potent mechanism for subverting the hegemony of the clerical class, which demanded a rigid traditionalist application of religion. Rejecting jurisprudence (*shar'*) as archaic and retrograde, the Hafezis as Baha'is undermined the foundation of clerical power and age-old, religious and racial segregation. Such conversions can be seen as a critical intermediate stage in Iran's development of modernity. At least until the mid-twentieth century, Baha'is tolerated dual communal loyalties and in so doing arguably helped subvert traditional religion. Some Jewish converts to Islam later adopted a Baha'i identity. Even more remarkable were those Jews who accepted in turn Christianity, Islam, and the Baha'i faith, and whose public practice of Islam did not affect their commitment to other communities.

This brings us back to the question of why Jewish converts to Islam, who supposedly enjoyed the advantages of being part of the majority religion, became committed members of a new and persecuted faith. Despite its many disadvantages, a continued attraction to the Baha'i alternative may be attributed to a need to connect with a universal worldview free from legalistic restraints, clerical authority, and what were seen as archaic fixations. In a social environment where self-definition was inconceivable outside of a religious community, faith became a vital link to the emerging modern, secular mindset. The advent of the

Pahlavi regime, with an agenda for advancing modernity, legitimized the alternative of a modern self, less constrained by traditional religious loyalties.

EPILOGUE

Faced with the challenges of Western hegemony and besieged by internal predicaments, Iran in the nineteenth century was in crisis. A legalistic reading of Shi'ism demanded strict religious conformity and constrained the diversity that had historically characterized Iran's religious landscape. Partly as a reaction to these pressures, traditional interpretations of religion came into question, new belief systems were constructed, and fluid, multiple identities became more common. Such mechanisms offered believers the necessary latitude to negotiate the modern situation and to make sense of the changing world around them.

If conversion and multiple identities were a response to modernity and religious conformity in the nineteenth century, they found new forms and new meanings in the twentieth century. This was also a time of overwhelming challenge, with more Shi'i demands for uniformity and increasingly rigid dogmas and ideologies. The short-lived experiment in democracy during the Constitutional period soon gave way to the authoritarian Pahlavi state that promised security, stability, and progress at the price of suspending civil liberties and democratic institutions. This was a price that even many liberal reformists were willing to pay.

However, unlike the state's sometimes half-hearted schemes for secular change (such as laws against traditional veiling), other more disciplined, Western models for coming to terms with modernity demanded unyielding loyalty. Impassioned nationalists who sanctified Iran's past glory competed with the doctrinaire Left, which had its own cast of saints, heroes, and heretics, its own dogmas and authorities. Each of these came distinctly close to being a "secular religion," with their respective demands for rigid identities and sanctioned associations. A new political and revivalist form of Islam rejected the state's secular agenda. But nonetheless, most Iranians were able to present a public, secular presence while maintaining their private, personal faiths.

The Jewish community experienced fundamental changes under the Pahlavis. Some Iranian Jews, mostly those in larger cities who had access to trade networks and were exposed to Western-style education, benefited greatly from their relative freedom from traditional Shi'i restrictions. But for the majority of Jews, emergence from centuries of economic deprivation was more gradual. Economic improvement accompanied an increase in the rate of migration to Tehran, away from Jewish quarters in ancient communities scattered throughout the country.

Though some Jews had secularist tendencies or became active in leftist politics, most observed a somewhat altered, less rigid form of Judaism. Enthusiasm over the establishment of a Jewish state in the Holy Land replaced age-old messianic yearnings. Partly in response to this excitement, and pursing hopes for a prosperous future free of discrimination and humiliation, perhaps one-third of the Jewish population of Iran, many from disadvantaged communities, migrated to Israel during the first few years of its establishment. Even today, despite political tensions between the Islamic Republic and Israel, Persian Israelis have managed to maintain a closer connection with their ancestral homeland than have their European counterparts. Later, as their concerns over discrimination and occasional use of anti-Jewish rhetoric by Islamic leaders increased, some two-thirds of the Jewish community left the country. This trend intensified as exile communities, mostly in the United States, became more able to provide supportive environments and better economic opportunities for the new immigrants.

Iran's Baha'is in the second half of the twentieth century were even more drastically influenced by the rise of Islamic revivalism. Mindful of its own religious legitimacy, the Pahlavi state adopted a general policy of denying Baha'is any recognition in the public sphere, regarding all reference to them as a taboo of sorts. The Iranian public subconsciously accepted the negation of the Baha'i presence and often euphemistically referred to them as those outside of "official religions" (*mazaheb-e rasmi*). The word "Baha'i" could rarely be uttered. Nonetheless, exemptions from this policy of avoidance were common in polemical, religious literature refuting Baha'i doctrine and impugning the community. Reference to Babi-Baha'i history in school textbooks was limited to a single paragraph under the heading "The Bab's sedition" (*fetneh-ye Bab*). There was no mention of the fact that the Baha'is were Iran's largest non-Muslim community, nor any explanation of their beliefs. The Baha'i response to these polemics was not given a public hearing, and defamation of the Baha'is was carried on as a hostile monologue.[§] During the anti-Baha'i persecutions of 1955, when an alliance between the ulama and the state threatened the lives of Baha'is, in particular those living in small towns and villages, neither the Left nor the nationalists voiced their protest against this religious persecution.

Yet despite their pariah status, through education and entrepreneurship, a small urban Baha'i bourgeoisie emerged. A few among them rose in the ranks of the military and occasionally used their influence to protect their marginalized coreligionists or to promote a few prominent, wealthy Baha'is. In a familiar pattern, questions relating to the past record of such prominent Baha'i members are often used to justify mistreatment of the entire community. Under the Islamic Republic, the anti-Baha'i polemics took on a more disturbing dimension which included trials and executions of Baha'i leaders and randomly selected members of the community. Restrictions on Baha'is in the areas of education, employment, and freedom of assembly remain in force.

The environment of fluidity and openness that was present in Iran around the turn of the twentieth century may now seem remote and beyond reach. Extremist and exclusivist views of religion continue to be dominant, at least on the surface. Yet as evidenced in the 2009 "Green Movement," the government's heavy-handed deployment of the apparatus of the modern state (such as mass education and mass media, not to mention state violence) to reverse secular trends and impose an "Islamic" identity may yield under the pressures of globalization. And while a "reformist Islam" seeking a pluralistic approach and respect for civil rights may be possible, it remains vulnerable to the familiar challenges of a literalist reading of Shi'i Islam.

In the aftermath of the Islamic Revolution, the preeminence of Shi'ism has meant the weakening of non-Shi'i communities and the exclusion of alternative secular voices—including the Left—from public life. The

---

[§] In the post-World War II period and before the Islamic Revolution, Baha'is were granted permission to publish using "offset" printing, but circulation had to be limited to the Baha'i community.

Jewish community is drastically reduced in size and, influenced by the wider religious environment, has adhered more fervently to its ritualistic observances. The Baha'i reformist message has been reduced to a forbidden memory associated with a marginalized and constitutionally "unrecognized" minority. This tendency toward conformity may prove to be a serious threat to Iran's cultural ecosystem. A vital question for Iran's future might be whether the country can rejuvenate within itself the sense of cultural diversity that has been a central part of its past.

NOTES

Introduction

1   Walter J. Fischel, "The Jews of Persia, 1795–1940," *Jewish Social Studies*, vol. 12, no. 2 (Apr., 1950) p. 154; Walter Fischel, "The Baha'i Movement and Persian Jewry," *Jewish Review*, vol. 2 (December-March 1934) p. 52.

2. For a history of messianic trends within Judaism, see Harris Lenowitz, *The Jewish Messiahs: From the Galilee to Crown Heights* (Oxford, 1998).

3   For a classic study of religion under Ilkhanid rule, see Alessandro Bausani, "Religion under the Mongols," in *The Cambridge History of Iran*, vol. 5, ed. by J. A. Boyle (Cambridge, 1968). For a study of religion in the Safavid period, see Rula Jurdi Abisaab, *Converting Persia: Religion and Power in the Safavid Empire* (London, 2004). For a Weberian analysis of Shi'ism in the Safavid and Qajar periods, see Said Amir Arjomand, *The Shadow of God and the Hidden Imam: Religion, Political Order, and Societal Change in Shi'ite Iran from the Beginning to 1890* (Chicago, 1984). For a survey of the role of the ulama in the Qajar period (with a somewhat overstated case for the opposition of the ulama to Qajar rule), see Hamid Algar, *Religion and State in Iran, 1785–1906* (Berkeley, 1969).

4   For a full exposition of Shi'i legal opinions concerning the impurity of non-Muslims, see Mohsen al-Tabataba'i al-Hakim, *Mustamsak al-'urwat al-wuthqa*, vol. 1 (Qom, 1404 SH [1983/4]) pp. 367–404.

5   For a general survey of the second half of the nineteenth century, see Abbas Amanat, *Pivot of the Universe: Nasir al-Din Shah Qajar and the Iranian Monarchy, 1831–1896* (Berkeley, 1997); Ann K. S. Lambton, *Qajar Persia: Eleven Studies* (Reprint: Austin, 1988); Nikki R. Keddie, *Sayyid Jamal ad-Din "al-Afghani": A Political Biography* (Berkeley, 1972); idem., *Modern Iran: Roots and Results of Revolution* (New Haven, 2003).

6   Ephraim Neumark, *Masa'be-erets ha-qedem* (Journey in the countries of the East), with Introduction and Notes by Avraham Ya'ari (Jerusalem, 1947) p. 80. His estimate of number of Babi/Baha'is in Iran is most likely an exaggeration. Abraham J. Brower, *Mi-Parashat Mas'otay be-Paras* (Jerusalem, 1937–38) pp. 22, 24, and 31. (I am indebted to Dr. Daniel Tsadik for translating passages from the Hebrew.) See also idem., *Avak darakhim* (Dust of roads) (Tel Aviv, 1944–46), vol. 2, pp. 146–53, cited in Hayyim J. Cohen, *The Jews of the Middle East: 1860–1972* (New York and Jerusalem, 1973) p. 162; George N. Curzon, *Persia and the Persian Question* (London, 1892) p. 496. Only a few families of Golpaygani Jewish Baha'is can be traced in Baha'i sources. One

can only speculate that many may have renounced their Baha'i identities. See also Fischel, "The Baha'i Movement," p. 54.

7 For a list of Jewish Baha'i families of Kashan and Hamadan, see Mousa Amanat, "Abna'-e Khalil-e Kashan" (unpublished manuscript, 1988) in Mousa Amanat Papers (hereafter referred to as MAP); idem., "Ahebba-ye kalimi- nejad-e Hamadan," (unpublished manuscript, 2000) in MAP. For the Kashan Jewish population, see Mousa Amanat, *Bahai'yan-e Kashan* (forthcoming); Yazghel Yerushalaymi, "Sharh-e qesmi az Yahudot-e Kashan va sayer-e shahrestanha-ye keshvar-e Iran" (1985 photocopy of manuscript in private hands) in MAP. For the Hamadan Jewish population, see Brawer, *Mi Parashat*, vol. 22, and sources cited in *Encylopedia Iranica*, Ehasan Yarshater, (1982–) (hereafter, *EIr*) s.v. "Hamadan Jewish Community" (Houman Sarshar).

8 The list of political figures who have been called new-Muslims has grown relentlessly. It includes the Islamic Republic's first president Abulhasan Bani-Sadr and the conservative religious leader Ayatollah Mesbah Yazdi. Astonishingly, President Ahmadinejad, as well as his advisor in matters relating to the Holocaust, Muhammad Ali Ramin, and his controversial minister, Esfandiyar Rahim-Masha'i, have also been accused of being new converts. Mehrdad Amanat, "Set in stone: religious ambiguity and postmortem identity in Iran" (forthcoming).

9 Rayhan Rayhani Memoirs (Tehran, 1939?) photocopy of handwritten original in MAP. A translation of the Rayhani Memoirs in Mehrdad Amanat, "Negotiating Identities: Jews, Muslims and Baha'is in the memoirs of Rayhan Rayhani," Ph.D. Dissertation (UCLA, 2006) is hereafter referred to as *Rayhani Memoirs.*

10 Aqajan Shakeri, "Shakerinameh" (unpublished manuscript, 1961), transcription of manuscript in MAP, hereafter referred to as *Shakerinameh.*

11 Yuhanna Khan Hafezi, "Tarikh-e zendegani-ye Haj Yuhanna Khan Hafezi (Hafez ul-Sehheh)," hereafter referred to as *Tarikh* photocopy of typed manuscript by the author's son 'Ezzatullah Hafezi (1950), in MAP. This author only had access to 197 of 420 pages of this manuscript.

12 Mirza Mohammad Taqi Sepehr (Lesan al-Mulk), *Nasekh al-tawarikh*, 4 vols., ed. by M. B. Behbudi, (Tehran, 1965). Reza Qoli Khan-e Hedayat, *Tarikh-e rowzat al-safa-ye Naseri*, 3rd ed. (Tehran and Qom, 1959/60). Mohammad Hasan Khan-e E'temad al-Saltaneh, *Matla' al-shams*, 3 vols. (Tehran, 1884-86. Reprint: 3 vols. in 2, Tehran, 1983).

13 Hasan Naraqi, *Tarikh-e ejtema'i-ye Kashan* (Tehran, 1345 SH [1967]) and idem., *Kashan dar jonbesh-e mashruteh-ye Iran* (Tehran, 2535 [1976/7]). Hasan Naraqi was the father of Dr. Ehsan Naraqi, the controversial author and public intellectual.

14 'Abd ul-Rahim Kalantar Zarrabi, *Mer'at ul-Qasan* (*Tarikh-e Kashan*), ed. by Iraj Afshar (Tehran, 1335 SH [1956/7]). It is worth noting that the author's son

'Ali-Qoli Khan, a prominent Baha'i, later became an Iranian envoy in Washington. See Marzieh Gail, *Summon Up Remembrance* (Oxford, 1987) and idem., *Arches of the Years* (Oxford, 1991). See also Chapter 7.

15 Muhammad 'Ali Ghaffari, *Khaterat va asnad-e Muhammad 'Ali Ghaffari (Tarikh-e Ghaffari)*, ed. by Mansureh Etehadiyyeh (Tehran, 1361 SH [1982/3]).

16 Aqa Najafi Quchani, *Siyahat-e sharq*, ed. by R. A. Shakiri (Mashhad, 1351 SH [1972]). Khaterat-e 'Abd ul-Hosein Owrang in Sayfullah Vahidnia, *Khaterat-e Vahid*, 2 vols. (Tehran, 1985). Ahmad Kasravi, *Zendegani-ye man* (Tehran, 1323 SH [1944]). 'Abd ul-Hosein San'atizadeh-Kermani, *Ruzegari keh gozasht* (Tehran, 1346 SH [1968]).

17 Gholam-Hosayn Mirza-Saleh, ed., *Sargozashte zendegie man, khaterat-e shaykh Ebrahim Zanjani* (Tehran, 2000, 2001, Reprint: Los Angeles, 2009). This auto- biography was reportedly banned after two Tehran editions. For a critique of Zanjani's views using numerous methods to discredit him, see 'Ali Abolhasani, *Shaykh Ebrahim Zanjani zaman zendegi khaterat* (Tehran, 2005).

18 Mo'ez al-Din Mahdavi, *Dastanha-'i az panjah sal*, Tehran, 1969.

19. Mashalah Farivar, *Hadis-e yek farhang*, edited by Goel Cohen (Los Angeles, 2007). Despite its recent publication date, this work is generally unavailable.

20. Muzaffar Berjis, "Khaterat-e Muzaffar-e Berjis" (unpublished manuscript, 1977), photocopy of manuscript transcribed by Hesam Noqaba'i in MAP.

21 It is possible that Hafezi's account was also initiated through this same project to collect local Baha'i histories.

22 Mohammad Nateq-e Isfahani, "Tarikh-e amri-ye Kashan va qora'-e tavabe'" (unpublished manuscript, 1309 SH [1930]), ms. no. 2016D, National Baha'i Library, Iran.

23 Asadullah Fazel Mazandarani, *Tarikh-e zohur ul-haqq*, vol. 3 (Tehran, n.d. [1320 SH/1942?]. Reprint, Hofheim, 2008), and vol. 8, parts 1 and 2 (Tehran, 1976). The other seven volumes have not yet been pub- lished, presumably at least in part because of inconsistencies with the "authoritative" Baha'i narratives. For online versions of Fazel-e Mazan- darani's unpublished works, see http://www.h-net.msu.edu/~bahai/ index/diglib/mazand1.htm.

24 Yazghel Yerushalaymi, "Sharh-e qesmi." For a detailed discussion of this source see Haideh Sahim, "Khaterat-e yahudiyan-e Iran" in *Iran Nameh*, vol. 15, no. 1 (Winter1996).

25 Yedidia Shofet, *Khaterat-e hakham Yedidia Shofet*, ed. by Manuchehr Kohan (Los Angeles, 2000).

26 Heshmatullah Kermanshahchi, *Tahavvolat-e ejtema'i-ye yahudiyan-e Iran dar qarn-e bistom* (Los Angeles, 2007).

27 Yousef Cohen, *Gozaresh va khaterat: fa'aliyyatha-ye siasi va ejetma'i* (Los Ange- les, 1995). Only 40 pages of the 320-page book is devoted to the author's memoirs. Cohen's unexpected victory over the more established and favored

candidate represented the ascendancy of a younger, more educated community leader.

28 Some Jewish converts did invest in Tehran's post-war real estate speculation and development. Many others became professionals, small businessmen, and even major industrialists. For examples of accounts by former Baha'is, see Fazlullah Sobhi, *Payam-e pedar* (Tehran, 1955) and Hasan Borujerdi Niku, *Falsafeh-ye Niku, dar paydayesh-e rahzanan va badkishan*, 4 vols. in 2 (Tehran, 1960?). For an example of pejorative anti-Baha'i accounts, see Mohammad Baqer Najafi, *Bahaiyan* (Tehran, 1979).

29 Fereydun Adamiyat, *Amir Kabir va Iran* (Tehran, 1323 SH [1944]) pp. 457–58. See also Esma'il Ra'in, *Enshe'ab-e Baha'iyyat* (Tehran, 1978?). For Adamiyat's anti-Jewish views, see the introduction to his *Shuresh bar emtiyaz-nameh-ye Rezhi* (Tehran, 1360 SH [1981]).

30 For a complete list of works by 'Abdullah Shahbazi, including *Jostarha-i az tarikh-e baha'igari dar Iran*, see www.shahbazi.org. For a reading of modern Iranian history with anti-Jewish themes, see his *Zarsalaran-e Yahudi va Parsi, Este'mar-e Britania va Iran*, 5 vols. (Tehran, 1377 SH [1998]).

31 For a positivist critique of Baha'is, see Ahmad Kasravi, *Baha'igari* (Tehran, 1956).

32 http://www.drsoroush.com/Persian/By_DrSoroush/P-NWS-13880718-HaghVaTaklifVaKhoda.html (October 2009).

33 One example of simplified religious obligation is the evolution of the Baha'i obligatory prayer (*salaat*). The original prayer requiring nine prostrations ordained in the *Ketab-e Aqdas* was replaced by Baha'u'llah himself with a long, medium, or short obligatory prayer, the choice of which is left to the individual. The last of the three is as short as one sentence. Complicated rules relating to inheritance, also part of the *Ketab-e Aqdas*, were later abrogated by Baha'u'llah. See Anthony A. Lee, "Choice Wine: The Kitab-i Aqdas and the Development of Baha'i Law," http://www.bahai-library.org/conferences/wine.html.

34 Among recent studies of Iranian Jewry, Daniel Tsadik's *Between Foreigners and Shi'is* (Stanford, 2007) offers a rare up-to-date, comprehensive, and well-researched account of the Jewish community of Iran in the nineteenth century. Tsadik uses a wide variety of British and French archival material as well as Shi'i legal treatises and other historical and legal sources in Arabic and Persian to demonstrate the interaction of Jews with the state and the ulama.

35 Fischel, "Baha'i Movement," pp. 47–55.

36 Cohen, *Jews of the Middle East*, p. 54.

37 For a discussion of the protection of Jewish converts by other Baha'is, see Chapter 4.

38 Cohen, *Jews of the Middle East*, pp. 162–63.

39 Fischel, "Baha'i Movement," p. 55.

40 Habib Levy, *Tarikh-e yahud-e Iran*, 3 vols. (Tehran, 1334 SH [1956]. Reprint in 2 vols., Los Angeles, 1984). A new, abridged edition of this work has recently been published in Los Angeles.

41 Idem., *Khaterat-e man* (Los Angeles, 2002) p. 183.

42 Personal interview with Mrs. Huri Enayati in Tehran in the 1970s.

43 Elyeh Khalili, *Yahudiyan-e kurd-e Iran* (Los Angeles, 2004) p. 88.

44 Mercedes Garcia-Arenal, "Jewish Converts to Islam in the Muslim West," in *Dhimmis and Others: Jews and Christians and the World of Classical Islam*, Israel Oriental Studies, vol. 17, ed. by Uri Rubin and David J. Wasserstein (Tel Aviv, 1997); idem. and Gerard Wiegers, *A Man of Three Worlds: Samuel Pallache, a Moroccan Jew in Catholic and Protestant Europe*, trans. by Martin Beagles (Baltimore and London, 2003).

45 For a discussion of Karaites, see Chapter 1.

46 See *Encyclopaedia Judaica* (hereafter cited as *EJ*), s.v. "Persia" (Walter Fischel). Fischel later asserted that Communism was an equally potent threat.

47 Amnon Netzer, "Conversion of Jews to the Baha'i Faith," in *Irano-Judaica*, vol. 6 (Jerusalem, 2008) pp. 290–323.

48 Mirza Mehdi Arjomand, *Golshan-e haqa'eq* (Reprint, Los Angeles, 1982).

Chapter 1

1 For general surveys of the history of Jews in Iran, see Walter J. Fischel, *Jews in the Economic and Political Life of Mediaeval Islam* (London 1937); Vera Basch Moreen, trans., *In Queen Esther's Garden: An Anthology of Judeo-Persian Literature* (New Haven, 2000); and D. E. Spector, "A History of the Persian Jews" (Ph.D. dissertation, University of Texas, 1975).

2 Amnon Netzer, "Sayri dar tarikh-e Yahud-e Iran," pt. 1, in *Padyavand*, ed. by A. Netzer, vol.1 (Los Angeles, 1996) pp. 3–7.

3 The large body of literature on Jews in ancient Iranian lands includes Mary Boyce, *History of Zoroastrianism*, vol. 3 (Leiden, 1991), chap. 2; idem, *Zoroastrianism: A Shadowy But Powerful Presence in the Judaeo-Christian World* (London, 1987); Jacob Neusner, *Israel and Iran in Talmudic Times: A Political History* (Lanham, MD, 1986); and Shaul Shaked, "Iranian Influence on Judaism: First Century BCE to Second Century CE," *Cambridge History of Judaism*, ed. by Louis W. D. Davies and Louis Finkelstein (Cambridge, 1984) vol. 1, pp. 308–25.

4 Netzer, "Sayri dar tarikh-e Yahud," p. 11. See also Richard C. Foltz, *Spirituality in the Land of the Noble: How Iran Shaped the World's Religions* (Oxford, 2004) pp. 46–47.

5 Ezra 1:1–4 (relating to the reign of Cyrus); Chron. 36:23.

6 R. N. Frye, "Iran und Israel," in *Festschrift für Wilhelm Eilers* (Wiesbaden, 1967) pp. 74–85.

7 L. Honarfar, *Ganjineh-ye asar-e tarikhi-ye Isfahan*, 2nd ed. (Tehran, 1971) pp. 68–69.

8 Geo Widengren, "The Status of the Jews in the Sassanian Empire," *Iranica Antiqua*, vol. 1 (1961) pp. 117–62. Antonio Panaino, "Trends and Problems Concerning the Mutual Relations between Iranian Pre-Islamic and Jewish Cultures," *Melammu Symposia*, vol. 4 (Milan, 2004) pp. 214.

9 Widengren, "Status of the Jews," pp. 139–41.

10 Nina Garsoian, "The Aršakuni Dynasty," in *The Armenian People from Ancient to Modern Times*, ed. by Richard G. Hovannisian, vol. 1 (New York, 1997) p. 90.

11 'Abd ul-Hosein Zarrinkub, "The Arab Conquest of Iran and Its Aftermath," in *The Cambridge History of Iran*, vol. 4, ed. R. N. Frye (Cambridge, 1975) pp. 1–56.

12 For nineteenth-century Jewish economic participation, see Spector, "History of the Persian Jews," chap. 7. See also Bernard Lewis, *The Jews of Islam* (Princeton, 1984). For a comparison with Jewish participation in the Levantine trade, see S. D. Goitein, *A Mediterranean Society: The Jewish Communities of the Arab World as Portrayed in the Documents of the Cairo Geniza* (Berkeley, 1967–88).

13 Laurence D. Loeb, "The Jewish Musician and the Music of Fars," *Asian Music*, vol. 4 (1972). A close reading of studies of Persian music, such as Ruhullah Khaleqi's, *Sargozasht-e musiqi-ye Iran* (Tehran, 1335 SH [1956]) reveals many references to Jewish musicians and instructors.

14 Shoja' al-Din Shafa, *Iran va Espania, farhang-nameh-ye Jahan-e Iran-shenasi*, vol. 1 (n.p., n.d.) pp. 226–36.

15 Parviz Azka'i, *Tarikhnegaran-e Iran* (Tehran, 1994) pp. 311–15. Amnon Netzer has disputed this relationship, basing his argument in part on the assumption that the conservative Isma'ilis would not have welcomed Jewish scholars among their number. See Netzer, "Rashid al-Din and His Jewish Background," in *Irano-Judaica*, vol. 3 (Jerusalem, 1994) p. 122. However, Chirine Bayani's assertion of the Isma'ilis' acceptance of all other sects and creeds, including the Jews, contradicts Netzer's assumption. See her, *Din va dowlat dar Iran-e ahd-e Moghol*, vol. 1 (Tehran, 1367 SH [1988/9]) p. 202.

16 See Netzer, "Sayri dar tarikh-e Yahud," p. 18.

17 See Vera Basch Moreen, *Queen Esther's Garden*; idem, "The 'Iranization' of Biblical Heroes in Judeo-Persian Epics: Shahin's Ardashir-Namah and Eza-Namah," *Iranian Studies*, vol. 29, no. 3–4 (1996) pp. 321–38.

18 See L. P. Elwell-Sutton, ed., *Bibliographical Guide to Iran* (Suffolk, 1983) pp. 20–21.

19 A. J. Arberry, *British Contributions to Persian Studies* (London, 1942) p. 9.

20 For details of this relatively recent discovery, see Parviz Azka'i, *Hamadan-nameh* (Hamadan, 2001) pp. 403–16. For a history of earlier translations of the New Testament, see Abbas Amanat "Mujtahids and Missionaries: Shi'i Responses to Christian Polemics in the Early Qajar Period" in *Apocalyptic*

Islam and Iranian Shi'ism (London, 2009) pp. 127–48. For details of Fazel Khan Garrusi's life, see *EIr*, s.v. "Fazel Khan Garussi" (Iraj Afshar).

21 See Norman Cohn, *Cosmos, Chaos and the World to Come: The Ancient Roots of Apocalyptic Faith* (New Haven, 1993); Shaked, "Iranian Influence on Judaism"; and K. D. Irani, "The Conceptual Basis for the Interaction between the Ancient Traditions of the Jews and the Iranians," in *Irano-Judaica*, vol. 3 (Jerusalem, 1994) pp. 90–98. For a useful introductory summary, see Foltz, *Land of the Noble*, pp. 45–56.

22 A. V. Williams, "Zoroastrian and Judaic Purity Laws: Reflections on the Viability of a Sociological Interpretation," in *Irano-Judaica*, vol. 3 (Jerusalem, 1994) pp. 72–89; Sorour Soroudi, "The Concept of Jewish Impurity and Its Reflection in Persian and Judeo-Persian Traditions," in *Irano-Judaica*, vol. 3 (Jerusalem, 1994) pp. 142–70.

23 Cohn, *Cosmos, Chaos*, p. 224, n. 4.

24 See Robert Wilson, "The Biblical Roots of the Apocalyptic," in *Imagining the End: Visions of Apocalypse from the Ancient Middle East to Modern America*, ed. by Abbas Amanat and Magnus Bernhardsson (London, 2002) pp. 56–66.

25 Cohn, *Cosmos, Chaos*, p. 225, and Jacob Neusner, "Jews in Iran," in *The Cambridge History of Iran*, vol. 3, part 2, ed. by Ehsan Yarshater (Cambridge, 1983) pp. 909–923.

26 The notion of a humanized deity did not disappear entirely from Iranian religious discourse. For a discussion of similar Baha'i views rooted in the revival of the Iranian Sufi tradition, see Chapter 3.

27 Cohn, *Cosmos, Chaos*, p. 221.

28 For the Mazdakite legacy in the early Islamic period, see *Encyclopedia of Islam, New Edition* (1960–) (hereafter *EI²*), s.v. "Khurramiyya" (W. Madelung); *EIr*, s.v. "Babak Khorrami" (G. H. Yusofi); Sa'id Nafisy, *Babak khurram-din, delavar-e Azarbayjan* (Tehran, 1342 SH [1963]).

29 For a survey of the heresiographical literature, see *EI²*, s.v. "al-Milal wa al-Nihal" (D. Gimaret).

30 See, for instance, *EJ*, s.v. "Persia" (W. Fischel).

31 See *EIr*, s.v. "Abu-'Isa Esfahani" (J. Lassner); and *EJ*, s.v. "Abu-'Isa" (W. Fischel).

32 *EJ*, s.v. "Karaites" and "Persia." Amnon Netzer, "*Sayri dar tarikh-e Yahud-e Iran*," pt. 2, in *Padyavand*, ed. by Amnon Netzer, vol. 2 (Los Angeles, 1997) pp. 1–65. For a collection of Islamic Karaite writings, see Leon Nemoy, *Karaite Anthology: Excerpts from the Early Literature*, Yale Judaica Series 7 (New Haven, 1952). See also Steven M. Wasserman, *Between Muslim and Jew: The Problem of Symbioses under Early Islam* (Cambridge, 1997). For the influence of the Karaites in Kashan through the twentieth century, and in Baha'i conversions, see Mousa Amanat, "Abna'-e Khalil-e Kashan" (1998, manuscript) MAP, p. 334.

33 See Richard W. Bulliet, "Conversion Stories in Early Islam," in *Conversion and Continuity: Indigenous Christian Communities in Islamic Lands, Eighth to Eighteenth Centuries*, Papers in Medieval Studies, vol. 9, ed. by Michael Gervers and Ramzi Jibran Bikhazi (Toronto, 1990) pp. 123–33. For a critique of Bulliet's views based on the need to consider regional differences, see Michael Morony's chapter in the same volume.

34 Claude Cahen, "Tribes, Cities and Social Organization," in *The Cambridge History of Iran*, vol. 4, ed. by R. N. Frye (Cambridge, 1975) p. 308.

35 Richard W. Bulliet, *Conversion to Islam in the Medieval Period: An Essay in Quantitative History* (Cambridge, MA, 1979). For an estimate of the size of important Jewish communities, see Zabihullah Safa, *Tarikh-e adabiyat dar Iran*, vol. 1 (Tehran, 1972) p. 232. Based on numerous medieval sources, Safa estimates the number of Jews in Hamadan, Isfahan, Shiraz, Ghazneh, and Samarghand as 30,000, 10,000, 8,000 and 30,000 respectively. He also reports substantial numbers of Jews in Khorasan and Khuzestan. To these estimates one might add the substantial rural Jewish population scattered throughout the region.

36 Zarrinkub, "The Arab Conquest of Iran," pp. 30–31.

37 For a full discussion of religious trends during the Ilkhanid period, see Alessandro Bausani, "Religion under the Mongols," *The Cambridge History of Iran*, vol. 5, ed. by J. A. Boyle (Cambridge, 1968) pp. 538–49.

38 Rashid al-Din, *Majma' al-tawarikh*, ed. by Alizadeh, pp. 396–97, cited in Bausani, "Religion under the Mongols," p. 542.

39 Ghazan owed his success in defeating his cousin Baydu to the assistance of the long-standing Muslim convert and Mongol commander Nowruz and to a loan from a local merchant.

40 A specific decree banned Muslims from filling any high administrative (*divani*) office. According to 'Abd ul-Muhammad Ayati, many Muslim notables were murdered on the specific orders of Sa'd al-Dowleh. (*Tahrir-e tarikh-e vassaf* [Tehran, 1967] p. 146)

41 For a concise and mostly balanced account of Sa'd al-Dowleh's career, see 'Abbas Eqbal, *Tarikh-e Moghol*, 3rd ed. (Tehran, 1347 SH [1968]) pp. 238–43.

42 Most sources date Rashid al-Din's conversion to the period between 1294 and 1298. The later date (not surprisingly) corresponds to Sa'd al-Dowleh's execution. See Netzer, "Rashid al-Din," p. 125.

43 Parviz Azka'i, *Tarikhnegaran-e Iran*, p. 317, dates Rashid al-Din's conversion to 1277, when at the age of 30 he joined Abaghan's (r. 1265–82) court.

44 Tusi's field of expertise extended far beyond medicine to include physics, astronomy, mathematics, logic, and literature. For a summary of his life, see introduction by S. J. Badakchani, *Nasir al-Din Tusi: Contemplation and Action: The Spiritual Autobiography of a Muslim Scholar* (London, 1998). Although we cannot be certain of the extent of the two brothers' collaborations with Tusi

in fields other than medicine, administration, and literature, it would be fair to assume that they in fact associated with him in other areas of scientific exploration. More to the point, it is fair to conclude that Tusi had a tolerant view of his Jewish colleagues.

45 Parviz Azka'i, *Tarikhnegaran-e Iran*, pp. 313–15; 'Abbas Eqbal, *Tarikh-e Moghol*, rev. ed. (Tehran, 1997) pp. 176, 181, 488.

46 Cited in J. A. Boyle, "Dynastic and Political History of the Ilkhans," in *The Cambridge History of Iran*, vol. 5, ed. by J. A. Boyle (Cambridge, 1968) p. 407.

47 See Dowlatshah Samarqandi, *Tadkerat al-Sho'ra* (Leiden, 1901) p. 330, cited in Netzer, "Rashid al-Din," p. 125.

Chapter 2

1 I am grateful to Dr. Afshin Matin for bringing my attention to this terminology. See his *Both Eastern and Western; The construction of Modern Iran's National and Islamic Identities* (forthcoming).

2 For an overview of the Safavid period, see Roger Savory, *Iran under the Safavids* (Cambridge, 1980); Amin Banani, "Reflections on the Social and Economic Structure of Safavid Persia at Its Zenith," *Iranian Studies*, vol. 11 (1978) pp. 83–116; and Rudolph P. Matthee, *The Politics of Trade in Safavid Iran: Silk for Silver, 1600–1730* (Cambridge, 1999).

3 Rula Jurdi Abisaab, *Converting Persia: Religion and Power in the Safavid Empire* (London, 2004) p. 27.

4 Vera Basch Moreen, *Iranian Jewry's Hour of Peril and Heroism: A Study of Babai ibn Lutf's Chronicle, 1617–1662* (New York, 1987) p. 85.

5 Ibid., p. 116.

6 Pietro della Valle, *Viaggi di Pietro della Valle* (Brighton, 1843), vol. 1, p. 598, cited in Matthee, *Politics of Trade*, p. 76; Persian translation by Mahmud Behforuzi, *Safarnameh-ye della Valle* (Tehran, 2001) pp. 604–609.

7 The entire population of the Georgian capital Zargam, consisting of Muslims, Armenians, and Jews, and numbering almost 15,000, was transported to Mazandaran to help develop the area. One thousand Jewish households were transported to Farahabad from the Georgian city of Kakht. See Matthee, *Politics of Trade*, p. 76.

8 See Moreen, *Iranian Jewry's Hour*, p. 71.

9 Rudolph P. Matthee, "Merchants in Safavid Iran: Participants and Perceptions," in *Journal of Early Modern History*, vols. 3–4 (1999–2000) pp. 233–68.

10 According to the Jewish source *Ketab-e Anusi*, tax revenues collected from Jews were assigned to a sister of Shah Abbas I. See Moreen, *Iranian Jewry's Hour*, p. 86.

11 Petro della Valle, *Safarnameh*, pp. 604–609.

12 Ibid., pp. 83–85.

13 Matthee, *Politics of Trade*, p. 44, cites a reference in the Safavid chronicle *Afzal*

al-tawarikh to Elezar (Lalezar Yahud) as "a loyal servant of the shah to whom silk from Gilan was to be consigned following the institution of the royal silk export monopoly in 1619." The group participation in the crime may have been a means of reducing the burden of the punishment, which according to Muslim law would be divided among the perpetrators.

14 See Matthee, *Politics of Trade*, pp. 20, 42.

15 According to Moreen, *Iranian Jewry's Hour of Peril*, pp. 90ff., the main text in question was *Sefer razim*, an early Jewish mystical work containing information about magic, the supernatural, and angelology.

16 The status of "People of the Book" was not granted to the Zoroastrian community until several decades after the establishment of Islamic rule in Iran. The debate continued among Muslim scholars as to whether or not Zoroastrian dualist beliefs should qualify them for such (monotheistic) status. See Chapter 1.

17 Moreen, *Iranian Jewry's Hour*, pp. 90–92.

18 Matthee, *Politics of Trade*, p. 83.

19 Ibid., citing Pietro della Valle, *Viaggi*, vol. 2, pp. 214–17.

20 Ezra Spicehandler, "The Persecution of the Jews of Isfahan during the Reign of Shah 'Abbas II (1642–1666)," *Hebrew College Union Annual*, vol. 46 (1975) p. 110, quoting Tavernier, *Voyages en Perse et description de ce royaume par Jean-Baptiste Tavernier* (Paris, 1930).

21 Roger Savory, "Relations between the Safavid State and Its Non-Muslim Minorities," *Islam and Christian-Muslim Relations*, vol. 14, no. 4 (October 2003).

22 Moreen, *Iranian Jewry's Hour*, pp. 71–74.

23 Ibid., pp. 101–102.

24 Ibid., p. 66.

25 See Matthee, "Merchants in Safavid Iran," p. 246.

26 See Savory, "Relations between the Safavid State," p. 445.

27 Bernard Lewis, *The Jews of Islam* (Princeton, 1984) p. 3.

28 Hosein Sa'adat-Nuri, *Rejal-e dowreh-ye Qajar* (Tehran, 1985) pp. 211–39.

29 Arman Estepanian, ed., *Aqa Reza 'Akkasbashi* (Tehran, 2007).

30 Kermanshahchi, *Tahavolat*, pp. 347–49. According to this source, Esma'il Khan converted to Islam after a love affair with the Imam Jom'eh's daughter put his family at great risk. The only solution found resulted in the family's conversion and his marriage to the daughter. However, this account may be an attempt to discount Esma'il Khan's own desire to convert.

31 For more details on Esma'il Khan, see Mohammad 'Ali Khan Faridul-Molk Hamadani, *Khaterat-e Farid* (Tehran, 1975), especially p. 274; 'Ali Akbar Khan Sardar Moqtader Sanjabi, *Il-e Sanjabi va mojahedat-e melli-ye Iran* (Tehran, 2001) pp. 446–47. For an extended report by Esma'il Khan on Kermanshah during the pro-German government in exile, see Movarrekh al-Dowleh

Sepehr, *Iran dar jang-e bozorg* (Tehran, 1957) pp. 305–308.

32 There is a substantial literature on the 1839 Mashhad persecutions and forced conversions. However, this study uses Qajar sources seldom used for this episode as well as a new primary source by a certain Mirza 'Azizullah Jazzab, whose family was victim of the persecution, but later became Baha'is.

33 Azaria Levy, *The Jews of Mashhad* (Jerusalem, 1998) p. 2.

34 See Chapter 2.

35 Levy, *The Jews of Mashhad*, pp. 1–3.

36 This estimate may be too low. The Qajar chronicler Reza Qoli Khan-e Hedayat reports the seemingly exaggerated figure of 1,000 families for the population of Mashhad Jews, in *Tarikh-e rowzat al-safa-ye Naseri*, 3rd ed. (Tehran and Qom, 1959/60) vol. 10, pp. 248.

37 'Abd al-Amir Muhammad Amin, *British Interests in the Persian Gulf* (Leiden, 1967) pp. 15–18, cited in Levy, *The Jews of Mashhad*.

38 See *EIr*, s.v. "Bukhara Jews" (Michael Zand).

39 Joseph Wolff, *Researches and Missionary Labours among the Jews, Mohammedans, and Other Sects* (Philadelphia, 1837) p. 106.

40 Ibid., p. 115.

41 Arthur Conolly, *Journey to the North of India: Overland from England, through Russia, Persia, and Affghaunistaun* (London, 1838) pp. 253.

42 According to Wolff, *Researches and Missionary Labours*, p. 91, the Turkomen accepted the Jews as "People of the Book" and never took them into slavery, while they considered the Persian Shi'is to be infidels who deserved to be enslaved.

43 Joseph Pierre Ferrier, *Caravan Journeys and Wanderings in Persia, Afghanistan, Turkistan, and Beloochistan* (London, 1857. Reprint: Karachi, 1976) p. 121.

44 See *EIr*, s.v. "The Herat Question" (Abbas Amanat).

45 Levy, *The Jews of Mashhad*, p. 6.

46 For the destructive effects of the *Nezam-e Jadid* troops in Khorasan, see James Baillie Fraser, *A Winter's Journey from Constantinople to Tehran* (London, 1838) pp. 256–86.

47 Conolly, *Journey to the North of India*, vol. 1, pp. 247–52.

48 Wolff, *Researches and Missionary Labours*, pp. 100–101.

49 For details of this incident, see Levy, *The Jews of Mashhad*, pp. 1–12; Patai, *Jadid al-Islam*, pp. 51–64; and Jaqleh Pirnazar, "Yahudiyan-e jadid al-Islam-e Mashhad," *Iran Nameh*, vol. 19, no. 1–2 (Winter and Spring 2001) pp. 41–60. See also Walter J. Fischel, "Secret Jews of Persia," *Commentary*, vol. 7 (1949) pp. 28–33.

50 At least two non-Jewish Persian sources are known to have referred to this incident, yet both report the seemingly exaggerated figure of 200 lives lost. This figure seems unrealistically high considering the estimated Mashhad Jewish population of 1,000. See Reza Qoli Khan-e Hedayat, *Tarikh-e rowzat,*

vol. 10, p. 248, and Mohammad Hasan Khan-e E'temad al-Saltaneh, *Matla ' al-shams* (Tehran, 1884–86. Reprint: 3 vol. in 2, 1983) p. 651.

51 The confusion over the date of the incident, being the holy day of 'Ashura, is particularly noteworthy. A number of studies, following confused European sources, date the incident to the Festival of 'Eid-e Qorban, on 11 Di Hajja 1255 SH (February 15, 1840). The date of 'Ashura in 1255 reported in Persian chronicles almost exactly agrees with the date of 12 Nisan 5999 (March 27, 1839) reported in Jewish sources. The Jewish and Muslim calendar dates differ by one day, a discrepancy within the margin of error for the two lunar calendars. See Habib Levy, *Tarikh-e Yahud-e Iran*, vol. 3 (Tehran, 1334 SH [1956]) pp. 113; Pirnazar, "*Yahudiyan-e jadid ul-Islam*," p. 46; and Patai, *Jadid al-Islam*, p. 57.

52 Fischel, "Secret Jews"; Levi, *Tarikh-e Yahud*, vol. 3; Patai, *Jadid al-Islam*; Pirmazar, "Yahudiyan."

53 It is not quite clear which Muslim holiday was in question, although Conolly reports observations of Muharram ceremonies in Mashhad. The *darugheh*'s curious request for alcohol was reportedly settled by a cash payment. See Conolly, *Journey to the North of India*, p. 255.

54 For an example of similar accusations made against the Babis of Kashan in the1850s, see Muhammad 'Ali Ghaffari, *Khaterat va asnad-e Muhammad 'Ali Ghaffari (Tarikh-e Ghaffari)*, ed. by Mansoureh Etehadiyyeh (Tehran, 1361 SH [1982/3]) p. 19. For a more recent case in which Jews were accused of sexual misconduct and became the victims of persecution during the constitutional period, see Chapter 6.

55 Mirza 'Azizullah Jazzab, "Tafsil-e fowz beh iman hazrat-e abawi," known as "Khaterat-e Jazzab," photocopy of manuscript, MAP, p. 3. See also 'Azizullah Solaymani, *Masabih-e hedayat*, vol. 7 (Tehran, 1976) pp. 451–52.

56 Allahyar Khan Asef al-Dowleh was an influential member of the Qajar elite and a close relative of Mohammad Shah. See Mehdi Bamdad, *Sharhe-e hal-e rejal-e Iran*, vol. 1, 2nd ed. (Tehran, 1978/9) pp. 154–58.

57 Ferrier, *Caravan Journeys*, p. 122.

58 E'temad al-Saltaneh, *Matla' al-shams*, 685, identifies the commander as Sam Khan Ilkhani. It was the Bahadoran regiment that on July 9, 1850, was given the task of executing the Bab in one of Iran's first public executions by firing squad. Abbas Amanat, *Resurrection and Renewal: The Making of the Babi Movement in Iran, 1844–1850* (Ithaca, 1989. Reprint: Los Angeles, 2002) p. 402.

59 See Conolly, *Journey to the North of India*, p. 276; E'temad al-Saltaneh, *Matla'al-shams*, pp. 644–47.

60 E'temad al-Saltaneh, *Matla' al-shams*, p. 652. For the role of the ulama in the Salar rebellion, see Hamid Algar, *Religion and State in Iran*, p. 125.

61 Ferrier, *Caravan Journeys*, p. 122.

62 Levy, *Jews of Mashhad*, p. 7.

63 'Abd al-Rahman Mudaress, *Tarikh-e ulama-ye Khorasan* (Mashhad, 1962) p. 95.
    E'temad al-Saltaneh, *Matla'al-shams*, p. 685.

64 Ferrier, *Caravan Journeys*, p. 122.

65 Hajji Mirza Musa Khan is reported to have resigned from "high-level ad-
    ministrative positions to serve the holy threshold of the shrine." E'temad
    al-Saltaneh, *Matla'al-shams*, pp. 514–15. For his public buildings, including
    dormitories offering free room and board to the orphan among the *sadat*
    (descendants of the Prophet Mohammad) who at times were organized as
    private militias, see *Matla' al-shams*, p. 523. Musa Khan had a long relation-
    ship with his one-time tutor and his half brother's rival and successor, Chief
    Minister Hajji Mirza Aqasi.

66 Ibid., p. 651.

67 The family name of "Jadid" was found in Mashhad as recently as the 1960s.
    Interview with Professor Ahmad Karimi-Hakkak, Manhattan Beach, Cali-
    fornia, September 11, 2005.

68 For the history of Jewish migration to Central Asia, see *EIr*, s.v. "Bukharan
    Jews" (Michael Zand), esp. pp. 536–37.

68 For the full text in Persian and a Hebrew translation, see Amnon Netzer,
    "Orot anuse Meshhed l'fi Ya'aqov Dilmanian" (The History of the forced
    converts of Mashhad according to Jacob Dilmanian), *Pe'amim*, vol. 42 (1990)
    p. 138, cited in Patai, *Jadid al-Islam*, p. 59.

70 As examples of his strict observance of the Sabbath during this period,
    Jazzab reports not wearing nailed shoes in order to avoid the possibility of
    sparks and staying at home so as not to encounter non-Jews on the sacred
    day. See Jazzab, "Khaterat."

71 Ibid., p. 2. Wolff, *Researches and Missionary Labours*, p. 99.

72 Jazzab, "Khaterat," p. 2. Wolff, *Researches and Missionary Labours*, pp. 93–95.

73 Wolff, *Researches and Missionary Labours*, p. 101.

74 Wolff reports his encounter with Hedayatullah in 1832 when the latter
    seemed to be genuinely interested in converting the former to Islam. (Ibid.)

75 Ibid., p. 102.

76 Jazzab, "Khaterat," p. 4.

77 Published works of Malamed Simantub (Simantov) (cited in Patai, *Jadid
    al-Islam*, p. 39) include a multilingual work in Hebrew, Aramaic, and Judeo-
    Persian entitled *Azhurat in the Holy Tongue and in the Persian Tongue* (Jerusalem,
    1896) and *Sefre hayat al-ruh* (Jerusalem, 1898). For a pseudo-historical debate
    between Simantub and Muslim ulama and Jewish converts, see Patai, *Jadid
    al-Islam*, p. 39. Amnon Netzer reports the date of Simantub's death as 1828.
    See Netzer, ed., *Padyavand*, vol. 1 (Los Angeles, 1996) p. 77. In a more recent
    study, Netzer speculates that he may have died as early as 1800. *Padyavand*,
    vol. 3 (Los Angeles,1999) p. 131. I am grateful to Dr. Nahid Pirnazar for
    bringing these last two sources to my attention.

78 Wolff, *Researches and Missionary Labours*, p. 128.
79 Ibid., p. 159.

Chapter 3

1   For surveys of the Baha'i faith and its teachings written from a Baha'i perspective, see J. E. Esslemont, *Bahá'u'lláh and the New Era* (London,1923); John Ferraby, *All Things Made New: A Comparative Outline of the Baha'i Faith* (London, 1957); William S. Hatcher and J. Douglas Martin, *The Baha'i Faith: The Emerging Global Religion* (San Francisco, 1984); John Huddleston, *The Earth Is But One Country* (London, 1976); Moojan Momen, *A Short Introduction to the Bahá'í Faith* (Oxford, 1997). For more academic treatments, see Peter Smith, *A Short History of the Bahá'í Faith* (Oxford, 1996) and *The Bábí and Bahá'í Religions: From Messianic Shi'ism to a World Religion* (Cambridge,1987); Juan R. I. Cole, *Modernity and the Millennium: The Genesis of the Baha'i Faith in the Nineteenth-century Middle East* (New York, 1998); Margit Warburg, *Citizens of the World A History and Sociology of the Baha'is from a Globalisation Perspective* (Leiden, 2006); William Garlington, *The Baha'i Faith in America* (Westport, CT, 2005); and Michael M. J. Fischer and Mehdi Abedi, *Debating Muslims: Cultural Dialogues in Postmodernity and Tradition* (Madison, 1990).

2   See Sabir Afaqi, ed., *Tahirih in History: Perspectives on Qurratu'l-'Ayn from East and West*, Studies in the Bábí and Bahá'í Religions, vol. 16 (Los Angeles, 2004).

3   For the history of the Babi movement, see Abbas Amanat, *Resurrection and Renewal*, also the preface to the paperback edition (Los Angeles, 2005), which discusses the Babis' unique message in terms of offering a drastic break with Islam; H. M. Balyuzi, *The Bab: The Herald of the Day of Days* (Oxford, 1973); Mangol Bayat, *Mysticism and Dissent: Socioreligious Thought in Qajar Iran* (Syracuse, 1982); E. G. Browne, *Materials for the Study of the Babi Religion* (Cambridge, 1918, repr. 1961); D. M. MacEoin, *The Messiah of Shiraz: Studies in Early and Middle Babism* (Leiden, 2009); and Shaykh Mohammad Nabil Zarandi, *The Dawn-breakers: Nabil's Narrative of the Early Days of the Baha'i Revelation*, trans. and ed. Shoghi Effendi (Wilmette, IL., 1932). For a recent survey of the Bab's writing and philosophy, see Nader Saiedi, *Gate of the Heart: Understanding the Writings of the Bab* (Waterloo, ON, 2008).

4   For surveys of Shi'ism in nineteenth-century Iran, see Hamid Algar, *Religion and State in Iran*; Mangol Bayat, *Mysticism and Dissent*; Said Amir Arjomand, *The Shadow of God and the Hidden Imam: Religion, Political Order, and Societal Change in Shi'ite Iran from the Beginning to 1890* (Chicago, 1984).

5   For surveys of Shaykhism, see Amanat, *Resurrection and Renewal*; MacEoin, *The Messiah*; Vahid Rafati, "The Development of Shaykhi Thought in Shi'i Islam" (Ph.D. dissertation, UCLA, 1979).

6   See Nikki R. Keddie, "Religion and Irreligion," in *Iran, Religion, Politics and Society: Collected Essays* (London, 1980); Bayat, *Mysticism and Dissent*.

7   For a translation of selections from these "tablets," see *The Proclamation of*

Baha'u'llah (Haifa, 1967). For Baha'u'llah's more developed social teachings, again in translation, see *Tablets of Baha'u'llah revealed after the Kitab-i-Aqdas* (Haifa, 1978).

8   For numerous references to the issue of obedience to state authority in the writings of Baha'u'llah, see Asadullah Fazel Mazandarani, *Amr va khalq*, vol. 3, reprint (Langenhain, 1986) pp. 275–81.

9   Moojan Momen, "The Social Bases of the Babi Upheavals in Iran (1843–53): A Preliminary Analysis," in *International Journal of Middle East Studies*, vol. 14 (1983) pp. 157–83.

10 For Baha'u'llah's life and teachings, see Cole, *Modernity and the Millennium*; H. M. Balyuzi, *Baha'u'llah, the King of Glory* (Oxford, 1980). For a more recent study of Baha'u'llah's ideas, see Nader Saiedi, *Logos and Civilization: Spirit, History, and Order in the Writings of Baha'u'llah* (Bethesda, 2000).

11 For 'Abdu'l-Baha's early writings advocating radical change in Iran see *Asrar al-ghybiyya li asbab al-madaniyya*, later known as *Resalihy-i Madaniyyih* (Bombay, 1882 [written in 1875]. Reprint: Darmstadt, 2006). There is a vast literature on 'Abdu'l-Baha's life and teachings. For a Baha'i perspective, see H. M. Balyuzi, *'Abdu'l-Baha: The Centre of the Covenant of Baha'u'llah* (London, 1971), reviewed by L. P. Elwell-Sutton in *Journal of the Royal Asiatic Society* (1973) pp. 166–68. For a study by a non-Baha'i contemporary, see Myron H. Phelps, *Life and Teachings of Abbas Effendi: A Study of the Religion of the Babis, or Beha'is Founded by the Persian Bab and by his Successors, Beha Ullah and Abbas Effendi*, 2nd rev. ed. (London, 1912), reprinted in abridged form as *The Master in 'Akka* (Los Angeles, 1985). For conversion of Zoroastrians to the Baha'i faith see Fereydun Vahman, "The conversion of Zoroastrians to the Baha'i faith", in Dominic Parviz Brookshaw and Seena B. Fazel ed. *The Baha'is of Iran, Socio-historical studies* (London, 2008) pp. 30–48; and Susan Stiles, "Early Zoroastrian Conversions to the Baha'i Faith in Yazd, Iran" in Juan Cole and Moojan Momen, *From Iran East and West*, Studies in Babi and Baha'i History, vol. 2 (Los Angeles, 1984).

12 See *Najm-e bakhtar (Star of the West)*, vol. 2, no. 4 (May 1911) p. 1, and 'Abdu'l-Baha, *Makatib-e 'Abdu'l-Baha*, vol. 2 (n.p., n.d.) p. 263.

13 For a detailed account of these events see Mohammad Taher Malmiri, *Tarikh-e shohad-ye Yazd*. 2 vol. (Cairo, 1922).

14 Homa Rezvani, *Lavayeh-e Shaykh Fazlullah Nuri* (Tehran, 1984) pp. 30–33, 40–44. Such warnings were eventually used to prohibit Baha'i political activity in the West by 'Abdu'l-Baha's successor, Shoghi Effendi. (See for example, Shoghi Effendi, *The World Order of Baha'u'llah*, pp. 64–66, 199.)

15 See 'Abd ul-Hamid Eshraq-Khavari, *Ma'edeh-ye Asmani* (Reprint: 9 vols. in 3rd reprint [New Delhi, 1984] vol. 2, pp. 409, 179.

16 For Ehsanullah Dustar, see *EIr.* s.v. "Ehsanullah Dustar" (K. Chakeri); Parviz Azka'i, *Hamadannameh* (Tehran, 2001) pp. 399–400. For an example of 11 Baha'is who fought governmental forces in Siahkal, in the province of Gilan, during the post constitutional period and were later executed by firing squad,

see *Yadegarnameh, majmo'eh-ye maqalat-e tahqiqi taqdim shodeh beh ostad Ebrahim Fakhra'i* (Tehran, 1984) pp. 40–42. I am grateful to Professor Houchang E. Chehabi for bringing this source to my attention.

17 Among Shoghi Effendi's works defining his vision of the Baha'i faith, see his *Baha'i Administration* (New York, 1928; Revised edition, Wilmette, IL, 1974); *The Promised Day is Come* (Wilmette, IL, 1941); and *The Advent of Divine Justice* (Wilmette, IL, 1939); and *God Passes By* (Wilmette, IL, 1944).

18 Among treatises developing Baha'i views, two are noteworthy: *Dala'il al-Bahiyya* by Mirza Abul-Faza'el Golpaygani (Cairo, 1898); and *Golshan-e haqaeq* by the Jewish convert Mehdi Arjomand (Reprint: Los Angeles, 1982).

19 In addition to Abul-Fazl Golpaygani, some of the more prominent among them were Mirza Hasan Adib Taleqani and Sadr al-Sodur Hamadani. Jamal Borujerdi, who later broke with mainstream Baha'ism, also played an important role during this period.

20 Juan Cole has argued that this change of attitude toward the Baha'is among the Qajar elite can be pinpointed to the 1882 arrest of nearly the entire Baha'i leadership of Tehran. The lengthy interrogations that followed proved that they were uninterested in political agitation. Juan Cole, "Religious Dissidence and Urban Leadership: Baha'is in Qajar Iran," *Journal of the British Institute of Persian Studies*, vol. 37 (1999) pp. 123–42. For Baha'u'llah's political ideas, see Cole, *Modernity and the Millennium*. For an early example of progressive democratic ideas, see 'Abdu'l-Baha, *Resala-ye siyahsiyeh* (Treatise on Politics), translated into English by Sen McGlinn as *Sermon on the Art of Governance*, with a Dutch translation by Marjolijn van Zutphen (np., nd. [2002?]).

21 Solyaman Shavar, *The Forgotten Schools: The Baha'is and Modern Education in Iran, 1899–1933* (London, 2009). Other Baha'i schools were established in Kashan (1898), Qazvin (1908), Hamadan (for boys, 1909; for girls, 1913), Ardestan (1913), Barforush (1912), and the village of Najaf-abad (for boys, 1912, for girls, 1928). See *EIr*, s.v. "Baha'i Schools" (Vahid Rafati). See also A. Sabet, *Tarikhche-ye Madreseh-ye Tarbiyat-e Banin* (New Delhi, 1997). Tehran's first official "modern" school was opened in 1898 by the reformist educationalist Hajji Mirza Hasan Roshdiyyeh and under the supervision of the Anjoman-e Ma'aref. See *EIr*, s.v. "Anjoman-e Ma'aref" ('A. Anwar). See also Monica Ringer, *Education, Religion, and the Discourse of Cultural Reform in Qajar Iran* (Costa Mesa, 2001).

22 Around 1904, the Baha'i Charitable Fund made a two hundred *toman* loan to the Baha'i assembly to purchase a property next to the new Baha'i center, perhaps in an attempt to provide more protection for the center. This land was used for building the Ta'id school and the Baha'i library. 'Abdul-Hamid Eshraq-Khavari, *Tarikh-e Hamadan* (Hofheim, 2004) p. 126; 'Abdullah Abizadeh, "Negahi beh vaqaye'-e tarikhi-ye amr dar ostan-e Hamadan," unpublished manuscript, pp. 141–42 cited in Eshraq-Khavari, *Tarikh-e Hamadan*, p. 310. After the closure of the library, the Baha'i books were preserved in the

Baha'i archive but "the rest of the library was destroyed," perhaps out of sheer neglect. Hafezi, *Tarikh*, p. 161.

23 Edward G. Browne, *The Persian Revolution* (Cambridge, 1910) p. 116.

24 William Garlington, *The Baha'i Faith in America*, p. 91. Homa Nateq gives important details about the society but curiously leaves out the obvious Baha'i connection. See "Tarikhcheh-ye Alians-e esra'ili dar Iran" in *Yahudian-e Irani dar tarikh-e mo'aser*, vol. 2, (Los Angeles 1997) p. 84, notes. For the Baha'i connections to the society, see Edward G. Browne, *Press and Poetry*, p. 59; Samuel Graham Wilson, *Bahaism and its Claims*, p. 154.

25 R. Jackson Armstrong-Ingram, "American Baha'i Women and the Education of Girls in Tehran, 1909–1934," in *In Iran*, Studies in Babi and Baha'i History, vol. 3, ed. by Peter Smith (Los Angeles, 1986) pp. 181–212; Baharieh Rouhani Ma'ani, "The Interdependence of Baha'i Communities: Services of North American Baha'i Women to Iran," in *Journal of Baha'i Studies*, vol. 4, no. 1 (March–June 1991) pp. 23–28, 30.

26 Farzin Vejdani, "Persian Baha'i Publishing in the late 19th and early 20th Century: Some Preliminary Remarks," unpublished paper presented at MESA 2008.

27 *EIr.* s.v. "'Akkas-Bashi" (Farrokh Gaffari).

28 A collection of Mirza Hasan's work has been published, though proper credit has been edited out. See *Shiraz-e Qadim* (Tehran, 2002). Mansur Sane' ed., *Beh yad-e Shiraz* (Tehran, 2002).

29 Among early amateur photographers is Ebrahim, son of the aforementioned Mirza Khalil. Arjomand, *Cheragh-e por forugh* (Ontario, 2002) pp. 93–94. One could add to this list one of Iran's first woman filmmakers Marva Nabili.

30 Ahmad 'Ata'i, *Nasabnameh-ye Hajji Mirza Kamal al-Din Naraqi*, unpublished manuscript, 117 pages and supplements, in private hands, pp. 25–27. For the Naraqi family, see Chapter 5.

31 Margaret L. Caton, "Baha'i Influences on Mirza 'Abdu'llah, Qajar Court Musician and Master of the *Radif*" in *From Iran East and West*, Studies in Babi and Baha'i History, vol. 3, ed. by Moojan Momen (Los Angeles, 1984) pp. 31–66.

32 F. Behgara, "Pay-e Sohbat-e Bijan Khadem-Misaq," *Payam-e Baha'i*, vol. 321–22 (August-September 2006) pp. 73–77. Bijan Kahdem-Misaq is an accomplished musician in Austria and is 'Ali Muhammad's nephew.

33 Another iconic musical figure, Ruhullah Khaleqi (1906–65), never formally became a Baha'i but has nevertheless been associated with the Baha'i community through his Baha'i brother. Khaleqi was a leading composer, educator, and scholar. His affiliation with the Baha'i faith, through his relatives, was significant enough in the eyes of the officials of the Islamic Republic to cause the cancellation of a commemoratory celebration of his 100th birthday, some forty years after his death. In a letter to a Tehran musical publication, his expatriate

relatives have denied "accusations" of his Baha'i association with harsh words calling them attempts aimed at "staining the pure name of Khaleqi" (*nam-e nik-e khaleqi ra aludeh sazand*). See Golnush Khaleqi, "Pasokh-e khanevadeh-ye Ruhullah Khaleqi beh maqaleh-ye vahi va takhribi-ye tohmat-e baha'igari," in *Honar-e Musiqi*, vol. 9, no. 78 (Jan-Feb 2007) pp.16–17. I am grateful to Dr. Manuchehr Sadeqi for bringing this source to my attention.

34 See 'Ali-Asghar Hekmat, *Rahamuz-e hekmat* (Tehran, 2003) pp. 324–25. Peter Smith estimates that Iran's Baha'i population in the 1920s was nearly 2 per cent of the country's population. See "A Note on Babi and Baha'i Numbers in Iran," *Iranian Studies*, vol. 15, no. 2–3 (1984) pp. 295–301. Judging by the figures available in the 1970s, a large percentage of Baha'is must have left the community, presumably due to social pressures, but also at least in part as a result of the tightening of membership rules within the community itself that began in the 1930s.

35 Nissim Levy to President, Tehran (November 27, 1901), Archive of the Alliance Israelite Universelle, Paris.

36 For a study of secular anti-Baha'i attitudes and mindsets, see Chehabi, "Anatomy of prejudice: reflections on secular anti-Baha'ism in Iran," in Brookshaw and Fazel, *Baha'is of Iran*, pp. 184–99.

37 For an example of a new style of opposition organized in the form of an economic boycott against the Baha'i villagers of Najafabad, near Isfahan, in the 1950s, see Ayatollah Montazeri, *Khaterat-e Ayatollah Hosein-Ali Montazeri* (Los Angeles, 2001) pp. 87–90. For a Baha'i perspective, see Fathullah Modarres, *Tarikh-e amr-e Baha'i dar Najaf-abad* (Darmstadt, 2004) pp. 145–51, 313–17. For an original survey of traditionalist opposition to the Baha'i faith in the 1950s, see Mohammad Tavakoli-Targhi, "Baha'i-setizi va Eslam-gara'i," *Irannameh* vol. 19, no. 1–2 (2001) p. 91. For an assessment of Iran's Islamic traditionalist opposition to the Baha'i faith, see Mohamad Tavakoli-Targhi, "Anti-Baha'ism and Islamism in Iran," in *Baha'is of Iran*, pp. 200–231. For an excellent case study of the 1955 campaign, see Shahrough Akhavi, *Religion and Politics in Contemporary Iran* (New York, 1980) pp. 76–90.

38 Formed in 1953, Hojjatiya is the quintessential post-war anti-Baha'i organizations. See *EIr*, s.v. "Hojjatiya" and "Halabi, Mahmud"(Mahmoud Sadri). Although the author acknowledges the significance of the anti-Baha'i mission in the inception of the Hojjatiyeh, he has not elaborated on their later connections with the secret police (SAVAK) and their organizational role in Iran's post-Revolutionary Baha'i persecutions. See also, Abbas Amanat, *Apocalyptic Islam and Iranian Shi'ism* (London and New York, 2009) pp. 224–25.

Chapter 4

1   Ephraim Neumark, *Masa'be-erets ha-qedem* (Journey in the countries of the East), with Introduction and Notes by Avraham Ya'ari (Jerusalem, 1947) p. 80. His estimate of the number of Babi/Baha'is is most likely an exaggeration. Abraham J. Brower, *Mi-Parashat Mas'otay be-Paras* (Jerusalem, 1937-8) pp. 22, 24, 31. I am indebted to Dr. Daniel Tsadik for translating passages from Hebrew. See also his *Avak darakhim* (Dust of roads) (Tel Aviv, 1944-46) vol. 2, pp. 146–53, cited in Hayyim J. Cohen, *The Jews of the Middle East: 1860–1972* (New York and Jerusalem, 1973) p. 162. George N. Curzon, *Persia and the Persian Question* (London, 1892) p. 496. Only a few families of Golpaygan Jewish Baha'is can be traced in Baha'i sources. One can only speculate that they may have retracted their Baha'i identity. See also Walter Fischel, "The Baha'i Movement and Persian Jewry," *Jewish Review*, vol. 7 (December-March 1934) p. 54.

2   A photograph of an elite Jewish family, the Hajji Lalezars, along with an explanation of their various religious convictions, is presented in Houman Sarshar, ed., *Esther's Children: A Portrait of Iranian Jews* (Beverly Hills, 2002) p. 201.

3   For patterns of Baha'i conversion, see Peter Smith and Moojan Momen, "The Bahá'í Faith 1957-1988: A Survey of Contemporary Developments," in *Religion*, vol. 19 (January 1989); and James J. Keen "Baha'i World Faith: Redefinition of Religion," in *Journal for the Scientific Study of Religion*, vol. 6, no. 2 (1967). For a brief critical response to this piece, see Agehananda Bharati, "Baha'i Statistics and Self-Defining Design," in *Journal for the Scientific Study of Religion*, vol. 7 (1968).

4   For an early example of materialist tendencies among lay Muslims, see *Rayhan Memoirs*, in Mehrdad Amanat, "Negotiating Identities," p. 191. For the attraction of some Jews to Sufism, see Chapter 2.

5   Elkan Nathan Adler, *Jews in Many Lands* (Philadelphia, 1905) p. 181.

6   Henry A. Stern, *Dawnings of Light in the East* (London, 1854) pp. 254–60. For a study of Baha'i debates with Christian missionaries, see Moojan Momen, "Early Relations between Christian Missionaries and the Babi and Baha'i Communities," in *Studies in Babi and Baha'i History*, ed. Moojan Momen (Los Angeles, 1982).

7   This practice is reported to have taken place in the latter part of the nineteenth century. See Asadullah Fazel Mazandarani, *Tarikh-e zohur ul-haqq*, vol. 8, pt. 2 (Tehran, 1976) p. 713.

8   Amanat, *Resurrection and Renewal*, p. 96, citing Qatil al-Karbala'i. For a discussion of the preoccupation with the idea of the Return among popular and Sufi figures, see pp. 70–105.

9   Oded Irshai, "Dating the Eschaton: Jewish and Christian Apocalyptic Calculations in Late Antiquity," in Albert I. Baumgarten, ed., *Apocalyptic Time*

(Leiden, 2000) p. 143. I am thankful to Professor Ra'nan Boustan for bringing this source to my attention.

10 See Parviz Azkar'i, *Hamadan-Nameh* (Tehran, 2001).

11 Benayahu, M. "Hezyonot ha-Qets shel 'Mashiah' me-Azarbaijan, TaQSaB-TaQTSaB," *Asufot*, vol. 2 (1988) pp. 285–344. Information is based on a text by Mosheh Mizrahi. I am thankful to Dr. Daniel Tsadik for bringing this source to my attention and for his summary translation of it.

12 See Daniel Tsadik, "Religious Disputations of Imami Shi'is against Judaism in the Late Eighteenth and Nineteenth Centuries," *Studia Iranica, vol.* 34, no. 1 (2005).

13 *Shant tarmad* in Hebrew, *tarmad* being the numerical equivalent of the year 644, which implies the year 5644 (1883/4). For an example from an earlier period, see Henry A. Stern, *Dawnings of Light in the East* (London, 1854) pp. 254–60.

14 *Rayhani Memoirs*, p. 183.

15 A. Cohen, *Qol Qara va-Elekh* (Tel-Aviv, 2000), pp. 7, 13, 22, 24. The author's main source is based on interviews with his own uncle. I am grateful to Dr. Daniel Tsadik for bringing this source to my attention. For Shiraz persecutions, see Tsadik, *Between Foreigners and Shi'is* (Stanford, 2007) pp. 120–137.

16 Hafezi, *Tarikh*, p. 127. One can only speculate that the date of Musa's claim may be around the turn of the century.

17 On famines, see Shoko Okazaki, "The Great Persian Famine of 1870–71," *Bulletin of the School of Oriental and African Studies, vol.* 49, no. 1 (1986) pp. 183–92. For the state of the economy, including the adverse effects of European influence, see Charles Issawi, ed., *The Economic History of Iran, 1800–1914* (Chicago, 1971) pp. 70–151, 258–309. For treatments of Iran's social and political conditions in the mid-nineteenth century, see Juan Cole's Introduction to his *Modernity and the Millennium*, and Abbas Amanat's Introduction to C. J. Wills, *In the Land of the Lion and Sun* (1883, 1891. Reprint: Washington, DC, 2004).

18 Muhammad 'Ali Sayyah, *Khaterat-e Hajji Sayyah, ya dawreh-ye khawf va vahshat* (Tehran, 1967) and Aqakhan Kermani, *Seh maktub* (Reprint: n.p., 1991).

19 The Sabbath ritual was conducted on Friday evening and Saturday morning, leaving the afternoon for leisure.

20 See Bassan to President, "Babism" (December 5, 1901), Archive of the Alliance Israelite Universelle, Paris. For Jewsih rabbis' negative attitude toward the Alliance, see A. 'Azizi, *Khatirat-i 'Azizullah 'Azizi, ya Taj-e vahhaj* (Reprint: New Delhi, 1994) p. 34. For a similar negative reaction to the Alliance around 1906 in Urumiyeh, see Khakshuri, R. S., "Yahoudiyan-e Urumiyeh" in Homa Sarshar, et. al., eds., *Yahoudiyan-e Irani dar tarikh-e mo'aser*, vol. 4 (Beverly Hills, 2000) pp. 209–24 especially pp. 209–10.

21 *Rayhani Memoirs*, pp. 259–60.

22 Bird, whose interest was the conversion of the Jews, may have had an interest

in seeing all the women as Jews. Isabella Bird, *Journeys in Persia and Kurdistan*, vol. 2 (London, 1891) p. 163. For women of the Naraqi family, see Eshraq-Khavari, *Tarikh-e Hamadan*, pp. 37, 49 notes.

23 Shofet, *Khaterat*, pp. 90–94.

24 Yazqel Yerushalaymi, "Sharh-e qesmi," pp. 44–52. For an account of the life of Qa'em-Maqami, including a lengthy extract from his autobiography, see Mazandarani, *Tarikh-e zohur ul-haqq*, vol. 8, pt. 1, pp. 267–278.

25 William Sims Bainbridge, "The Sociology of Conversion," in *Handbook of Religious Conversion*, ed. by H. Newton Malony and Samuel Southard (Birmingham, 1992) pp. 178–91. I am grateful to Professor Mehdi Bozorgmehr for pointing out this source to me.

26 Michael Ragussis, *Figures of Conversion* (Durham, 1995).

27 An example of this cultural transformation can be observed in Rayhani's son Na'im, an assimilated second-generation Baha'i who also commissioned his father's memoirs. A poet and man of letters, Na'im was educated at Vahdat-e Bashar, the Baha'i school in Kashan.

28 'Azizullah Solaymani, *Masabih-e hedayat*, vol. 9 (Tehran, 1976) p. 485.

29 Examples of family names adopted by Baha'is include Misaqiyeh (devotee of the Covenant) and Iqani (associated with Certitude).

30 For a study of the concept of manifestation, see Juan Cole, "The concept of manifestation," in *Baha'i Studies* monograph, vol. 9 (1982) pp. 1–32. Also available at: http://www-personal.umich.edu/~jrcole/bhmanif.htm.

31 Alessandro Bausani, *Religion in Iran, from Zoroaster to Baha'ullah*, Trans. by J. M. Marchesi (New York, 2000) p. 396.

32 Baha'u'llah, *Kitab-i Iqan* (Cairo, 1933) pp. 150–54.

33 *Rayhani Memoirs*, p. 221. For another example of discrimination against Jewish converts to Islam being called "half Jews" (*nim-Johud*), see Shofet, *Khaterat*, p. 62.

34 Homi K. Bhabha, "Unsatisfied: Notes on Vernacular Cosmopolitanism," *Text and Nation: Cross-Disciplinary Essays on Cultural and National Identities*, Laura Garcia-Moreno and Peter C. Pfeiffer, eds. (Columbia, SC, 1996) pp. 191–207 and idem., "Unpacking my library…again," in *The Post-colonial Question: Common Skies, Divided Horizons*, Iain Chambers, Lidia Curti, eds. (New York, 1996) p. 210.

35 For a case of nominal conversion to protect family assets, see the account of the Nur-Mahmud family in Chapter 5.

36 One indication of tensions between Jews and Mashhad's Jewish nominal-converts who later reverted to Judaism is the fact that the latter still do not intermarry with Jews from other communities, even when they live outside of Mashhad. See Raphael Patai, *Jadid al-Islam*, p. 104.

37 For a letter by 'Abdu'l-Baha warning the Baha'is against racial prejudice among Baha'is, see Eshraq-Khavari, *Ma'edeh-ye Asmani*, vol. 3, p. 96.

38 For another example of conversion to Islam involving a financial dispute,

and leading in turn to a Baha'i conversion, see 'Ata'ullah Eqrari, *Panjah va haft bahar* (Los Angeles, 2004) p. 22.

39 Shofet, *Khaterat*, pp. 62–104.

40 The famous Mongol statesman, physician, and historian Rashid al-Din Fazlullah, was killed on the order of the monarch in 1318. Several decades later, his body was exhumed, burned and reburied in the Jewish cemetery (see Chapter 1).

41 'Abbas Amir-Entezam, *An su-ye etteham*, vol. 2 (Tehran, 2002) p. 423. *Kayhan* (daily paper), *Nimeh-ye penhan, sima-ye kargozaran-e farhang va siyasat* (Tehran, 1378 SH [1999]), vol. 4. I am grateful to Dr. Jalal Jalali for bringing these sources to my attention. For a discussion of this relatively new obsession with finding a Jewish new-Muslim enemy of Islam one's political opponents or competitors and a relentlessly growing list of "accused" officials, see Mehrdad Amanat, "Set in Stone: Religious Ambiguity and Postmortem Identity in Iran" (forthcoming).

42 *Rayhani Memoirs*, p. 214.

43 The first known case of marriage between Baha'is of Muslim and Jewish backgrounds from Kashan was performed in Tehran around 1930 to avoid controversy. Correspondence with Bahereh Rastegar, January 2005.

44 Mousa Amanat, "Abna'-e Khalil-e Kashan" (1998) manuscript, MAP, pp. 36–38.

45 Letter dated June 2, 1903, in *Najm-i Bakhtar* (*Star of the West*). I am grateful to Dr. Fereydun Vahman for pointing out this source to me.

46 For a dignified biography of Mirza Mehdi see Azizullah Solaymani, *Masabih-e Hedayat*, vol. 4 (Tehran, 1960) pp. 4–91. For a somewhat vexed critical account, see Sobhi, *Payam-e pedar*, Reprint in: Sobhi, *Khaterat-e zendegi* (Tehran, 2007) pp. 287–90.

47 According to Solaymani, p. 7, these diaries, which are written in a telegraphic style and include a collection of Baha'i tablets and poems, are 825 pages in length. Lacking proper handwriting skills, Mirza Mehdi dictated his diaries to others such as Mirza Habibullah Samimi, another itinerate teacher who accompanied him in his journeys. A sample of the diaries is included in Solaymani's account. A. Solaymani, *Masabih-e Hedayat*, vol. 4, pp. 4-91. A photocopy of a portion of these diaries relating to the author's stay in Hamadan is in MAP.

48 Shoghi Effendi discouraged Baha'is from attending non-Baha'i religious ceremonies, such as *Rowzeh-khani*. Eshraq-Khavari, *Ma'edeh-ye Asmani*, vol. 3, p. 14.

49 Baha'i marriage laws include requirements for the consent of both parties and their parents, the attainment of the minimum legal age of 15, the limitation of the engagement period to 95 days, and the performance of the Baha'i ceremony in the presence of two lay witnesses. Divorce is permitted after a

"year of patience" (separation) aimed at reconciliation. See 'Abd ul-Hamid Eshraq-Khavari, *Ganjineh-ye hodud va ahkam* (Reprint: New Delhi, 1980) pp. 159–88. Baha'i holidays when work must be suspended consist of nine days which include the commemoration of festivals such as Now Ruz (March 21) and Rezvan (April 21-May 1), as well as the commemoration of the proclamation and martyrdom of the Bab, and of the passing of Baha'u'llah, and both of their birthdays. Iranian Baha'is were restricted from traveling to the United States without permission from Baha'i institutions from 1944 to 1957.

Chapter 5

1   For Christian proselytizing efforts among Jews of Isfahan, see Heidi Walcher, *In The Shadow of the King: Zil al-Sultan and Isfahan under the Qajars* (London, 2008), pp. 244-65.

2   Elezar collaborated with the French diplomat and historian Comte de Gobineau (1816–1882) in his pioneering work on the Babi movement, *Les Religions et philosophies dans l'asie centrale* (1865). He later moved to Baghdad and died there in 1881, apparently from alcoholism. See Yuhanna Khan Hafezi, *Tarikh*, pp. 12 and 36. For details of Tahereh's stay in Hamadan, see Eshraq-Khavari, *Tarikh-e amri-ye Hamadan*, pp. 28–30; Abbas Amanat, *Resurrection and Renewal*, p. 315.

3   The subtle difference between *Mashiah* (Messiah), not an unusual choice of name among Iranian Jews, and *Masih* (Christ), together with the physician's interest in Islamic religious concerns and Babi debates points to an unconventional believer, or perhaps a convert to Christianity or Islam. For Hakim Masih's brother and his sons see Amnun Netzer, "Yahudiyan-e Tehran az ebteda to enqelab-e mashrutiyyat" in *Padyavand*, vol. 3.

4   For Golpaygan Jewish converts, see above Introduction. For details of Hakim Masih's conversion, see an account by Mirza 'Ali-Muhammad Ibn-e Asdaq, son of Mulla Sadeq Muqaddas, in Vahid Rafati, ed., *Payk-e rastan* (Darmstadt, 2005) p. 395; Fazel Mazandarani, *Zohur al-haqq*, vol. 6 (unpublished manuscript) pp. 442–44; Hasan Balyuzi, *Eminent Baha'is*, p. 18. Some members of Hakim Masih's family became committed Baha'is, and his grandson, Lutfullah Hakim, was elected to the Baha'i Universal House of Justice in 1963.

5   Cited in Introduction. Curzon's numbers may include many sympathizers or early believers who later reverted to Judaism.

6   Nur Mahmud's son, Ayyub, visited Baha'u'llah in Palestine and received two tablets from him. Ayyub was an accomplished calligrapher, and he transcribed a number of Baha'i scriptures including the *Ketab-e Aqdas* in Judeo-Persian, many with illuminations as works of art. This author has seen some of this artwork, which is in the possession of his descendants. Considering his wealth,

his vast knowledge and his artistic work, all of which made him a prominent member of the community, his artwork can be seen as an indication of his devotion to the new religion, even though he is not known to have publicly proclaimed his Baha'i conviction.

7   *Rayhani Memoirs*, p. 207.

8   It was common practice in nineteenth-century Iran to take protective sanctuary in a mosque or in the royal stable, and civil and religious authorities were usually banned from intervening. *EIr*, s.v. "Bast" (J. Calmard).

9   Tavus was the daughter of the aforementioned Hakim Aqajan. She later married an apothecary seller (*'attar*), a predictable social demotion for a second marriage. Hafezi, *Tarikh*, pp. 23, 36.

10   Ayyub died some time in the late 1880s. Ibid., p. 101. His first wife is not named in the sources. She also must have been subject to Ayyub's difficult demeanor and a victim of his decision to marry a second wife whom he banished. Ibid., p. 33.

11   *Rayhani Memoirs*, p. 208. Rayhani identifies the Russian trade representative as Aqa 'Ali Haydar, but he does not name the Foreign Ministry official in question.

12   "One day he converted [to the Baha'i faith], and on the following Thursday he decided to fast. 'It isn't necessary to fast,' I told him.
'My sins are many,' he replied. 'I must fast.'" *Rayhani Memoirs*, p. 209

13   Ibid.

14   Khalil's commentary, referred to by other Baha'i authors, is presently unavailable and may have been lost. Arjomand, *Cheragh-e porforugh*, p. 21. According to Arjomand, Khalil's visit to 'Akka took place in 1888. Ibid., p. 14.

15   Khanom reportedly donated 900 *tomans* of this sum to the Baha'i fund as *huququllah* (the right of God), a Baha'i tithe. See Arjomand, *Cheragh*, p. 22. According to Hafezi, Khalil had collected a net 10,000 *tomans* and had paid legal fees to Sadr al-Sodur. Hafezi, *Tarikh*, p. 54.

16   Hafezi cites nine men, including three of the youth, who were "directed" by Khalil. Hafezi, *Tarikh*, p. 101.

17   Ibid., p. 33.

18   For Hakim Harun's family tree, see Levy, *Tarikh-e Yahud-e Iran*, vol. 3, p. 747.

19   Hafezi, *Tarikh*, p. 118, 135.

20   Interview with Besharat Kahvari-Amanat, May 25, 2009.

21   Hafezi, *Tarikh*, pp. 133–37.

22   Hafezi, *Tarikh*, pp. 129–30. 'Azizullah worked for Yuhanna Hafezi's pharmacy and later for a certain Mirza Ebrahim Morad Rashti.

23   Ibid.

24   'Azizi, *Taj-e vahhaj*. According to the editor, the Baha'i institutions did not authorize publication of approximately one third of the original manuscript

for reasons having to do with existing "governmental and Baha'i circumstances and necessities." According to the volume's editor, the complete manuscript was kept in Iran's Baha'i archives, which was confiscated after the 1979 revolution. The manuscript's present whereabouts and whether or not it has survived are not known. See editor's introduction to 1994 edition.

25 Ibid. p. 38.

26 Ibid. pp. 19–27, 49, 54.

27 Ibid. pp. 36–37; Eshraq-Khavari, *Tarikh-e Hamadan*, p. 71. For Baha'u'llah's prohibition against shaving one's head, see the *Ketab-e Aqdas*, K44 and Q10.

28 One notable associate was Fath 'Ali Shah's daughter and mother of Hesam al-Molk, Zobaydeh Khanom (also known as Fereshteh), of the prominent landowning Qaragozlu family. She was instrumental in hosting Tahereh after she was forced to leave the Jewish physician's house. Hajiyeh Khanom was the wife of the foreign minister, Mahmud Khan Naser al-Mulk. Amanat, *Resurrection and Renewal*, pp. 305, 314; *Tarikh-e Hamadan*, pp. 28–29.

29 Eshraq-Khavari, *Tarikh-e Hamadan*, pp. 48–49, notes.

30 Ibid. pp. 37–38 notes. Gowhar Khanom, wife of Aqa Mohammad Hasan Isfahani, is listed in Yuhanna Khan Hafezi's history as the other early Babi/Baha'i woman. Hafezi, *Tarikh*, p. 22. It is plausible that Isabella Bird's reference to a "Jewish women" Bible study group in Hamadan was not limited to Jewish Baha'i participants and included other learned women. Isabella Bird, *Journeys in Persia and Kurdistan*, vol. 2 (London, 1891) p. 163.

31 This account is related by Nabil Zarandi who met the two brothers in Asadabad on his tour of Iran in 1283/1866-7. References to Baha'is by Nabil (or Mazandarani) in the mid-1860s when a Baha'i identity had not yet been shaped may be anachronistic. See Fazel Mazandarani, *Zuhur al-Haqq*, vol. 6, http://www.h-net.org/~bahai/arabic/vol13/tzh6/tzh6.htm, pp. 705–706 notes. This account is not included in the published translation of Nabil's Narrative, which ends with the events of the year 1852. See Shoghi Effendi, ed., *The Dawn-Breakers*. The original manuscript of Nabil's Narrative in the Baha'i International Archives is generally not available to researchers.

32 Hafezi identifies the two Baha'i women as Gohar Khanum, the wife of Aqa Muhammad Hasan Isfahani, and Sakineh Khanum, the wife of Aqa Sayyed Yahya Naraqi, known as Nabil or Mosaafer. Hafezi, *Tarikh*, p. 22.

33 The twelve Baha'is and one Azali were arrested on March 14, 1881, by the order of the governor 'Ezz al-dowleh's son, who presided in the absence of his father. A number of the prisoners paid heavy fines, up to 150 *tomans*, but others were released after the intervention of the prominent land owner Zayn al-'Abedin Khan Qaraguzlu. Eshraq-Khavari, *Tarikh-e Hamadan*, pp. 48–49.

34 Ibid., pp.40–42; Amanat, *Resurrection*, pp. 269–71.

35 Having lost his father at a young age, Aqajan was known by his mother's name, Valad-e Misha (son of Misha). Hafezi, *Tarikh*, pp. 19–21.

36 Hakim Aqajan must have been mindful of such risks, as his own maternal grandfather, Musa, had died from injuries resulting from a beating by family members of a Muslim patient after competitor Jewish physicians ruled that the patient's death was due to medical malpractice. Ibid., pp. 5–6.

37 Yuhanna Khan Hafezi, son of Hakim Rahamim, refers to him as Hamadan's "chief physician" (*riyasat-e atebba*). Ibid., p. 36. See also Chapter 8 for more detail.

38 Hafezi reports his cousin Aqa Hayyem's salary from the Presbyterian mission as being three to four *tomans* (10–13 pounds) per month. Ibid., p. 24.

39 M. Stern, "The state of the Jews in Hamadan" in *The Jewish Herald and Record of Christian Effort for the Spiritual Good of God's Ancient People*, Vol. 6 (London, 1852) p. 317.

40 Both Christian and Baha'i sources report on the number of converts. Yuhanna Khan's account tries to discount the converts' level of commitment and claims the true attraction to have been to the Baha'i religion. Hafezi, *Tarikh*, pp. 22–26.

41 James Hawkes (d. 1932) was a Princeton graduate who came to Iran in the early 1880s to perform missionary activities. Both his young wife and their infant son died in Iran. His *Qamus-i kitab-i muqaddas* (Beirut, 1928. Reprint: Tehran, 1998) is a monumental work of Persian biblical studies. He lived in Iran for 52 years. Robin Waterfield, *Christians in Persia* (New York, 1973) p. 136.

42 William Thomas Gidney, *The History of the London Society for Promoting Christianity Amongst the Jews* (London, 1908) p. 467.

43 Hafezi, *Tarikh*, p. 24.

44 Hafezi reports that by 1878, "a small group of Jews were attracted, first in the name of Christianity, but in reality to the cause of Baha'u'llah." Ibid., pp. 22–23. Prominent Baha'i teachers who visited Hamadan included Mirza 'Ali Mohammad Ibn-e Asdaq, Jamal Borujerdi, and Aqa Shaykh Mohammad 'Arab. Hafezi, *Tarikh*, p. 26.

45 The description given of Aqajan and Rahamim by the Nestorian preacher, Sham'un, almost certainly confirms the identity of the two Jewish Baha'i leaders referred to in Baha'i sources. *The Gospel in All Lands*, Methodist Episcopal Church Missionary Society, New York, vol. 3 (January–June 1881) p. 176; James Bassett, *Persia: Eastern Mission* (Philadelphia, 1890) p. 176.

46 Hafezi, *Tarikh*, p. 34; Eshraq-Khavari *Tarikh-e Hamadan*, p. 47.

47 Benjamin Labaree, "The conversion of a Persian Jew" in *The Gospel in All Lands*, vol. 3 (January–June 1881) p. 176.

48 Ibid. This detail has not been confirmed by other sources.

49 See Chapter 7.

50 *Persia: Eastern Mission*, p. 175.

51 Hafezi , *Tarikh*, pp. 23–24. Hafezi generally understates the significance of Jewish conversions to religions other than the Baha'i faith.

52 Ibid., p. 25. Hafezi reports fines of ten *tomans* (approximately 20 pounds) per person were extorted from the prisoners by the governor. James Basset most likely reports the same incident, even though there are differences in his account. Basset reports that only two Christian converts were persecuted and that the converts were released after payment of seventy five *tomans*. Bassset, *Persia: Eastern Mission*, pp. 219–20.

53 The number of Jewish Christian converts is reported to be 55. Albert Edward Thomson, *A Century of Jewish Missions* (Chicago, 1902) p. 200.

54 Hafezi, *Tarikh*, pp. 24.

55 Ibid., p. 28. Hafezi's telescoped narrative of the process of the break with the Christian community minimizes its significance. A more reliable account by Abolfazl Golpaygani dates the final break to 1887, some ten years after the first Baha'i conversions. Ruhollah Mehrabkhani, *Sharh-e ahval-e jenab-e Mirza Abulfazl Golpaygani* (Tehran, 1975) p. 130. For Golpaygani's articulation of the Baha'i debate, see Golpaygani, *Dala'il al-Bahiyya*.

56 Hajji Mehdi Arjomand, *Golshan-e Haqa'eq*. For details of the debates, see *Zohur al-Haqq*, vol 8, II, p. 887; Hafezi, *Tarikh*, pp. 136–37.

57 According to Hafezi (*Tarikh*, pp. 56–57), Mohammad Mehdi Mirza Mu'ayyad al-Saltaneh's brother in law prince Meshkat al-Mulk also became a Baha'i after debates with Abulfazl Golpaygani.

58 For an account of rivalries between Rahamim's father, Hakim Elyahu, and the family of Hamadan physicians who had an exclusive claim to the profession, see Hafezi, *Tarikh*, p. 15. For a case of rivalries among Jewish physicians reportedly leading to a physician's death, see above note 36.

59 Hafezi, *Tarikh*, p. 28.

60 Feraydun Adamiyyat and Homa Nateq, eds., *Afkar-e ejtema'i va siasi va eqtesadi dar noskheh-haye montasher nashodeh-ye dowran-e Qajar* (Tehran, 1976/77) p. 309.

61 The myth of Jews killing gentile children to use their blood to make Matzo for Passover rituals has deep roots in medieval Europe and may have been introduced to Iran by sixteenth-century Christian missionaries.

62 Eshraq-Khavari, *Tarikh-e Hamadan*, pp. 44–46; Hafezi, *Tarikh*, pp. 26–28.

63 James Bassett, *Persia Eastern Mission*, pp. 175–57.

64 This incident took place on March 14, 1881. Eshraq-Khavari, *Tarikh-e Hamadan*, pp. 77–79.

65 Ibid. The sources do not specify which Jewish laws Baha'is (or Christians) were breaking other than the Kosher laws and Sabbath observance.

66 Hafezi, *Tarikh*, pp. 15, 71.

67 Report by Bassan to President (December 5, 1901), Archive of the Alliance Israelite Universelle, Paris, "General Situation of the Jews, Hamadan,

1875–1933." I am grateful to Dr. Daniel Tsadik for making these documents available to me.

68 Nasrullah Rastegar, *Tarikh-e hazrat-e Sadr al-Sodur* (Tehran, 1948/49) pp. 21–28; Fazel Mazandarani, *Tarikh-e Zohur al-Haqq*, vol. 8, I, pp. 480–81.

69 Since this study is not concerned with contemporary personalities, the issue of Jewish-Baha'is' contribution to the field of scholarship will have to be dealt with in a separate study.

70 In a visit to Palestine around 1920, Eshaq Anvar (d.1975), a convert from Hamadan, asked for 'Abdu'l-Baha's guidance to improve his family's dire economic condition. He was advised to move to Tehran where, using Baha'i contacts, he built a successful business distributing modern pharmaceuticals. See his autobiography, three-page Xeroxed manuscript, MAP.

71 'Abd ul-Misaq Misaqiyyeh (1893–1981), a nephew of Hakim Nur Mahmud, is known to have donated most of his fortune, which he earned in Tehran's post-World War II real estate market, to religious and philanthropic causes, including a major Tehran hospital in his name in 1945 and a nursing school. See his autobiography, "Kholaseh-i az khaterat-e jenab-e Misaqiyyeh va nemuneh-i az nikugariha-ye ishan," edited and transcribed by Muhammad 'Ali Fayzi, Xeroxed manuscript, 199 pages, (Tehran, 1977) MAP.

72 Manuchehr Hakim was a descendant of the aforementioned Hakim Masih. For more details on his life and services, see Christine Hakim-Samandari, *Les Baha'is: ou victoire sur la violence* (Paris, 1982).

73 Eskandar and Jalal were sons of Tehran's early Jewish convert, the aforementioned 'Azizullah 'Azizi.

74 For an account of one such Baha'i physician and medical entrepreneur, see 'Ata'ullah Eqrari, *Panjah va haft bahar*.

75 Both Khalil Arjomand and Habib Sabet were descendants of the aforementioned ambitious physician Mirza Khalil ('Aqiba). Arjomand, *Cheragh-e por-forugh*, pp. 38–48, 62–66. See also, Habib Sabet, *Sargozasht-e Habib-e Sabet beh qalam-e khod-e ishan* (Los Angeles, 1993).

76 In a survey of Iranian immigrants to Los Angeles, based on 1980 Census Data, Baha'is ranked second in education level after Muslims. (Many Muslims were foreign students who chose to stay in the U.S.) See Mehdi Bozorgmehr, et al., "Beyond Nationality: Religo-ethnic Diversity" in *Irangeles: Iranians in Los Angeles*, Ron Kelley, ed. (Los Angeles, 1993) p. 73.

Chapter 6

1 Rayhani was not an experienced writer and, as he indicates at the conclusion of his account, he struggled with issues of organization, footnoting, chronology, and even spelling. He nevertheless assures us that certain seemingly vague passages will become clear once they are read a few times, a fact to which this author can attest.

2 For examples of this genre of Baha'i narrative, see Adib Taherzadeh, *The*

Revelation of Baha'u'llah, 4 vols. (Oxford, 1974-87), and William S. Hatcher and J. Douglas Martin, *The Baha'i Faith: The Emerging Global Religion* (San Francisco, 1984).

3 Among the Jewish poets of Kashan were Babai ben Lutf (1617–62), his grandson Babai ben Farhad (d.1700), Benyamin ben-Mishael (Amina) (1672–1732), Yehuda Lari (sixteenth century), and the eccentric convert to Islam Sa'id Sarmad ('Aref-e Sarmadi) (seventeenth century). One recognized Jewish musician from Kashan was Musa Khan-e Kashi (Kamanchchkesh). Sarshar, *Esther's Children*, pp. 418–23.

4 For Kashan's economy during the second half of the nineteenth century, see Charles Issawi, ed., *The Economic History of Iran, 1800–1914* (Chicago, 1971), and Abbas Amanat, ed., *Cities and Trade: Consul Abbot on the Economy and Society of Iran, 1847–1866* (London, 1983).

5 For Rayhani's early life, see *Rayhani Memoirs*, pp. 179–83.

6 Ibid., pp. 188–89.

7 Ibid., pp. 267–68, 282–83. Shofet, *Khaterat*, p. 91 refers to Rayhani as a Sufi who became a Baha'i. Later in his memoirs, Shofet confuses Rayahan Rayhani with his son Na'im.

8 For the life and accomplishments of the Hakim Nur Mahmud family, see Habib Levy, *Tarikh-e Yahud-e Iran*, vol. 3, pp. 753–56. See also Chapter 5.

9 For evidence of the nominal conversion of Nur Mahmud's sons (for the purpose of, among other reasons, protecting the family estate against potential claims by a single family member who might convert to Islam and claim ownership of the entire estate), see the text of an 1899 ruling by Mozaffar al-Din Shah confirming an earlier ruling under Naser al-Din Shah which divided Hakim Harun's estate among his sons, in Mousa Amanat, "Abna'-e Khalil-e Kashan," manuscript, 1998, MAP, p. 425. Earlier, on July 11, 1889, the Paris office of the Alliance Israelite Universelle (AIU) had received a petition from Hakim Harun's grandson, the aforementioned 'Aqiba, later known as Mirza Khalil, who requested that the AIU present his petition to Naser al-Din Shah when the shah arrived in the French capital. Archive of the Alliance Israelite Universelle, Paris: Iran.II.C.6, Tehran. I am indebted to Dr. Daniel Tsadik for sharing these documents.

10 *Rayhani Memoirs*, pp. 184–86.

11 Ibid., p. 193.

12 Ibid., p. 195.

13 Ibid., p. 206.

14 Ibid., pp. 186–88; Jamal Borujerdi, a prominent *mojtahed* from Borujerd, became Iran's leading Baha'i advocate, community leader and head of the council of the "Hands of the Cause of God" in the latter decades of the nineteenth century. His later disagreements with 'Abdu'l-Baha and Baha'i leaders in Tehran resulted in his gradual disengagement. He was eventually declared a "Covenant Breaker." Rayhani's account supports the conven-

tional Baha'i view of Borujerdi as a manipulative leader focused on his own power and financial gain.

15 *Rayhani Memoirs*, pp. 179–80. Shah Mirza was a Babi *luti* rebel from Kashan with ties to the ulama and notables. He collaborated with another presumably Babi *luti* named Yahya Sayyed-e Babr (Tiger). Both were arrested and imprisoned in Tehran in 1863, on typical trumped up charges of raping women during the most holy Shi'i ceremony of 'Ashura. Nevertheless, their rebellion continued at least through 1870. Mansureh Etehadiyyeh, ed., *Khaterat va asnad-e Mohammad 'Ali Ghaffari* (Tehran, 1361 SH [1982/3]), pp.19–20. For Baha'u'llah's disapproval of his rebellious activities and the injustice by the local officials see Asadullah Fazel Mazandarani, *Asrar ul-asar*, vol. 3 (Tehran, 1973) pp.186–87. The Shaykh of Mazgan (Shaykh Abolqasem) was originally from Nushabad, northeast of Kashan. He had moved to the nearby village of Mazgan to escape persecution and lead the local Babi community. He was in his eighties when he was executed at Government House (later, Tekyeh Hajji Mohammad Ja'far Khan). The execution took place early in the morning, but the shaykh was left there for hours. His last wishes were that he be given water for his ablutions, so that he could say his last prayer, and that his body not be dragged around town as was customary for Babi victims. The reported date of 1870 for the execution is inconsistent with the author's recollection (since he would have been 10 years old in 1870). Mousa Amanat, "Ahebba-ye qora' va tavab'e-e Kashan," manuscript, MAP, pp. 264–73; 'Abd ul-Hosein Ayati Avareh Tafti, *Al-Kavakeb al-dorriyyeh*, vol. 1 (Tehran, 1923), pp.438–40; and Nateq-e Isfahani, "Tarikh-e amri-ye Kashan va qora'-e tavab'e'" (1309 SH [1930]) MS no. 2016D, National Baha'i Library, Iran, pp. 13–14.

16 Rayhani also reports on the reaction of one of Tehran's leading Shi'i clerics (and later constitutionalist) Sayyed 'Abdullah Behbahani to this incident. Behbahani publicly protested the execution of Mulla 'Ali Jan calling it a violation of the sanctity of the station of a *mojtahed. Rayhani Memoirs*, pp.190–91; 'Azizullah Solaymani, *Masabih-e hedayat*, vol. 4, pp. 499–537. According to one Baha'i observer, Mazandarani's instructions based on his understanding of the new faith included rules of cleanliness as well as covering for women peasants. Mirza Haydar 'Ali Isfahani, *Behjat al-sodur* (Bombay, 1331 [1913]) pp. 237–39, and translation by A. Q. Faizi, S*tories from the Delights of Hearts* (Los Angeles, 1980).

17 *Rayhani Memoirs*, p. 192.

18 Hajji Elyahu was one of the earliest and most enigmatic Jewish Baha'is of Kashan. He is reported to have converted in Hamadan in 1296 (1879) and to have gone to Palestine two years later. In Palestine he wrote a treatise arguing the validity of the new religion. He returned to Iran to practice medicine in Qom, where he met Rayhani and traveled with him to Tehran. He is also

reported to have returned to Palestine after the passing of Baha'u'llah. See Mazandarani, *Tarikh-e zohur ul-haqq*, vol. 6, p.671.

19 Hebrew, *kohanim*; Persian, *kuhen*. Descendents of Aaron.

20 For details of Hajji Elyahu's life, including his medical problems and financial demands on Baha'is, see *Rayhani Memoirs*, pp. 201–205. According to Rayhani, Elyahu's sons remained active Baha'is.

21 *Rayhani Memoirs*, p. 205.

22 For an account of Hajji Elyahu's activities and persecution in Tehran at the hands of other Jews, see, 'Azizi, *Taj-e vahhaj*, pp. 28–29. Baha'u'llah's tablet addressed to Hajji Elyahu appears in the revised edition, p. 27a.

23 *Rayhani Memoirs*, pp. 234–35.

24 For one example of protection extended to Jews by Muslims, see Chapter 7.

25 *Rayhani Memoirs*, pp. 255–56.

26 Ibid., p. 265.

27 For an example of unruly chaos and infighting among warlords in the Arak region in this period including murder of Ayatollah Khomeini's father, see *Khaterat-e Ayatollah Pasandideh*, ed. by Javad Muradinia (Tehran,1375/1996), especially pp. 28–30.

28 Asadullah Fazel Mazandarani, *Tarikh-e zohur ul-haqq*, vol. 8, pt. 1, pp. 267–73.

29 Jewish peddlers like Rayhani at times took on the role of traditional physician, fortune-teller, or soothsayer, and occasionally became intimate with women in the towns and villages they visited. Sorour Soroudi, "The Concept of Jewish Impurity and Its Reflection in Persian and Judeo-Persian Traditions," in *Irano-Judaica*, vol. 3 (Jerusalem, 1994) pp. 164–65.

30 The use of wine in rituals was a point of contention between Jews and Muslims that preceded the debates with the Baha'is. Daniel Tsadik, "Religious Disputations of Imami Shi'is against Judaism in the Late Eighteenth and Nineteenth Centuries," *Studia Iranica*, vol. 34, no. 1 (2005).

31 For an example (by a Jewish author) of dissatisfaction with the rabbis, whom some Jews considered "treacherous liars," see Yazghel Yerushalaymi, "Sharh-e qesmi," p.44.

32 *Rayhani Memoirs*, p. 256. The use of a sack for beating a woman in public must have served to cover her body. As a poor and apparently unmarried immigrant woman, she may have been a potential threat to the rabbi's sense of social control and was easily ostracized.

33 *Rayhani Memoirs*, pp. 213–15. Mulla Solayman's identity crisis seems to have been passed on to his son, Sha'ban, who went through a number of different names and occupational changes in his life. Amanat, "Abna'-e Khalil," p. 70.

34 Mazandarani, *Tarikh-e zohur ul-haqq*, vol. 8, pt. 2 (Tehran, 1976) p. 712, cites

Mulla Solayman's attachment to his leadership position as the reason for the reversal of his Baha'i identity, but does not mention the mulla's followers.

35 Although there are numerous provisions for capital punishment in the Torah, they are distinctly rare in the Talmud, even for those who deliberately commit murder. See Moreen, *Iranian Jewry's Hour of Peril*, p. 72 ff.

36 Mazandarani, *Zohur ul-haqq*, vol. 8, pt. 2, pp. 713–15; Amanat, "Abna'-e Khalil," p. 70.

37 Mazandarani, *Zohur ul-haqq*, vol. 8, pt. 2, pp. 702–703.

38 *Rayhani Memoirs*, p. 243.

39 Ibid., pp. 223–29. Some sources have dated this incident to 1318 SH (1900/1). See Nateq-e Isfahani, "Tarikh-e amri-ye Kashan," and the account of Mehdi Towfiq, son of Hakim Faraj, cited in Amanat, "Abna'-e Khalil," p. 430. Mazandarani has dated the incident to 1319 SH (1901/2). See *Zohur ul-haqq*, vol. 8, pt. 2, p. 706. These dates seem more credible than the one cited by Rayhani as 1904/5.

40 Three instrumental leaders are reported to have been Hakim Elyas, a son of aforementioned Hakim Harun; Mulla Eshaq, Kashan's leading Jewish rabbi; and Kadkhoda Musa (see the memoirs of Mozaffar Berjis). According to a different account, the Jewish leaders' motive stemmed from an incident at a Baha'i gathering where a certain one-eyed Ebrahim performed a program of entertainment that was offensive to the Jews. After Ebrahim was released from prison, he joined the town's security force, an unusual occupation for a Jew or even a convert. See Amanat, "Abna'-e Khalil," p. 430.

41 Amanat, "Abna'-e Khalil," pp. 293–94.

42 *Rayhani Memoirs*, p. 227. Rayhani seems to have been concerned about the possibility of the young converts recanting their new faith and did not mind being imprisoned.

43 Babis and Baha'is ascribed a symbolic religious significance to the number 19. The prisoners also paid three additional *tomans* probably to the guards as their share of the fine. Such a demonstration of independence by young Jews, which later became common during the Constitutional period, was an indication of the rising awareness of individual rights.

44 The minister's reaction was supposedly provoked by the governor's seemingly hypocritical demonstration of support and protection for the Jewish religion. The governor in question was apparently Mirza Ja'far Khan Mostowfi, who held the post from 1316 to 1320 (1898–1902) at the behest of Sayyed 'Abdu'l-Karim Shoja' Lashkar. Hasan Naraqi, *Tarikh-e ejtema'i-ye Kashan* (Tehran, 1345 SH [1967]) pp. 298–9.

45 Sayyed Mohammad-e Karvansara was a man of wealth and influence with close ties to the ruling elite and the later renegade *luti*, Nayeb Hosein. The latter was at first friendly with the Baha'is. Through contacts with provincial

governors, Sayyed Mohammad was on occasion influential in releasing some Baha'i prisoners.

46 *Rayhani Memoirs*, pp. 212–13.

47 The sources are understandably mostly silent about secular Jews in Qajar Iran. However, this silence does not preclude the existence of such beliefs among Jews and even (the above-mentioned) ex-Baha'is.

48 As Rayhani reports, "the *darugheh* was a daring and reputable man named Mashdi Mohammad who had recently become a Baha'i," *Rayhani Memoirs*, pp. 239–40.

49 Farrokh Khan Amin al-Dowleh (1812–71) was a reform-minded and influential high-ranking Qajar official. He held a number of governorships and important court positions and headed various ministries. As a skilled diplomat, he was responsible for a number of important treaties during the reign of Naser al-Din Shah. His construction projects in Kashan are among the most notable in the Qajar period.

50 Mokhber al-Saltaneh Hedayat, *Khaterat va khatarat* (Tehran, 1965) pp. 108, 113; Mohammad Hasan Khan E'temad al-Saltaneh, *Ruznameh-ye khaterat-e E'temad al-Saltaneh*, ed. Iraj Afshar (Tehran, 1966) pp.774, 822, 932.

51 For a positive portrayal of Vazir Homayun by a Shi'i cleric who was close to him during his governorship of Zanjan in 1903 and was influenced by his reformist ideas, see Shaykh Ebrahim Zanjani, *Sargozasht*, pp. 208–12. For a less sympathetic treatment, see 'Ali Abolhasani, *Shaykh Ebrahim Zanjani; zaman, zendegi, khaterat* (Tehran, 2005) pp. 51–59.

52 Hedayat, *Khaterat va khatarat*, p. 144.

53 *Rayhani Memoirs*, pp. 298–303.

54 Among Hajji Mohammad's business associates were Qajar notables and relatives of Vazir Homayun including Amin Khalvat and Eqbal al-Dowleh. Mohammad Khan Eqbal al-Dowleh (1848–1923/4), son of Hashem Khan Amin Khalvat, was a cousin of Vazir Homayun and a Qajar court official who became the governor of Kashan and in 1909, the governor of Isfahan. See Mehdi Bamdad, *Sharhe-e hal-e rejal-e Iran*, vol. 3, 2nd ed. (Tehran, 1978/9) pp. 214–15.

55 According to Rayhani this attack was with the support of the Shi'i cleric Mulla Habibullah Kashani and the influential merchant Mohammad Taqi Attarha. Mulla Habibullah Kashani (Sharif) (1845/6–1921/2) was a high-ranking ulama (*mojtahed*) with an inclination toward Sufism as well as mainstream Shi'ism. He joined the constitutionalists and was a member of Kashan's first provincial society (*anjoman*). He may have assumed the role of urban leader with the help of Kashan's *lutis*. See Naraqi, *Tarikh-e ejtema'i*, pp. 45–57, 304–305, and Kurosh Za'im, *Mardan-e bozorg-e Kashan* (Tehran, 1336 [1957]) pp. 119–20.

56 Rayhani identifies the merchant rival as the influential Mohammad Taqi Attarha.

57 Abul-Faza'el Golpaygani, *Kashf ul-gheta'* (Tashkent, 1919?) pp. 42–43.

58 *Rayhani Memoirs*, pp. 303–306.

59 *Rayhani Memoirs*, pp. 236–37. Rayhani mistakenly identifies the governor in question as Rokn al-Dowleh, who was Naser al-Din Shah's brother and who died around 1900. It is likely that he was referring to Mohammad Reza Rokn al-Saltaneh, who was Naser al-Din Shah's son and the governor of Kashan in 1320 SH (1902/3). See Mirza Ebrahim Shaybani, *Montakhab al-tavarikh-e Mozaffari* (Tehran, 1366 SH [1987]) p. 395. For an account that confirms details of the governor's abuses, see Hasan Naraqi, *Kashan dar jonbesh-e mashruteh-ye Iran* (Tehran, 2535 [1976/7]) p. 29.

60 See, for example, E. G. Browne, *The Persian Revolution of 1905–1909* (Cambridge, 1910) pp. 112–13.

61 The emissary was a certain Mulla Taher who reported the plans to the Baha'is. He "was quite friendly with the Baha'is. They would give a robe and a water pipe every year." *Rayhani Memoirs*, p. 237.

62 Ten *shahis* was approximately the equivalent of 25 cents. The incident reportedly took place a short while prior to May 1892. *Rayhani Memoirs*, pp. 253–54.

63 *Rayhani Memoirs*, pp. 217–23. Although there were a few clerics with the same title, the reference here is probably to Sayyed Ja'far Sadr ul-Ulama, the son of Sayyed Mohammad Baqer, a leading member of the pro-constitutional ulama whose role was especially important during the early part of the protest movement. His Babi-Azali connection is referred to by Rayhani: "There was a mulla who lived in Sadr ul-Ulama's house who was said to be Azal's deputy (*vakil*)." Ibid., p. 220.

64 For a biography of an important constitutional figure with Baha'i associations and multiple identities, see Juan Cole, "The Provincial Politics of Heresy and Reform in Qajar Iran: Shaykh al-Rais in Shiraz, 1895–1902," in *Comparative Studies of South Asia, Africa and the Middle East*, vol. 22, no. 1–2 (2002 [2003]) pp. 119–26.

65 Hosein Partow-Bayza'i, *Tarikh-e varzesh-haye bastani-ye Iran* (Tehran, 1958) p. 204.

66 Khavari Kashani, *Ketab-e Mahmud* (Tehran, 1329 SH [1911]). Khavari also served as editor of two progressive newspapers *Mizan* and *Sorayya*. See Sadr-e Hashemi, *Tarikh-e jara'ed va majellat*, 2nd ed. (Tehran, 1984). The poem which refers to 'Abdu'l-Baha appears in Ne'matullah Zoka'i-Bayza'i's biography of Khavari Kashani in *Sho'ara-ye qarn-e avval-e Baha'i*, vol. 1 (Tehran, 1965) pp. 315–23. Bayza'i obtained this poem through his brother Adib Bayza'i, the renowned poet of Kashan and a friend of Khavari. For a biography of Khavari Kashani, see Hasan Naraqi, *Zendegi nameh-ye Khavari-ye Kashani* (Tehran, 1977). *EIr.* s.v. "Khavari" (Mehrdad Amanat). Given the lack of transparency of the sources on his religious convictions, and perhaps his own

secrecy on this issue, one can only speculate about the Babi or Baha'i affiliations of such close associates of Khavari and noteworthy constitutionalist figures as Aqa 'Ali Naraqi. The biographer Hasan Naraqi does not discuss any Babi/Baha'i affiliations among any of these close associates.

67 These titles emulated those of the Qajar ruling establishment.

68 *Rayhani Memoirs*, pp. 283–84. Rayhani may be referring to the popular uprising in reaction to the anti-constitution agitation got up by Nayeb Hosein and his gang in the form of extortion, rape, and indiscriminate killing, most likely financed and orchestrated by anti-constitutionalists in Tehran. After a group of Kashan ulama issued a *fatva* on February 14, 1908, Nayeb Hosein and his son Mashallah (Sardar) were driven out of the area and their strongholds were demolished. Nayeb took sanctuary in Qom, while his son was arrested in Tehran and sentenced to death. But he soon escaped from prison, presumably with support from Tehran anti-constitutionalists. Naraqi, *Tarikh-e ejtema'i*, pp. 304–305; idem, *Kashan dar jonbesh*, pp. 45–57; and Za'im, *Mardan-e bozorg*, pp. 119–20.

69 For documentation of Nayeb Hosein's atrocities, see 'Abdulhussein Nava'i, et al., ed., *Nayebiyan-e Kashan* (Tehran, 2000).

70 *Rayhani Memois*, pp. 265, 295.

Chapter 7

1 For a comprehensive study of Iran's autobiographies see Bert, G. Fragner, *Persische Memoirenliteratur als Quelle zur neueren Geschichte Irans,* Persian translation by Majid Jalilvand Reza'i, *Khaterat nevisi Iranian* (Tehran 1998).

2 Aqajan Shakeri, *Shakerinameh*, photocopied manuscript, 246 pages plus appendices (Tehran?, 1961) MAP. The copy used by this author was made for the purpose of legibility by Mousa Amanat and 'Enatyullah 'Alizadeh around 1987. Parts of the original photocopied manuscript remain illegible due to the poor condition of the copy and the author's handwriting. All cited pages are according to the author's page numbers.

3 For a study of Hamdan in this period, see *EIr* s.v. "Hamadan Jewish community" (Hooman Sarshar); Haideh Sahim, "Jews of Iran in the Qajar Period: Persecution and Perseverance," in Robert Gleave, ed., *Religion and Society in Qajar Iran* (London, 2003) pp. 293–310.

4 *Shakerinameh*, p. 2.

5 Ibid., pp. 10–11.

6 Interview with Mrs. Jalalat Javid-Setareh, August 30, 2008.

7 *Shakerinameh*, p. 2.

8 Ibid., p. 5.

9 Within thirty years, the *qeran* (one tenth of a *toman*) lost half its value, from 25 *qeran* per English pound in the 1860s to around 50 by 1890. Issawi, *The Economic History*, pp. 344–45.

10 *Shakerinameh*, pp. 4–5.

11 Ibid, pp. 7–8.

12 Ibid, p. 6. For Hamadan's labor migration to Russia and migrant participation in construction of the Trans-Caspian Railway in the 1890s, see Hassan Hakimian, "Wage Labor and Migration: Persian Workers in Southern Russia, 1880–1914," *International Journal of Middle East Studies*, vol. 17, no. 4 (November 1985) pp. 443–62.

13 Shakeri's extended family fed Hatan and found him a job. He later remarried and lived in Hamadan. *Shakerinameh*, pp. 123,126.

14 Ibid, pp. 3–5.

15 The traditional *maktab*, often held in the teacher's home or in a synagogue, consisted of a group of students of varying ages who sat in a circle and learned the Hebrew letters and vowels. These were used to read and write Judeo-Persian. The students also memorized passages from the Torah, prayers, and sermons. The *maktab* system relied heavily on the repetition of verses combined with a heavy dose of corporal punishment and some tutoring by more advanced students. For a more positive description of *maktab*, see Mahdavi, *Panjah sal*, pp. 4–27.

16 *Shakerinameh*, pp. 3–4.

17 Ibid., p. 3.

18 For Alliance schools, see *EIr.* s.v. "Alliance" (A. Netzer).

19 Since soil conditions in Hamadan did not allow for cesspools, sewage had to be manually removed by sewage removers (*khala pak-kon*) and was used as fertilizer.

20 *Shakerinameh*, pp. 5–6, 45.

21 Ibid., p. 45.

22 Ibid., p. 45 (notes).

23 Ibid., p. 63.

24 Ibid., supplement to page 115.

25 For an example of the unruly chaos in the Arak region, see Chapter 6.

26 *Shakerinameh*, pp. 9–10.

27 For another example of women's conversion due to domestic strife or "deception" by a *luti*, see Hafezi, *Tarikh*, pp. 132–133.

28 *Shakerinameh*, p. 10.

29 Ibid., p. 8. Shakeri's claim of daily fights among the women is probably an overstatement.

30 Ibid., p. 9. A petition dated 1884 from Hamadan Jews to Tehran's "Investigation of Grievances Commission" (*majles-e tahqiq-e mazalem*) requested assistance from the government in rebuilding a burnt synagogue. If this was the same synagogue, Shakeri may be referring to an earlier incident he had heard about. In any case, such incidents were not too unusual. *Afkar-e ejtema'i*, ed. by F. Adamiyyat and H. Nateq, p. 309.

31 Prior to Sara's death, Shakeri (now a Baha'i) came to Hamadan for a last

visit. He engaged her in religious debates (*mozakerat-e amri*), and she accepted the Baha'i beliefs. "She suffered a great deal all her life and for a long time her husband was an itinerate merchant (*gharib*) in Zanjan. Just as they became relatively comfortable, she became ill and died. She asked me to take care of her second son, who was very intelligent. He is now known as Farajullah Khan and has become an erudite rabbi in Shiraz." Despite Sara's knowledge of the scripture and perhaps because of her Christian connection, few attended her funeral. "We moved her body. Despite all the hospitality she had provided in the community, none of the [Jewish] men offered to help out to carry her body from her home to the cemetery. The coffin stayed on my shoulder all the way. I was broken into pieces." *Shakerinameh*, p. 126.

32 Ibid., p. 49.

33 Ibid., p. 50.

34 Ibid., pp. 38–39. In a supplement apparently written at a later date, Shakeri dates his conversion to 1911, indicating a gradual process of acceptance of his faith. For the role of family support in his process of conversion, see 'Ataullah Abizadeh, "Sharh-e hal-e seh baradar, va do khawhar va madar," five-page manuscript (May 10, 1983) in MAP.

35 *Shakerinameh*, p. 51.

36 His old boss, Hajji Mehdi Aqa Refu'a (Arjomand) had offered him 70 *tomans*, but he settled for 25 *tomans* from his cousin. Other reasons Shakeri cites for not accepting the job had to do with "difficult working conditions" in the silver rending shop and his desire to say daily prayers for his recently deceased father. As an apprentice, some of his chores included bringing drinking water from far distances, grocery shopping, cleaning, cooking, walking to nearby villages to collect debts, and attending to the shop. Ibid., p. 31.

37 Ibid., pp. 32–33.

38 Shakeri's defense was to point out the similar method of producing yogurt that was widely consumed by the Jews. Ibid., pp. 22–23.

39 Ibid., pp. 51–52. This amount was twice the value of the house the Shakeris purchased around the same time.

40 For economic changes, see Issawi, *The Economic History of Iran*. For Iraqi Jews in Hamadan, see Elie Kedourie and H. D. S., "The Jews of Baghdad in 1910," *Middle Eastern Studies*, vol. 7, no. 3 (Oct., 1971) pp. 355–361.

41 For an example of a dispute resolution in Hamadan, see the case of two Jewish-Baha'i goldsmiths in *Masabih-e Hedayat*, vol. 6, pp. 448–50.

42 Of course, his marriage was in itself an example of traditional rather than modern behavior. Shakeri also cites careless spending patterns as one of the reasons for his father-in-law's bankruptcy. *Shakerinameh*, p. 115 (supplement).

43 Ibid., p. 52.

44 Ibid., pp. 65–66. According to Shakeri, "Manchester products were reduced to less than half a qeran [per meter]."

45 Solayman was Yuhanna Hafezi's maternal uncle. Hafezi, *Tarikh*, p. 135.

46 *Shakerinameh*, pp. 127–30.

47 Shakeri returned to Tehran in November 1936. After a short failed joint venture, his first job in Tehran was as an apprentice, earning a meager 19 *tomans* per month plus room and board. A few years later, he moved his family to Tehran permanently.

48 Ibid., p. 75.

49 Ibid., p. 58. According to Rayhani, Malayer Baha'is had considerable freedom of association in the 1880s, some thirty years before. He attended Baha'i gatherings in the home of the influential Baha'i Prince Mozun, where debates were conducted. *Rayhani Memoirs*, pp. 193–95. For an account of the 1910 Malayer persecutions and their aftermath, see *Kavakeb al-Doriyyeh*, vol. 2, pp. 234–37. A similar case of disintegration of a Baha'i community is the rural community of Uzman, near Malayer, where Shakeri visited a sizeable new Baha'i community in the 1910s. He reports the community had mostly disintegrated by 1935. *Shakerinameh*, p. 181.

50 Ibid., p. 58. Shakeri's friend and mentor, Aqa Sayyed Hosayn Hashemizadeh, later known as Motevajjeh, was a prominent Baha'i teacher. For his biography, see *Masabih-e Hedayat*, vol. 6.

51 *Star of the West* or *Najm-e Bakhtar*, a bilingual periodical publication from Washington, DC, was published in 25 volumes (1910–1925).

52 "We had clout" (*Zur-e ma ziyad bud*). *Shakerinameh*, p. 61. Elsewhere (p. 78) Shakeri refers in passing to the chief of Malayer's gendarmerie as a Baha'i.

53 At this stage of his life, Shakeri seems to have been inspired by his charismatic friend and new convert Eshaq Anvar. The rabbi was hired from the Jewish community of Tuyserkan with a salary of ten *tomans* per month. Ibid., pp. 61–62. Shakeri does not state whether or not he himself kept kosher at this time.

54 Ibid., pp. 78–79 and notes. For Shakeri's efforts in transporting the peddler's decomposed body, see below.

55 Ibid., pp. 62–64.

56 Ibid., p. 151. The choice of the name is interesting, not only because it is not a Jewish name, but also for its possible Baha'i connotations.

57 The number nine has sacred significance to Baha'is. The fine was paid by an officer, Ajoodan Hosein Khan, who was accused of trying to recruit Baha'is into the (Democrat) Party. Membership in political parties was religiously forbidden to Baha'is. Hosein Khan's title suggests association with the military or the gendarmerie. Shakeri's detailed description of how he prepared "the three fine chickens" they bought with the fine is valuable to a student of culinary material culture. Ibid., pp. 58–60. For an example of a composition from Rumi's poetry which Baha'is derived references to the coming of Baha'i prophets, see ibid., p. 130.

58 "*Ba 'adl raftar nafarma'id balkeh beh fazl.*" The three Baha'is in the photo were

Sayyed Asadullah Qomi, an elderly Baha'i teacher who had accompanied 'Abdu'l-Baha to America; Fazlullah Mohatadi Sobhi, previously 'Abdu'l-Baha's secretary, who was expelled from the Baha'i community some time after the photo was taken (see introduction); and Shakeri who held "a large portrait of 'Abdu'l-Baha next to his chest," presumably as a sign of loyalty. The photographer was a certain Shaykh Saleh Maraqeh'i who was also expelled from the Baha'i community. Prior to his expulsion, he taught the craft to Sayyad Asadullah. Shakeri and his friends had invested 60 *tomans* in a camera to make Sayyed Asadullah financially independent. *Shakerinameh*, pp. 133–34, 142–43. Expulsion or excommunication (*tard-e rohani*) was not unusual during Shoghi Effendi's ministry, but has since been increasingly rare. Expulsion meant that all loyal Baha'is were required to shun the expelled party, including the individual's own family.

59 Ibid., pp. 151–52. Baha'i laws forbid men from both shaving their heads and growing their hair beyond ear's length. *Ketab-e Aqdas*, K44.

60 Ibid., pp. 214–15.

61 For the Qaragozlu-Babi connections and his role as a staunch defender of Baha'is, see Eshraq-Khavari, *Tarikh-e Hamadan*, pp. 49–53, 127–28. For more details on the family, see Chapter 8.

62 According to Shakeri, Nayeb Mirza became a Baha'i after Shakeri arranged a meeting with the Baha'i leader, Hand of the Cause and custodian of the Baha'i religious tax (*hoququllah*), Hajji 'Abd ul-Hasan Ardakani, also known as Hajji Amin (1838?–1927/28). He reports that Nayeb was particularly impressed by the Hajji's lucidity at his advanced age. *Shakerinameh*, pp. 66–69. For an account of Mulla Baba Khan Malayeri, a Malayer *luti* who reportedly became a pious Baha'i, see Eshraq-Khavari, *Tarikh-e Hamadan*, p. 37 (notes).

63 During the famine of 1917–18, Shakeri helped to establish a bakery, on condition that he receive six kilos of bread per week to feed his family of six. *Shakerinameh*, pp. 88–89.

64 The contract to employ Morgan Shuster to help develop Iran's modern financial system was negotiated by the Persian Charge d'Affaires in Washington, Mirza Ali Qoli Khan, who was a Baha'i. Upon their arrival in Tehran, the American experts employed "fifteen or twenty very efficient servants" whom they met through their unnamed host and who soon after became known as Baha'is. Shuster rebuffed Iran's finance minister's efforts to fire his employees despite rumors that Baha'is were trying to take over Iran's finances. It is possible that from the inception of the gendarmerie (by the Shuster mission) a number of Baha'is were attracted to become officers through these or other Baha'i connections. W. Morgan Shuster, *The Strangling of Persia* (New York, 1920) pp. 4, 21–22,

65 Land for the Baha'i cemetery was first purchased in 1915. Eshraq-Khavari, *Tarikh-e Hamadan*, p. 148.

66 *Shakerinameh*, p. 76. Although no requirement for circumcision exists in Baha'i law, this custom continued to be observed.

67 Ibid., p. 140.

68 Ibid., pp. 169–70.

69 Ibid., p. 104. Baha'i law limits the engagement period to 95 days possibly to prevent child marriages through engagements that often lasted for many years. *Keteb-i Aqdas*, Q43.

70 For details of the wedding ceremonies and associated inter-communal conflicts, see *Shakerinameh*, pp. 103–112, 111 and supplement starting on pp. 115, 120. Given Hamadan's cold climate, girls there reached puberty at a later age as compared to girls in other parts of the country. Recourse to the mysterious "other" in times of desperation made fortune telling one of the few areas of cultural exchange between Jews and Muslims. Their mutual estrangement allowed them to ascribe supernatural powers to one another.

Chapter 8

1   See Mehrdad Amanat, "Set in Stone: Religious Ambiguity and Postmodern Identity in Iran" (forthcoming).

2   Anonymous (Nurullah Ehteshami?), *Sharh-e ahval-e marhum hazrat-e Hajji Mirza 'Abd-al Rahim Khan-e Hafez al-sehheh*, 20 pages (incomplete?) xeroxed handwritten manuscript, MAP, p. 2. The author was one of Hakim Rahamim's many grandsons and was a devoted Christian. It is worth noting that Mushe was also the maternal grandfather of the aforementioned Hakim Aqajan.

3   Sufi biographical dictionaries do not seem to acknowledge even the existence of Sufis of Jewish or other persuasions. This silence is significant in face of a long tradition of Jewish mysticism especially among the Kraites (Qara'is), which since the early middle ages had a prominent presence in Iran. See for example Muhammad Ma'sum Shirazi, *Tarae'q al-Haqae'q* (Tehran, nd). This question deserves further investigation. See also Chapter 2 on Mashhad Jews' association with the local Sufis.

4   Hafezi, *Tarikh*, pp. 4–5.

5   Ibid., pp. 5–6.

6   Elyahu is reported to have quit his job after his boss, Hakim Danial, scoulded him for having done a poor job of grooming his donkey. The name of the pharmacist, Karbala'i Taqi 'Attar's father, was apparently illegible to the transcriber of Hafezi's *Tarikh*. Among the medical texts he studied were: 'Aqili 'Alavi Shirazi, Mohammad Hoseini ibn Mohammed, fl.1772, *Khulasat al-hikmah* and Tonkaboni, Mohammad Mo'men Hoseini, fl. 1670, *Tohfeh-ye hakim-e mo'men*. Both of the above texts belong to the late Safavid period. Hafezi, *Tarikh*, p. 6.

7   The fact that Elyahu preserved his Jewish name (at least as far as the narrative tells us) implies that he maintained his mainstream Jewish appearance. Nonetheless, a nominal conversion to Islam, which would allow his close

contact with a Muslim master, cannot be ruled out.

8   Hafezi, *Tarikh*, pp. 9, 11–12; Amanat, *Resurrection and Renewal*, p. 315 note 124. For more details on Lazar see Chapter 5.

9   Hafezi, *Tarikh*, p. 12. On Haqq Nazar's close court connections especially with the women of the royal harem, see Amanat, *Pivot of the Universe*, pp. 336–37.

10 Gobineau's theory of inequality of the races was highly influential in the development of racial theories in nineteenth-century Europe.

11 Gobineau, *Religions et philosophies dans l'asie centrale*, p. 101. See also the introduction to the Persian translation by M. F. [Muhammad Ali Farahvashi] (n.p., nd).

12 *Hekmat-e Naseriyyeh: tarjomeh-ye resaleh-ye Descartes* (Tehran?, 1853) cited in, Khanbaba Moshar, *Fehrest-e Ketabha-ye Chappi-ye Farsi* (Tehran, 1973) p.1203. For the reported burning of the first edition and a summary of the translator's attempts to persuade authorities to publish the text, see Feraydun Adamiyyat, *Andisheh-ye Taraqqi va Hokumat-e Qanun* (Tehran, 1973) pp. 18–22.

13 For a comprehensive summary of the literature relating to this translation, see Mohammad Tavakoli Tarqi, "The homeless texts of Persianate modernity" in *Iran: Between Tradition and Modernity*, ed. by Ramin Jahanbegloo (Lanham, 2004) pp. 315–17.

14 Hafezi, *Tarikh*, pp. 19–20; Mazandarani, *Tarikh-e Zuhur al-Haqq*, vol. 6 (unpublished manuscript) p.706. Mazandarani does not specify his source for this information.

15 He earned the sizable amount of 1,000 *tomans* or 400-pounds sterling in fees from his Azerbaijan journey. Hafezi, *Tarikh*, pp. 19–20.

16 For details of the two physicians' debate with Nur Mahmud, see Chapter 5. This is the same occasion when Rayhani was first introduced to the Baha'i message.

17 Hesam al-Molk's sister Nimtaj, who was married to chief minister Hosein Khan Moshir al-Dowleh, is reported to have been instrumental in bringing this matter to a peaceful end. Hafezi, *Tarikh*, p. 29.

18 The transcription of Hafezi's *Tarikh* is not clear on the exact nature of other charges against the rebellious physicians. According to Hafezi, one of the Tehran Jewish elders, a certain Ezra, son of Yusef Esfahani, added the following to the petition: "As I sign this petition, my tears are falling on this page." Ibid., p. 28.

19 Moshir al-Dowleh's close family connections with the prominent Hamadan elite family of Qaragozlu, with whom Rahamim had close connections, may have helped bring a peaceful end to this affair. Ibid., pp. 28–30.

20 Ibid., p. 30. For E'tezad al-Saltaneh's life and career, see *EIr* s.v. "E'tezad al-Saltaneh" (Abbas Amanat).

21 As a sign of his disappointment, Nur Mahmud is said to have factiously asked his son Ayyub to have all his medical books thrown in the pool. Ibid., p. 32.

22 One possible influence on Hakim Rahamim may well have been Dr. Justin Perkins. He came to Iran in 1835 and lived there for 36 years. He was stationed in Urumiyyeh but made occasional visits to Hamadan. J. Christy Wilson, "A Persian apostate: Benjamin Badal," *Muslim World*, vol. 21, no. 3 (1931) p. 224.

23 He is reported to have earned "five times as much as he earned in Hamadan." Hafezi, *Tarikh*, p. 37.

24 Ibid. Hafezi identifies some of the Baghdad Babis or Baha'is as being from Hoveyd (Hovayzeh?) and 'Avasheq. Their out of control behavior may well have contributed to Baha'u'llah's decision to leave Baghdad in 1854, and to take refuge in isolation with Sufis of the Sulaymaniya region. For more details of circumstances leading to Baha'u'llah's departure, see Balyuzi, *Baha'u'llah*, pp. 115–122; Juan Cole, "Baha'u'llah and the Naqshbandi Sufis in Iraq, 1854–1856." in *From Iran East and West*.

25 The Ottoman council in Hamadan took the position that the female slave, Salameh (Salumeh?), had a different owner. Hafezi, *Tarikh*, p. 37.

26 Ibid., p. 75.

27 Ibid., p. 123. According to Hafezi, Baha'u'llah reportedly discouraged Iranian Baha'is from obtaining foreign citizenship.

28 Hafezi (*Tarikh*, p. 62) dates his conversion to a trip to the countryside on September 12, 1892. For an excellent treatment of this tragic episode of persecution, mostly based on reports by foreign officials and correspondence from Jewish leaders, see Daniel Tsadik, *Between Foreigners and Shi'is* (Stanford, 2007) pp. 155–74. The Hafezi account represents the converts' narrative and adds a valuable dimension to record of events.

29 The possible influence of European anti-Semitism on the revival and development of anti-Jewish discriminatory laws in Iranian Shi'ism has not been established and is worthy of further investigation.

30 The extended list of some thirty prohibitions included: wearing "fine" clothing or robes (*aba*), a visible sign of wealth; riding horses or mules within city limits; and a prohibition against leaving home on rainy days (supposedly meant to protect Muslims against transfer of impurities (*tarrashoh*) through splashing. This last was a particularly harsh requirement for physicians, who were dependant on house visits, and for business owners and peddlers. The prohibition against holding shop in the main bazaar had major economic significance. The prohibition against the height of houses exceeding those of the Muslim neighbors was a common Shi'i requirement applied universally. Having the entrances much lower in height may have been intended to distinguish a lower status. Women were not allowed the facial veil or black chador, a sign of prestige for the urban, privileged classes during the nineteenth century. For a complete list of new restrictions on the Jews, see Tsadik, *Between Foreigners*, p. 161.

31 Hafezi, *Tarikh*, p. 65.

32 Ibid., p. 62.

33 On one occasion around 1892/3, 'Abdullah is reported to have demanded that "the government has to first seek the ulama's seal of approval before being able to govern." Muhammad-Baqir Khurasani al-Qa'eni, *Tarikh-i i'brat-e leman i'tabara: dar vaqay'e-e 1315 Hijri dar Hamadan* (Tehran, 1946) p. 31. For details of a feud between two of Hamadan's landed notables, Mansura al-Dowleh and Zia' al-Molk, see Ibid., p. 27.

34 On the public ban of opium in coffee houses of Hamadan by Mulla 'Abdullah, see James W. Hawkes, "Religious conditions in Hamadan field," in *The Church at Home and Abroad*, vol. 16 (1894) p. 313.

35 *Tarikh-i 'ibrat*, pp. 24–26.

36 For examples of domestic abuse within the Jewish community see Chapter 7.

37 It is possible that both incidents played a part in instigating riots. Hafezi identifies the accused Jews as Neftali (?) Isfahani and Mushe Babajan Qassab. The latter was a handsome entertainer (*motreb*) with a pleasant voice who worked as a butcher at his day job. The victims are identified as two Lori charcoal porters. Hafezi, *Tarikh*, pp. 63–64.

38 A letter in Judeo-Persian in collection of Baron Rosen, dated October 17, 1892, written by a certain Aqa Sulayman 'Attar Hamadani was sent to another Jewish Baha'i, Aqa Sulayman Shalforuoush Hamadani who was living in Ashkabad. The letter dates the incident to a month prior to when it was written, September 17, 1892. The fact that a complaint was made to Mulla 'Abdullah about "drunken Jews" harassing Muslims in the Hamadan countryside is further referred to in a second undated letter which also dates the incident to (25 Elul=September 17). However, what appears to be second-hand information relayed by the author cannot by itself confirm the validity of the charges. See Youli A. Ioannesyan, *Baron Victor Rosen and the Baha'i Faith*, Studies in the Babi and Baha'i Religions, Vol. 23 (Los Angeles: Kalimat Press, forthcoming).

39 Hafezi, *Tarikh*, p. 63.

40 Tsadik, *Between Foreigners*, p. 159.

41 See for example, Habib Levi, *Tarikh-e Yahud-e Iran* and Walter J. Fischel, "The Jews of Persia."

42 Hafezi, *Tarikh*, p. 64; Tsadik, *Between Foreigners*, p. 156, cites documents which date the incident to late-September, 1892. See also, Sahim, "Jews of Iran," pp. 293–310.

43 Hafezi, *Tarikh*, p. 64.

44 The ritual ablution (*taharat*) was required even for Shaykhis who adopted the *usuli* form of Shi'ism during anti-Shaykhi persecutions instigated by Mulla 'Abdullah. *Tarikh-e 'ibrat*, p. 63. In the case of the Jews, the ritual also had the function of legitimizing the converts' use of the public bathhouse, which was strictly closed to Jews.

45 Hafezi, *Tarikh*, pp. 62–64. Hafezi dates his conversion to a trip to the countryside on September 12, 1892

46 Ibid. p. 65.

47 Ibid.

48 James W. Hawkes, "Religious conditions in Hamadan," p. 313 claims the conversions to Christianity were genuine because of their timing, a year after the commencement of persecutions.

49 Hafezi, *Tarikh*, p. 126.

50 In addition to Haji Aqa Mohammad, Hafezi identifies Mulla 'Abdullah's rivals as Sayyed Abd al-Majid, who was an ally of the Kababian Sadat, and two newly arrived Borujerdi mujtaheds, Sayyed Muhammad and Aqa-ye Fazel. Hafezi, *Tarikh*, pp. 65–66

51 Ebrahim Safa'i, *Panjah Nameh-ye Tarikhi* (Tehran, 1972) pp. 80–82. The liaison with the Ottoman consul may have been arranged by Hakim Rahim, himself now an Ottoman subject.

52 Safa'i, *Panjah*, p. 82; Hafezi, *Tarikh*, p. 66; 'Ayn al-Saltaneh, *Ruznameh-ye khaterat 'Ayn al-Saltaneh*, Qahreman Mirza, I. Afshar and M. Salur, eds., vol. 1 (Tehran, 1995) pp. 504–506.

53 Mulla 'Abdullah left Hamadan on October 7, 1892, but was "returned" by his followers briefly thereafter. He finally left for Tehran in mid-December 1892, after hearing the shah's plans to send troops to Hamadan to capture him. Tsadik, *Between Foreigners*, pp. 159–64; 'Ayn al-Saltaneh, *Ruznameh*.

54 The shah initially demanded 100,000 *tomans* in fines from the three khans. However, Sa'ed al-Saltaneh, Hesam al-Mulk, and Ziya' al-Mulk were released after they paid 7,000, 14,000 and 2,000 *tomans* respectively. 'Ayn al-Saltaneh, *Khaterat*, vol. 1, (Tehran, 1995) p. 509.

55 Remarkably, Mulla 'Abdullah apparently had good relations with both of the rival *mujtaheds*. His association with Mirza Hasan Ashtiyani is evidenced by an undated letter to Amin al-Sultan where Ashtiyani defends him as having "no intention to force the Jews into becoming Muslims (*beh jabr*)." Ebrahim Safa'i, *Panjah Nameh*, p. 85. According to Hafezi (*Tarikh*, p. 63), Mulla 'Abdullah's friendship with Dowlatabadi went back to their seminary years.

56 For Mulla 'Abdullah's anti-Babi sentiments see Bamdad, *Tarikh-e Rejal*, vol. 6, pp. 145–46. Hafezi on the other hand, claims that his own suspicions about Mulla 'Abdullah's Azali sentiments were confirmed by no other than the celebrated Malek al-Mutekallemin, the radical constitutional leader who was among the seven activists executed by Muhammad 'Ali Shah after the bombardment of the *majles* in 1908. Hafezi, *Tarikh*, p. 65. A leading scholar of Shi'ism also believes Mulla 'Abdullah's Azali affiliations as highly unlikely, if not impossible. (Personal communication.)

57 The other instigator of anti-Jewish persecution with alleged Azali affiliation was the aforementioned Sadr ul-Ulama in Tehran (see Chapter 6). Sayyed

Rayhanullah (1848–1910) was responsible for anti-Jewish persecutions in Tehran in 1897–98, which forced the Jews to wear the patch. Levi, *Tarikh-e yahud*, vol. 3, pp. 773–82. Rayhanullah's association as a Babi or Azali is limited to his family history. He was the brother of the Babi leader Sayyed Yahya Darabi (Vahid) and the son of Sayyed Javad Darabi Kashfi (intuitionist), himself an Akhabri thinker whose main preoccupation was with the Return of the Hidden Imam. Amanat, *Resurrection*, pp. 46–47, 247–48; Mohammad-Hosein Roknzadch-Adamiyat, *Daneshmandan va sokhanvaran e Fars* (Tehran, 1958–61) vol. 2, p. 90.

58 Hafezi, *Tarikh*, pp. 67–8

59 Ibid., pp. 72–74.

60 Ibid. Yuhanna Khan established his herbal and Western-style pharmacy around 1890, with the help of an apprentice by name of 'Azizullah whom he paid 18 *tomans* a year. By the year's end, his income from the pharmacy was 600 *tomans*.

61 Ibid., p. 74.

62 The minimum age for marriage according to Baha'i law is 15. *Ketab-e Aqdas*, Q43. The minimum age for marriage in Islam is 9.

63 Hafezi, *Tarikh*, pp. 89–90.

64 Ibid., p. 77.

65 Mirza Nabi's son, Manuchehr, was married to Tavus, the author's paternal cousin. Ibid., p. 93.

66 Ibid., p. 188.

67 Ibid., pp. 92–94; Eshraq-khavari, *Tarikh*, pp. 137–41. For the ulama's role in replacing governor Muzaffar al-Mulk with Sardar-Lashgar, see *Khaterat-e Farid*, p. 428.

68 Hafezi, *Tarikh*, pp. 74–75.

69 Hafezi identifies a certain Yequtiel as the assaulted party, whose son had allegedly insulted Mirza Baba, son of Aqa Shalom. Ibid., p. 75.

70 Ibid. The title *Kargozar* referred to the foreign ministry representative and prosecutor in charge of dealing with cases involving foreign consuls. The capitulatory obligations required that complaints relating to foreign subjects be processed through the foreign ministry. Baba Khan was the nephew of Mirza 'Abdullah Khan, son of ex-foreign minister Qavam al-Dowleh. Upon arrival in Hamadan, Baba Khan stayed with a close ally of Ya'qub, Hosein Khan Yavar.

71 Ibid., pp. 75–77.

72 Eshraq-Khavai, *Tarikh*, p. 71. This source does not identify the *Kargozar* and refers to him as *Sarparast*.

73 *EIr* s.v. "Amir Nezam Garrusi" (Abbas Amanat).

74 Hafezi, *Tarikh*, p. 78, cites the names of the *lutis* under "the mujtahed's employment" as: "Sayyed Vahhab who could commit every kind of mischief;

Solyaman Sardamdar, son of Ja'far , an alcoholic who carried out all kinds of wickedness and harassment. The same was true of Hashem Khan Asadabadi and a certain Haydar."

75 Ibid., pp. 80–83; 87

76 Ibid., pp. 83–85.

77 Ibid.

78 Hafezi estimates his family's business assets as 1,000 *tomans* and their debts over 1,300 *tomans*. The Ottoman representative had issued a plea to postpone demands on the family's debt until after the settlement of their claim against the Persian government. Ibid., p. 106.

79 Ibid., pp. 137–140.

80 Perhaps mindful of the treasury's chronic cash shortages, Rahim requested the annual stipend was to be paid part in cash and the remainder in grain. Ibid., p. 123.

81 Ibid., p. 140. Hafezi refers to a weekly income around 1899, of 300 to 400 *tomans* from *sarf va nozool* (the cash sale of merchandise, plus interest) in Tehran.

82 Ibid., pp. 140–41. An important center of trade in Tehran's bazaar was Saray-e Amir. It was under the control of Hajji Hosein Malek, who himself was a central part of the protest.

83 Ibid.

84 Ibid., pp. 147–48; 154.

85 Ibid., p. 154.

86 Ibid., pp. 156–57.

87 According to Hafezi, a group of Jews and converts contributed 600 *tomans* to "hire Mr. Bassan and his wife as teachers from Paris." He does not specify the details of this contribution or the level of Alliance contribution. Ibid., p. 164.

88 'Azizullah Mirza Zafar al-Saltaneh, son of the celebrated Prince Jalal al-Din Mirza was a notable military commander of the western frontiers. He was Hamadan's governor for three years (1900–1903). George Percy Churchill, *Biographical notices of Persian statesmen and notables August 1905* (London, 1906) trans. by Gholam Hosein Mirza Saleh, *Farhang-e Rejal-e Qajar* (Tehran, 1990) pp. 116–117.

89 Hafezi, *Tarikh*, pp. 164–65. Eshraq-Khavari, *Tarikh-e Hamadan*, p. 105 reports the less likely scenario of the Baha'is merely stating to the governor "the account of the Jews hostility and their strict enforcement of their superstitions (*omur-e vahmiyyeh*)."

90 The boys school was later moved to the Baha'i center. Hafezi, *Tarikh*, p. 165; Eshraq-Khavari, *Tarikh-e Hamadan*, pp. 116–133. Rafati gives 1909 as the opening year for both schools. *EIr s.v.* "Baha'i Schools" (Vahid Rafati).

91 For details of the 1913 school parade in Hamadan in which Alliance and

Nosrat schools also participated, see *Tarikh-e Hamadan*, pp. 143–46. See also, Mirza Muhammad 'Ali Khan Farid al-Mulk, *Khaterat-e Farid* (Tehran, 1354/ 1975–76) pp. 421–22.

92 Muhammad 'Ali Khan Farzin (Kolup), the head of Hamadan treasury and a notable nationalist is quoted in Eshraq-Khavari, *Tarikh-e Hamadan*, p. 144. For the education ministry's letter of formal recognition, see Abbas Sabet, *Tarikhch-ye Madreseh-ye Tarbiyat-e Banin* (New Delhi, 1997) p. 86.

BIBLIOGRAPHY

Manuscripts held in Iran's National Baha'i Library, cited as INBA Library, are no longer accessible. Documents in the Mousa Amanat Papers, Santa Monica, California, are cited as MAP. All quotes from Rayhan Rayhani's "Memoirs" are taken from the English translation in Mehrdad Amanat, "Negotiating Identities" (2006).

'Abdu'l-Baha. *'Abdul-Baha's Sermon on the Art of Governance = Resala-ye siyahsiyeh* (Treatise on politics). With English trans. by Sen McGlinn and Dutch trans. by Marjolijn van Zutphen. N.p., n.d. (2002?).

———. *Asrar al-ghybiyya li asbab al-madaniyya* (written in 1875; later known as *Resalihy-i Madaniyyih*). Bombay, 1882. Reprint, Darmstadt, 2006.

———. *Makatib-e 'Abdu'l-Baha*, vol. 2. N.p., n.d.

———. *Resala-ye siyahsiyeh* (Treatise on politics). Bombay, 1894. Reprint, Darmstadt, 2006.

Abisaab, Rula Jurdi. *Converting Persia: Religion and Power in the Safavid Empire.* London, 2004.

Abizadeh, 'Abdullah. Negahi beh vaqaye'-e tarikhi-ye amr dar ostan-e Hamadan. Unpublished manuscript, n.d., MAP.

Abizadeh, 'Ataullah. Sharh-e hal-e seh baradar, va do khawhar va madar. Unpublished manuscript, 5 pp., May 10, 1983, MAP.

Abolhasani, 'Ali. *Shaykh Ebrahim Zanjani zaman zendegi khaterat.* Tehran, 2005.

Adamiyat, Fereydun. *Amir Kabir va Iran.* Tehran, 1323 SH (1944).

———. *Andisheh-ye Taraqqi va Hokumat-e Qanun.* Tehran, 1973.

———. *Shuresh bar emtiyaz-nameh-ye Rezhi.* Tehran, 1360 SH (1981).

Adamiyat, Fereydun, and Homa Nateq, eds. *Afkar-e ejtemai va siasi va eqte-sadi dar noskheh-haye montasher nashodeh-ye dowran-e Qajar.* Tehran, 1976/7.

Adler, Elkan Nathan. *Jews in Many Lands.* Philadelphia, 1905.

Afaqi, Sabir, ed. *Tahirih in History: Perspectives on Qurratu'l-'Ayn from East and West.* Studies in the Bábí and Bahá'í Religions 16. Los Angeles, 2004.

Algar, Hamid. *Religion and State in Iran, 1785–1906: The Role of the Ulama in the Qajar Period.* Berkeley, 1969.

Akhavi, Shahrough. *Religion and Politics in Contemporary Iran.* New York, 1980.

Amanat, Abbas. *Apocalyptic Islam and Iranian Shi'ism.* London and New York, 2009.

————. Mujtahids and Missionaries: Shi'i Responses to Christian Polemics in the Early Qajar Period. In *Apocalyptic Islam and Iranian Shi'ism*. London and New York, 2009.

————. *Pivot of the Universe: Nasir al-Din Shah Qajar and the Iranian Monarchy, 1831–1896*. Berkeley, 1997.

————. *Resurrection and Renewal: The Making of the Babi Movement in Iran, 1844–1850*. Ithaca, 1989. 2nd ed., Los Angeles, 2005.

Amanat, Abbas, ed. *Cities and Trade: Consul Abbott on the Economy and Society of Iran, 1847–1866*. London, 1983.

Amanat, Mehrdad. Negotiating Identities: Jews, Muslims and Baha'is in the Memoirs of Rayhan Rayhani. Ph.D. dissertation, University of California, Los Angeles, 2006.

————. Set in Stone: Religious Ambiguity and Postmortem Identity in Iran. Forthcoming.

Amanat, Mousa. Abna'-e Khalil-e Kashan. Unpublished manuscript, 1998, MAP.

————. Ahebba-ye kalimi-nejad-e Hamadan. Unpublished manuscript, 2000, MAP.

————. Ahebba-ye qora' va tavab'e-e Kashan. Unpublished manuscript, 2000, MAP.

————. Ahl ul-Kaf. Unpublished manuscript, 1998, MAP.

————. *Bahai'yan-e Kashan*. Forthcoming.

Amin, 'Abd al-Amir Muhammad. *British Interests in the Persian Gulf*. Leiden, 1967.

Amir-Entezam, 'Abbas. *An su-ye etteham*. Tehran, 2002.

'Aqiba (Mirza Khalil). Petition to Naser al-Din Shah in Paris, July 11, 1889. Archives of the Alliance Israélite Universelle, Paris: Iran.II.C.6, Tehran.

'Aqili 'Alavi Shirazi, Mohammad Hoseini ibn Muhammad. *Khulasah al-hikmah*. India, 1851.

Arberry, A. J. *British Contributions to Persian Studies*. London, 1942.

Arjomand, Amir. *Cheragh-e por-forugh*. N.p., 2002.

Arjomand, Mirza Mehdi. *Golshan-e hqa'eq*. Reprint, Los Angeles, 1982.

Arjomand, Said Amir. *The Shadow of God and the Hidden Imam: Religion, Political Order, and Societal Change in Shi'ite Iran from the Beginning to 1890*. Chicago, 1984.

Armstrong-Ingram, R. Jackson. American Baha'i Women and the Education of Girls in Tehran, 1909–1934. In *Iran: Studies in Babi and Baha'i History 3*. Ed. Peter Smith. Los Angeles, 1986.

'Ata'i, Ahmad. *Nasabnameh-ye Hajji Mirza Kamal al-Din Naraqi*. Unpublished manuscript, 117 pp. and supplements, n.d., private collection.

Ayati, 'Abd al-Hosein Avareh Tafti. *Al-Kavakeb al-dorriyyeh*, 2 vols. Cairo, 1923–24.

Ayati, 'Abd ul-Muhammad. *Tahrir-e tarikh-e vassaf*. Tehran, 1967.

'Azizi, 'Azizullah. *Khaterat-e 'Azizullah 'Azizi ya taj-e vahhaj*. Reprint, New Delhi, 1994.

Azka'i, Parviz. *Hamadannameh*. Tehran, 2001.

———. *Tarikhnegaran-e Iran*. Tehran, 1994.

Badakchani, S. J. *Nasir al-Din Tusi: Contemplation and Action: The Spiritual Autobiography of a Muslim Scholar*. London, 1998.

Bahá'u'lláh. *Kitab-e Aqdas*. Haifa, 1995.

———. *Kitab-i Iqan*. Cairo, 1933.

———. *The Proclamation of Bahá'u'lláh to the Kings and Leaders of the World*. Haifa, 1967.

———. *Tablets of Baha'u'lláh: Revealed after the Kitáb-i-Aqdas*. Haifa, 1978.

Bainbridge, William Sims. The Sociology of Conversion. In *Handbook of Religious Conversion*. Ed. H. Newton Malony and Samuel Southard. Birmingham, 1992.

Balyuzi, H. M. *'Abdu'l-Baha: The Centre of the Covenant of Baha'u'llah*. London, 1971.

———. *The Bab: The Herald of the Day of Days*. Oxford, 1973.

———. *Baha'u'llah, the King of Glory*. Oxford, 1980.

———. *Eminent Baha'is in the Time of Baha'u'llah*. Oxford, 1985.

Bamdad, Mehdi. *Sharhe-e hal-e rejal-e Iran*, 6 vols. Tehran, 1347 SH (1968). 2nd ed., Tehran, 1978/9.

Banani, Amin. Reflections on the Social and Economic Structure of Safavid Persia at Its Zenith. *Iranian Studies* 11 (1978).

Bassan. Report to the President [of the Alliance Israélite Universelle (?)] on Babism (in French). December 5, 1901. Archives of the Alliance Israélite Universelle, Paris.

———. Report to the President [of the Alliance Israélite Universelle (?)] on the general situation of the Jews in Hamadan (in French). December 5, 1901. Archives of the Alliance Israélite Universelle, Paris.

Bassett, James. *Persia, Eastern Mission*. Philadelphia, 1890.

———. *Persia: The Land of the Imams*. London, 1887.

Bausani, Alessandro. *Religion in Iran, from Zoroaster to Baha'u'llah*. Trans. J. M. Marchesi. New York, 2000.

———. Religion under the Mongols. In *Cambridge History of Iran*, vol. 5. Ed. J. A. Boyle. Cambridge, 1968.

Bayani, Chirine. *Din va dowlat dar Iran-e ahd-e Moghol*, vol. 1. Tehran, 1367 SH (1988/9).

Bayat, Mangol. *Mysticism and Dissent: Socioreligious Thought in Qajar Iran*. Syracuse, 1982.

Behgara, F. Pay-e Sohbat-e Bijan Khadem-Misaq. *Payam-e Baha'i* 321–322 (August–September 2006).

Benayahu, M. Hezyonot ha-Qets shel "Mashiah" me-Azarbaijan, TaQSaB-TaQTSaB. *Asufot* 2 (1988).

Berjis, Mozaffar. Khaterat-e Muzaffar-e Berjis. Photocopy of manuscript transcribed by Hesam Noqaba'i, 1977, MAP.

Bhabha, Homi K. "Unpacking My Library... Again." In *The Post-colonial Question: Common Skies, Divided Horizons*. Ed. Iain Chambers and Lidia Curti. London and New York, 1996.

———. Unsatisfied: Notes on Vernacular Cosmopolitanism. In *Text and Nation: Cross-Disciplinary Essays on Cultural and National Identities*. Ed. Laura Garcia-Moreno and Peter C. Pfeiffer. Columbia, SC, 1996.

Bharati, Agehananda. Baha'i Statistics and Self-Defining Design. *Journal for the Scientific Study of Religion* 7/2 (1968).

Bird, Isabella L. *Journeys in Persia and Kurdistan*, 2 vols. London, 1891.

Boyce, Mary. *History of Zoroastrianism*, vol. 3. Leiden, 1991.

———. *Zoroastrianism: A Shadowy But Powerful Presence in the Judaeo-Christian World*. London, 1987.

Boyle, J. A. Dynastic and Political History of the Ilkhans. In *Cambridge History of Iran*, vol. 5. Ed. J. A. Boyle. Cambridge, 1968.

Bozorgmehr, Mehdi, et al. Beyond Nationality: Religio-ethnic Diversity. In *Irangeles: Iranians in Los Angeles*. Ed. Ron Kelley. Los Angeles, 1993.

Brower, Abraham J. *Avak darakhim* (Dust of roads). Tel Aviv, 1944–46.

———. *Mi-Parashat Mas'otay be-Paras*. Jerusalem, 1937–38.

Browne, Edward Granville. *Materials for the Study of the Babi Religion*. Cambridge, 1918. Reprint, 1961.

———. *The Persian Revolution of 1905–1909*. Cambridge, 1910.

———. *The Press and Poetry of Modern Persia*. Cambridge, 1914. Reprint, Los Angeles, 1983

Bulliet, Richard W. *Conversion to Islam in the Medieval Period: An Essay in Quantitative History*. Cambridge, MA, 1979.

———. Conversion Stories in Early Islam. In *Conversion and Continuity: Indigenous Christian Communities in Islamic Lands, Eighth to Eighteenth Centuries*. Papers in Medieval Studies 9. Ed. Michael Gervers and Ramzi Jibran Bikhazi. Toronto, 1990.

Cahen, Claude. Tribes, Cities and Social Organization. In *Cambridge History of Iran*, vol. 4. Ed. R. N. Frye. Cambridge, 1975.

Caton, Margaret L. Baha'i Influences on Mirza 'Abdu'llah, Qajar Court Musician and Master of the Radif. In *From Iran East and West, Studies in Babi and Baha'i History*, vol. 3. Ed. Moojan Momen. Los Angeles, 1984.

Chehabi, H. E. Anatomy of Prejudice: Reflections on Secular Anti-Baha'ism in Iran. In *Baha'is of Iran: Socio-historical Studies*. Ed. Dominic Parviz Brookshaw and Seena B. Fazel. London and New York, 2008.

Churchill, George Percy. *Farhang-e Rejal-e Qajar*. Trans. Gholam Hosein Mirza Saleh. Tehran, 1990. Originally published as *Biographical Notices of Persian Statesmen and Notables August 1905* (London, 1906).

Cohen, A. *Qol Qara va-Elekh*. Tel Aviv, 2000.

Cohen, Hayyim J. *The Jews of the Middle East: 1860–1972*. New York and Jerusalem, 1973.

Cohen, Yousef. *Gozaresh va khaterat: Fa'aliyyatha-ye siasi va ejetma'i*. Los Angeles, 1995.

Cohn, Norman. *Cosmos, Chaos and the World to Come: The Ancient Roots of Apocalyptic Faith*. New Haven, 1993.

Cole, Juan R. I. Baha'u'llah and the Naqshbandi Sufis in Iraq, 1854–1856. In *From Iran East and West*. Ed. Moojan Momen. Los Angeles, 1984.

———. *The Concept of Manifestation in the Bahá'i Writings*. Baha'i Studies 9. Ottawa, 1982. Also available at http://www-personal.umich.edu/~jrcole/bhmanif.htm.

———. *Modernity and the Millennium: The Genesis of the Baha'i Faith in the Nineteenth-century Middle East*. New York, 1998.

———. The Provincial Politics of Heresy and Reform in Qajar Iran: Shaykh al-Rais in Shiraz, 1895–1902. *Comparative Studies of South Asia, Africa and the Middle East* 22/1–2 (2002 [2003]).

———. Religious Dissidence and Urban Leadership: Baha'is in Qajar Iran. *Journal of the British Institute of Persian Studies* 37 (1999).

Conolly, Arthur. *Journey to the North of India: Overland from England, through Russia, Persia, and Affghaunistaun*, 2 vols. London, 1838.

Curzon, George N. *Persia and the Persian Question*. London, 1892.

Ehteshami, Nurullah (?). Sharh-e ahval-e marhum hazrat-e Hajji Mirza 'Abd-al Rahim Khan-e Hafez al-sehheh. Photocopy of autograph manuscript, 20 pp. (incomplete?), n.d., MAP.

Ekhvan al-Safa, Mirza Mehdi. Khaterat. Manuscript, n.d., MAP.

Elwell-Sutton, L. P., ed. *Bibliographical Guide to Iran*. Suffolk, 1983.

———. Review of Balyuzi, *'Abdu'l-Baha*, 1971. *Journal of the Royal Asiatic Society* (1973).

The Encyclopaedia of Islam (EI²). New ed., Leiden and London, 1960–.

Encyclopaedia Judaica (EJ). Jerusalem and New York, 1971–72. 2nd ed., Detroit, 2007.

Eqbal, 'Abbas. *Tarikh-e Moghol*. 3rd ed., Tehran, 1347 SH (1968). Rev. ed., Tehran, 1997.

Eqrari, Ata'ullah. *Panjah va haft bahar*. Los Angeles, 2004.

Eshraq-Khavari, 'Abd ul-Hamid. *Ganjineh-ye hodud va ahkam*. Reprint, New Delhi, 1980.

———. *Ma'edeh-ye Asmani*. Reprint, 9 vols. in 3, New Delhi, 1984.

———. *Tarikh-e Hamadan*. Hofheim, 2004

Esslemont, J. E. *Bahá'u'lláh and the New Era*. London,1923.

Estepanian, Arman, ed. *Aqa Reza 'Akkasbashi*. Tehran, 2007.

E'temad al-Saltaneh, Mohammad Hasan Khan. *Matla' al-shams*, 3 vols. Tehran, 1884–86. Reprint, 3 vols. in 2, Tehran, 1983.

———. *Ruznameh-ye khaterat-e E'temad al-Saltaneh*. Ed. Iraj Afshar. Tehran, 1966.

Farahvashi, Muhammad 'Ali. Introduction. In *Dinha-ye Asiya'i* (?), n.p., n.d., Persian translation of Comte Joseph de Gobineau, *Les Religions et philosophies dans l'asie centrale* (Paris, 1865), by M. F.

Farid al-Molk Hamadani, Mohammad 'Ali Khan. *Khaterat-e Farid*. Tehran, 1354 SH (1975/6).

Farivar, Mashalah. *Hadis-e yek farhang*. Ed. Goel Cohen. Los Angeles, 2007.

Fazel Mazandarani, Asadullah. *Amr va khalq*, vol. 3. Reprint, Langenhain, 1986.

———. *Asrar ul-asar*, 3 vols. Tehran, 1973.

———. *Tarikh-e zohur ul-haqq*, vols. 1–2, 4–7, 9. http://www.h-net.msu.edu/~bahai/index/diglib/mazand1.htm.

———. *Tarikh-e zohur ul-haqq*, vol. 3. Tehran, n.d. (1323 SH [1944] [?]). Reprint, Hofheim, 2008.

———. *Tarikh-e zohur ul-haqq*, vol. 8. Tehran, 1976.

Ferraby, John. *All Things Made New: A Comparative Outline of the Baha'i Faith*. London, 1957.

Ferrier, Joseph Pierre. *Caravan Journeys and Wanderings in Persia, Afghanistan, Turkistan, and Beloochistan*. London, 1857. Reprint, Karachi, 1976.

Fischel, Walter J. The Baha'i Movement and Persian Jewry. *Jewish Review* 7 (December–March 1934).

———. *Jews in the Economic and Political Life of Mediaeval Islam*. London, 1937.

———. The Jews of Persia, 1795–1940. *Jewish Social Studies* 12/2 (April 1950).

———. Secret Jews of Persia. *Commentary* 7 (1949).

Fischer, Michael M. J., and Mehdi Abedi. *Debating Muslims: Cultural Dialogues in Postmodernity and Tradition*. Madison, 1990.

Foltz, Richard C. *Spirituality in the Land of the Noble: How Iran Shaped the World's Religions*. Oxford, 2004.

Fragner, Bert G. *Khaterat nevisi Iranian*. Trans. Majid Jalilvand Reza'i. Tehran, 1377 SH (1998). Originally published as *Persische Memoirenliteratur als Quelle zur neueren Geschichte Irans* (Wiesbaden, 1979).

Fraser, James Baillie. *A Winter's Journey from Constantinople to Tehran*. London, 1838.

Frye, R. N. Iran und Israel. In *Festschrift für Wilhelm Eilers*. Wiesbaden, 1967.

Gail, Marzieh. *Arches of the Years*. Oxford, 1991.

———. *Summon Up Remembrance*. Oxford, 1987.

Garcia-Arenal, Mercedes. Jewish Converts to Islam in the Muslim West. In *Dhimmis and Others: Jews and Christians and the World of Classical Islam*. Israel Oriental Studies 17. Ed. Uri Rubin and David J. Wasserstein. Tel Aviv, 1997.

Garcia-Arenal, Mercedes, and Gerard Wiegers. *A Man of Three Worlds: Samuel*

Pallache, a Moroccan Jew in Catholic and Protestant Europe. Trans. Martin Beagles. Baltimore and London, 2003.

Garlington, William. *The Baha'i Faith in America*. Westport, CT, 2005.

Garsoian, Nina. The Aršakuni Dynasty. In *The Armenian People from Ancient to Modern Times*, vol. 1. Ed. Richard G. Hovannisian. New York, 1997.

Ghaffari, Muhammad 'Ali. *Khaterat va asnad-e Muhammad 'Ali Ghaffari (Tarikh-e Ghaffari)*. Ed. Mansureh Etehadiyyeh. Tehran, 1361 SH (1982/3).

Gidney, William Thomas. *The History of the London Society for Promoting Christianity Amongst the Jews*. London, 1908.

Gobineau, Comte Joseph de. *Les Religions et philosophies dans l'asie centrale*. Paris, 1865.

Goitein, S. D. *A Mediterranean Society: The Jewish Communities of the Arab World as Portrayed in the Documents of the Cairo Geniza*. Berkeley, 1967–88.

Golpaygani, Abul-Faza'el. *Dala'il al-Bahiyya*. Cairo, 1898.

———. *Kashf ul-gheta'*. Tashkent, 1919 (?).

Hafezi, Yuhanna Khan. Tarikh-e zendegani-ye Haj Yuhanna Khan Hafezi (Hafez ul-Sehheh). Photocopy of typed manuscript, 1950–61 (?), MAP.

Al-Hakim, Mohsen al-Tabatab'i. *Mustamsak al-'urwat al-wuthqa*, vol. 1. Qom, 1404 SH (1983/4).

Hakimian, Hassan. Wage Labor and Migration: Persian Workers in Southern Russia, 1880–1914. *International Journal of Middle East Studies* 17/4 (November 1985).

Hakim-Samandari, Christine. *Les Baha'is ou victoire sur la violence*. Paris, 1982.

Hatcher, William S., and J. Douglas Martin. *The Baha'i Faith: The Emerging Global Religion*. San Francisco, 1984.

Hawkes, James. *Qamus-i kitab-i muqaddas*. Beirut, 1928. Reprint, Tehran, 1998.

———. Religious Conditions in Hamadan Field. *The Church at Home and Abroad* 16 (1894).

Hedayat, Mokhber al-Saltaneh Mehdi Qoli. *Khaterat va khatarat*. Tehran, 1965.

Hedayat, Reza Qoli Khan-e. *Tarikh-e rowzat al-safa-ye Naseri*. 3rd ed., Tehran and Qom, 1959/60.

Hekmat, 'Ali-Asghar. *Rahamuz-e hekmat*. Tehran, 2003.

Honarfar, L. *Ganjineh-ye asar-e tarikhi-ye Isfahan*. 2nd ed., Tehran, 1971.

Huddleston, John. *The Earth Is But One Country*. London, 1976.

Ibn-e Asdaq, Mirza 'Ali-Muhammad. *Payk-e rastan*. Ed. Vahid Rafati. Darmstadt, 2005.

Ioannesyan, Youli A. *Baron Victor Rosen and the Baha'i Faith*. Studies in the Babi and Baha'i Religions 23. Forthcoming.

Irani, K. D. The Conceptual Basis for the Interaction between the Ancient Traditions of the Jews and the Iranians. *Irano-Judaica* 3 (1994).

Irshai, Oded. Dating the Eschation: Jewish and Christian Apocalyptic Calculations in Late Antiquity. In *Apocalyptic Time*. Ed. Albert I. Baumgarten. Leiden, 2000.

Isfahani, Mirza Haydar 'Ali. *Behjat al-sodur*. Bombay, 1331 SH (1913). Also published in abridged English translation by A. Q. Faizi as *Stories from the Delights of Hearts* (Los Angeles, 1980).

Issawi, Charles, ed. *The Economic History of Iran, 1800–1914*. Chicago, 1971.

Jazzab, Mirza 'Azizullah. Tafsil-e fowz beh iman hazrat-e abawi (known as Khaterat-e Jazzab). Photocopy of manuscript, n.d., MAP.

Kashani, Khavari. *Ketab-e Mahmud*. Tehran, 1329 SH (1911).

Kasravi, Ahmad. *Baha'igari*. Tehran, 1956.

———. *Zendegani-ye man*. Tehran, 1323 SH (1944).

Kayhan (publisher of the daily paper). *Nimeh-ye penhan, sima-ye karkozaran-e farhang va siyasat*, vol. 4. Tehran, 1378 SH (1999).

Keddie, Nikki R. *Modern Iran: Roots and Results of Revolution*. New Haven, 2003.

———. Religion and Irreligion. In *Iran, Religion, Politics and Society: Collected Essays*. Ed. Nikki R. Keddie. London, 1980.

———. *Sayyid Jamal ad-Din "al-Afghani": A Political Biography*. Berkeley, 1972.

Kedourie, Elie, and H. D. S. The Jews of Baghdad in 1910. *Middle Eastern Studies* 7/3 (October 1971).

Keen, James J. Baha'i World Faith: Redefinition of Religion. *Journal for the Scientific Study of Religion* 6/2 (1967).

Kermani, Aqakhan. *Seh maktub*. Reprint, n.p., 1991.

Kermanshahchi, Heshmatullah. *Tahavvolat-e ejtemai-ye yahudiyan-e Iran dar qarn-e bistom*. Los Angeles, 2007.

Khakshuri, R. S. Yahoudiyan-e Urumiyeh. In *Yahoudiyan-e Irani da tarikh-e mo'aser*, vol. 4. Ed. Homa Sarshar et al. Beverly Hills, 2000.

Khaleqi, Golnush. Pasokh-e khanevadeh-ye Ruhullah Khaleqi beh maqaleh-ye vahi va takhribi-ye tohmat-e baha'igari. *Honar-e Musiqi* 9/78 (January–February 2007).

Khaleqi, Ruhullah. *Sargozasht-e musiqi-ye Iran*. Tehran, 1335 SH (1956).

Khalili, Elyeh. *Yahudiyan-e Kurd-e Iran*. Los Angeles, 2004.

Khavari Kashani, Sayyed Ahmad Fakhr al-Va'ezin. *Ketab-e Mahmud*. Tehran, 1329 SH (1911).

Khurasani al-Qa'eni, Muhammad-Baqir. *Tarikh-i i'brat-ee leman i'tabara: Dar vaqay'e-e 1315 Hijri dar Hamadan*. Tehran, 1946.

Labaree, Benjamin. Conversion of a Persian Jew. *The Gospel in All Lands* 3 (January–June 1881), pp. 175–176.

Lambton, Ann K. S. *Qajar Persia: Eleven Studies*. Reprint, Austin, 1988.

Lee, Anthony A. Choice Wine: The Kitab-i Aqdas and the Development of Baha'i Law. http://www.bahai-library.org/conferences/wine.html, n.d.

Lenowitz, Harris. *The Jewish Messiahs: From the Galilee to Crown Heights*. Oxford, 1998.

Levy, Azaria. *The Jews of Mashhad*. Jerusalem, 1998.

Levy, Habib. *Khaterat-e man*. Los Angeles, 2002.

———. *Tarikh-e Yahud-e Iran*, 3 vols. Tehran, 1334 SH (1956). Reprint in 2 vols., Los Angeles, 1984.

Levy, Nissim. Letter to the President. Tehran, November 27, 1901. Archives of the Alliance Israélite Universelle, Paris.

Lewis, Bernard. *The Jews of Islam*. Princeton, 1984.

Loeb, Laurence D. The Jewish Musician and the Music of Fars. *Asian Music* 4 (1972).

Ma'ani, Baharieh Rouhani. The Interdependence of Baha'i Communities: Services of North American Baha'i Women to Iran. *Journal of Baha'i Studies* 4/1 (March–June 1991).

MacEoin, D. M. From Shaykhism to Babism: A Study in Charismatic Renewal in Shi'i Islam. Ph.D. dissertation, Cambridge University, 1979.

———. *The Messiah of Shiraz: Studies in Early and Middle Babism*. Leiden, 2009.

Mahdavi, Mo'ez al-Din. *Dastanha'i az panjah sal*. Tehran, 1969.

Malmiri, Mohammad Taher. *Tarikh-e shohad-ye Yazd*, 2 vols. Cairo, 1922.

Ma'sum 'Ali Shah, Muhammad Ma'sum Shirazi. *Tarae'q al-Haqae'q*. Tehran, n.d.

Matin, Afshin. *Both Eastern and Western: The Construction of Modern Iran's National and Islamic Identities*. Forthcoming.

Matthee, Rudolph P. Merchants in Safavid Iran: Participants and Perceptions. *Journal of Early Modern History* 3–4 (1999–2000).

———. *The Politics of Trade in Safavid Iran: Silk for Silver, 1600–1730*. Cambridge, 1999.

Mehrabkhani, Ruhullah. *Sharh-e ahval-e jenab-e Mirza Abulfazl Golpaygani*. Tehran, 1975.

Misaqiyyeh, 'Abd ul-Misaq. Kholaseh-i az khaterat-e jenab-e Misaqiyyeh va nemuneh-i az nikugariha-ye ishan. Photocopy of manuscript edited and transcribed by Muhammad 'Ali Fayzi, 199 pp., Tehran, 1977, MAP.

Modarres, 'Abd al-Rahman. *Tarikh-e ulama-ye Khorasan*. Mashhad, 1962.

Modarres, Fathullah. *Tarikh-e amr-e Baha'i dar Najaf-abad*. Darmstadt, 2004.

Mo'men Hoseini. *Tohfeh-ye hakim-e mo'men*. N.p., 1670.

Momen, Moojan. The Bahá'í Faith 1957–1988: A Survey of Contemporary Developments. *Religion* 19 (January 1989).

———. Early Relations between Christian Missionaries and the Babi and Baha'i Communities. In *Studies in Babi and Baha'i History*. Ed. Moojan Momen. Los Angeles, 1982.

———. *A Short Introduction to the Bahá'í Faith*. Oxford, 1997.

———. The Social Bases of the Babi Upheavals in Iran (1843–53): A Preliminary Analysis. *International Journal of Middle East Studies* 14 (1983).

Montazeri, Ayatollah. *Khaterat-e Ayatollah Hosein-'Ali Montazeri*. Los Angeles, 2001.

Moradinia, Mohammad Javad, ed. *Khaterat-e Ayatollah Pasandideh*. Tehran, 1997.

Moreen, Vera Basch. *Iranian Jewry's Hour of Peril and Heroism: A Study of Babai ibn Lutf's Chronicle, 1617–1662*. New York, 1987.

———. The "Iranization" of Biblical Heroes in Judeo-Persian Epics: Shahin's Ardashir-Namah and Ezra Nameh. *Iranian Studies* 29/3–4 (1996).

Moreen, Vera Basch, trans. *In Queen Esther's Garden: An Anthology of Judeo-Persian Literature*. New Haven, 2000.

Moshar, Khanbaba. *Fehrest-e Ketabha-ye Chappi-ye Farsi*. Tehran, 1973.

Mudaress, 'Abd al-Rahman. *Tarikh-e ulama-ye Khorasan*. Mashhad, 1962.

Nafisy, Sa'id. *Babak khurram-din, delavar-e Azarbayja*. Tehran, 1342 SH (1963).

Najafi, Mohammad Baqer. *Bahaiyan*. Tehran, 1979.

Najm-e bakhtar = *Star of the West* 2/4 (May 1911).

Naraqi, Hasan. *Kashan dar jonbesh-e mashruteh-ye Iran*. Tehran, 2535 (1976/7).

———. *Tarikh-e ejtema'i-ye Kashan*. Tehran, 1345 SH (1967).

———. *Zendegi nameh-ye Khavari-ye Kashani*. Tehran, 1977.

Nateq, Homa. Tarikhcheh-ye Alians-e esra'ili dar Iran. In *Yahudian-e Irani dar tarikh-e mo'aser*, vol. 2. Los Angeles, 1997.

Nateq-e Isfahani, Mohammad. Tarikh-e amri-ye Kashan va qora'-e tavabe'. INBA Library, ms no. 2016D, 1309 SH (1930).

Nava'i, 'Abdulhosein, et al., eds. *Nayebiyan-e Kashan*. Tehran, 2000.

Nemoy, Leon. *Karaite Anthology: Excerpts from the Early Literature*. Yale Judaica Series 7. New Haven, 1952.

Netzer, Amnon. Conversion of Jews to the Baha'i Faith. *Irano-Judaica* 6 (2008).

———. Orot anuse Meshhed l'fi Ya'aqov Dilmanian (The History of the forced converts of Mashhad according to Jacob Dilmanian). *Pe'amim* 42 (1990).

———. Rashid al-Din and His Jewish Background. *Irano-Judaica* 3 (1994).

———. Sayri dar tarikh-e Yahud-e Iran, parts 1 and 2. In *Padyavand*, vols. 1 and 2. Ed. Amnon Netzer. Los Angeles, 1996–97.

———. Yahudiyan-e Tehran az ebteda to enqelab-e mashrutiyyat. In *Padyavand*, vol. 3. Ed. Amnon Netzer. Los Angeles, 1999.

Netzer, Amnon, ed. *Padyavand*, vol. 1. Los Angeles, 1996.

———. *Padyavand*, vol. 3. Los Angeles, 1999.

Neumark, Ephraim. *Masa'be-erets ha-qedem* (Journey in the countries of the East). With Introduction and Notes by Avraham Ya'ari. Jerusalem, 1947.

Neusner, Jacob. *Israel and Iran in Talmudic Times: A Political History*. Lanham, MD, 1986.

———. Jews in Iran. In *Cambridge History of Iran*, vol. 3, part 2. Ed. Ehsan Yarshater. Cambridge, 1983.

Niku, Hasan Borujerdi. *Falsafeh-ye Niku, dar paydayesh-e rahzanan va badkishan*, 4 vols. in 2. Tehran, 1960 (?).

Okazaki, Shoko. The Great Persian Famine of 1870–71. *Bulletin of the School of Oriental and African Studies* 49/1 (1986).

Panaino, Antonio. Trends and Problems Concerning the Mutual Relations between Iranian Pre-Islamic and Jewish Cultures. In *Melammu Symposia IV: Proceedings of the Fourth Annual Symposium of the Assyrian and Babylonian Intellectual Heritage Project.* Ed. Antonio Panaino. Milan, 2004.

Partow-Bayza'i, Hosein. *Tarikh-e varzesh-haye bastani-ye Iran.* Tehran, 1958.

Patai, Raphael. *Jadid al-Islam: The Jewish "New Muslims" of Meshhed.* Detroit, 1997.

Phelps, Myron H. *Life and Teachings of Abbas Effendi: A Study of the Religion of the Babis, or Beha'is Founded by the Persian Bab and by his Successors, Beha Ullah and Abbas Effendi.* 2nd rev. ed., London, 1912. Abridged as *The Master in 'Akka,* Los Angeles, 1985.

Pirnazar, Jaqleh. Yahudiyan-e jadid ul-Islam-e Mashhad. *Iran Nameh* 19/1–2 (Winter and Spring 2001).

Quchani, Aqa Najafi. *Siyahat-e sharq.* Ed. R. A. Shakeri. Mashhad, 1351 SH (1972).

Rafati, Vahid. The Development of Shaykhi Thought in Shi'i Islam. Ph.D. dissertation, University of California, Los Angeles, 1979.

Ragussis, Michael. *Figures of Conversion.* Durham, 1995.

Ra'in, Esma'il. *Enshe'ab-e Baha'iyyat.* Tehran, 1978 (?).

Rastegar, Nasrullah. *Tarikh-e hazrat-e Sadr al-Sodur.* Tehran, 1948/9.

Rayhani, Rayhan. Memoirs (in Persian). Photocopy of autograph manuscript, Tehran, 1939 (?), MAP.

Rezazadeh Langarudi, Reza. *Yadegarnameh, majmo'eh-ye maqalat-e tahqiqi taqdim shodeh beh ostad Ebrahim Fakhra'i.* Tehran, 1984.

Rezvani, Homa. *Lavayeh-e Shaykh Fazlullah Nuri.* Tehran, 1984.

Ringer, Monica. *Education, Religion, and the Discourse of Cultural Reform in Qajar Iran.* Costa Mesa, 2001.

Roknzadeh-Adamiyat, Mohammad-Hosein. *Daneshmandan va sokhanvaran-e Fars.* Tehran, 1958–61.

Sa'adat-Nuri, Hosein. *Rejal-e dowreh-ye Qajar.* Tehran, 1985.

Sabet, A. *Tarikhche-ye Madreseh-ye Tarbiyat-e Banin.* New Delhi, 1997.

Sabet, Habib. *Sargozasht-e Habib-e Sabet beh qalam-e khod-e ishan.* Los Angeles, 1993.

Sadr Hashemi, Muhammad. *Tarikh-e jara'ed va majellat,* 4 vols. 2nd ed., Tehran, 1984.

Safa, Zabihullah. *Tarikh-e adabiyat dar Iran,* vol. 1. Tehran, 1972.

Safa'i, Ebrahim. *Panjah Nameh-ye Tarikhi.* Tehran, 1972.

Sahim, Haideh. Jews of Iran in the Qajar Period: Persecution and Perseverance. In *Religion and Society in Qajar Iran.* Ed. Robert Gleave. London and New York, 2005.

———. Khaterat-e yahudiyan-e Iran. *Iran Nameh* 15/1 (Winter 1996).

Saiedi, Nader. *Gate of the Heart: Understanding the Writings of the Báb*. Waterloo, Ontario, 2008.

———. *Logos and Civilization: Spirit, History, and Order in the Writings of Baha'u'llah*. Bethesda, 2000.

Salur, Qahraman Mirza. *Khaterat-e 'Ayn al-Saltaneh*, vol. 1. Ed. Iraj Afshar. Tehran, 1995.

Samarqandi, Dowlatshah. *Tadkerat al-Sho'ra*. Leiden, 1901.

San'atizadeh-Kermani, 'Abd ul-Hosein. *Ruzegari keh gozasht*. Tehran, 1346 SH (1968).

Sane' Mansur, ed. *Beh yad-e Shiraz*. Tehran, 2002.

Sanjabi, 'Ali Akbar Khan Sardar Moqtader. *Il-e Sanjabi va mojahedat-e melli-ye Iran*. Tehran, 2001.

Sarshar, Houman, ed. *Esther's Children: A Portrait of Iranian Jews*. Beverly Hills, 2002.

Savory, Roger. *Iran under the Safavids*. Cambridge, 1980.

———. Relations between the Safavid State and its Non-Muslim Minorities. *Islam and Christian-Muslim Relations* 14/4 (October 2003).

Sayyah, Muhammad 'Ali. *Khaterat-e Hajji Sayyah, ya dawreh-ye khawf va vahshat*. Tehran, 1967.

Sepehr, Mirza Mohammad Taqi (Lesan al-Mulk). *Nasekh al-tawarikh*. 4 vols. Ed. M. B. Behdudi. Tehran, 1965.

Sepehr, Movarrekh al-Dowleh. *Iran dar jang-e bozorg*. Tehran, 1957.

Shafa, Shoja'eddin. *Iran va Espania, farhang-nameh-ye Jahan-e Iran-shenasi*, vol. 1. N.p., n.d.

Shahbazi, 'Abdullah. *Zarsalaran-e Yahudi va Parsi; Este'mar-e Biritania va Iran*, 5 vols. Tehran, 1377 SH (1998).

Shaked, Shaul. Iranian Influence on Judaism: First Century BCE to Second Century CE. In *Cambridge History of Judaism*, vol. 1. Ed. Louis W. D. Davies and Louis Finkelstein. Cambridge, 1984.

Shakeri, Aqajan. Shakerinameh. Transcription of manuscript, Tehran (?), 1961, MAP.

Shavar, Solyaman. *The Forgotten Schools: The Baha'is and Modern Education in Iran, 1899–1933*. London, 2009.

Shaybani, Mirza Ebrahim. *Montakhab al-tavarikh-e Mozaffari*. Tehran, 1366 SH (1987).

Shofet, Yedidia. *Khaterat-e hakham Yedidia Shofet*. Ed. Manuchehr Kohan. Los Angeles, 2000.

Shoghi Effendi. *The Advent of Divine Justice*. Wilmette, IL, 1939.

———. *Baha'i Administration*. New York, 1928. Rev. ed., Wilmette, IL, 1974.

———. *God Passes By*. Wilmette, IL, 1944.

———. *The Promised Day is Come*. Wilmette, IL, 1941.

———. *The World Order of Bahá'u'lláh*. Wilmette, IL, 1955. 2nd rev. ed., Wilmette, IL, 1974.

Shuster, W. Morgan. *The Strangling of Persia.* New York, 1920.

Simantub (Simantov), Malamed. *Azhurat in the Holy Tongue and in the Persian Tongue.* Jerusalem, 1896.

——. *Sefre hayat al-ruh.* Jerusalem, 1898.

Smith, Peter. *The Bábí and Bahá'í Religions: From Messianic Shi'ism to a World Religion.* Cambridge,1987.

——. A Note on Babi and Baha'i Numbers in Iran. *Iranian Studies* 15/2–3 (1984).

——. *A Short History of the Bahá'í Faith.* Oxford, 1996.

Smith, Peter, and Moojan Momen. The Bahá'í Faith 1957–1988: A Survey of Contemporary Developments. *Religion* 19 (January 1989).

Sobhi, Fazlullah. *Khaterat-e zendegi.* Tehran, 2007.

——. *Payam-e pedar.* Tehran, 1955.

Solaymani, 'Azizullah. *Masabih-e hedayat,* 9 vols. Tehran, 1958–77.

Soroudi, Sorour. The Concept of Jewish Impurity and Its Reflection in Persian and Judeo-Persian Traditions. *Irano-Judaica* 3 (1994).

Spector, D. E. A History of the Persian Jews. Ph.D. dissertation, University of Texas, 1975.

Spicehandler, Ezra. The Persecution of the Jews of Isfahan during the Reign of Shah 'Abbas II (1642–1666). *Hebrew Union College Annual* 46 (1975).

Stern, Henry A. *Dawnings of Light in the East.* London, 1854.

Stern, M. The State of the Jews at Hamadan. *The Jewish Herald and Record of Christian Effort for the Spiritual Good of God's Ancient People* 6 (1852), pp. 317–320.

Stiles, Susan. Early Zoroastrian Conversions to the Baha'i Faith in Yazd, Iran. In *Studies in Bábí and Bahá'í History,* vol. 2, *From Iran East and West.* Ed. Juan R. Cole and Moojan Momen. Los Angeles, 1984.

Taherzadeh, Adib. *The Revelation of Baha'u'llah,* 4 vols. Oxford, 1974–83.

Tavakoli-Targhi, Mohammad. Anti-Baha'ism and Islamism in Iran. In *Baha'is of Iran: Socio-historical Studies.* Ed. Dominic Parviz Brookshaw and Seena B. Fazel. London and New York, 2008.

——. Baha'i-setizi va Eslam-gara'i. *Irannameh* 19/1–2 (2001).

——. The Homeless Texts of Persianate Modernity. In *Iran: Between Tradition and Modernity.* Ed. Ramin Jahanbegloo. Lanham, 2004.

Tavernier, Jean Baptiste. *Voyages en Perse et description de ce royaume par Jean-Baptiste Tavernier.* Paris, 1930.

Thomson, Albert Edward. *A Century of Jewish Missions.* Chicago, 1902.

Tsadik, Daniel. *Between Foreigners and Shi'is: Nineteenth-Century Iran and Its Jewish Minority.* Stanford, 2007.

——. Foreign Intervention, Majority, and Minority: The Status of the Jews during the Latter Part of Nineteenth-century Iran (1848–1896). Ph.D. dissertation, Yale University, 2002.

——. Religious Disputations of Imami Shi'is against Judaism in the Late

Eighteenth and Nineteenth Centuries. *Studia Iranica* 34/1 (2005).

Vahidnia, Sayfullah. *Khaterat-e Vahid*, 2 vols. Tehran, 1985.

Vahman, Fereydun. The Conversion of Zoroastrians to the Baha'i Faith. In *The Baha'is of Iran, Socio-historical Studies*. Ed. Dominic Parviz Brookshaw and Seena B. Fazel. London, 2008.

Valle, Pietro della. *Viaggi di Pietro della Valle*, 2 vols. Brighton, 1843. Translated as *Safarnameh-ye della Valle* by Mahmud Behforuzi. Tehran, 2001.

Velasco, Ismael. Academic Irrelevance or Disciplinary Blind-Spot? Middle Eastern Studies and the Baha'i Faith Today. *Middle East Studies Association Bulletin* 35/2 (Winter 2001).

Walcher, Heidi. *In The Shadow of the King: Zil al-Sultan and Isfahan under the Qajars*. London, 2008.

Warburg, Margit. *Citizens of the World: A History and Sociology of the Baha'is from a Globalisation Perspective*. Leiden, 2006.

Wasserman, Steven M. *Between Muslim and Jew: The Problem of Symbioses under Early Islam*. Cambridge, 1997.

Waterfield, Robin E. *Christians in Persia: Assyrians, Armenians, Roman Catholics and Protestants*. New York, 1973.

Widengren, Geo. The Status of the Jews in the Sassanian Empire. *Iranica Antiqua* 1 (1961).

Williams, A. V. Zoroastrian and Judaic Purity Laws: Reflections on the Viability of a Sociological Interpretation. *Irano-Judaica* 3 (1994).

Wills, C. J. *In the Land of the Lion and Sun*. London, 1883, 1891. Reprint, Washington, DC, 2004.

Wilson, J. Christy. A Persian Apostate: Benjamin Badal. *Muslim World* 21/3 (1931).

Wilson, Robert. The Biblical Roots of the Apocalyptic. In *Imagining the End: Visions of Apocalypse from the Ancient Middle East to Modern America*. Ed. Abbas Amanat and Magnus Bernhardsson. London, 2002.

Wolff, Joseph. *Researches and Missionary Labours among the Jews, Mohammedans, and Other Sects*. Philadelphia, 1837.

Yarshater, Ehsan, ed. *Encyclopaedia Iranica* (*EIr*). London and Boston, 1982–.

Yerushalaymi, Yazghel. Sharh-e qesmi az Yahudot-e Kashan va sayer-e shahrestanha-ye keshvar-e Iran. Photocopy of manuscript, 1985, MAP.

Za'im, Kurosh. *Mardan-e bozorg-e Kashan*. Tehran, 1336 SH (1957).

Zanjani, Ebrahim. *Sargozasht-e zendegani-ye man, khaterat-e shaykh Ebrahim Zanjani*. Ed. Gholam-Hosein Mirza-Saleh. Tehran, 2000, 2001. Reprint, Los Angeles, 2009.

Zarandi, Shaykh Mohammad Nabil. *The Dawn-breakers: Nabil's Narrative of the Early Days of the Baha'i Revelation*. Trans. and ed. Shoghi Effendi. Wilmette, IL, 1932.

Zarrabi, 'Abd ul-Rahim Kalantar. *Mer'at ul-Qasan (Tarikh-e Kashan)*. Ed. Iraj Afshar. Tehran, 1335 SH (1956/7).

INDEX